Adoption Matters

Adoption Matters

PHILOSOPHICAL AND FEMINIST ESSAYS

Edited by

SALLY HASLANGER

AND

CHARLOTTE WITT

CORNELL UNIVERSITY PRESS

Ithaca and London

The following were published in earlier versions and are used here with permission.

Anita L. Allen, "Open Adoption Is Not for Everyone," appeared in a different version as "Accountability to Family and Race," in *Why Privacy Isn't Everything: Feminist Reflections on Personal Accountability*, by Anita L. Allen, published by Rowman & Littlefield, 2003.

Elizabeth Bartholet, "Abuse and Neglect, Foster Drift, and the Adoption Alternative" is a revised excerpt of chapter 2 of *Nobody's Children: Abuse and Neglect, Foster Drift, and the Adoption Alternative*, by Elizabeth Bartholet. Copyright © 1999 by Elizabeth Bartholet. Reprinted by permission of Beacon Press, Boston.

Drucilla Cornell, "Adoption and Its Progeny: Rethinking Family Law, Gender, and Sexual Difference" appeared in *At the Heart of Freedom: Feminism, Sex, and Equality*, by Drucilla Cornell. Copyright © 1998. Princeton University Press.

Hawley Fogg-Davis, "Racial Randomization: Imagining Nondiscrimination in Adoption," appeared as "Racial Randomization," in *The Ethics of Transracial Adoption*, by Hawley Fogg-Davis. Copyright © 2001 by Cornell University. Used by permission of the publisher, Cornell University Press.

First published 2005 by Cornell University Press
First printing, Cornell Paperbacks, 2005

Printed in the United States of America

Library of Congress Cataloging-in-Publication Data

Adoption matters : philosophical and feminist essays / edited by Sally Haslanger and Charlotte Witt.
    p. cm.
    Includes bibliographical references and index.
    ISBN 0-8014-4194-3 (cloth : alk. paper) — ISBN 0-8014-8963-6 (pbk. : alk. paper)
    1. Adoption.   I. Haslanger, Sally Anne.   II. Witt, Charlotte, 1951–
    HV875.A3425   2005
    362.734′01—dc22   2004015589

Cornell University Press strives to use environmentally responsible suppliers and materials to the fullest extent possible in the publishing of its books. Such materials include vegetable-based, low-VOC inks and acid-free papers that are recycled, totally chlorine-free, or partly composed of nonwood fibers. For further information, visit our website at www.cornellpress.cornell.edu.

Cloth printing   10 9 8 7 6 5 4 3 2 1

Paperback printing   10 9 8 7 6 5 4 3 2 1

For
Anna and Jonathan
Isaac and Zina

Contents

Acknowledgments

Thanks to Clare Batty for her excellent work in preparing the final manuscript. We are also grateful to the MIT Department of Linguistics and Philosophy and to the College of the Liberal Arts at the University of New Hampshire for research funding. We would also like to thank Mark Googins for his generous and timely legal advice.

Special thanks to Stephen Yablo and to Mark Okrent for their support of the project, and their devotion to our families.

S.H. and C.W.

Notes on Contributors

ANITA L. ALLEN is the Henry R. Silverman Professor of Law and Professor of Philosophy at the University of Pennsylvania. She holds a Ph.D. in Philosophy from the University of Michigan and a Law degree from Harvard. Her recent books include *The New Ethics: A Guided Tour of the 21st-Century Moral Landscape* (Miramax, 2004) and *Why Privacy Isn't Everything: Feminist Reflections on Personal Accountability* (Rowman and Littlefield, 2003). She is the mother of two mixed-race children adopted in Washington, D.C.

ELIZABETH BARTHOLET is the Morris Wasserstein Public Interest Professor of Law at Harvard Law School, where she teaches civil rights and family law, specializing in child welfare, adoption, and reproductive technology. Before joining the Harvard Faculty, she was engaged in civil rights and public interest work, first with the NAACP Legal Defense Fund, and later as founder and director of the Legal Action Center, a non-profit organization in New York City focused on criminal justice and substance abuse issues. Her publications include *Family Bonds: Adoption, Infertility, and the New World of Child Production* and *Nobody's Children: Abuse and Neglect, Foster Drift, and the Adoption Alternative*. She is the mother of three boys, one by birth and two by adoption.

DRUCILLA CORNELL is Professor of Political Science, Women's Studies, and Comparative Literature at Rutgers University. Cornell was a union organizer before becoming an academic, and is also a produced playwright. She is the author of numerous acclaimed works of feminist theory, continental thought, and political philosophy, including *Beyond Accommodation: Ethical Feminism, Deconstruction, and the Law; The Philosophy of the Limit; Transformations: Recollective Imagination and Sexual Difference; The Imaginary Domain: Abortion, Pornography, and Sexual Harassment; At the Heart of Freedom: Feminism, Sex, and Equality; Just Cause: Freedom, Identity, and Rights;* and *Between Women and Generations: Legacies of Dignity*. Her newest book is *Defending Ideals* (Routledge, 2004). She is also an adopting mother.

HAWLEY FOGG-DAVIS is Assistant Professor of Political Science at the University of Wisconsin–Madison. Her research and teaching interests are in political theory and public law, in particular philosophical race theory, and ethics and public policy. Her most recent publications include *The Ethics of Transracial Adoption* (Cornell University Press, 2002) and "Navigating Race in the Market for Human Gametes" in the *Hastings Center Report.*

HARRY FRANKFURT is Professor Emeritus of Philosophy at Princeton. He works mainly on Descartes, moral philosophy, and the theory of action. His most recent publication is *The Reasons of Love* (Princeton University Press, 2004). His interest in adoption, such as it is, derives entirely from the fact that when he was thirty-six years old his mother told him, shortly before she died, that he had been adopted.

SONGSUK HAHN is Assistant Professor of Philosophy. She specializes in 19th-Century Continental Philosophy, and is currently visiting Kenyon College. She was adopted as an infant from Seoul, Korea, along with her two full-blooded sisters. She is presently looking into the possibility of adopting a child from China.

SALLY HASLANGER is Professor of Philosophy and Women's Studies at the Massachusetts Institute of Technology. Her publications have addressed topics in metaphysics, epistemology, and feminist theory, with a recent emphasis on the social construction of gender and race. She is the adoptive mother of two children in open domestic transracial adoptions.

KIMBERLY LEIGHTON, a Mellon Humanities Fellow, is a Visiting Assistant Professor of Philosophy at Cornell University. A Sarah Lawrence College graduate, she received her Ph.D. in philosophy from the University of Massachusetts at Amherst. Her current research investigates the relationship between the capacity for self-knowledge and the constitution of political legitimacy. She is presently working on a book manuscript, "Adopted Knowing: Claiming Self-knowledge in the Age of Identity," which considers how a valuation of the self's desire to know itself might be useful for a politics of resistance. An adoptee, Kimberly includes in her family her (adoptive) parents and her birth mother, whom she found in 1994.

SHELLEY PARK is Associate Professor of Philosophy at the University of Central Florida. Her teaching and research focus on feminist theory, especially as this intersects with issues of family and memory. She lives in Orlando, Florida, with her partner and two pre-teen daughters, and enjoys an open adoptive relationship with the birth mother of her eldest daughter.

DOROTHY ROBERTS is the Kirkland and Ellis Professor at Northwestern University School of Law and a faculty fellow of the Institute for Policy Research. She has written and lectured extensively on the interplay of gender, race, and class in legal issues concerning reproduction, motherhood, and child welfare. She is the author of *Killing the Black Body: Race, Reproduction, and the Meaning of Liberty* (Pantheon, 1997), *Shattered Bonds: The Color of Child Welfare* (Basic Books, 2002), and more than fifty articles and essays in books and scholarly journals, as well as the coauthor of casebooks on constitutional law and women and the law. She serves as a member of the board of directors of the National Black Women's Health Initiative and the National Coalition for Child Protection Reform.

JANET FARRELL SMITH, Associate Professor of Philosophy at University of Massachusetts Boston, has held the Liberal Arts Fellowship in Law and Philosophy at Harvard Law School, and has written articles about adoption, property, and personhood. She is the sole parent of her daughter, adopted in Beijing, China.

JACQUELINE STEVENS is the author of *Reproducing the State* (Princeton University Press, 1999). Her work has appeared in *Political Theory*, the *American Political Science Review*, the *Journal of Political Philosophy*, *Social Text*, and many other publications. Her interest in the topic of adoption was first engaged when her mother's second husband adopted her.

SARAH TOBIAS is a coauthor, with Sean Cahill and Mitra Ellen, of *Family Policy: Issues Affecting Gay, Lesbian, and Transgender Families* (New York: National Gay and Lesbian Taskforce Policy Institute, 2002). She has a Ph.D. in Political Science from Columbia University and has written widely on the subject of feminist ethics, including "Toward a Feminist Ethic of War and Peace" in *The Ethics of War and Peace*, edited by Terry Nardin (Princeton University Press, 1996), and "Coexisting with Cacophony: Affirming Discordant Voices in Feminist Ethics and Politics" (Ph.D. diss., Columbia University, 2001). Her articles and op-eds about GLBT families have appeared in the gay press around the country, as well as on Alternet and Commondreams.org.

CHARLOTTE WITT is Professor of Philosophy and Humanities at the University of New Hampshire. She is the author of *Substance and Essence in Aristotle* and *Ways of Being: Potentiality and Actuality in Aristotle's Metaphysics*. She is co-editor of *A Mind of One's Own: Feminist Essays on Reason and Objectivity* and *Feminist Reflections on the History of Philosophy*. Her family includes an adopted daughter.

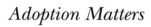

Adoption Matters

Introduction: Kith, Kin, and Family

SALLY HASLANGER AND CHARLOTTE WITT

As a social and legal institution of family formation, and as a personal experience of members of the adoption triad (adoptee, birth parents, adoptive parents), adoption provides a fresh vantage point on an important set of philosophical and feminist issues. Although the family is often thought to be the basic and natural form of social life for human beings, adoption highlights the powerful role that law and politics play in shaping families and our ideas about those families. As a result, attention to the practices of adoption sheds light upon deeply held but often tacit assumptions about what in human life is natural and what is social.

Adoption books come in many varieties. Some of them provide "how to adopt" strategies; others provide personal narratives of the adoption experience. More academically oriented volumes consider the psychological impact of being a member of an adoption triad, or perhaps they consider the strengths and weaknesses of current adoption policy. Although this collection of essays includes both moments of personal reflection and discussion of policy, its goal is to bring together an interdisciplinary group of scholars to explore and critique how adoption is situated within mainstream conceptual frameworks and to consider how a reorientation towards a less stigmatizing understanding of adoption has repercussions for other parts of the frameworks, even parts not explicitly concerned with families. For example, what do we learn about love by considering an adopted person's feelings for the biological parents she has never met? What do we learn about knowledge by exploring an adopted person's desire to know her biological ancestry? What do we learn about race by reflecting on the relationships formed within transracial adoptions?

The etymologies of "kith" and "kin" support the suggestion that beliefs about adoption are interwoven with topics in epistemology and metaphysics, e.g., about knowledge and essence that extend well beyond questions of public policy. Who are one's kith and kin? The original meaning of "kith," though now obsolete, is defined by the *OED* as "knowledge, acquaintance with something; knowledge communicated, information." From here, the word took on the sense of "a place known or familiar, one's native land, home," and then to the people of that place, one's friends, or family. The *OED* suggests that eventually there came to be a confusion of "kith" with "kin" and the two words are now often treated as equivalent.

Etymologically the term "kin" has its roots in the word "kind," designating simply a "class, group, or division"; "kin" is also used for any class of things with common attributes. The preference for defining one's "kinsfolk" by common *biological* attributes—kin as species or ancestral groups—echoes the assumption that real kinds must be natural kinds, that real kinds share an essence. But what, if anything, are the common attributes that constitute families as groups? Those who share a home, in potentially a broad sense of home, are kith. Is there something more or something less to being kin?

Our book explores the contrast and overlap between the family viewed as a social association (a view suggested by the original meaning of "kith") and the family viewed as a natural or biological entity (a view suggested by the original meaning of "kin"). The essays in this volume trace three central themes concerning adoption and families that center on the contrast between what is (considered to be) social and what is (considered to be) natural: (1) Natural and Unnatural Families, (2) Familial Relationships and Personal Identities, and (3) Constructions of Race and Constructions of Family.

Before discussing the essays in this volume, it is useful to sketch out some background information on the social and legal context of adoption in the contemporary United States, given that this is the complex, though limited, perspective from which our contributors approach the institution of adoption.

ADOPTION IN THE UNITED STATES

Although informal practices of adoption have always existed, the institution of legal adoption is a relatively recent phenomenon. In 1851, Massachusetts passed the first modern adoption statute in the United States. (Adoption was not part of English common law. Prior to 1851, state legislatures would sometimes pass a private adoption act to formalize the transfer of a particular child to a new family.) The Massachusetts Adoption Act formalized the process by which custody of a child could be transferred—severing all legal ties to the biological parents—and clarified the child's inheritance rights. The move to such legislation was caused by a number of factors: increasing urbanization and industrialization created a large number of orphaned and homeless children; the privatization of the family and an increasingly sentimental attitude towards children encouraged the formation of nuclear families in which a mother in the home cared for "her" children (Berebitsky 2000, chap. 1, esp. 20–21).

Since 1851, the legal, social, and cultural understandings of adoption have gone through many changes. Currently, there are several different forms of adoption in the United States (National Adoption Information Clearinghouse 2002c). One major distinction falls between *domestic* and *international* adoption. Shortly after World War II, a significant number of Americans began to adopt from abroad, reaching out to war orphans, those in poverty, and others facing unmanageable social conditions. Between 1971 and 2001, U.S. citizens adopted 265,677 children from abroad, the large majority (156,491) being from Asia, though this trend is changing: in 2001, 22 percent were adopted from Russia (The Evan B. Donaldson Adoption Institute 2002a). The U.S. State Department estimates that there were 20,099 international adoptions in FY2002 (Office of Children's Issues n.d.). Approximately 90 percent of children adopted internationally are under five years old (The Evan B. Donaldson Adoption Institute 2002a).

Within the category of domestic adoptions, there are also several different kinds: stepparent adoption, second-parent adoption, foster care adoption, private adoption, and independent adoption. *Stepparent adoption,* i.e., cases in which the child is adopted by the spouse of a biological parent, is the most common form (42 percent of domestic adoptions in 1992);[1] intra-family adoptions on the whole comprise over half of all adoptions. *Second-parent adoptions* provide a way, at least in some states, for same-sex couples to adopt. In a second-parent adoption one member of the couple gains legal custody of the child (by birth or single-parent adoption) and the second parent petitions the court to become a second parent. Twenty-one states have court precedents that allow such adoptions in which the second parent is not a spouse; in four states (Vermont, New York, Massachusetts, and New Jersey) the option of second-parent adoption is binding law (National Adoption Information Clearinghouse 2002b).

Foster care adoption (also known as "public" adoption) is carried out by

1. Adoption statistics have not been comprehensively compiled since 1992. The 42 percent figure is an estimate suggested in a study conducted by the National Center for State Courts. For further information, see The Evan B. Donaldson Adoption Institute (2002b).

state agencies and occurs when the child cannot be reunified with the biological parents for safety or other reasons. The U.S. Department of Health and Human Services estimates that in FY1999 there were 581,000 children in foster care in the United States; 127,000 of them were waiting for adoption.[2] The average age of waiting children was 7.9 years; the average time in continuous foster care was 44 months. In that same year, 46,000 children were adopted from the system, 50 percent of them male, 50 percent female (Administration for Children and Families 2003).

In *private agency adoptions* biological parents choose to place their child through an agency (either non-profit or for-profit) licensed by the state. *Independent adoptions* occur through an attorney or facilitator and do not involve an agency. (Independent adoption is also sometimes called "private adoption"; this creates potential confusion with private *agency* adoption.) Independent adoptions are legal in all but four states (Connecticut, Delaware, Massachusetts, Minnesota). Because reporting is not required for private agency or independent adoption, it is difficult to estimate the prevalence of each. However, some have suggested that independent adoptions comprised at least one-half of adoptions in 2000 (Gilman and Freivalds 2002).

Gathering data on adoption has been a longstanding problem (Stolley 1993). For decades, adoption was something to be hidden; adoptees themselves were not always told of their adoptive status, and few studies were conducted. Although currently statistics are kept on international and foster care adoptions, states are not required to keep statistics on other forms of adoption (The Evan B. Donaldson Adoption Institute 2002b). Some estimate, however, that there are close to six million adoptees in the United States (Pertman 1998), 1.2 million being children aged 18 and under (Fields 2001, 9).[3]

During most of the 20th century, adoption was largely hidden because it was a source of shame for all those involved: the birth parents for what was often an "out of wedlock" pregnancy, the adoptive parents for their presumed infertility, and the child for being "unwanted" or "rejected." As a result, adoption was shrouded in secrecy: birth certificates listed the names of adoptive, not biological parents; adopted adults had no access to agency or court documents concerning their biological parents; adoptees were placed with adoptive families who, as far as possible, "could have

---

2. Waiting children are those in foster care who have a goal of adoption and/or whose parental rights have been terminated. However, children aged 16 and over whose parental rights have been terminated are not included if their goal is emancipation. See Administration for Children and Families (2003).

3. "Children" encompasses individuals aged 18 and under. The total includes the approximately 500,000 children living with one biological parent and a stepparent who adopted them.

4

been" their biological parents (i.e., were of the same race or ethnicity); and in most cases there was no contact between the biological parents and either the adoptive parents or adoptee.

Although adoption remains a source of shame and the shroud of secrecy has not been fully lifted, over the last twenty years there has been a substantial shift in the adoption climate. For example, there has been a steady trend away from confidential adoption towards openness, i.e., direct or indirect contact between adoptive families and birth families. In cases of private and independent adoption, it is now common for the birth mother to choose the adoptive parents for her child from a portfolio of waiting families. In the case of "semi-open" or "mediated" adoption, the birth family and adoptive family do not share identifying information, but communicate through an agency or other third party; in "fully open" or "fully disclosed" adoptions there is direct contact ranging from occasional phone calls to lengthy and regular visits.

Single parent adoptions are also becoming more common. According to the Department of Health and Human Services, in 2000, 33 percent of the children adopted from foster care were adopted by single parents. This is up from 0.5–4 percent in the 1970s (National Adoption Information Clearinghouse 2002a). Moreover, approximately 25 percent of children adopted with special needs are adopted by single parents (Piasecki 1987). (Recall also that the only option for gay and lesbian couples to adopt is for one of the couple to adopt as a single parent, possibly followed by a second-parent adoption.) The picture is not quite as rosy as this might suggest, however, for one explanation of these numbers is a strong bias in adoption agencies and amongst social workers in favor of white, heterosexual, married, middle or upper-middle class couples as the first choice for a placement. Children who are harder to place—due to age, race, disability—are designated for the "lower-ranked" homes of unmarried couples, single parents, lesbians and gays, and those with lower incomes, even though such families may be ideal for certain children (National Adoption Information Clearinghouse 2000b).

The past twenty years have also shown a marked increase in domestic transracial adoptions and international adoptions in which adoptees and adoptive parents are not of the same race or ethnicity. Both international and transracial adoptions made up for 8 percent of adoptions in 1993 (National Adoption Information Clearinghouse 2002c). Such "visible" adoptions disrupt the norm of secrecy; plausibly, they have been made possible by and contributed to a cultural shift in our understanding of families (Pertman 2000). However, domestic transracial adoptions are a source of controversy (Liem 2000). In 1972 the National Association of Black Social Workers issued a statement condemning the adoption of Black children by Whites, and continues (as of 1994) to hold that transracial adoptions are unnecessary and should be treated as a last resort (Neal 1996). However, federal legislation passed in 1994 (MEPA 94) forbids federal agencies from delaying or denying adoption of a child on the basis of race (Hollinger 2001). In 1996, MEPA was amended to forbid agencies from taking race into account in making placement decisions.[4]

Last but not least, economic factors play a substantial role in the adoption world. Undoubtedly, one of the major factors in a woman's (or a couple's) decision to relinquish a child is their financial situation. This is true in both international and domestic adoptions. The cost of adopting varies tremendously, depending on a variety of factors. According to the NAIC, factors affecting the cost of adoption include the following (National Adoption Information Clearinghouse 2003):

- the type of adoption
- the area of the United States where the adoption occurs
- whether or not the agency charges a sliding-scale fee based on family income
- the country of origin of a foreign-born child
- the amount of state or federal subsidy available for a child with special needs
- federal or state tax credits available for reimbursement of adoption expenses
- employer adoption benefits
- state reimbursement for non-recurring expenses for the adoption of a child with special needs

They estimate that currently one can expect to pay:

Domestic public agency adoption: Zero to $2,500
Domestic private agency adoption: $4,000 to $30,000+
Domestic independent adoption: $8,000 to $30,000+
Intercountry private agency or independent adoption: $7,000 to $25,000

Some employers provide adoption benefits to help defray the costs; some states provide subsidies and tax benefits. Nonetheless, one can expect that in the large majority of adoptions, the adoptive family is financially more secure than the birth parents, and in the adoption world, as elsewhere, the more economically privileged have more options.

4. Thanks go to Elizabeth Bartholet for clarification of the differences between MEPA 94 and MEPA 96.

ADOPTION, FEMINIST THEORY, AND PHILOSOPHY

The essays in this volume are interdisciplinary, and interdisciplinary research begins as a collective enterprise with a common subject matter serving as the focus for different disciplinary paradigms. For example, in women's studies, scholars trained in a broad array of fields—not only in the humanities, but in the social sciences, biology, law, divinity, medicine, public health, social work—bring the expertise of their discipline to consider the phenomenon of gender and its manifestation in their domain. The complexity of gender is not adequately understood by any of these disciplines taken individually; hence an exchange across disciplines becomes essential to developing adequate theories. As interdisciplinary exchange occurs, scholars not only learn about new aspects of gender, eclipsed within their discipline, but also new ways to ask questions that inform their own inquiry. This often prompts critical reflection on traditional or mainstream disciplinary methods and assumptions.

Feminists engaged in interdisciplinary research take gender as their common subject matter and, more specifically, gender injustice. Over the past several decades, feminist research has developed its own strategies of inquiry and methods of analysis, and it has brought these back to the mainstream disciplines. It may be helpful to make explicit two ideas that have played an important role in feminist theorizing and that emerge in the essays collected in this volume: the interdependence of a society's social institutions and its psycho-cultural forms, and the phenomenon of situated knowledge.

First, consider the relationship between institutions and identities. Social categories such as gender and race, but also more specific categories such as citizen, professor, student, wife and adoptee, position one within a structure of social institutions. The different positions carry distinct sets of expectations, entitlements, material benefits, and costs; and in some cases, rights and obligations. In formal institutions the social categories and their implications are explicitly defined; in informal contexts the structure of social positions is more implicit. Those who live within a particular structure of social categories tend to carry with them an understanding of how the system works and their place in it. For example, they expect themselves and others to behave in certain ways; they feel entitled to certain benefits, are willing to act in accordance with even quite harsh norms. To lubricate the interplay between social institutions and each individual's interpretation of their role in them, cultural forms in the arts, literature, and media provide resources for situating the individual within the structure. Cultural narratives take shape in response to institutional and structural pressures (for example, the economy, political events such as war or welfare reform, developments in technology) and in response to individual (and collective) creativity and resistance.

For example, consider marriage. It is surely the case that marriage is a legal and political institution. It is also, however, the lived experience of millions of heterosexual couples, and an experience denied to homosexuals. It is the subject matter of novels and plays; it is a background rite of passage assumed in many layers of our culture. An interdisciplinary feminist discussion of marriage that focused entirely on its legal and political aspects would be lacking. In particular, one would want and expect discussion of issues such as: how are assumptions about marriage revealed in other cultural forms like literature, the arts, etiquette? How might living within (or without) such an institution affect one's subjectivity (as a "wife" or a "husband")? How does the normative weight of marriage frame cultural understandings of love, knowledge, and family? How have bans on interracial marriage affected our understanding of race and our identities more generally? These questions become feminist as they incorporate a critical concern with gender justice; they become philosophical as they question the (often unstated) assumptions behind our ordinary practices and interrogate them.

Many of the essays in this collection raise the same range of questions for the institution of adoption. Questions that concern the law and politics of adoption, in particular, and family, more generally, are central to the discussion. However, for philosophers and feminists, analysis of the phenomenon of adoption cannot end there, because of the complex interplay between social institutions and our individual and collective interpretations of them. We need to ask of families: how have the institutions shaped our understandings of family, and how might critical reflection on these understandings help us reshape the institutions to be more just?

The second theme that deserves note is an attention to situated knowledge. Situated knowledge is a term that one often finds associated with *standpoint epistemology,* a cluster of views according to which a particular socially situated perspective is granted epistemic privilege or authority with respect to a particular domain. *Feminist* standpoint theories, in particular, typically grant such privilege to members of subordinated groups. Usually the privilege in question is granted over the domain of social relations that oppress them. A commitment to *situated knowers* is, however, a weaker commitment (Anderson 2002). To claim that knowers are situated is to claim that what we believe or understand about something is affected by how we are related to it. This is consistent with the other feminist theme just discussed: if being a member of a certain social category brings with it pressure to learn the practices and internalize the norms and expectations of that category, it is not surprising that this process would reveal some phenomena and obscure others.

A commitment to situated knowers does not commit one to *privileging* any particular perspective; nor is it to claim that one is unable to "step outside" one's perspective; nor is it to claim that an objective viewpoint is impossible. In fact, one might argue that any plausible empiricism has to take into account the situatedness of knowing in order to address the potential for bias: the idea that multiple observers of a phenomenon are desirable in order to increase objectivity is itself an acknowledgement of the situatedness of perception and cognition.[5]

Many of the authors in our collection, including ourselves, believe that knowers are situated; more specifically, that those in the adoption triad typically have available to them a different perspective on family, love, race, and knowledge than those who are not. This is not to say that everyone in the triad sees things the same way, or that triad members can only see family, love, and so forth in some "different" way. It is simply to say that those in the adoption triad, more often than those outside it, develop a perspective on family that fully accommodates the process of adopting, growing up adopted, or placing a child for adoption. This perspective, we believe, offers something intellectually and philosophically valuable because of the challenges it poses to certain dominant ideas.

Of course, some scholars *not* in the triad are *more expert* on some aspects of adoption. Given that knowers are situated, a full understanding of adoption would have to take into account the insights gained from (and limitations intrinsic to) many different theoretical approaches, and many different relationships to the phenomena. In the context of feminist and philosophical work, the perspectives of those familiar with adoption have not been prominent (in fact they've been almost entirely missing!). We hope that the essays in this volume will demonstrate to those who have never thought carefully about adoption or see it as theoretically uninteresting that reflection on and from the adoption triad is of significant value.

Some of the essays have a more self-disclosive style than one typically finds in philosophy. In keeping with the idea of knowers as situated, one should not take this self-disclosure as a claim of authority. We interpret this style against the backdrop of work in feminist philosophy that questions the impersonal voice and cautions us to beware of presumed but false objectivity. The alternative to the impersonal is not an utterly personal voice, but philosophical argumentation that makes explicit its sources and its ba-

---

5. The commitment to situated knowers is not standpoint epistemology as typically described. Rather, the idea behind the volume follows a paradigm of feminist intervention in many fields of science: when women scientists enter the field, they notice things that the male scientists didn't notice. Their observations generate new data that have to be taken into account. Or they notice biased background assumptions that structure the theoretical model, and these assumptions are called into question. Note that the new observations and criticisms must also withstand scrutiny—they aren't granted a privileged status—and if a revised theory is to be adequate, it must satisfy a range of familiar epistemic criteria. Although the authors in our volume are humanists, and not scientists, the structure of their argumentation is consistent with the scientific model broadly construed.

sis in experience, so that its strengths and limitations, bias and insight, can be better evaluated (Anderson 1995, esp. 63–64; Diamond 1991). This style of inquiry may not be rhetorically effective in certain contexts or in certain disciplines. But this methodology both draws on and speaks to an ongoing interdisciplinary discussion about how to do feminist research.

This book looks at families, and our assumptions about families, with a critical and questioning eye; what results is an engaging set of essays that address feminist and philosophical topics far beyond the confines of the family and family life. Feminist theorists should be especially interested in the way that certain practices of adoption undercut the legitimacy of the patriarchal family. For feminists, the family plays a central role both as the location of gender injustice, and as the primary scene of moral development and gender identification. Feminists have been quick to question the way in which traditional conceptions of marriage and family have excluded gays and lesbians. Hence there are good reasons for feminists to be wary of the assumption that the traditional family is a natural unit immune to political criticism. And, there is a robust feminist literature critical of the traditional family. Surprisingly, there has been relatively little attention paid to adoption and adoptive families by feminists, and much of what is there is either tacitly or overtly critical of adoption. Our collection begins with what we call "unnatural families" and the light that thinking about them can shed on feminist topics like justice in the family and justice for all families.

NATURAL AND UNNATURAL FAMILIES

Several important philosophical and feminist issues cluster around the natural/social distinction as it functions in relation to adoption and how we think about families. First, there is the question of how to conceptualize families and kinship relations once the existence of adoptive families throws open to question their presumed natural (biological or genetic) basis. Since the family is often taken to be the basic unit of social and political life, the importance of this issue for political philosophy and legal theory is clear. In "Adoption and Its Progeny: Rethinking Family Law, Gender, and Sexual Difference," Drucilla Cornell argues on moral grounds for a rejection of "the state-enforced heterosexual, nuclear, monogamous family" and on feminist grounds against "relinquishment," the widespread, though not universal, practice of requiring birth mothers to give up all contact with their children upon adoption. Claiming that there should be no state intervention into the sexual and intimate relationships that we might choose to inhabit, Cornell argues for a revision of family law which bases the parent-child relationship on a contract model. This way of revisioning families would leave private space for negotiating contacts between birth mothers, their children, and parents-by-contract. In "Open Adoption Is Not for Everyone," Anita L. Allen investigates the ethical dimensions of open adoption. In particular, she asks whether there is a moral obligation for adoptive parents to include birth parents (and their families) in their lives. She argues, against Cornell, that openness is a legitimate option for adoptive families, but not a moral necessity.

In "Methods of Adoption: Eliminating Genetic Privilege," Jacqueline Stevens provides a systematic criticism of the dichotomy between genetic and adoptive families. Stevens argues that the narrative of the genetic family is a myth which is neither numerically nor normatively established despite the extensive support of law and politics. Stevens argues for a thoroughgoing revision of family law in order to establish laws which are both more reflective of actual family life and better able to protect the needs of children than the current system. Like Cornell, Stevens proposes that all parents contract (or adopt) children independently of their genetic relationships. Unlike Cornell, Stevens recognizes the category of mothers, who carry and give birth to children, and on that basis have a privileged status with regard to contracting to parent their gestational child.

The legal and political support given to the married, heterosexual family discussed and criticized by Cornell and Stevens unjustly penalize lesbian and gay families whether formed through adoption or by other means. In "Several Steps Behind: Gay and Lesbian Adoption," Sarah Tobias details the unjust discrimination faced by lesbians and gays seeking to form families, and she argues that a rejection of the hetero-normative conception of the family should be endorsed by feminists on the grounds that it reinforces pernicious gender stereotypes and is harmful to women. Janet Farrell Smith, in "A Child of One's Own: A Moral Assessment of Property Concepts in Adoption," provides a criticism of the assumption that a child is a kind of property or possession where that status is determined by a biological or genetic tie. The property-based view of parental rights, together with its genetic underpinning, is morally unacceptable because it contributes towards the stigmatization and unequal treatment of certain children (orphaned, adopted, and foster children).

FAMILIAL RELATIONSHIPS AND PERSONAL IDENTITIES

The standard philosophical topics of personal identity and self-knowledge have also become central to feminist theorizing in recent years. Interesting and important questions about personal identity, self-knowledge, and the emotions are highlighted in the experience of adoptees, birth parents, and adoptive parents. For example, the assumption that our identities are secured by the genetic tie (and the related thesis of biological essentialism) becomes available for critical evaluation in the context of adoption. And, the Socratic injunction to self-knowledge is complicated in interesting ways for both adoptees and their parents. How is the desire for self-knowledge to be understood in relation to both adopted and non-adopted selves? Even an apparently straightforward issue like the question of maternal identity—who counts as a mother?—becomes complex, disputed, and interesting in relation to adoption. Parental love, sometimes idealized as absolute, unconditional, and unitary, reveals a more complex, less unified dynamic when viewed from the perspective of adoption.

In "Family Resemblances: Adoption, Personal Identity, and Genetic Essentialism," Charlotte Witt considers the problematic issue of the sense of self and identity of adoptees in relation to both Saul Kripke's metaphysical theory of personal identity based on genetic essentialism, and a relational theory of the self, which has been advanced recently in feminist theory. Witt argues that genetic essentialism fails as a theory of personal identity and that the relational theory of the self is more adequate to the experience of adoptees. The discourse of family resemblances is one aspect of personal identity which is particularly charged for adoptees and their families. Witt explores the role that narratives of family resemblance play in families, and the extent to which they provide tacit support for genetic essentialism.

Identity and self-knowledge are the themes of Kimberly Leighton's essay, "Being Adopted and Being a Philosopher: Exploring Identity and the 'Desire to Know' Differently." Leighton uses the notion of being an *adopted self* to question whether or not the self is a stable entity capable of being fully known. According to Leighton, it is the *desire* to know, and the *process* of coming to know, that is crucial to self-knowledge, which is always open-ended and contingent. According to Leighton, being adopted is both a real, lived experience and a metaphor for the contingency of individual identity and the uncertainty of self-knowledge.

The complexity and fluidity of identity—in this case maternal identity—is also the theme of Shelley Park's essay, "Real (M)othering: The Metaphysics of Maternity in Children's Literature." Park uses the multiplicity of mothers in adoption to question standard views of maternity in which genetic, gestational, and social mothering typically coincide in a single person. Arguing for a more fluid and inclusive notion of maternity, and, indeed, for the possibility of multiple mothers, Park uses the narrative of "real motherhood" provided by children's literature to illustrate the shortcomings of standard conceptions of maternity. And she turns to another children's classic, *The Velveteen Rabbit,* to illustrate her proposal that real mothers are those that are loved by their children. This notion of motherhood is both fluid and inclusive; and it is one which makes the child the author of his or her maternal reality.

Songsuk Hahn's paper, "Accidents and Contingencies of Love," explores the idea of unconditional love as the philosopher Harry Frankfurt has developed it. The central example of unconditional love, according to Frankfurt, is the love that a parent feels for a child, who is loved unconditionally, disinterestedly, and not for any particular reason or characteristic. Using examples of the failure of love and connection within the world of adoption (in the phenomenon of abdication) as well as among genetically related parents and children (deadbeat dads), Hahn makes the case that unconditional love is, in fact, interwoven with conditions and contingency in a way that Frankfurt's concept does not acknowledge. Moreover, Hahn explains that, in the sphere of adoption, a child's characteristics (and sometimes lack of characteristics) often serve as reasons which can condition the love between parent and child. The accidents and contingencies of love not only make the notion of unconditional love overly simple and problematic, but they also provide conceptual space for freedom and choice in our loving attachments. Harry Frankfurt replies by distinguishing the notion of unconditional love, which is loving without reasons for our love, from the contingent, causal factors that might affect the existence and persistence of any instance of unconditional love.

CONSTRUCTIONS OF RACE AND CONSTRUCTIONS OF FAMILY

As mentioned earlier, there has been a history of controversy over the issue of race in adoption. This is not surprising. The concept of race and the concept of kin or kind are intertwined, for races are often assumed to be biological kinship groups; and the idea of distinct racial essences corresponding to these groups has been invoked historically to defend anti-miscegenation law (Novkov 2002; Moran 2001).

Contemporary scholars working on race do not assume that races are biological kinds; nonetheless, it can hardly be denied that race remains a social category that carries with it different social and material consequences due to ongoing racism. The family is a primary site where one's identity is formed, where the framework for one's individual relationship to one's social group and the broader society is established; so it is also the site where one develops basic resources to navigate the racial terrain—whether in complicity or not. Yet due to the ongoing effects of racism, many families and communities of color are struggling to cope with devastating poverty, violence, and disenfranchisement; as a result, families and communities differ dramatically in the resources and opportunities they offer to children. What policies should be in place to achieve justice for the children, the families, and the communities whose lives are at stake? How should the social reality of race be taken into account?

Elizabeth Bartholet's essay "Abuse and Neglect, Foster Drift, and the Adoption Alternative" argues that policies that prioritize "family preservation" often do so at the expense of children languishing in foster care or in group homes, and being returned to unsafe or severely disadvantaged circumstances. Drawing on lessons from the battered women's movement, Bartholet argues that more should be done to protect children from maltreatment, both by increasing family support services and by using coercive measures to remove children and more quickly freeing them for adoption. Dorothy Roberts's "Feminism, Race, and Adoption Policy" takes issue with Bartholet's interpretation of the problem, highlighting the role of racism in decisions to remove children from homes, in the lack of support and services provided to families, in the disrespect shown to families and communities of color. Describing Bartholet's approach as overly focused on the individual—the abusive parent(s), the child, the adoptive parents— Roberts argues that a feminist analysis should attend to and seek to eliminate the racial hierarchy that gives rise to the numbers of children in crisis; in her view, coercive intervention only reinforces that hierarchy rather than dismantles it.

Child welfare policy must evolve within the constraints of law and morality. Hawley Fogg-Davis's essay, "Racial Randomization: Imagining Nondiscrimination in Adoption," steps back from debates over family preservation to consider what is legally and morally at stake in the practice of transracial adoption. Employing a strict interpretation of equal protection law, Davis argues that there's a case to be made that prospective adoptive parents should not be allowed to designate the race of the child they are willing to adopt. Although Davis does not support this as policy, she uses the thought-experiment of racial randomization (placing children with otherwise qualified families without regard to race) as a way to explore our assumptions about racial justice and ongoing race-based social aversion.

Over the past thirty years there has been significant progress in reducing institutional racism. It is less clear what progress we have made with race-based aversion. Davis's essay illustrates continued anxiety about cross-racial intimacy and family formations; it suggests that a deep racism remains. In "You Mixed? Racial Identity without Racial Biology," Sally Haslanger draws on her experience as a White mother of Black children to consider how life within such a racially complex category can disrupt racial identity. She argues, in particular, that racial identity—understood as the individual's incorporation of his or her racial position—should not be understood as a conscious identification with a race, but as more literally an incorporation or embodiment of racial norms in the practices of everyday life. Because racial identity in this sense is not fully conscious, the aversions and other manifestations of racism easily remain even after one's racist beliefs are changed.

The essays in this volume show how interdisciplinary thinking about adoption can reveal new perspectives on the institution of adoption itself. Not surprisingly perhaps, unstated assumptions concerning race, identity, and the natural form of family life shape the tacit norms and explicit rules governing adoption and adoptive practices. Through uncovering these unstated assumptions and critically evaluating the explicit rules, our contributors provide a context for rethinking family and adoption, and the norms and rules that govern them, in a more humane and just fashion.

The essays also contribute to the exploration of traditional philosophical and feminist issues. This is hardly surprising, since the family lies at the intersection of nature and culture, and it embodies, and is shaped by, both social and legal norms. Given the richness of topics and the complexity of discussion in these papers, however, we collect them with the hopes of opening up new avenues of philosophical and feminist thought concerning the ethical, political, and—even—metaphysical and epistemological issues that emerge once we begin to think about the family from a new perspective.

Part I

"NATURAL" AND
"UNNATURAL" FAMILIES

CHAPTER ONE

Adoption and Its Progeny: Rethinking Family Law, Gender, and Sexual Difference

DRUCILLA CORNELL

Why have feminists been reluctant participants in the politics of adoption? Today, the law in most states pits the two mothers against each other while the media dramatizes the purportedly hostile relationship between the two. Think of the "heart-tugging" pictures of baby Jessica as she is removed from her adoptive parents to be given back to her birth mother and father. The press in general has never shown much sympathy for birth mothers. Nor has the feminist press, wherein for years members of the various birth mothers' associations have tried without success to publish.[1] These organizations have accused feminists of favoring adopting mothers, either because they are adopting mothers themselves or because, like the public in general, they have disdain for the birth mother who gave up her baby.

This reluctance may not spring from conscious attitudes about birth mothers. There are real difficulties raised by adoption when a custody battle is fought. Such battles challenge one of our culture's deepest fantasies—that there can only be one mother and, therefore, that we have to pick the "real" mother. Picking one mother over another is a harsh judgment not easily reconciled with feminist solidarity, which supposedly grows out of the shared experience of our oppression as women, uncovered through consciousness raising that gives new meaning to what we have had to endure under male domination (MacKinnon 1989). At first glance, however, the so-called birth mother and the adopting mother do not share the same reality with respect to treatment. More often than not the privi-

1. See generally the work of Lorraine Dusky.

lege of class separates the two mothers. In numerous contemporary movies we see the scene of the two warring mothers played out in its most stereotypic form: the responsible, married white woman vying against the young, sexually irresponsible, crack-addicted black woman. The woman who is picked by law as the "real" mother is the one privileged by class and race. The politics of imperialist domination and the struggle of postcolonial nations to constitute themselves as independent nations are inevitably implicated in international adoptions. Hence, it is not surprising that one of the first steps in the constitution of nationhood is an end to international adoptions (Schemo 1996). Adoption is fraught with issues of race, class, and imperialist domination that have persistently caused divisions in the second wave of feminism.

The language of adoption is the language of war. In most states the "birth mother" surrenders her child to the state, which then transfers the child to the adopting, predominantly white, middle-class, heterosexual parents. A recent change is that single mothers are allowed to adopt. There are almost no states in the United States that allow a gay or lesbian couple to openly adopt a baby as a couple. Single or coupled, gay men are almost entirely excluded from access to legally recognized parenthood. It is still the exception to the rule that a lesbian can adopt a child born into the relationship by one mother but raised by both women and ascend to the status of legally recognized parent.

According to current law, what the "birth mother" surrenders is not just primary custodial responsibility of her child, but her entitlement to any kind of relationship with him or her in the future. She is denied even the most basic kind of information as to the child's well-being. In states where records are closed, adopted children have to "show cause" to get any information about their heredity or the whereabouts of their "birth mother" and/or their biological father. For decades now, birth mothers' organizations have militantly protested against the surrender of their entitlement to the status of mother, even if they chose or were forced by circumstances to forsake formal primary custodial responsibility of their child. Lorraine Dusky eloquently writes:

> They call me "biological mother." I hate those words. They make me sound like a baby machine, a conduit, without emotions. They want me to forget and go out and make a new life. I had a baby and gave her away. But I am a mother. (Dusky 1979)

Adopted children are now in the process of challenging as unconstitutional their unequal treatment at the hands of the legal system. After all, nonadopted children have access to information about themselves and their genealogy. On the one hand, it seems obvious that adopted children are indeed being treated unequally. Could there be a compelling state interest that would legitimate such unequal treatment? A feminist answer to that question has to be that there could be no compelling state interest that could legitimate the relinquishment of the birth mother's entitlement to any kind of access to her child or to the child's access to her. We need to have a deeper analysis of why that relinquishment has historically been enforced and felt by many to be so necessary to the protection of "family values." Without this analysis we will continue to establish victors and vanquished in a war that is usually portrayed as being one between women. The issue of adoption demands that we examine our entire family law system from the ground up. In spite of attempts at feminist reform, our family law remains grounded in enforced heterosexuality with its inscription of rigid gender identities and corresponding familial roles and duties.

This chapter will argue that the state-enforced heterosexual, nuclear, monogamous family cannot be sustained under an equivalent law of persons. Enforced monogamous heterosexuality makes the state and not the person the source of moral meaning of her sexuate being and how it should be lived with "all our kin."[2] It is time that we recognize that governmentally enforced sexual choices, let alone the outright denial of the right to parent to some persons because of their sexual lives, is inconsistent with the equal protection of their imaginary domain. Feminists have a strong political interest in insisting that the right to build families and to foster our own intimate lives be privileged over the state enforcement of any *ideal* of the good family. I will conclude with my own proposed guidelines for family law reform, which would change the very meaning of adoption as it now is legally and culturally understood.

Many birth mothers who have given up their babies for adoption have undergone trauma. A legal system that makes the cut from her child absolute blocks any hope for the recovery from this trauma, for the mother certainly, and maybe for the child. The best law can do for adopted children and birth mothers who feel compelled to seek out one another is to provide them with the space to work through the traumatic event that has to some extent formed them. Law cannot erase the past. It certainly cannot provide a magical "cure" to the emotional difficulties we all face in our intimate associations. Some adopted children will want to search for their birth parents and some will not. Some birth parents will want to be found; others will not. Law cannot take the passion and complexity out of emotionally fraught situations. Still, the imaginary domain will give to the persons involved in an adoption the moral and psychic space to come to terms

2. I borrow this phrase from Carol Stack's well-known book. Stack's ethnographic study of African American families showed that "kin" was a much broader concept than that which has dominated the white middle-class community. Stack's ethnographic work showed that biological ties do not define the parameters of the family (Stack 1974).

with their history, the meaning it has for them, and the possibilities it yields for new ways of imagining themselves.

THE MEANING OF MODERN ADOPTION

Why has adoption come to be understood as requiring complete relinquishment of all access to or even information about the child? We can see all the contradictions wrought by this demand for absolute surrender in recent lesbian coparent adoptions. In such adoptions, the last thing the "birth" mother wants is to give up all access to her child. She wants to share childrearing responsibilities within the relationship. Long before lesbian adoptions became possible to the limited degree they are now, informal "adoptions" in African American communities kept families together by extending them, rather than by shutting out the birth mother. In these communities there are often two mothers, which avoids the demand to pick one as the "real" mother (Stack 1974).

Modern legal adoptions are only one form of adoption and are a recent historical event (Klibanoff and Klibanoff 1973, chap. 16). We have to ask what legal interests are at stake in these adoptions and why adoption has come to demand total surrender of both the child and of all information about her. Why not identify adoption as only the signing away of primary custody? To understand why we define adoption as we do, we need to look at the intersection between women's legal standing in society as a whole and the residues of patriarchy in family law as they effectuate an unjust limit on women's right to claim their own person.

THE RELATIONSHIP BETWEEN WOMEN'S CIVIL
STANDING AND THEIR ROLE IN THE FAMILY

The imaginary domain gives to women, as well as to men, the chance to become a person, to interiorize and cohere the identifications that make us who we are into a self. Hegel argued that the modern civil law (and in the case of a common law country like our own, the constitutional law) received its only justification and legitimacy because it was the guardian of man's subjectivity (Hegel 1967). When Hegel wrote "man," he specifically meant men because it was only they who were accorded status as persons in the civil law.

For Hegel, in the genealogically male family, the woman remains bound by her duties in the family as the servant of man's needs. She has no independent standing in civil society. According to Hegel, ethical life includes family life as well as life in the organizations of civil society—corporations, unions, and the like. But unlike the other organizations, the family is natural. Women can participate in ethical life because of their central role in the family. Their nature makes them duty bound, and indeed, their sense of duty to their family is one reason why women as women could play an important role in the ethical life of society (Hegel 1967, 10–22).

Man, on the other hand, is able to find his freedom and exercise his subjectivity as both a citizen and a member of civil society, because his "natural" side is cared for in the family. Further, the law is the guardian of his subjectivity, because it protects the space for man to interiorize his identity as an individuated human being who is irreducible to his social role. For Hegel, the crowning achievement of the modern legal system was the reconciliation of the objective power of the state with the legal freedom of individuals.

But the law could not be the guardian for woman's subjectivity, since woman was defined by her exteriority, that is, by state-imposed duties. The state realized her nature by imposing womanly duties on her. Thus, only by taking up her properly allotted role—that is, as wife and mother—did she warrant protection by the state.

Obviously, as a feminist I strongly disagree with Hegel's conclusions that a woman's true nature is to be duty bound to the family and that the state owes allegiance to her only in her role as wife and mother. But his description of how a woman's legal identity is intertwined with her duties to the family, and not in her entitlement as a person, remains a powerful explanation, in spite of his own intent to justify it, of why it has been so difficult to adequately challenge family law. Obviously things have changed since Hegel's time. Women are public citizens. Women can vote. Women can run for public office. They have some independent standing in civil society when unmarried. Women can own property in their own name and can obtain credit. But these changes have been piecemeal because they have not adequately challenged the basis of the legal problem sweepingly called patriarchy.

Patriarchy and Its Legal Effects

For my purposes, the word *patriarchy* indicates the manner in which a woman's legal identity remains bound up with her duties to the state as wife and mother within the traditional heterosexual family. Our feminist demand must be for the full release of women from this legal identity that is wholly inconsistent with the recognition of each one of us as a free and equal person.

We cannot demand release from a legal identity that defines and limits what it means to be a woman through state-imposed duties without chal-

23

lenging the legal institution of the monogamous heterosexual family. The duties that define woman in her social identity are inseparable from the conjugal institution of the heterosexual family. The demand for women's release from the bonds of duty demands the reform of our family law system from the ground up. Furthermore, it is inseparable from the demands of gays and lesbians to be free and equal to create their own persons.

If we understand that women's legal identity in both family life and civil society remains bound up with an externally imposed set of duties, we can at least make sense of why it is that the so-called birth mother is deemed as giving up all entitlement to any kind of relationship with her child when she yields her duty to be the child's caretaker. Under the patriarchal scheme that Hegel so accurately describes, a woman is entitled to protection by the state because she takes up her duties as caregiver to her family. If she forsakes those duties, she is denied any of the protection given to mothers. Since she has no independent standing in civil society, she has no social life. In Hegel's state, women are mothers, not persons. Let me put this as clearly as possible: it is only in the context of a system of duties that remains bound up with women's legal identity in the heterosexual family that we can even begin to understand the unequal treatment of birth mothers and adopted children.

The relationship between legal identity in civil society, or "social life,"[3] and the system of duties in the heterosexual family can help us understand the driving anxiety about infertility that has haunted the history of modern adoptions. If a woman's social worth is inseparable from the fulfillment of her duty as a mother, then if she cannot live up to that duty, she is confronted with the loss of her only social status. Of course, the obsession with genetic ties is also tied into unconscious fantasies about the meaning of masculinity and racial superiority (Roberts 1995). The protagonist of the film *The Official Story* sees herself as worthless because of her inability to meet her duty to biologically reproduce her husband's line. She and her husband adopt a child, but the adoption is kept secret to protect her from public notice of her failure. The symbolic reduction of woman to the maternal function is intimately tied to the sexual shame experienced because of infertility (Cornell 1991).

This protection from public exposure of the adopting mother's failure to be a woman because she has failed to meet the symbolic meaning of womanhood demands the erasure of the birth mother. It is not entitlement but rather the terror before the loss of identity that explains so much of the secrecy that surrounds adoption and, in the case of *The Official Story,* allows the woman to blind herself to the reality of her daughter's tragic history. She discovers that her daughter is a child of a missing person, prob-

---

3. Please refer to Cornell (1998), chap. 2 for what I mean by "social life."

ably one of those murdered by the Argentinean government. It is only by slowly freeing herself from the imprisonment of imposed duties in the family that she can see her way to her responsibility as a citizen of Argentina. She sheds her exteriorized feminine identity, and in a profound sense becomes a person for herself when she dons the identity of a citizen responsible for the fate of her country as well as for the destiny of her adopted daughter. Before, she left the world of politics to men. She dons her identity as citizen by taking her place in a demonstration beside the grandmother of her daughter. Her prior life in the conjugal institution of the heterosexual family does not survive her insistence of her political responsibility as citizen and her ethical responsibility to her daughter's grandmother. What relationship the two women will have to one another is left open, but it is clear that there can be no going back once the grandmother is accepted and embraced. The woman's embrace of the grandmother as someone entitled to a relationship to her daughter left nothing in its place. It ended her life in the traditional family.

The Official Story presents in an extreme form the continuing presence of kidnapping disguised as an economic transaction in an adoption. *The Official Story* also graphically demonstrates the ability of the rich and powerful in many of the world's nations to steal children of the poor or the politically dispossessed. This phenomenon is well documented in heartwrenching stories of the mothers of "the disappeared." The dictatorship in Argentina that allowed babies to be stolen for adoption is not an isolated event. Indeed, the open stealing of a person's children is part of the enactment of psychic as well as physical torture (Daniel 1996). *The Official Story* is clear: disappeared persons do not *have* children because they are deemed socially dead; their social death is a preliminary obliteration foreshadowing their actual murder.

The scene of adoption is ensnared in imposed roles associated with women's legal identity within the heterosexual family. The first step in untangling oneself from these imposed roles is to don the identity of citizen and to demand a full civil identity as a person. Simply put, as feminists we must demand that we are entitled to rights, not because we are mothers, but because we are persons.

The Imaginary Domain and the Right of Birth Mothers and Adopted Children

My argument so far has been that, even now, the way in which women have been symbolically sexed is partly constituted by legal duties that have been imposed upon them, so that the very idea of the equal protection of women's imaginary domain challenges the legitimacy of those state-

DRUCILLA CORNELL

imposed duties. Our "selves" have been buried under these duties for far too long. As Irigaray has written:

> Valorized by society as a mother, nurturer, and housewife (the community needs children to make up the future work force, as defenders of the nation and as reproducers of society, aside from the fact that the family unit is the most profitable one for the State in that much of the work that is done within it goes unpaid, for example), woman is deprived of the possibility of interiorizing her female identity. (Irigaray 1996)

The value of privacy is expanded and not curtailed in the ideal of the imaginary domain. First, it challenges the idea that heterosexuality has ever been truly privatized. Obviously it has not, since it has been enforced by the state; thus, violation of heterosexuality has meant criminalization of nonconformist sexuality and, in many cases, enforced exile from a home country. Second, it recognizes that we need not only actual physical space, but also psychic space in which to struggle to become a person. The individual, not the state, should be the normative "master" of this kind of struggle in which we seek to make sense of the identifications that make up who we are.

THE RIGHTS OF BIRTH MOTHERS

Would the equal protection of the imaginary domain give rights to birth mothers and adopted children? First, let us take the example of so-called birth mothers. It is only too evident that the struggle of every woman to become who she is demands a confrontation with the connection between femininity and motherhood. For some women, oppressions imposed by race, class, national, and sexual identity have forced absolute separation from their children upon them. Carol Austin, who had to hide her own relationship to her lesbian lover in order for them to successfully complete an international adoption, describes the situation of the "birth mother" of their first adopted child as follows:

> A real joy for us was being able to spend a lot of time with Catherine's birth mother, Violetta, a twenty-two-year-old Quechua Indian who was also Julie's maid. When Violetta had become pregnant out of wedlock, she had been taken in by some distant members who struggled to care for their own five children. Living in a crowded, dirt-floored home in a poverty-ridden neighborhood in Lima, the family was not willing to care for another child. And if Violetta decided to keep her child, she could not work. Violetta's and her child's survival depended on her giving up this firstborn baby to adoption. (Austin 1995)

26

Violetta did not have the economic option to take custodial responsibility for her child. Austin was only too well aware that Violetta's decision to give up her child was not a choice, and Austin knew that no amount of emotional support from her could make up for Violetta's loss and sorrow that she could not keep her baby. Still, to whatever degree it might help Violetta, both Austin and her partner wanted her to get to know them—wanted her to know that her baby would be safe. They showed her pictures of where the baby was to live; they left their address with her so that she could check on her baby's well-being.

Certainly, these measures, as reassuring as they may have been, could not make up for Violetta's terrible either/or, a forced sexual choice in the worst sense. Some adopting mothers have spoken of their feeling that their babies were destined for them. Austin was well aware that if this baby was destined for her and her lover, then Violetta was destined to be deprived of her child by economic circumstances. Measures could be taken to ameliorate Violetta's pain, but the poverty of her life circumstances still remained. Austin's sensitivity to Violetta's horrible either/or, and the economic poverty and oppression that imposed it, came in part from her own struggle as an adopting lesbian parent.

Austin described her pain at having to be disappeared in order to adopt a child for herself and her lover. Again, economics played a major role in the lovers' choice of who was to appear as a mother. Austin's circumstances were in no way comparable to Violetta's, but she did not have the same kind of professional job as her lover did, who was put forward as most suitable for the role of (supposedly) single mother because of her professional and financial standing. But, in spite of her realization that this was the best way for the two of them to adopt a baby, Austin rebelled:

> I soon found myself emotionally stranded between anger and guilt. I felt angry and totally left out by my externally forced, yet self-imposed, invisibility, And right on the heels of my anger came my guilt! It was, after all, Jane who was putting in hours of meeting time, and it was her financial and personal history that was being dissected. I didn't envy her, yet I began to have an all or nothing reaction . . . Finally immersion at *any* level, without recognition of my existence, became impossible. How naïve I had been to assume, only a few months before, that my invisibility would be no problem. The entire adoption situation had forced open some of my raw childhood wounds. (p. 106)

Austin's emotional pain at being forcibly rendered invisible sensitized her both to a birth mother's need to be seen and understood and to the adopted child's need to be in touch with her national heritage.

Could a birth mother who chose or was forced to give up primary custody still know herself at the deepest recesses of her person to be a mother?

Birth mothers' testimonies have answered yes to that question. To rob her of her chance to struggle through what meaning being a mother still has for her is to put the state, and not the woman, as the master over the construction of her sense of who she is. Birth mothers have rights, not as birth mothers, but as persons who, like all others, must be allowed the space to come to terms with their own life-defining decisions about sexuality and family.

Lorraine Dusky is only one of many birth mothers who have described their anguish at the enforced separation between them and their children. In her case, she knew that there was crucial information that the adopted parents needed to have about her daughter. Dusky had taken birth control pills during the early stage of her pregnancy, before she realized that she was pregnant. Studies later found that the pills could cause serious gynecological problems in the next generation. She tried to get the agency that had handled the adoption to pass the crucial information on to the adopting parents; she was desperate to know that her daughter received the proper medical attention. The agency told her that her daughter was fine. Tragically, the information was in fact never passed along to her daughter's adopting parents. As it turned out, the adopting parents were trying to locate Dusky because, although Dusky's daughter did not suffer from gynecological problems, she had suffered severe seizures, almost drowning twice; the adopting parents urgently needed to communicate with Dusky about her medical history. Dusky finally found her daughter through the adoption underground. The adopting mother recognized her as Jane's other mother, and Dusky has for many years had a relationship with her daughter.

Dusky's story had a happy ending. But why did Dusky—white, middle class, and on her way to becoming a successful journalist—give her baby up in the first place? The story of her decision is inseparable from the sexual shame imposed upon women in the 1950s who did not get pregnant in the proper way: that is, within legal marriage. Abortion was illegal, and, like many women who hoped against hope that they were not pregnant, she put off searching for alternative routes to get an abortion. By the time she found access to an illegal abortion in Puerto Rico, it was too late. Adoption was her only option, because abortion was illegal, and because the blending of personal and political morality made it nearly impossible at that time for an unmarried, white, middle-class woman to be a single mother. Dusky's decision exemplifies what I mean when I say that enforced sexual choice arises from denying women their equivalent chance to claim their person and to represent their own sexuate being.[4]

4. See chapter 1 of my *Imaginary Domain* (New York: Routledge, 1995) for a discussion of how I use the term "sexuate being."

What should a birth mother relinquish when she relinquishes primary custody of her child? Only that—primary custody. The equal protection of the birth mother's imaginary domain at least demands that she be allowed access to any information she desires to have about her child, and to have the chance to meet and explore with the child what kind of relationship they can develop.

The child should have the same right to access information about his or her biological mother and father as the biological parents have with respect to their child. Again, once we accept that even a primordial sense of self is not just given to us, but is a complicated lifelong process of imagining and projecting ourselves over time, we can see how important it is to have access to one's family history if one feels the need to have it. If the meaning of that history is inseparable from the struggle of postcolonial nations to achieve meaningful economic and political independence, then that history is political from the outset. Heritage has a genetic component, but not only that. The break with the nation, culture, and language of one's birth inevitably imposed by an international adoption involves factors that must be made available for symbolization. Under our current law, an internationally adopted child is already subjected to second-class citizenship. Certain rights of citizenship, including the right to run for the presidency of the country, are denied.[5] But even if we were to remove the taint of second-class citizenship, the child still needs to make sense of the break, to have the chance to recover herself and the meaning of keeping in touch with the linguistic and cultural traditions of her country of origin through her own imaginary domain.

Children should not have to show cause, let alone show that they are emotionally disturbed because of their adoptive status. The demand to show cause is just one more way in which people who do not fit neatly into the purportedly natural heterosexual family are pathologized. Again, the imagined heterosexual adopting family is privileged as the one deserving of protection of the state, even against the child who is a member of it. My only serious disagreement with some of the literature written by birth mothers is the idealization of biological ties. There is an old Italian saying that blood seeks blood. But blood also robs, rapes, and murders blood. Moreover, as Dorothy Roberts has eloquently argued, the idealization of genetic ties is intertwined with the most extreme racist fantasies, including the desire for racial purity (Roberts 1995).

To conclude, adopted children and birth mothers should be allowed access to each other as part of the equal protection of their imaginary domain. We should have public records in which all adopted children and

---

5. The imposition of this second-class citizenship itself needs to be reformed in the name of equality.

birth parents can register. A birth mother who was forced to give up her child obviously was not granted the protection of her right to represent her own sexuate being. She had a decision thrust upon her either by economic circumstances or, as in Dusky's case, because of the sexual hypocrisy that dominated this country in the 1950s. *Her right should be based not on the fact of her biological motherhood but on her personhood.* If, in spite of circumstances, she still represents herself as a mother who has given up on primary custody, but only that, she should be allowed to follow through in her efforts to reach her child. The fear of the hysterical birth mother is just that, fear. The adoption resolves the issue of primary custody, except in the few states where lesbian lovers are allowed joint custody; custody laws should be tailored to meet the needs of lesbian joint custody, all the while protecting the established custody of adopting mothers who are not in lesbian relationships. Dusky did not try to steal her daughter Jane from her adopting parents. She knew she could not undo what she had done, that Jane now had two mothers, and she had to come to terms with that. Jane calls Lorraine by her first name and not "mother," perhaps to recognize the differential relationship between the two mothers. Yet everyone agrees that it is better this way.

What of the woman who, when she gives up primary custody, also wishes to escape entirely from any imposition on her self of the role of mother? Such a woman should be allowed her refusal to register. But the law cannot make it illegal for the child to track down the birth mother. In the end it is between them. This is an example of why I argue that we should not expect the law to do more than provide us with the space to work through and personalize our complicated life histories. It cannot heal trauma. It cannot protect a birth mother who is tracked by her child from the pain of confrontation with her child. Such a confrontation with her child could undoubtedly challenge her sense of who she has struggled to become. The protection of the imaginary domain demands that space be open to explore and establish relationships, but cannot provide the moral content of those relationships without delimiting the space that its justification demands to be kept open.

THE IMAGINARY DOMAIN AND FAMILY LAW REFORM

My defense of the imaginary domain insists that the law protect it as a right. This breaks even with feminists who agree with me that our family law needs to be reconceptualized from the ground up. Recognition of the suffering that formal equality brings in its wake in hierarchically arranged families has led many in the international human rights movement to return to the idea of the expansion of state duties to women and children as part of an overarching concept of the good, which can provide a solution to the continuing reality of inequality between the sexes. Such expanded, affirmative duties are seen as necessary for the protection of women and children. But there are serious problems with the establishment of these kinds of duties. Legislation in some postcolonial nations has attempted to stabilize heterosexual families against the informal sexual arrangements that had previously reigned.[6] One aspect of this legislation, often articulated in terms of the need to protect the reproduction of the next generation of workers, has seemingly had the progressive aspect of imposing affirmative duties on the state to protect women and children, for example, from abuse within the family. But, as Jacqui Alexander has argued, a severe price has been paid for this legislation. As she has effectively demonstrated, the protection from abuse was conditioned on the mandate to marry:

> For most women who stand outside the legal definitions of "party to a marriage," no such claims can be made for relief from the court. Domestic violence as a legal construct—or more accurately, women's experience of physical, sexual and psychic violence together, in a space that has been designated as private—operates as a proxy to ensure the allocation of private property within disruptive hetero-sexual marriage (70% of children in the Bahamas are brought into being outside of hetero-sexual marriage) might both increase the state's anxiety around questions of hetero-sexual respectability as well as threaten the ideology of primogeniture. (Alexander 1997, 76–77)

Because she is a lesbian, Alexander has been outlawed from her own country on the basis of legislation that mandates a return to the patriarchal family structure in which a woman's legal identity is bound up with her duties within the traditional heterosexual family (Alexander 1994). Duty to the nation and duty to be heterosexual are conflated. Alexander writes:

> The nation has always been conceived in hetero-sexuality, since biology and reproduction are at the heart of its impulse. The citizenship machinery is also located here, in the sense that the prerequisites of good citizenship and loyalty to the nation are simultaneously sexualized and hierarchized into a class of good, loyal, reproducing, hetero-sexual citizens, and a subordinated marginalized class of new citizens who by virtue of choice and perversion choose not to do so. (Alexander 1997, 84)

Since Alexander failed to live up to the nation's demand to be a good heterosexual woman, she lost her legal identity, her very right to citizen-

6. See generally the work of M. Jacqui Alexander.

ship. She was not just rendered socially dead; she was literally banished. So, the beginning of a program of family reform must begin with the recognition of women as persons whose citizenship and civil standing are not bound by traditional female duties within the family.

LIMITING FREEDOM: PROBLEMATIC
FEMINIST REFORM PROGRAMS

Before turning to my own guidelines for family law reform, I need to discuss and critique programs of reform offered by Martha Fineman and Luce Irigaray, since both thinkers argue that our current family law must be radically transformed. Although each offers visionary alternatives to our current family law, my disagreement with both is that their programs controvert women's freedom by limiting their right to represent their own sexuate being.

Martha Fineman argues masterfully that the entitlement of women as mothers demands that we replace the sexual family altogether. To do so would abolish marriage as a legal category:

> In other words, I suggest that all relationships between adults be non-legal, and therefore, non-privileged—unsubsidized by the state. In this way, "equality" is achieved in regard to all choices of sexual relational affiliations. I suggest we destroy the marital model altogether and collapse all sexual relationships into the same category—private—not sanctioned, privileged or preferred by law. (Fineman 1995, 5)

For Fineman, then, once marriage is no longer legally recognized as the core unit privileged in law, the baseline norm for the family would be the mother/child dyad. To the response, "but that's sexist—it excludes men," Fineman reminds us that there are other roles for men besides lovers and sexual reproducers. Describing a typical exchange in class, Fineman constructs her response to that charge as follows:

> "Why," I respond, "do you think that men's major, definitive role in the family is only expressed in terms of their sexual affiliation with women? Don't men also find their places within units as sons, or as a mother's brother, as uncles to her children? What about grandfathers? Why are you disturbed by a paradigm that challenges the way we typically think about intimacy between men and women—a vertical rather than a horizontal tie; a biological rather than sexual affiliation, an intergenerational organization of intimacy?" (Fineman 1995, 5)

Fineman would give fathers rights, but these rights would be based on neither a simple biological connection nor a man's marital relationship to the child's mother. Instead, both married and unmarried fathers would have to show "biology plus" in order to claim a parental right to their child. Moreover, paternal responsibility would no longer be coterminous with economic support. Although fathers could claim parental rights by showing an actual caretaking role, they would not be included in the baseline norm for the family as *fathers*. To be included in that norm, a man would have to show that he was a committed primary caregiver, taking on the features we stereotypically associate with the mother. The mother/child dyad functions as a metaphor, which is why Fineman can argue that men could potentially be "mothers." Indeed, for Fineman, men can fully come into the family only as mothers.

> First, I believe that men can and should be Mothers. In fact, if men are interested in acquiring legal access to children (or other dependents), I argue they *must* be Mothers in the stereotypical nurturing sense of that term—that is, engaged in caretaking. (235)

The dyad is a metaphor for the practice of care for dependents that all societies demand. The "child" does not need to be a literal child, but can be anyone who is dependent in the ways children are dependent on adult care and management. Fineman's dyad would be a core family protected by a redefined doctrine of entity privacy. Aware of its patriarchal roots, Fineman is careful to unhook her own concept of entity privacy from its traditional conceptualization as the protection of the man as the head of his household. Still, the inadequacies of individual privacy are only too evident in the case of single mothers who, because they are dependent on the state, cannot claim "privacy" as autonomous individuals. As Fineman rightfully notes, their dependence has left them prey to state violations of their dignity and the dignity of their families.

According to Fineman, her redefinition would end public persecution of single mothers and would instead recognize them for the valuable and inevitable labor they perform:

> Under my intimacy scheme, however, single mothers and their children and indeed all "extended" families transcending generations would not be "deviant" and forgotten or chastised forms that they are considered to be today because they do not include a male head of household. Family and sexuality would not be confluent; rather, the mother-child formation would be the "natural" or core family unit—it would be the base entity around which social policy and legal rules are fashioned. The intergenerational, nonsexual organization of intimacy is what would be protected and privileged in law and policy. (5–6)

Fineman has written a brave book that challenges us to redefine the family. My disagreement with her is that there can be *no state imposed* baseline norm that privileges one kind of intimacy over another. For some people, and not just heterosexuals, horizontal sexual intimacy is how they wish to represent their sexuate being. They should be legally allowed to express their horizontal love whether it is called marriage or some newly created legal name for horizontal love that does not proceed by contract alone. Obviously, to the degree that there is marriage, it should be open to us all—gays and lesbians, as well as straight men and women. I agree with Fineman that intimacy and sexuality should not be forced by the state into confluence through recognition of the heterosexual family as the natural family. However, it is one thing to argue that there should be no state-enforced confluence between sexuality and intimacy, and another to defend the proposition that the two *must* be separated in a new legally privileged baseline for the family.

It is these state-imposed "must be's" that violate the sanctuary of the imaginary domain. If men must be mothers in order to have parental rights, then the state is inescapably in the business of defining those who meet the required level of care. How much caretaking does it take for a man, or for that matter, a woman, to become a mother? What about women who do not meet the standard of the stereotypical caretaker? What of, for example, the lesbian lover in a relationship where one partner not only did not give birth, but where she, with her lover's agreement, took over the financial responsibility for the family? What if her responsibility to her family was primarily financial? Should we let the state define her as less of a mother, and therefore deny her rights to the child whom she considers her own even though she has no biological connection and has not related to the child in a way typical to women?

We all know such families in the lesbian and gay community. We know nontraditional heterosexual families as well. The problem here is that the deviant mother is let in the back door in Fineman's scheme by imposing a "must be" on fathers, which inevitably demands that we define how much care it takes to be a mother. As we will see shortly, my own guidelines for family law reform would define these "must be's" as narrowly as possible.

Although Fineman seeks to denaturalize the heterosexual family, she still privileges the biological family in her scheme of intimacy. This privilege has imposed untold suffering on gays and lesbians who, because they had no biological connection to their child, lost "custody" when their beloved partner died, in spite of the explicitly stated contractual desires of the departed lover.[7] This is the case not only for gays and lesbians. Many

---

7. The outcomes of custody battles involving gay and lesbian coparents vary greatly state to state and according to the individual judge who hears the case. For example, in *McGuffin v. Overton* 542 N.W.2d 288 (Mich. Ct. App. 1995), the court held that the lesbian partner of a deceased mother lacked standing to challenge the father's custody petitions. The deceased mother had executed a will making her partner the guardian of the children, while the fa-

straight couples use marriage as a shield to shut abusive biological transgenerational relatives out of their child's life, ensuring that custody will go
to the lover or spouse upon death and not to the biological family.

Dependency is undoubtedly a reality in the rearing of children and in
the care of the ill. But there are many transgenerational members of families, spry men and women in their seventies and eighties who would not
be adequately described as "dependents." What can make grandparents,
biological or adopted, so special is that they do not give the same kind of
care as parents. In many societies the aged are viewed as a source of wis-
dom and valued for their role in moral education. Even when an older person becomes ill and in need of care, she is still not reducible to the status
of a child. The dependency of an ill adult and that of a child should be differentiated in part to preserve the dignity of the adult, who needs to be
recognized and respected for their maturity despite the fragility imposed
by age. Thus, I would argue against Fineman's analogizing all dependency
through the figure of the child.

Children should also be recognized as persons with rights and responsibilities appropriate to their age. I am aware of the appropriation of children's rights rhetoric in the fathers' movement. Still, children should be
recognized as persons and as members of the moral community from
birth, with the scope of their rights increasing with maturity. Some rights,
especially what Amartya Sen has called "capability rights" (Sen 1992)—the
rights to develop the basic skills necessary to become an individuated person—would be given to the child so that she can set out on life's way as her
own person.

The mother/child dyad exists only in fantasy. The fantasy, if taken as
truth, corrodes the possibility of a mother/child relationship, since the
very idea of a relationship demands two differentiated beings. Traditional
psychoanalysis suggests that the dyad as fantasy is perpetuated by both in-
fantile and feminine narcissism (Freud 1957). Fineman argues that it is
only because of the degradation of the mother that most schools of psychoanalysis define individuation as against the mother, rather than with
the mother's support of her daughter's personhood. However, the beginning of a *relationship* between mother and daughter, and the celebration of
a symbolic distance that makes recognition possible, can occur only once
the fantasy that we ever were a dyad is dissolved. Trying to simply reenact
the dyadic fantasy gets us nowhere new. That is why I disagree with Fine-

---

ther was twenty thousand dollars in arrears in child support. The court concluded that Michigan law and case law dictated against permitting the partner to proceed with a petition for
guardianship. In *Guardianship of Aston H. v. Sofia D.*, 635 N.Y.S.2d. 418 (N.Y. Family Court,
1995), however, the court awarded custody to the lesbian life partner of the deceased mother,
ruling that this was in the best interest of the child. See also Lambda Legal Defense and Education Fund (1996).

man's enactment of the mother/child dyad as a metaphor for what loving care might be in a transformed society.

Sex cannot be legislated out of families, because it is irreducible to literal sex acts between adult lovers. In efforts to combat sexual abuse within the family, feminist reforms have at times fallen short by failing to acknowledge the presence of eroticism in familial relationships. Because relationships in families are erotically charged, awareness of that eroticism is what makes sexual responsibility on the part of the adult possible. Unlike Fineman, I suggest that it is only through acknowledgment of this eroticism in the family that transformation is possible.

In poems that seem daring 2700 years later, Sappho describes her own erotic celebration of her daughter's "magnificence." She expresses joy in her daughter's stride because it expresses a freedom Sappho has never known and mourns as lost. Sappho's erotic appreciation of her daughter is inseparable from the celebration of her daughter's physical freedom, her strength. Sappho sings of the distance between the two that makes a mother's joy in her daughter's singularity possible. The daughter "whose skin of burnished gold pales the magnificence of the sun"[8] is uncapturable by the mother who cannot keep up with her daughter as she runs down the beach. The mother joys in the stride that takes her daughter into her own future as she stays behind, marveling at the play of lights illuminating her daughter's beauty.

The most profound lore of heterosexuality may well be that daughters and mothers are sexual rivals: the mother wanting to hold her daughter to her or subject her to the plight of femininity. Our feminist lore should at least begin with the other tale, with the affiliations with, rather than appropriations against, the daughter's freedom.

I agree with Jacqui Alexander when she writes,

One would urgently need an emancipatory praxis that deconstructs the power of heterosexual lore that positions women as their own worst erotic enemies and rivals, that might explode mothers' inherited discomfort with the emerging, restless sexuality of their own daughters, a sexuality that is often viewed as threatening and anxious to usurp. We might have to speak the unspeakable and name the competitive heterosexuality, an unnamed homosexual desire between mother and daughter, its complicated, as yet unspecified origins, and its contradictory societal sanctions and approbations. (Alexander 1997, 99)

Eroticism is what gives "life" to intimacy. Yes, there is work to be done to provide the necessary care for young children, lots of it—lots and lots and

8. Excerpts from the poems of Sappho, trans. Emma Bianchi, unpublished manuscript on file with author (Sappho n.d.).

lots of it—but there is also sometimes a joyous, often frustrating, frequently heart-wrenching passionate engagement in the cooperative, interactive endeavor I would call a family.

Luce Irigaray's entire program of legal reform is rooted in the need for women to achieve a legally recognizable civil identity so that they can transmit to their daughters the symbolic meaning of being a woman precisely so that the two will not be collapsed in a fantasized dyad. That is certainly the strength of her program, for Irigaray argues that we need to reinterpret the great myths of creation:

> The daughter's words to the mother may represent the most highly evolved and most ethical modes of language, in the sense that they respect the intersubjective relationship between the two women, express reality, make correct use of linguistic codes and are qualitatively rich. (Irigaray 1994, 111)

For Irigaray, the story of Hades is the mythical expression of the condition of mothers and daughters who are forbidden to symbolize their erotic joy in one another. As for modern patriarchal cultures, Irigaray writes:

> For the little girls, education, the social world of men-amongst-themselves and the patriarchal culture function as Hades did for Kōrē/Persephone. The justifications offered to explain this state of affairs are inaccurate. The traces of the story of the relationship between Demeter and Kōrē/Persephone tell us more. The little girl is taken away from her mother as part of the contract between men-gods. The abduction of the daughter of the great Goddess serves to establish the power of the male gods and the structure of patriarchal society. But this abduction is a rape, a marriage with the consent of neither the daughter nor the mother, an appropriation of the daughter's virginity by the god of the Underworld, a ban on speech imposed on the girl/daughter and the woman/wife, a descent for her (them) to the invisible, oblivion, loss of identity and spiritual barrenness. (111)

Irigaray then finds patriarchy symbolically inseparable from the sacrifice of the virgin and the mother's submission or banishment if she resists. Hades represents the spiritual oblivion of a placated masculine sexuality that is the compensation for men's acceptance of their inevitable castration. But this compensation demands sacrifice:

> Patriarchy has constructed its heaven and hell upon this original sin. It has imposed silence upon the daughter. It has dissociated her body from her speech, and her pleasure from her language. It has dragged her down into the world of male drives, a world where she has become invisible and blind to herself, her mother, other women and even men, who perhaps want her that way. Patriarchy has thus destroyed the most precious site of love and its fidelity: the relationship between mother and daughter, the mystery which is guarded by the virgin daughter. (112)

37

To Irigaray, a new culture, a new symbolic peace between the sexes, would exist thanks to Aphrodite's female *philotes,* which Aphrodite interpreted as "the spirit made flesh" (p. 95). A new civil law that could recognize women's sexual difference would begin then with the explicit reversal of the mythological foundation of patriarchy. It would do so first by granting to the girl the right to her virginity and the right to the mother to defend her children against any unilateral decision based on men's law. Patriarchy in its most traditional sense made the girl's virginity a "thing" owned by the father. The civil law would break with its patriarchal origins by giving virginity as a right to an identity to the girl, and giving the right to protect her to the mother as her guardian.

But Irigaray's new civil law is not against men or fatherhood. For her, the recognition of the right of the daughter to her virginity is the law that "civil" men would want, because only such a law would end the "thingification" (Sheila Rowbotham, quoted in MacKinnon 1989, 124) of women and so could be the basis for a possible reciprocity between the sexes. The granting to women of a civil identity objectified in law is the beginning of a peaceful civilization between the sexes.

Further, the cost to women of a legally recognized civil identity should not be the forced repudiation of their sexual difference:

> Women must obtain the right to work and to earn wages, as civil persons, not as men with a few inconvenient attributes: menstrual periods, pregnancy, child rearing, etc. Women must not beg or usurp a small place in patriarchal society by passing themselves off as half-formed men in their own right. Half the citizens of the world are women. They must gain a civil identity with corresponding rights; human rights, as well as rights respecting work, property, love, culture, etc. (Irigaray 1994, 63)

Men will no longer be cast into "incivility" either. A new "balance" has to be created. Irigaray takes Hegel's insight to the conclusion he would have reached if he had not been blinded in his vision of love by patriarchal assumptions. Until the law recognizes that there are *two* sexes, each recognized as having a civil identity with rights and duties, proper to the recognition of their sexual difference, the law makes true love impossible. To quote Irigaray,

> The fact that the girl as a minor becomes an adult "through marriage" manifests yet again the female gender's subjection to existing institutions and customs rather the girl's civil recognition as an autonomous person.
>
> Therefore, the law has to be changed for love. So that lovers remain two in love, woman and man have to be civil adults and their alliance has to be guaranteed by words that have a value for both of them. (Irigaray 1996, 132–33)

For Irigaray, following Hegel, sexuate rights turn on the recognition of sexual difference as a universal. The law has to be made appropriate to the natural reality of human beings in the sense of their sexed identity:

> By virtue of this law: Universal and particular are reconciled, but they are two. Each man and each woman is a particular individual, but universal through their gender, to which must correspond an appropriate law, a law common to all men and to all women. (51)

I strongly disagree with Irigaray that our sexed identity is a natural reality and that our particularity as a person can be adequately expressed through legally defining gender as a universal. Thus, I reject her conceptualization of sexuate rights in spite of the advance she has made by insisting on a women's right to a civil identity that recognizes the inviolability of their persons. The problem, philosophically, is found in Irigaray's own appropriation of Hegel. Although women would be given a civil identity, the attempt to give rights, thought through gender differences as a universal, denies women the freedom to reimagine their sexual difference. For Irigaray, there are naturally two sexes. Her ontologization of the two denies that women live their biology in infinitely different and original ways. In the imaginary domain, sexes cannot be counted because what we will become under freedom cannot be known in advance. As Ursula Le Guin has beautifully written, "it is in our bodies that we lose or begin our freedom, in our bodies that we accept or end our slavery" (Le Guin 1995, 280).

FAMILY LAW AND AN EQUIVALENT LAW OF PERSONS

In spite of my fundamental disagreement with her, Irigaray is absolutely right to insist that family law reform must be rooted in the transformation of women's civil identity and must be rid of all traces of patriarchy as well. What would be fair family law guidelines that would encompass the equivalent law of persons and protect the full civil identity of all who fell under its governance? First and foremost, the state could not impose any form of family as *the* good family, and so could not reinforce the heterosexual and monogamous nuclear family, even if such families continued to be one way in which people organized their sexual lives and their relationships to children. Gays, lesbians, straights, and transgendered would all be able to organize their sexuality as it accorded with their own self-representation at the time.

But what about intergenerational relationships? Obviously, children need care. A considerable amount of time and devotion is needed to bring up a child. In our society the nuclear heterosexual family has been the institution assigned primary, if not the entire, responsibility for the raising of children.

One popular justification for the heterosexual family is that it is in the best interests of the child to have two parents, a man and a woman, who live together. Statistically, we know that the divorce rate means that many children of heterosexual parents do not live in such families (Stacey 1996). Is there any reason to think that living as a heterosexual makes one a better parent? There is absolutely no evidence other than that grounded in homophobia that this is the case.[9] Open gay and lesbian parenting is so new that there are few studies available. Those that exist show that gay and lesbian parents tend to have less conflict in the family, and that in itself may benefit children; as to why that is the case, some have guessed that there is greater ease in communication between members of the same sex. Since gay and lesbian parenting often involves access to costly reproductive technology and is a difficult row to plow, those parents overall are economically more stable than their heterosexual counterparts. Their children are wanted. Both the economic stability and the intense desire to parent have been noted as factors that have helped create healthy and happy children in these families (Stacey 1996, chap. 5; Due 1996).

Lesbian partners show the most egalitarian patterns in sharing household responsibilities. This example of integrating work and home life has seemed to be particularly beneficial to the self-esteem and general life-outlook of girls raised by lesbians (Stacey 1996; Due 1996). These preliminary studies should certainly assuage any legitimate fears that gays and lesbians will not be committed parents. Long-term commitment to children is clearly necessary. How are we, as a society, to provide for the reproduction of the next generation, given the need young children have for stable, lasting relationships? The interests of the state would have to be consistent with the equivalent evaluation of each one of us as a free and equal person, and children would be recognized as persons whose scope of rights would mature with time. I am only describing a reform structure consistent with the limit that must be placed on family law by the recognition of our full equality as persons; I am not making specific legislative proposals. But I would argue that, to be legitimate, specific proposals would have to be guided by this structure.

First, regulation of the family should protect all lovers who choose to register in civil marriage, or some other form of domestic partnership. Many gays and lesbians have argued against the mimicry of heterosexuality inherent in the very idea of marriage (Kaplan 1997, chap. 7). I am sympa-

9. See testimony in *Baher v. Miike*, WL 694235 (Hawai'i Cir. Ct. 1996).

thetic to this line of reasoning. But it is still consistent to demand as a right that which you personally do not choose to exercise. The denial of this legal recognition is an illegitimate incorporation of moral or religious values into the basic institutions of a constitutional government. Moreover, because the government has no legitimate interest in monogamy, it cannot enforce coupling. Simply put, in the name of equality, if polygamy is to be allowed, so is polyandry, as well as multiple sexual relationships among women and among men.

Second, the government must provide a structure for custodial responsibility for children. If the government has no legitimate interest in a particular form of family life, it should also have no legitimate interest in linking custodial responsibility only to those people who are in a sexual relationship. Thus, Fineman's goal of separating parental responsibility from its inherent relation with the heterosexual couple would be achieved: two women friends who were not sexually involved could assume parental responsibility for a child; three gay men could assume parental responsibility for a child; and finally, a traditional heterosexual couple could also assume parental responsibility for a child. The difference would be that custody would not be a given fact of their sexual unit. In other words, a man skittish about becoming a parent could choose to stay married to his partner and yet also choose not to share full custodial responsibility for his child, leaving his partner to take on custodial responsibility with another friend or, for that matter, a lover other than himself.

To achieve the needed stability for children, the assumption of custodial responsibility would carry with it all that it does now—financial support, limits on movement, and so forth. Parents would be legally established at the time they assumed custodial responsibility; each child would have a legally recognized family. If there were others who, because of sexual affiliation with one of the custodial parents, wanted to assume legal status as a parent, it would be up to the initial group to decide whether or not they should be allowed to do so. The procedure would be similar to that of current stepparent adoptions. Custodial responsibility would remain for life; legal responsibility to custodial children would continue regardless of the sexual lives of the members of the custodial partnership or team. From my standpoint as a mother, I would prefer a "team," but I understand that to be only my preference.

Those persons who have recently argued against divorce have done so because the stability of children is often profoundly undermined in divorce, let alone in an ugly custody battle (Gallagher 1996). Divorce, or an end to a sexual liaison of one of the partners in the team, would not in any way affect custodial responsibility. The only reason for a partner or a team to legally sue to terminate someone else's custodial responsibility in the partnership, or team, would be what we now call the doctrine of extraordinary circumstances, for example, sexual or physical abuse. Children could also sue to separate themselves from one custodial partnership or team, but under the same doctrine. If minors, the only requirement would be that they choose another custodian. Would adults owe financial support to other adults in this arrangement, if for example one member of the partnership or the team chose to stay home during the early years of the child's life? My answer would be only by contract.

Once you have signed on, you have signed on for life, which is why I believe that this conception of custodial responsibility meets the state's as well as the children's interest in stability. But could you add on? I have already advocated that you should be able to do so. For example, could you, as an adopting mother, embrace the birth mother in a relationship of shared custody? Could it be the other way around? It already is the other way around in lesbian couples, where the birth mother and her lover seek joint custody together. The situation of lesbian lovers obviously demands that we reenvision the meaning of adoption, for in these cases the two lovers seek to parent together. The tortuous process of adoption has been eloquently described by lesbian parents. The birth mother is a mother by birth. Her lover is denied parental status in most states, and in states where she can achieve it, the birth mother must give up her rights in order for her lover to adopt. This case forces us to confront how difficult it is for our society to conceive of two mothers raising a child together. We keep imposing one choice, which is the last thing the mothers want.

The problem is inseparable from a culture that imposes monogamous heterosexuality, because it is only in that culture that the existence of two mothers is such a problem.[10] Patriarchy, as Irigaray eloquently describes, lets the man, not the woman, determine his line. The existence of two mothers causes a problem only when a society is organized around patrilineal lineage. If both women are to be accorded civil status, then it follows that they are free as persons to assume custody together. This would end the pain associated with lesbian adoption.

Lesbian mothers are obviously in a relationship with one another. But so are adopting mothers who never meet the birth mother. The fear of the "return of the birth mother" haunts adoptions. But why? If she has signed away primary custody, she cannot take the child back. Why wouldn't this return be envisioned as a good thing, as it turned out in the case of Lorraine Dusky? As Dusky describes, "all of us long ago made peace with our places in Jane's life. She calls me Lorraine. 'Mom' is her other mother" (Dusky 1992).

10. Same-sex parenting seems incomprehensible only in a culture that imposed heterosexuality as the norm. Consider sociologist David Eggeben's testimony in *Baher v. Miike:* "'same-sex marriages where children [are] involved is by definition a step parent relationship' because there is one parent who is not the biological parent of the child" (7).

We cannot lose our children because they are not ours to have. That children are not property is recognized by their inclusion in the moral community of persons from birth. Obviously, this idea of custodial responsibility and children's rights demands that we stretch our imaginations. It demands that we struggle to free ourselves from the picture of the family as "Mommy and Daddy and baby makes three." But if we are truly to take seriously what it means to treat each one of us as an equal person and thus not insist on a "proper" family or "normal" sexual relations, then we have to have the courage to do so. It is what is demanded of us by our civic duty.

I have little doubt that it is in the best interests of the children. Certainly it would meet Fineman's goal of ending the horrendous tragedy of a woman losing her children because she does not live up to some fantasy conception of what her duty as a mother is. If a woman was living up to her custodial responsibility, it would not matter whether she had one lover or many. It certainly would not matter that she currently, or in the past, had another woman as a lover. But rather than entitling women through the reciprocal right of mothers and children, I would do so through the reciprocal right of custodial partners and children. I would advocate this conception of parental entitlement because any state regulation based on normalized conceptions of femininity, including those of the mother as caretaker, is inconsistent with the equal protection of the imaginary domain.

The third legitimate state interest is equitable distribution of the burdens of reproduction and the equal protection of the health of young children. Obviously, we would have to have provisions for health care for children. I would also argue that we would have to have income maintenance for families. Mothering should no longer be a class privilege. In order to support oneself beyond the level of guaranteed income, people have to work. Therefore, we would need to provide some kind of publicly funded child care as part of parental entitlement.

The structure of these reforms would provide stability to children and sexual freedom to adults. Since there would be no state-enforced normalized family, children who fell outside the norm would not be stigmatized. There would be no normal family, as if such a thing has ever existed. Part of the difficulty for adopted children is that they have fallen outside of the norm. By lifting the norm, we lift the stigma.

BRAVE NEW FAMILIES?

Are these brave new families? In *Brave New World* Aldous Huxley fantasized about the totalitarian horror of the state outlawing families as dangerous sites of intimacy. In Huxley's tale, embryos were processed in many duplicate prints to stamp out beings individuated enough to be persons. Love was outlawed, and indeed, the hero's great crime against the state was that, as a sign of individuality, he fell in love.

Like all totalitarian states, the brave new world fought valiantly to defeat the imaginary domain, the place of retreat that kept the person uncapturable, individuated from the regime. The torture of the regime, imagined in George Orwell's *1984* as well, articulates the centrality of defeating the imaginary domain in a totalitarian state. The state reaches into that sanctuary, breaking the divide between fantasy and reality, by actualizing the victim's worst nightmares. The message is clear—there is no sanctuary from the state.

A family law that insists that this sanctuary is crucial to the protection of our inviolability clearly and firmly rejects the state control of persons of the brave new world. That state fears eros. In contrast, an equivalent law of persons that would allow us to initiate and set forth our own lives as lovers and parents celebrates eroticism.

For some, the realization of their desire to parent demands reliance on technology: lesbian couples frequently rely on sperm banks; many gay and straight men have turned to surrogates. Straight couples have also sought out reproductive technology. This kind of technology is extremely costly, and economic class limits who has access to it. Dusky worries that human beings born of this new technology are missing a piece: "like androids out of science fiction, they lack a full human parentage, that connection with our past that forms such a large part of our present. They fill the hole in their identity with rage" (Dusky 1982, 30).[11]

11. The question of whether or not surrogacy should be outlawed deeply divided the feminist movement. Some feminists argued that surrogacy should be outlawed altogether, as an illegitimate aberration of the integral person. Others agreed that it should not be banished altogether, but regulated so that surrogates would not be so easily exploited. Others have argued against such regulation because it still involves the state in morally accepting surrogacy. Instead, surrogacy should remain completely deregulated. Others have insisted that in surrogacy there is a contract like any other but that we should not resort to the remedy of specific performance, a remedy that is disfavored in contract law.

The problem of surrogacy has intensified because such arrangements often end in custody fights. In such battles, the question of the surrogate mother's rights and the sperm donor's rights demand to be resolved. In the case of Mary Jo Whitehead, a surrogate who wanted desperately to keep her baby, her surrogacy was used in the custody case as evidence that she was a bad mother. What kind of mother would initially agree to selling her baby? Ultimately, the biological father, Joseph Stern, and his wife, Betsy, were given custody of the baby. The standards for so deciding were those that have often favored men with wives over single mothers in custody disputes. See Chesler (1986).

Some feminists argued that it should never have become a custody battle. It became such a battle only because the contract to sell the baby was not upheld in the New Jersey Supreme Court. If the contract was illegal, and Joseph Stern became a father only by contract, then he had no rights to his child simply because of his biological connection. The issue that haunted these debates was once again the question of the legal status of mothers. For example, Phyllis Chesler argued that what was denied Mary Jo Whitehead once she had changed her mind

But what is "full human parentage"? Isn't it better that we leave it to each of us to work through what it means to be lovers and parents, rather than have the state impose limits that will exclude some from representing their own sexuate being? Children born into love are the lucky ones. But I would at least hope that no one in this day and age would argue that sexual intercourse is necessarily loving. Can the act of artificial insemination be a loving act, as joyous to the lovers as any sex that transpires between heterosexual couples? The answer is: of course. It is not the body parts that makes the love. I find nothing "out of kilter" about planning babies.

The question of technology brings us back to an old argument in feminism that should be confronted. Over the last two hundred years, numerous feminists have contended that naturalized motherhood is the enemy. State-enforced denaturalization should then be *the* demand of feminism. Shulamith Firestone made that argument in the 1970s (Firestone 1970, chap. 10). Less extreme feminists like Simone de Beauvoir simply advocated the avoidance of motherhood in the name of freedom (Beauvoir 1974, 774). Cultural feminists have responded strongly that this is just more of the same degradation of women and everything they stand for, e.g., Ruddick (1989). But the equal protection of our imaginary domain insists that the individual woman be given the space to grapple with what motherhood means to her. State-imposed denaturalization would clearly controvert the imaginary domain.

Families are special because they offer a space for eroticism in which love and life can flourish.[12] Whether they are created through biology or adop-

---

was a violent patriarchal breaking of the "sacred bond" of motherhood. See Chesler (1988).

Things got even more difficult when the battle was not between a biological mother and biological father, but between a gestational mother and a biological mother. In *Anna J. v. Mark C.*, 286 Cal. Rptr. 369 (Cal. App. 1991), review granted, 822 p.2d.1317 (Cal. 1992), an African American woman was hired by a white couple to bear their child. After the birth, the gestational mother wanted to keep the child. The court decided in favor of genetics, saying that it was genetics, and not gestational history, that was formative to identity. The court's rhetoric mimics Dusky.

How do we decide cases when by all conventional meanings of the word, there are two mothers? Here we seem inevitably plunged into subtle judgments about what biological act is more important in the constitution of mothering. Rather than making law the determinant of whether gestation is more important than biological lineage in deciding who is the "real" mother, I would draw a simple, bright line: persons cannot be sold outright; that is slavery. An adult person can alleviate a part of herself as a representation of who she is. Many of us may view this as a bad moral judgment on the part of the individual who makes it. But a baby cannot alleviate a part of itself because she is not yet capable of making the judgment. A baby cannot represent itself. Entry into the moral community at birth means at least two things: you cannot be physically violated, let alone killed, and you cannot be sold.

Thus, the parent who does not come into its relationship to the child by buying it gets to keep the child. Contracts to sell children cannot be enforced. But, at the same time, surrogacy should be allowed as one way in which people make a family.

12. It is crucial to note that families have historically been sites of abuse and pain. See Gelles (1987); Felder and Victor (1996).

tion, or some combination of both, the specialness of erotic connection will obviously make families different from other associations in civil society, in and out of which people move freely.

I have argued strongly that adopted children and birth mothers should have access to each other if they seek it. The idea of the birth mother and adopting mother living together as lovers is still obviously a brave new family to some. And yet this is exactly what lesbian lovers seek to do. Indeed, the demand for open records has been deeply controversial because it challenges the patriarchal concept of entity privacy that Fineman so eloquently criticizes. All the imaginary domain can do is give us the space to try to dream up and live out love in our relationships to other adults and with our children. This recognition would be a big step toward the dissolution of the myth of Hades, where those who have been denied their right to represent their own sexuate being have been banished.

CHAPTER TWO

Open Adoption Is Not for Everyone

ANITA L. ALLEN

THE OPEN ADOPTION MOVEMENT

Adoption is undergoing significant change. "Open" adoption—also called "disclosed" and "cooperative" adoption—is gaining acceptance (Appell 1995; Brooks 2001; Hollinger 1998). The adoptions between strangers that took place in the United States in the decades after World War II were unduly "closed." The parties were anonymous, the procedures were confidential, the official records were sealed. In addition, birth parents legally transferred all parental rights and responsibilities respecting their offspring and were then expected to drop out of sight. Most did. The experts of yesteryear maintained that closed adoption hastened the end of birth mothers' grief, spared them shame, enabled them to go on with their lives, and ensured that their offspring would grow up with secure identities. Experts also maintained that closed adoptions would allow adoptive parents to maintain secrecy and bond more easily with their adopted children (Carp 1998).

The closed adoption regime and its ideologies of secrecy and shame are fading. A growing number of adoption professionals and legal experts now believe that the birth parents of children placed for adoption should not be forced out of sight and should be permitted to maintain a relationship with their offspring (Brooks 2001; Mangold 2000). Although some birth parents prefer that the legal termination of parental rights and responsibilities also terminate their relationship with their offspring and the adopting families, other birth parents welcome post-adoption contacts. Many adoptive parents reportedly value the information about their children's health and origins that contact with birth parents affords. Research by Harold D. Grotevant and Ruth G. McRoy (1998) discredits assumptions of the old, closed adoption regime. Dozens of adoptive parents, birth parents, and adoptees interviewed over a period of years report good experiences with open adoptions, including what Grotevant and McRoy (1998) refer to as "time-limited" and agency "mediated" open adoptions. "Time-limited" open adoptions are those in which the parties agree that for a limited time before and after birth, birth parents will have contact with the adoptive family. "Mediated" open adoptions are those in which the ongoing contact that birth parents have with the adoptive family is arranged or supervised by an adoption agency.

Domestic adoptions afford opportunities for one-time and ongoing interchange between birth and adoptive parents that international adoptions rarely do. In the case of international adoptions—that is, adoptions by United States citizens of infants or children who are foreign nationals— it is unusual for birth parents to have an opportunity to meet prospective adoptive parents. Post-placement contact of any type between, say, a Russian or Chinese birth parent and an American adoptive family would be unusual. In some cases, U.S. adoptive families maintain ties with adoption officials or others in their children's community or country of origin. By contrast, in the case of domestic adoptions of infants in the United States, it is no longer unusual for birth parents to meet adoptive parents prior to or shortly after the birth of the child. In some instances these meetings are conducted semi-anonymously on a first-name only basis by an adoption professional. It is common for birth parents to request and receive letters, photographs, and videos concerning their offspring. Some birth parents share special holidays, events, and vacations with adoptive families. A few even enjoy the unrestrained spontaneous intimacy we associate with family or close friends.

In some instances of domestic adoption, the open relationships between birth parents and adoptive families are secured by oral understandings; in other instances, they are secured by written agreements setting forth the terms of post-adoption contacts, such as the frequency of letters. Relationships cemented by oral or written agreements may be mediated and monitored on an ongoing basis by adoption agency social workers. While the parties to such agreements seldom intend to create legally binding contracts, the idea that courts should enforce agreements between birth parents and adoptive parents has adherents (Appell 1995).

Although greater openness in adoption has been a positive development, openness generates a number of difficult practical, ethical, and legal concerns. Legal concerns include whether courts must enforce open adoption agreements and whether authorities should unseal adoption records. Practical concerns include whether adoption agencies can effectively mediate potential conflicts between communicating birth and adoptive families. Ethical concerns include the limits of birth parents' responsibilities to provide information about their health, genes, and families to adoptive families. One ethical concern goes straight to the heart of the very idea of post-placement open adoption arrangements in domestic adoptions: whether adoptive parents are ethically bound significantly to include birth parents in their lives, after an otherwise successful placement and termination of birth parents' legal rights.

EXCLUDING THE BIRTH PARENTS: AN ILLUSTRATION

Should birth parents ever be excluded? Sue and Brad are the parents of two children, Sam and Lynn, whom they adopted as infants several years apart. Sam's adoption, their first, was facilitated by an agency that placed children anonymously and confidentially. Sue and Brad did not meet Sam's birth parents. Lynn's adoption, their second, was facilitated by an agency that encouraged open adoption practices. The agency asked birth parents to participate in the selection of adoptive parents. The agency encouraged prospective adoptive parents to meet birth parents and offer to provide letters and photographs throughout the child's life.

Fearful of not being selected to adopt, Sue and Brad reluctantly met Lynn's unmarried expectant birth parents, Jill and Chris. Jill was a retail clerk and Chris was a college student. The foursome "clicked" and agreed with enthusiasm and relief to proceed with the adoption. Sue and Brad offered to provide letters and photographs. After Jill gave birth to Lynn, Sue proposed that visits with Lynn might ease Jill's considerable emotional pain at being unable to muster the emotional and financial resources needed to keep her baby. Sue and Brad presumed that only a few visits would be required to assist Jill, while Jill presumed that the door had been opened to ongoing contact.

From the time of Lynn's birth, with the help of their adoption agency, Sue, Brad, Jill, and Chris coordinated meeting times and places consistent with the four adults' schedules. Sue and Brad lived fifty miles away from the two different towns in which Jill and Chris lived. To make the visits, it was necessary for Sue to skip work and arrange after-school care for Sam. Sam was never included in the visits out of concern that seeing Lynn with her birth parents would deepen his sadness about the irretrievable loss of his own birth parents. Once when scheduling was a problem for Sue and Brad, an agency social worker offered to take Lynn to visit with Jill and Chris without them. Sue and Brad were distressed and insulted by the suggestion that they might permit someone outside the family and not a personal friend to take their daughter anywhere.

49

Visitation was a logistical problem that became an emotional problem as well. Initially, Sue did not much mind the visits. Brad, though enthusiastic about adoption, was not keen on the visits. He was often unavailable or uninterested in getting together with Jill and Chris. An "on again/off again" couple, the young birth parents were unhappy when Sue and Lynn visited them without Brad. They explained that because they had both grown up with uninvolved fathers, they experienced Brad's absences as rejection. Sue felt awkward getting together with Chris without Brad, because she felt sexually attracted to the good-looking father of her daughter.

After the initial few visits, it seemed to the adoptive parents, Sue and Brad, that the birth parents' attention shifted away from their birth daughter Lynn, where they felt it should be. Jill, the birth mother, seemed to like to talk about herself and was kind but awkward handling Lynn. Jill clearly wanted more contact and connection among the group than the other three adults. For example, Jill wanted her stepsisters and an uncle in another state to meet Lynn. Jill wanted Brad and Sue to attend a musical event in another city in which Jill's best friend was performing. A college student still living at home with his mother, Chris had not expected post-adoption visits, only letters and photographs, as the four originally agreed. Chris was not especially attentive to Lynn. He fell asleep during one visit with Lynn and Sue. During another visit that Jill and Brad could not attend, Chris suggested that he, Sue, and Lynn go to a shopping mall. At the mall he made purchases, while Sue and Lynn, who by this time was a toddler, tagged along behind him.

Sue and Brad grew to feel that they were constructing a way of life that was unduly complex, confusing, and stressful. The lack of meaningful guidance or support from a changing array of agency social workers was discouraging. The adoptive parents' family and friends adored Lynn and Sam, but were suspicious of the birth parents. For their part, Sue and Brad came to doubt their abilities to raise Lynn competently, as one of four cooperating parents, each with issues and needs of his or her own. Sue and Brad had full-time professional careers, two adopted children, and large, close extended families that included aging parents, siblings, nieces, nephews, uncles, aunts, and cousins. Sue and Brad believed their family of four would be better if they limited contact with Chris and Jill to an exchange of letters and photographs a few times a year as originally agreed. There was no written agreement promising perpetual visitation. Sue and Brad met with their adoption agency to discuss discontinuation of face-to-face meetings before speaking to Jill and Chris. The agency advised them to do what they felt was best and what was most comfortable.

Perhaps not surprisingly, Jill, the birth mother, was upset by the decision to discontinue face-to-face visits. Neither Sue nor Brad felt that they had made promises. Jill felt that she had been misled by the agency, Sue, and

Brad—perhaps intentionally. The four parents nonetheless planned and participated in a final face-to-face visit, shortly after Lynn's second birthday. Thereafter, using the adoption agency as an intermediary, Sue sent photographs and letters to Jill and Chris two or three times a year. Brad was uninvolved. After nearly three years of silence, Sue and Brad received separate letters from Jill and Chris expressing love for Lynn and a desire that periodic updates on her development continue.

A Moral Question

Was it wrong for Sue and Brad to pull back from open adoption? Did they violate their moral obligations to Jill and Chris? In general, does excluding birth parents merit moral condemnation? I would like to argue that, as a general matter, adoptive parents are not ethically bound to include birth parents in their lives. Instead, adoptive parents are bound to do what they can do well toward providing a good life for their children. The discharge of this obligation may or may not entail birth parent inclusion, depending upon individual circumstances. Of course, many adoptive parents will want to include birth parents significantly in their lives, and many will have good reasons to attempt even painful and inconvenient inclusion. For example, those who adopt older children with healthy ties to their birth families (and possibly foster families or others) are likely to have good reason to attempt to maintain those ties through some form of inclusion.

I will argue that adoptive families who prefer to end, limit, or forgo post-adoption contact with birth parents should not be subjected to automatic moral condemnation; instead, they should be supported in their good faith decisions by adoption professionals and policymakers. Birth parents and their families do not have a *prima facie* moral right to maintain contact with adopted kin, because such an ascription of right would be inconsistent with adoptive parents' *prima facie* rights and responsibilities as caretakers. I expect that critics of the traditional, nuclear, privatized, and exclusive family will balk at the direction of my argument (Young 1998). Yet even proponents of non-traditional, alternative models of the family and birth parent rights must recognize the importance to effective caretakers of secure spheres of agency, autonomy, and well-being.

As I hope to make clear, I do not think legislators should outlaw contact between birth and adoptive families, or even discourage it. However, I disagree with Reuben Pannor's perspective that open adoption is obligatory because the adoptive parents' relationship with their children should be understood, by contrast to the biological parents' relationship with their children, as merely "a guardianship, a stewardship." Few practicing social workers explicitly portray adoptive parenting as mere "guardianship." But some social workers seem to believe that birth parents ought, in a moral sense, to have access to adopted children and adoptive families long after the judges' legal decrees are signed. They seem to urge thinking of adoption as enlarging the natural family to include birth parents and adoptive parents in a fused or blended family. But it remains plausible and morally legitimate to understand newborn adoption as configuring separate, new families altogether.

FUSION AND CONFIGURATION: TWO MODELS OF ADOPTION

Just what sort of event or process is adoption? I want to suggest two contrasting perspectives on the nature of adoption. I want to suggest that we can think of adoption either as a way of *configuring* a new parent-child family, or as a way of *fusing* two or more existing families and making them into a larger one. Some of the most thoughtful defenders of open adoption practices seem to urge that family fusion is a *fact* adoptive parents must accept as part of the territory of adoption (Cahn and Singer 1999). I believe family fusion is instead a *perspective* on adoption that need not be built into public policy and ethics. The two contrasting perspectives require elaboration.

Under the configuration model, which is the first perspective, adoption takes individual adults and children who may have no preexisting biological or social ties to one another and establishes them as a new primary social unit. Under the configuration model, the primary social unit created by adoption is a family, consisting of one or two heterosexual or homosexual parents and one or more dependent children. The resulting family is "nuclear" in the sense of being small, distinct, and central to the lives of its members. It is not necessarily "nuclear" in the sense of being lorded over by a husband and father who provides economically for a dependent wife and mother who is responsible for day-to-day care of dependent children. From a traditional legal point of view, it is easy to comprehend the sense in which adoption creates new families. On this view, adoption is an event or series of one-time events. The state issues new, fictitious birth certificates and reallocates actual rights and obligations for care. But from non-legal, social, and emotional points of view, adoption can be thought to create new families. New, primary, caregiver/dependent relationships modify and supplant old ones. Adoption configures new families by reconfiguring established ones: one or more families essentially lose a member (if only temporarily until the child matures) and another family gains a member (it is hoped, for a lifetime). Whether the two or more families involved in an adoption ought to maintain some sort of contact after configuration and reconfiguration is an open question. It is conceivable, under the configuration model, that the adult parties to adoption are and remain practically strangers.

Under the competing fusion model, which is the second perspective to be elaborated, adoption takes individual adults and children who may have no preexisting ties to one another, plus those children's biological parents and perhaps other kin and ties, and establishes them as a new social unit. Under the family fusion model, the social unit created is also a family, but like a stepfamily, the adoptive family is not simply or aptly characterized as "nuclear." Under the fusion model, adopting parents gain family members, but birth parents do not lose family members. Whether adopting parents and birth parents ought to maintain contact is an open question under the fusion model; and yet because cooperative contact is normative for functional, loving families, cooperative contact might be viewed as a legitimate expectation for families fused by the adoption of a child.

Advocates of open adoption who think that all adoptive parents have presumptive obligations of birth parent inclusion may be relying on the family fusion model of adoption. It is theoretically possible that both models of adoption would lead adoption professionals who embraced them to advocate the same kinds of adoption policies and practices. I believe, however, that post-placement open adoption will seem rather more compelling to those who are strongly drawn to the fusion model than to those who are strongly drawn to the configuration model. That is because with open adoption practices come intimate exchanges of personal information, intergenerational displays of emotion, and opportunities for relaxed, spontaneous physical contact most closely associated in our society with functioning family units.

FUSION AND OPENNESS

From an ethical point of view, much can be said in favor of the family fusion model of adoption and the open adoption practices for which it might be thought to call. Open adoption policies will be especially attractive to anyone who subscribes to the fusion model of adoption. In the field of bioethics, practices facilitated and encouraged by the helping professions—including obstetricians, social workers, psychologists, psychiatrists, the clergy—are commonly assessed by reference to whether they conform to broadly stated principles of autonomy, beneficence, non-maleficence, and justice (Beauchamp and Childress 2001). It would be useful to consider what such principles, along with the ideals of care and agency that feminists stress, might suggest about adoption (Noddings 1986). It could

ANITA L. ALLEN

be argued that the adoption-as-fusion model flows from and mandates a profound understanding of the rights and needs of all of the parties to an adoption, including the informational needs of maximally effective adoptive parents and birth parents. It can be argued that adoption is best viewed as a fusing or blending of families whose members subsequently acquire *prima facie* rights and obligations of intimate contact and disclosure. I will eventually argue that attention to autonomy and beneficence countermands an adoption regime in which adoptive parents are ascribed moral or legal obligations of post-adoption contact with birth parents. For now, though, let us see how an argument to the contrary would look: an argument that birth parent autonomy and societal beneficence entail obligations of post-adoption contact.

To respect autonomy, it can be argued, a society must at a minimum preserve meaningful choices for the men and women who create children they believe they cannot rear. Biological parents must be free to transfer custody of their children to responsible new adoptive parents; they must be free to select adoptive parents for their children or to delegate some or all of the powers of selection to a trusted fiduciary; they must be free to require of adopting parents a means of obtaining information about the continuing well-being of their children. If adoption is family fusion, it would seem to follow that the means by which birth parents obtain information should be means appropriate to intimates in our culture, rather than means open to strangers. Personal letters, personal conversations, and intimate direct contact could be expected.

To act with beneficence and without maleficence, it could be argued, the needs of birth parents who strongly desire to maintain ties with adopted children and their families ought to be accommodated, and that the needs of children for access to biological kin and information about them ought to be accommodated. To meet these relational needs it might be supposed that adoptions and adoption records should be more open than closed. And, again, if adoption is family fusion, modes of openness appropriate to families should be encouraged to the extent possible.

Finally, to do as justice requires, it is imperative that the adoption process treat birth families fairly and as the moral equals of adoptive families, despite typical disparities in education, income, class, and race. It is imperative, too, that the human rights of birth families be respected. Drucilla Cornell (2002) has powerfully argued that birth mothers have rights to "be allowed the space to come to terms with their own life-defining decisions about sexuality and family." These rights could justify ascription of generous rights to surrogate mothers, as well as other birth mothers. Cornell conceives of the ongoing interest of birth mothers for inclusion in the lives of adopted children in this way:

54

What should a birth mother relinquish when she relinquishes primary custody of her child? Only that—primary custody. The equal protection of the birth mother's imaginary domain at least demands that she be allowed access to any information she desires to have about her child, and to have the chance to meet and explore with the child what kind of relationship they can develop. (Cornell 2002)

Arguably, birth fathers have analogous equality interests in knowing their offspring. It would follow that a just society ought to honor fathers' interests as well. Grounded in the model of adoption as family fusion, there is an impressive ethical case for a duty of cooperative openness that extends beyond a one-time meeting at the adoption agency or lawyer's office.

In summation, if adoptive parents and birth families are construed as part of a single primary familial unit, whose members are to be treated with respect for their moral autonomy, with benevolent respect for their welfare, and with justice, it makes sense to think that, *prima facie*, adoptive parents have (1) a moral obligation of family-style inclusion to birth parents, and (2) a moral obligation to their children, for example, to meet with the children's birth parents, learn from them, and provide them with information. Adoptive parents have rights, too, on this conception. They have a right to birth parents' cooperation in some form of mutually acceptable ongoing contact, so that adopted children have meaningful opportunities to know their full ("true") genealogical identities and their entire ("real") parents and families.

As powerful as the family fusion-based case for open adoption arrangements can appear when viewed through the lenses of commonly held bioethical principles, I want to urge that those same principles ultimately compel a quite different view of things. Below I elaborate the case for the alternative, family configuration model of adoption, and then urge that we should view post-placement open adoption as an important option rather than a moral mandate.

THE PERMANENT ADOPTION IMPERATIVE

In the United States children of all ages often need homes because their parents are unable to provide for them. Ideally, no child would have to be placed for adoption; ideally, policymakers would devote more resources to measures that allow parents to care for the children they bear (Brooks 2001). It is especially heartbreaking that kind, employed, high school–educated birth parents, such as Jill and Chris, who figure in the story above, feel compelled to resort to adoption for primarily economic reasons.

ANITA L. ALLEN

In our less than ideal nation, welfare policies and practices enshrine the permanent adoption imperative: young children whose parents cannot, should not, or do not wish to rear them ought to be placed for adoption with minimal delay in permanent new homes with new parents (Brooks 2001). The permanent adoption imperative is reflected in, *inter alia,* the Adoption and Safe Families Act (1997) and the Adoption Assistance and Child Welfare Act (1980). It requires a pool of competent, loving adults willing to take on the time-consuming, expensive, and emotional process of qualifying for adoption, followed by the burdens of rearing children born to others. We are glad when new families competent to shelter children from harm, want, and uncertainty unconditionally embrace the children who need them. We are saddened when children spend a significant portion of their lives in neglect, abuse, and serial foster homes. Open record policies, face-to-face pre-adoption meetings, post-placement communication through letters and photos, and post-placement visits are four distinct varieties of open adoption, each of which requires separate analysis. The impact, if any, of each on (1) the size and welfare of the pool of prospective adoptive parents, and on (2) efficacious adoptive parenting must be part of the ethical calculus. I want to focus on post-placement contacts because they may be the forms of open adoption that are most likely to turn off or turn away prospective adoptive parents. They are also the form of open adoption most likely to increase the burdens of parenting for adults seeking to rear adopted children. I believe ethical respect for adoptive parents' agency and autonomy, when combined with considerations of beneficent regard for adoptive families and the pool of children needing homes, makes a strong case for a regime in which post-adoption contact is strictly optional. We do best by children when attempting to preserve varieties of non-disclosed adoption as meaningful options for the prospective parents who require it as a condition of adoption *and* for the actual adoptive parents who require it as a condition of what they believe to be responsible care.

PRESERVING THE POOL

Our domestic adoption practices thwart the permanent adoption policy imperative to the extent that concerns about adoption practices diminish the pool of prospective adoptive parents in the United States. Several practices could diminish the pool. Denying adoptive families the ability to express racial preferences in adoption might reduce the pool, much as requiring genetic testing to prove fitness to adopt. It is also possible that open adoption practices could reduce the pool of prospective parents. Should policymakers be worried about the size of the pool? At

56

present in the United States there are many more people seeking to adopt healthy white newborns than there are healthy white newborns available for adoption. With respect to the pool of potential parents for white American newborns, concerns about policies adversely affecting the size may be unwarranted. But the pool for non-white and at risk newborns is not so vast as to render concern moot. And I see no reason to think that the crowded pool for white parents could not be significantly emptied in the future by unappealing changes in adoption practices, coupled with appealing developments in biomedical technology. The felt needs and desire of whites to address infertility and incapacity through adoption will soon be addressed by cloning and other reproductive technologies on the horizon.

An attractive, workable option for some, open adoption is not for everyone. Not everyone who would otherwise make a terrific adoptive parent will want to adopt if he or she is expected to participate in open procedures. Some prospective adoptive parents may not be willing to adopt, particularly a child from their own locale, if they cannot do so anonymously or with complete confidence that they will not be compelled to interact with birth parents on an ongoing basis. According to Carol Sanger, open adoption "increases the number of children available," presumably by making adoption more attractive to birth parents (Sanger 1996). However, it is not clear that open adoption increases or preserves the number of families willing to adopt.

In the case of international adoptions, adoptive parents may be unable to avoid excluding birth parents' from their lives. Even where it is not literally unavoidable, birth parent exclusion can seem natural and justified by great geographic and cultural distances. But adoptive parents in the United States who adopt from their own localities would be expected to participate in a variety of open adoption practices, precisely because geographic or cultural barriers are perceived as minimal. Private adoption agencies commonly promote a degree of openness in their domestic adoptions. Adoptions Together, an agency that serves families throughout the greater Washington, D.C., and Baltimore region is just one example of a private adoption agency that for many years has encouraged birth parents to participate in the selection of adoptive families, and encourages adoptive families to meet and maintain contact with birth parents.

Counseling, education, and emotional support can convert some reluctant people into willing participants in open adoption practices. Private agencies officially committed to ideals of openness have reported success in persuading prospective adoptive parents to meet birth parents face-to-face, at least once. Some adoptive parents have agreed to one or more face-to-face meetings with birth parents partly out of curiosity and mainly out of fear that they would hurt their chances of obtaining a child were they

to insist upon complete anonymity. Private agencies report that when resisted initial face-to-face meetings finally happen, they are generally pleas-
ant and informational. Anecdotally, birth parents and adoptive parents
report feeling less anxious about adoption after meeting one another.

I would conjecture that only a small number of prospective adoptive
parents have been utterly unreceptive to the process of adoption by the
prospect of simply meeting with birth parents. Those who were unreceptive may have had concerns about being judged by and potentially rejected
by birth parents. They may have concerns about future emotional entanglement with birth parents who are not complete strangers. Some people
who eschew open adoption remain in the pool for domestic adoption, but
search for non-open adoption options. Others enter the pool for international adoptions from orphanages, where contact with birth parents is ex-
ceedingly rare.

The greatest threat to domestic adoption is not the one-time pre-adoption meeting. Instead it is the perceived threat of hardship potentially arising out of ongoing post-adoption intimate contact with birth families.
When it comes to newborn adoptions, few agencies actively encourage ongoing contact between birth families and unrelated adoptive families,
apart from occasional letters and photographs. The story is different when
it comes to domestic adoptions involving older children and minority children placed in white homes of dubious "cultural competence." Adoption
professionals often advise adoptive parents to maintain older children's social ties to prior families, caretakers, and friends, and minority children's
ties to appropriate minority communities. Yet, to maintain a clientele of
appealing prospective parents for same-race newborn adoptions, some
agency professionals reassure prospective adoptive parents that once an
adoption is final, they, the legal parents, will call the shots and need not do
anything that they find uncomfortable. This is what Sue and Brad, the
adoptive parents in my illustration, were told. Prospective parents quickly
figure out that in theory they can decline to deliver on promises about
post-adoption contact they make to the agency and to birth parents.

Adoptive parents should not make promises they do not plan to keep.
There is no reason to think many do. Nor should adoption professionals
directly or indirectly encourage insincere promises and promise-breaking.
Adoptive parents who do not make specific promises of ongoing contact
do not have ethical obligations of ongoing contact, for reasons I will describe below; but adoptive parents who make specific representations to
birth parents are obligated to make a good faith effort to adhere to them.
Sensible people will be reluctant to make promises to perfect strangers that
they are not sure they will want to keep, particularly promises about their
deepest emotional attachments and gravest responsibilities. Qualified pro-

spective adoptive families may therefore decline to get involved in adoption, fearing that open adoption will produce heartache for them rather than happy families of their own.

FAMILIES OF THEIR OWN

Not everyone wants to live in a parent-child family, and no adult is forced to. From this perspective, it is a good thing for the perpetuation of our society that many people want to bear children, and that many want to rear children, whether or not they bear them. Adults who rear children generally wish to imprint them with their core values, while creating a reciprocal loving bond that gives rise to special commitments. Two decades ago in a pair of provocative books, a group of New Haven researchers advanced a theory of limited state interference in the family; it was premised on the notion that children have a psychological need for a continuous relationship with autonomous parents who model responsibility and maturity through the exercise of independent judgment (Goldstein, Freud, and Solnit, 1997a,b). In a related vein, republican political theory advances a case for parental independence that emphasizes the family as a domain in which the young most effectively learn civic virtues of responsibility, cooperation, loyalty, and trust.

The parent-child family that most children need and that many adults want for themselves has constitutional dimensions. For better or for worse, we speak of "family privacy" in the United States to suggest that a substantial degree of freedom from governmental and other outside interference is fitting for the parent-child unit (Cahn 1999; Woodhouse 1999). Constitutional freedoms of association, marriage, parentage, religion, and education—along with a healthy dose of government welfare, protective services, and law enforcement—sustain private families of parents and children. The Supreme Court's decision in favor of the Amish in *Wisconsin v. Yoder,* 406 US 205 (1972) affirmed the constitutionally protected status of the parent-child relationship and the non-conforming decisions parents may elect to make on behalf of their minor children.

Presumptions of "family privacy" can be taken to harmful extremes (Cahn, 1999; Fineman 1999; Woodhouse 1999). This was the painful lesson of *Deshaney v. Winnebago Dep't of Social Services,* 489 US 189 (1989). Competent, consistent, accountable uses of government power to protect children from family violence and medical neglect are imperative limits on ideals of family privacy.

For many adoptive parents, the stated goal of adoption is to have a family *of their own.* Having a family of one's own means being able, within the usual constraints of law and society, to define the parameters of one's most intimate sphere and to make decisions about its course. People have and adopt children precisely to engage their intimacy-building, nurturing, and decisional capacities. Autonomy-related values support the right of adults to choose or refuse parenthood; and for those who choose it to be permitted a degree of independence and agency. Of course, beneficence and justice-related values require that society respond to the nesting and caretaking impulses of its citizens with care and caution. For while many efforts to form families are clearly ethical, as when consenting adults agree to have sexual intercourse and rear any resulting issue, some approaches to family formation enabled by recent reproductive technologies raise grave ethical concerns, as when families are formed in the context of commercial surrogacy arrangements (Allen 1989). The regime of closed adoptions and sealed records that forever severs the ties of adopted children and biological kin understandably raises ethical concerns, whatever its legal or constitutional status.

The desire of adoptive parents to have families of their own, and the desire of birth parents for access to their own children potentially are in tension. To address that tension, a number of theorists have begun to challenge the ideal of the nuclear family and propose in its place more inclusive notions of family (Cahn and Singer 1999; Young 1998). For these theorists, adoption, and especially open adoption that reserves a place at the table for birth mothers, is an example of the reconceived, deprivatized family. The post-nuclear family will have fluid, overlapping boundaries, not yet fully incorporated into law. Interestingly though, opponents of the nuclear, private family ideal continue to press for a sphere of decisional authority for primary caretakers. Thus Alison Harvison Young (1998) argues for a "reconceptualization of the family which would": (1) recognize the limitations of the ideology of the exclusive family and articulate a model that includes non-traditional family units, as well as the range of roles potentially played by various actors in the life of a child; and yet (2) allocate the ultimate decision-making authority to a particular sphere, such as the primary caretaker or caretakers, that is, the "core family unit." My argument here is that when adoptive parents have become the core family unit, their moral powers must include the power to substantially exclude birth parents, even kind and generous birth parents, from their daily lives.

It must be admitted that, despite their recognized virtues, open adoption practices can discourage and complicate adoption. For policymakers, this is a problem of perception and realities. The perception that post-adoption contact is expected but will lead to emotional entanglements and logistical nightmares can discourage adults from choosing domestic adoption. This perception can lead rational adults to conclude that adoption is not a way to have a happy family of one's own. When entanglements and nightmares do occur, the reputation of open adoption as a viable alternative is harmed.

In ways that open records and pre-placement meetings need not, ongoing post-adoption contact with birth parents can frustrate the ability of adoptive parents to achieve the genuine and selective intimacy many Americans associate with parent-child families. Many Americans think of the family as an intimate union formed around the core values and preferences of the adults who configure them. Parent-child families today are indeed *configured,* that is, intentionally shaped by knowing choices and deeply felt responsibilities. In important respects, marriage is a choice. Partnership is a choice. Divorce and remarriage are choices. Pregnancy can be a choice. Because of birth control, abortion, and prenatal testing, the number, sex, and health of one's children is subject to choice. Whether kin or close friends are part of one's home and family life are matters about which there is considerable choice. (None of this emphasis on the role of choice is intended to deny the major forces that shape motive and desire, and the acts of God that can overtake a family—an unexpected illness, a unanticipated genius, a disability.)

The wish for post-adoption birth parent exclusion may sometimes stem from insecurities about losing a child or losing powers of independent decision-making. Adoptive parents may fear the continuing moral influence of birth parents, even birth parents who do not intend or expect to monitor or influence adoptive parents' key child-rearing decisions. Adoptive parents may be made uncomfortable by the unequal relationships that often exist between themselves and birth parents. Economic and educational inequalities are typical, with adopting parents being more affluent and better educated than birth families. Informational inequalities are common. Birth parents disclose more information about themselves than adoptive parents do. After years of contact, birth parents may know only the first names of adoptive parents and their general line of work. Conversation, friendship, and trust are difficult when the norms of the disclosure of personal data are vague and nonreciprocal. The social discomforts that result, some of which can be overcome, are only a part of the story behind resistance to open adoption.

The bigger part of the story is an affirmative desire among adoptive parents for self-defined family privacy and intimacy. Open adoption practices strike some people as *dictating* the fusion of families and *mandating* specific intimacies. Adoptive parents may reject intimacy with birth parents, because they feel they have little in common with birth families. They may feel that attempts to fuse and blend are strained and stressful. This can easily be the case when birth and adoptive parents are far apart in age, education, or religion, and where they belong to different ethnic, cultural, and linguistic groups.

FACILITATING EFFECTIVE ADOPTIVE PARENTING

How hard can it be to open one's life to the people who are, after all, the biological kin of your children? The honest answer is that it can be very hard. It does not have to be hard, but it can be hard. Real open adoption stories like that of Jill et al. reveal the burdens that open adoption can present for everyone involved. Consider the uncertain degree of accountability; the mismatch of tastes and temperament; the generational differences; the lopsided, forced intimacy; the time, emotional work, and money. Such stories are dramatically not so close to the well-known family law sagas depicted in textbooks or television movies. Yet they smack of enough emotional confusion and entanglement to turn some prospective parents off to open adoption, if not to adoption altogether.

Adoptive parents who feel they should spend time with birth parents and incorporate them into their lives may find that they cannot easily do it. Time is a scarce commodity in many families. Emotional space is a scarce commodity as well. Adoptive parents may have two or more children, two careers, large, established extended families, and many close friends competing for their time and attention. Some birth parents easily blend into adoptive families. Yet these young birth parents may have unmet needs for parenting that leave adoptive parents bewildered, feeling like overburdened grandparents of their adopted children.

Adoptive parents may judge that contact with birth parents or a particular birth parent is unwise for a child evidencing special needs unrelated to adoption. Adoptive parents like Sue and Brad who have two or more adopted children with differently accessible birth parents may conclude that there are emotional risks entailed by post-placement openness. Highly contextual issues of intimate inclusion and exclusion loom especially large in families in which one or more adopted children suffer from attachment, conduct, or mood disorders.

Clinical studies may suggest that adopted children as a class, even including those who have not suffered grave deprivation or abuse, are at a higher risk than non-adopted children for mental illnesses (Brand and Brinich 1999). A study of adults who had been adopted as children found that they were more likely than other adults to have a history of conduct disorder, antisocial personality, and drug abuse. Clinical studies have concluded that disruptive behavior, conduct disorders, and attention deficit/ hyperactivity disorder are all more common among adopted children than non-adopted children (Moore and Fombonne 1999). Fortunately, a number of researchers are skeptical about studies linking adoption to mental illness. There is disputed evidence that mental illness affects a minority of adopted children and that the mental health problems of many adopted children resolve after childhood or adolescence (Lipman et al. 1993). In the face of ongoing research, however, one ought to respect the decision of adoptive parents who are reluctant to introduce or sustain open adoption practices that add stress into their families' lives. Adoptive parents need maximal flexibility to structure protectively the intimate realms of vulnerable children. While birth parent involvement may be a blessing in some instances, when children in the family are troubled or ill, it may also be a stressor and a curse.

No Going Back

One thing should be clear: the preference for preserving closed adoption options is not a desire to return to the complete closed adoption regime of the 1950s. A few short decades ago adoptive parents, adoption professionals, and the state collaborated to make it possible for adoptive parents to pretend that they were biological parents. Agencies placed children in families with whom the children bore physical resemblances. Adoptive parents often kept the fact of adoption a secret and passed adopted children off as their biological offspring. Having a family of one's own in the 1950s meant gaining social acceptance through a pretense of fertility and normalcy. Adoption was a secret kept from friends, neighbors, and even the adopted children themselves. The state supported this secrecy by issuing birth certificates naming the adoptive parents as the child's parents. Although some states still issue such certificates, they are intended to fool no one. I know a lesbian couple in Washington whose adopted son was issued a birth certificate bearing the names of two female parents.

Today's adoptive families show little interest in secrecy and fictional parenthood. Families send out adoption announcements proudly to herald their adoptions. Adopted children know that they are adopted, particularly if they are of a different race or ethnicity than their adoptive parents. The contemporary adoptive parent's desire for a happy family of his or her own has nothing to do with secrecy and pretense, and everything to do with family privacy, intimacy and the design of a healthy, workable private life. Not every prospective adoptive parent is prepared to meet or befriend birth parents. For this reason, a norm (or even a perceived norm) of open adoption could adversely affect the size, diversity, and welfare of the pool of prospective adoptive families. If open adoption practices are risky, America's most vulnerable children will pay the price. Children pay if open adoption reluctantly undertaken makes the adoption process and post-adoption family life significantly more taxing.

Continuity and Child Welfare

What, though, about the moral interests of children in identity and continuity? Debates about open adoption generally focus on the rights, needs, and interests of children. It could be argued from perspectives of beneficence and justice that adopted children are entitled to post-adoption access to their birth parents so as to provide social continuity and/or emotional continuity. By "social continuity" I mean continuities of kinship with others with roots in the same biological family, neighborhood, tribe, race, religion, ethnicity, history, or culture. By "emotional continuity" I mean continuities of love, affection, and mutual understanding arising out of shared experiences. Children plainly have a moral interest in social and emotional continuities. In the case of newborns adopted shortly after birth, the desirability of emotional continuity provides a weak argument for post-adoption contact, if any basis at all. After all, newborns have no emotional ties beyond the biological ties to the mothers who bear them. In the case of older children, adoption disrupts relationships and established patterns of life. Emotional and social continuities are disturbed. Beneficence, non-maleficence, and justice require attention to continuities.

It is widely believed that newborns, like older children, have an interest in social continuity after adoption, even where it is conceded that they have no interest or minimal interest in emotional continuity with families of origin (Perry 1993–1994). The ideal of social continuity is part of the thinking behind the federal restrictions on the adoption of Native American children by persons who are not themselves Native Americans (Smith 1996). It is why some African Americans vehemently oppose the adoption of black children by whites (Bowen 1987–88).

The social continuity argument for open adoption practices is based on the pervasive but mistaken view that children are born with certain thickly constituted social identities that ought to be reinscribed by an upbringing among or in the ways of their social similars (Holmes 1995). We are said to wrong children, to ignore their basic welfare interests, to mistreat them, when we thwart reinscription.

Thus biological parents raising their own children sometimes feel that they wrong their children to the extent that they do not rear them in a way that will assure them an appropriate racial or cultural identity. Orthodox Jews take pains to rear their children as Orthodox Jews. African American parents who live in predominately white communities sometimes take pains to expose their children to foods, rituals, music, and dance that will help their children to not only appreciate black culture in an aesthetic sense, but that will enable them to participate in and identify with black culture. Adoptive parents who adopt transracially may feel special incompetence and special pressures to rear their children in a way that will assure them their appropriate identities.

Open adoption seems to some as the most just and responsive form of domestic transracial adoption (Holmes 1998). It has been argued that if white people are going to adopt black newborns or older children, they should do so in a way that facilitates African American modes of kinship and black identity. I have heard white parents in non-disclosed transracial adoptions express a sense of obligation to their adopted children and the children's unknown and unknowable birth parents to rear and educate the children in a way that is consistent with the values and mores of an important branch of the child's ancestral family tree.

Indeed, I have on several occasions heard white adoptive parents explain why they are involved in open adoption, in effect by reference to what they felt were their Asian or Black or Mexican American child's social continuity needs. For example, a former colleague who has adopted a Mexican American girl maintains close contact with the girl's biological grandparents to assure social continuity. The child was adopted as a newborn and had no emotional relationship with the grandmother prior to adoption.

Some adoptive parents and perspective adoptive parents will conclude that neither emotional nor social continuity arguments are sufficiently strong to warrant open adoption. Some will reach such conclusions because they do not believe children are born with certain thickly constituted identities that merit reinscription. They may doubt that social categories of race and national origin, for example, are sufficiently meaningful to design their families' lives around them; they may view their obligations as parents as requiring that they seek to ensure that their adopted children have stable, secure, loving environments likely to give rise to stable personalities and secure individual identities. Others will conclude that seeking social continuity is impractical. Birth families may live in remote places or be deceased or be unknown. A child's biological parents may have come from two or more extremely different and even antagonistic cultural traditions. Which tradition gets reinscribed? What if adoptive parents know that the birth parents were indifferent to their own traditions (e.g., they were non-practicing Catholics, assimilated Cuban Americans or Jews)? What if the birth parents held offensive beliefs? Plainly there can be no categorical duty to maintain social continuity.

Is there a *prima facie* duty like this? Suppose, *arguendo,* that adoptive parents know precisely the social origins of their children and know how to contact birth parents and families. And suppose further that there is no history of abuse and neglect or criminality to warrant keeping children away from birth families. Do a child's interests in social continuity warrant viewing open adoption as a *prima facie* moral mandate? I propose that they do not, at least in the case of newborn adoptions. My proposal rests in part on a tenet, elaborated elsewhere, that no child has a right to a certain identity (Allen 1992–93). The parents of newborns have obligations of beneficence or care to rear their child in reasonably stable and loving environments that prepare the child for its adult roles. Concerns about "appropriate" identity formation often have more to say about adults' feelings of social isolation and insecurities about acceptance than about what an emotionally healthy and happy child actually requires. For children adopted as infants, the interests in social continuity are weak. My proposal also rests on a belief that the desire for a family of one's own is a legitimate one, and that it is at odds with expectations of family fusion or cooperative parenting. The intimidating notion that adoptive parents are morally obligated to provide social continuity in the form of family fusion and open adoptions *could* reduce the pool of willing adoptive parents.

I believe it would be a mistake to condemn categorically an adoptive parent's judgment that contact with birth families is—or is not—in his or her particular child's best interest. There are a number of good reasons to pursue open adoption, such as making it possible for one's child by adoption to locate birth parents later in life, and to communicate concerns about health and progress. It would appear that open adoption arrangements are called for in many circumstances, where adopted children have significant, otherwise beneficial emotional bonds with biological kin—parents, siblings, grandparents (Wiggins 2000). In these cases, however, adoptive parents are likely to conclude without coercion that, to the extent that they can have a happy family of their own, they must provide for the emotional continuity needs of their children.

The permanent adoption imperative instructs the just society to find families for young children who need them. Adoption must be kept attractive to prospective parents. Open adoption practices—such as unsealed records, face-to-face meetings between birth and adoptive families, and post-adoption contact between birth and adoptive families—may make domestic adoption less attractive and practical. Policymakers should avoid measures that make ongoing intimate contact between birth and adoptive families a precondition of adoption.

In the ideal world, prospective adoptive parents and birth parents would be able to negotiate and choose freely among various types of open adoption and traditional non-disclosed adoption options. Given choice, many adoptive parents will choose a degree of openness, because they believe it is something they can manage in the context of their unique lives and something from which their adopted minor child will benefit. Birth parents, adoption professionals, and policymakers do best by children when they help to make the adoption process attractive to as diverse and large a pool of qualified people as possible, including those who are not drawn to post-adoption contact. As a society, we should reserve the ability to enable effective parenting and to validate the desire for a secure realm of family intimacy.

CHAPTER THREE

Methods of Adoption: Eliminating Genetic Privilege

JACQUELINE STEVENS

This essay questions the legitimacy of a linguistic, legal, and social convention that seems so ordinary as to be beyond any serious critique: the contrast between the "natural" or "biological" family, on the one hand—referred to here as the "genetic family"—and the "adoptive family," on the other. This dichotomy, pervasive in adoption policies and widespread in intuitions about how families are formed, actually makes little sense in light of historical and present facts about child development, reproduction, genetics, and court decisions when custody is in dispute. Custodial relations for children based on anything except pregnancy are all rooted in legal and social conventions, not biology. Today any parent other than the pregnant mother has custodial prerogatives through legal sanction. Because the present idiomatic dichotomy between "genetic" and "adoptive" families causes many harms, it should be changed by revisiting legal definitions that at present serve men's egos and genetic iconography but do not advance the only state goal relevant to parenting laws: the end of raising healthy children with emotional, physical, and intellectual skills sufficient for them eventually to make their way on their own.

Such a claim as to the irrelevance of genetics for determining legal custody may strike some as odd in light of new techniques to test for paternal DNA. That is, until the last two decades, courts could easily exercise their prerogative to name legal familial statuses—in particular, that of pater-

Many thanks to Wendy Brown, Mary Coffey, and especially Sally Haslanger for the excellent questions and suggestions provided in response to earlier drafts of this essay.

nity—with little worry that their pronouncements would be undermined by other authorities. However, the widespread use of DNA tests in custody and paternal support cases is creating a parallel epistemological institution, a bioscientific knowledge that, it seems, demands to be recognized by courts. In situations where genetic fathers and mothers are not married, the courts are not moving en masse from the standard "best interest of the child" criterion to awarding custody based on DNA (Anderlik and Rothstein 2002).[1] Still, the very proliferation of paternal-rights claims based strictly on DNA, and the success of these in some cases, threatens not only maternal rights, but also adoptive families. If the "fathers' rights movement" successfully institutionalizes its goal of presumptive custodial rights, based on DNA,[2] the dichotomy between genetic and adoptive families will be even more stark, and hence the adoptive family will be further stigmatized.

The epistemology of states entails their prerogative to establish criteria, such as genetics, for defining the family and establishing terms for child custody.[3] The resulting contrast between biological or natural families and adoptive ones is a legal distinction and therefore a construction, one with the same power and effects as other myths whose acceptance shapes reality, even if they do not simply reflect underlying truths. The norm of a different-sexed genetic-parent family maintaining kinship ties through the adolescence of a child is not a fact of nature, a predominant practice, nor an obviously beneficent one. In light of this, we need to think about institutionalizing standards more consistent with and kind to our lived kinship experiences. The first part of this essay reviews tacit themes in prevailing adoption policy; the second part outlines alternative approaches.

1. A study of paternity testing in Canada from 1992 to 1998 "finds no significant increase in either the number of cases brought to court or the percentage of cases in which genetic testing was ordered. However, the author's analysis suggests that courts are placing a growing value on the importance of genetic evidence, and that they justify its use by reference to the importance of complete medical information for the future health of the child, to the state's interest in ensuring that a child receives financial support, and to the certainty which genetic evidence affords" (Caulfield 2000, 67).

2. Melanie G. McCulley argues that if women have the right to abortion, then genetic fathers should have the right to terminate their interests in unborn children, based on the notion of obligations imposed by not doing so. However, McCulley does not believe that women should have the right to abortions: "The author's purpose in writing this article is to demonstrate the inequities in the abortion decision and to propose legislation promoting male equality in the procreative decision. This article should not be construed to promote or advocate the women's right to abortion" (1999, 517).

3. For an excellent discussion of the constitutive role of law in creating behaviors it claims only to restrain, see Hunt (1993).

JACQUELINE STEVENS

TENSIONS IN INTUITIONS, THEORIES, AND LAWS
ABOUT PARENTAL CUSTODY

Definitions

In contrast with "adoptive parents," this essay refers to "genetic parents"—not the more idiomatic "birth parents," "natural parents," or "biological parents," as these latter categories are over-inclusive with respect to the practices they seek to name. "Genetic parents" is more accurate than the other labels because men never give birth, but they are often parents, and sometimes even claim that parental status, informally and legally, on the strict basis of genetics and no other more general biological or natural attribute. Excluding fathers from the category of a "birth parent" may appear pedantic, but it is necessary for the purpose of clarifying prevailing intuitions underlying longstanding patterns in adoption law. Birth is an activity yielding a bond to the fetus not present in a purely genetic tie, and hence it is necessary to consider a claim to parental status based on birth separately from claims based on genetics.

There are a variety of criteria that governments reasonably may consider for awarding the title "parent" to further the state's goal of raising healthy children. However, ejaculation of semen as an act that conveys DNA to an egg cannot be deemed to be a pertinent consideration. Nor do many courts tend to think so presently, as genetics alone largely is not a compelling de facto basis for parental rights. According to Stacia Gawronski, "the courts have not settled the problem of what to call these men" who impregnate women and then have no further relation with her or her child. Gawronski continues, "Courts generally refer to them as putative fathers or unwed fathers, but appellations such as 'fleeting impregnator' are not unknown" (2000, 554).

The term "genetic parent" for such men—and for women who are egg donors—as well as for parents who raise their genetic progeny, is useful because it highlights popular attitudes about the status of genetic ties. That is, the chief taxonomic difference between families is not "supportive families" and "mean families"; or "rich families" and "poor families"; or even just "good families" and "bad families," though these are revealing of important family practices and dynamics, much more so than the "genetic family" versus "adoptive family" distinction. In popular discourse and sometimes in law the sheer status of genetic relations is what drives the most overriding distinction, so that the absent genetic parent and the present genetic parent are both regarded as the "real" or "natural" parent, as opposed to the adoptive parent who is, well, adoptive. "Biological parent" is another phrase used to connote the real parent, but I find it unsatisfactory. It is not biological narratives but specifically genetic ones that

70

prompt women to want their own eggs, inseminated by their husbands' sperm, to be carried by others. After all, what could be more "biological" than carrying a fetus in one's womb for nine months and then giving birth? Yet these are considered "surrogate" and also not "real" mothers. And even though the children of such interventions may still have genetic ties to their parents, when procreation depends on technologies other than the penis and uterus, "natural" is simply confusing.

That American courts could even contemplate awarding custody based only on a sex act—an activity that in itself is more likely to be considered "dirty" or taboo than sacred in this Puritanical country—can be explained only by the disposition privileging genetics over other human connections, despite the fact that DNA is conveyed in what some might consider an unseemly manner. That rights may be contemplated—despite sex it seems, and only because of genes—is a habit of thought not captured by the vaguer references to a "biological" or "natural" parent. In other words, the preferred status of these categories is parasitic on acts thought "genetic," and hence this is the term that will be used and scrutinized.

Finally, I define a "family" as *a custodial group facilitated by the state for the purpose of providing care across generations,* a situation that may also require mutual financial and other support among caregiving members of the group. While it is currently colloquial to regard only two-generation households with genetic or legal ties as "family," this version is a subset of the more general definition offered above. Such a family can be construed as one attempt at family, one that has failed so frequently as to prompt a serious investigation into its continued desirability and even utility.

Common Intuitions about Adoption

Adoption seems to occur through three major routes in the United States. Some of us are adopted at or near birth by nongenetic parents. Many of us are adopted by the spouse of a genetic parent. Others of us are adopted later, often after spending significant time in foster care situations.[4] The reason it is imperative to question the dichotomy between adoptive and genetic families is not simply to correct poor taxonomic work in the past, but because the division marginalizes and stigmatizes those families, relations, and relatives called "adoptive."

The thinking—rarely articulated—leading to such a double standard is confused and unfair. Overtly or implicitly all families are adoptive, as all families depend on the legal institutionalization of rules that put children

---

4. For statistics on these different routes to adoption, see the well-documented web page for the National Adoption Information Clearinghouse (2003).

in relation to parents that the children themselves do not choose. That is, from the point of view of a newborn, the kinship practices resulting in her care by any particular individual or group are arbitrary. This is not horrible or even undesirable, but a necessary consequence of infant dependence, a biological fact limiting the range of family choice for all children. Nonetheless, strictly speaking, the only genetics influencing the necessity to be in a family are the ones we all share: we are mammals who as children have a long stage of dependency on adults. That any particular adult performs these tasks is not, however, a consequence of a genome particular to that person but, legally or informally, occurs when one or more adults take care of, or, we could say, adopt, a helpless creature who has no say in the matter. From the point of view of the dependent infant, the existence of a few mutations in DNA that she may or may not share with her caregiver is completely irrelevant. To survive, she needs at least nutrition, shelter, and emotional intimacy, none of which lead to requirements for a narrative distinguishing genetic parents from any others.

That the narrative that results in placing a child in one home and not another eludes genetics and depends on politics seems clear when we consider that some of the most resonant stories of Western civilization turn on discrepancies between heritage and identity, or the gulf between genetic ties and emotional affinities. The iconography of a genetic family is not overflowing with images of sentimental affection, but a conceit that works overtime to achieve this in the face of a canon brimming with fathers like King Lear and sons like Oedipus, or husbands like Henry VIII and wives like Loretta Bobbitt. That a human being would happen to be born into a particular family, much less a world populated with narratives about the meaning and shape of families, is not a choice or a necessary event—ask Anne Boleyn—but a discursive fact promoted and disavowed in a variety of texts and laws. Although much of sociobiology is devoted to convincing us that the patriarchal heterosexual family is adaptive, the actual historical and natural record suggests something quite the opposite.[5] Reproduction requires sperm and eggs, one may point out. Therefore, one might infer, it is nature, not laws, that determine parental status. The law, on this rendition of reproduction, is merely recognizing a natural, genetic imperative. That it does so inconsistently by sometimes awarding custody based on genetics and sometimes ignoring genetics does not obviate genetics but highlights the tomfoolery of courts, according to this view.

Such a story depends on assuming that whenever a biological event occurs, this event should produce the correct narrative for accommodating its obvious facts. In this narrative, genetic ties demand the utmost legal at-

---

5. For a review of claims about the family made by sociobiologists and the data refuting these, see Stevens, introduction (2004).

tention because they are there and it would just be strange to ignore such important biological truths.

Yet numerous biological cause-effect relations powerfully regulate our existence without demanding any legal or even social attention to our social status. We may notice, if it is pointed out, that oxygen has a huge influence on human survival. No human exists without the stuff. If legal and social attention follow from the importance of a biological need alone, then we would expect to see an abundance of oxygen cults or perhaps a hierarchy based on lung capacity, maybe a large think-tank devoted to discerning the social differences between those who easily metabolize oxygen and those whose oxygen use is not optimal—with the expectation we would find a strong prejudice against those who were bad metabolizers of oxygen, along the lines of those dedicated to glorifying the patriarchal family for supposedly achieving natural ends. Obviously there are numerous places where the analogy between parent-child relations and oxygen breathing breaks down, and, tellingly, it is hard to imagine such a study not eventually making its way around to implicating genetics. Still, the example teaches us that a biological fact, even one whose importance is signaled by public policies to protect or improve this function, e.g., to limit pollution, cannot explain the existence of a narrative whereby this function entails status differences among individuals.

That this myth of genetic families is at least as powerful in influencing our lives as the material conditions it implicates is clear once we recognize that most of us do not live in conformity with the norm putatively extrapolated from observations of how most of us live. As an empirical matter, it would actually be false to say most children are raised by two genetic parents who only reproduce other children in that family through monogamous sexual relations with each other. Nonetheless, despite the mythological quality of such a family, when it comes to adoption law, the state favors the genetic family, treating it as a norm, while the adoptive one is the deviant one demanding of special government regulation and scrutiny. Table 1 highlights some of the key differences in criteria used to recognize adoptive as opposed genetic parenthood.

Current Rules

Some U.S. states offer detailed adoption rules, while others, such as Minnesota, require simply the "Protection of the child's best interests" (Minnesota 2001). However, even this vague injunction goes beyond the requirements for genetic parents, who are legally prohibited only from negligence and abuse and are not affirmatively required to protect the child's best interests. With the exception of the statutes referring to same-

Table 1. Sample requirements for eligibility to be a genetic or adoptive parent in the United States

	Genetic	Adoptive
Age for mother	None	May be 21 for domestic adoptions in some states; 25 for some international adoptions; and no more than 45 in some cases; age often object of inquiry in home study.
Age for father	None	At least 21 for domestic adoptions in some states; no more than 45 for some international adoptions; father-daughter age difference may be required in international adoptions by single fathers, age often object of inquiry in home study.
Housing quality standards and inspections	None	Various safety provisions required. Home is inspected.
Income	If on welfare, mothers must name genetic fathers	Household finances reviewed.
Criminal record	None	Reviewed and shall or may eliminate one from eligibility, depending on state.
Religion	None	Reviewed and often required by religious denominational agencies. Massachusetts requires adoptive parents to have the religion requested by the parent surrendering the child.
Marital status	None	Married status increases likelihood of adoption. Utah and Nevada require this of couples cohabiting.
Citizenship	None	U.S. citizenship required of at least one parent if child is foreign born.
Health status	None	Health status reviewed.
Sexuality	None	In Mississippi "[a]doption by couples of the same gender is prohibited"; in Florida a "homosexual" may not adopt; and other states prevent second-parent adoptions in same-sex couples.
Race	None	Not a legally permissible consideration under federal adoption law; private agencies continue to facilitate racial preferences.
Presence of other children	None	Taken into account when reviewing suitability for placement.

sex prohibitions, the laws cited above are exemplary and not exhaustive. State laws differ, and they are somewhat of a moving target, both in terms of their substance (they are revised) and how they are interpreted. The table and notes merely illustrate some of the more obvious and common disparities between genetic and adoptive families, the point being that regardless of differences in the details, potential and actual adoptive families are subject to regulations and expectations that do not hold for genetic families.

Why Adoptive Parents Receive Special Scrutiny Genetic Parents Avoid

The obvious reasons for the different standards seem to be largely pragmatic. One follows from the difficulty of enforcing particular rules for genetic parents, and the second concerns whether they seem necessary. Even if society had an interest in allowing only certain types of people to raise children, it appears as though it would be as difficult to implement such rules as it would be to allow sleep only to people who use their time well. Because conception is something that occurs as a largely private activity, the government can prevent this, for the most part, no more easily than it can prevent us from taking naps.[6] When such interventions are attempted—for instance, when the state and the medical profession have legally and informally attempted to constrain reproduction by putatively irresponsible mothers—not only ethical but also practical problems ensue. Women can always violate court orders not to have more children and can even reverse tubal ligations. The more obvious exception to this thinking can be seen in something like China's "one child policy," though this has faced major hurdles in enforcement. Moreover, a flat rule such as this is far more easily implemented than one assessing the character of those who may reproduce.

A second reason for the disparity is that, in addition to pragmatic worries, prominent ideologies about heredity invite the belief that genetic parents have instinctual desires to do well by their children, rendering state interventions superfluous. Why force people to sleep or stay awake if you believe they will naturally do so as needed?

Finally, a related pragmatic reason for adoption rules that go above and beyond those for genetic parents comes from adoption's broader institutional context. For adoptions to be agreed to, birth mothers must have confidence that their infants will be adequately cared for by adoptive parents. (Unless married to the mother, the genetic father's consent to an adoption is required only under certain limited conditions.)[7] Guaranteeing certain attributes among adoptive parents should enhance the willingness of

---

6. For analyses and a review of state regulations of "unfit mothers," see Roberts (1991) and Gomez (1997).

7. According to the California Family Code: "A man is presumed to be the natural father of a child if he meets the conditions provided in Chapter 1 (commencing with Section 7540) or Chapter 3 (commencing with Section 7570) of Part 2 or in any of the following subdivisions: (a) He and the child's natural mother are or have been married to each other and the child is born during the marriage, or within 300 days after the marriage is terminated by

birth mothers to part in good conscience from their newborns. Legal criteria for anonymous adoptions and informal considerations in open adoptions tend toward scrutiny of adoptive parents that does not occur for genetic ones, and hence enhances the birth mothers' trust.

The above, apparently commonsensical formulations, are not false statements about the adoption practices in this country, but they comprise a partial story that reinforces practices at the level of individual families that lead to broader social harms. The notion of a "real family"—nurtured in the interstices of custody law—renders some families and ties authentic and others as copies that, as such, perform the superiority of the original. Judith Butler makes the point that homosexuality as even a convincing copy of heterosexuality does not destabilize heterosexuality. Although the ease of mimicry might be seen as a way to dislodge essentialist assumptions about sexual desire—if a "butch" or "femme" subject position follows from one's imagination and not specific genitalia, then anatomy seems not to be destiny—in fact the "copy" only serves to bolster the authority of the "original" (Butler 1991). Likewise for adoption practices: the variety and ubiquity of families that jumble the forms of being for subject positions in the U.S.-American family seem only to strengthen injunctions tending toward a single, correct fundamental family structure. The reproduction of a two-tier family structure, with one seemingly authentic and the other a copy, illogically and unfairly stigmatizes the latter families while affording irrational protections to genetic parents who may mistreat their children. Moreover, ideologies of the natural family underlie a spectrum of other irrational forms of oppression and hierarchies among ethnic and racial groups in this country. And, the biologized heterosexual reproductive family marginalizes those raising children with same-sex partners. Just as the

---

death, annulment, declaration of invalidity, or divorce, or after a judgment of separation is entered by a court. (b) Before the child's birth, he and the child's natural mother have attempted to marry each other by a marriage solemnized in apparent compliance with law, although the attempted marriage is or could be declared invalid, and either of the following is true: (1) If the attempted marriage could be declared invalid only by a court, the child is born during the attempted marriage, or within 300 days after its termination by death, annulment, declaration of invalidity, or divorce. (2) If the attempted marriage is invalid without a court order, the child is born within 300 days after the termination of cohabitation. (c) After the child's birth, he and the child's natural mother have married, or attempted to marry, each other by a marriage solemnized in apparent compliance with law, although the attempted marriage is or could be declared invalid, and either of the following is true: (1) With his consent, he is named as the child's father on the child's birth certificate. (2) He is obligated to support the child under a written voluntary promise or by court order. (d) He receives the child into his home and openly holds out the child as his natural child." A widely cited exception to the application of this law is *re Adoption of Kelsey S.* (1992) 1 Cal. 4th 816. For a discussion of the divided rulings in the aftermath of this case, see Alton (2000). For elaborations of continued legal liabilities of unmarried genetic fathers, see Wambaugh (1999), note 145.

copy of heterosexuality narrates and performs an authentic, original heterosexuality, the "adoptive" family creates the "real" one of genetics.

Hence by distinguishing between adoptive and genetic families, the laws outlined in table 1 falsely instantiate the view that the family is pre-political. That is, these differences imply that a legal order only formally ratifies a natural family that has long predated it, when the truth of the matter is that families have never existed without a political society providing the rules for what counts as a family, with patterns of endogamy and exogamy that vary across societies and within the same society over time (Levi-Strauss 1969; Stevens 1999, chapter 5). These rules, constructed by all political societies, ranging from tribes in New Guinea to the state marriage court in New York City, exist for two reasons alone. The first is to bring men into relation with children, which, absent kinship rules, would occur only at the whims of the mother. Significantly, these kinship rules do not require a genetic premise for a paternal relation to a child, only a formal relation to the mother.[8] And the second purpose of kinship rules is to allow societies to maintain their distinction as an intergenerational community. Membership in a particular family typically provides the route for membership in a larger tribe, nation, ethnicity, race, and so forth (Stevens 1999). Once we review the various ways that the state constructs the ostensibly natural family, we shall see how it is immanently reasonable to consider radically different alternative family rules that do not take myths about the genetic family as their starting point.

The U.S.-American Family

Perhaps the most salient fact about today's families in this country is that they do not conform to a common intuition that underlies ideas about what counts as natural, generally thought to include what is normal or common. If genetic families are natural, then one would expect to see them not only in a numerically hefty majority but ubiquitous, as are other behaviors called natural, e.g., eating, sleeping, drinking—natural behaviors that everyone, not just a majority, practice. Yet as the pie charts in figure 1 and other data indicate, only half the children in the United States will be raised by their two genetic parents.

While 71 percent of children are now living with two parents, not all of these parents are genetic parents. Eight percent are stepfamily situations and of the remaining 63 percent, about 3 percent of these will be adoptive parents, leaving a snapshot portrait of only 60 percent of children in two-

---

8. For an analysis of the contradictory claims in the political anthropology of paternity, see Stevens (1999), 224–26.

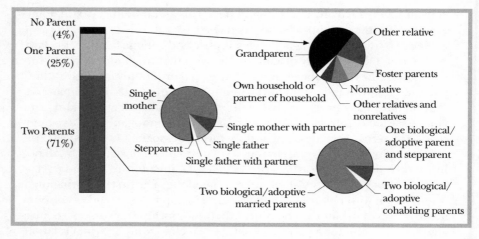

Figure 1. The U.S.-American Family. U.S. Census Bureau, Survey of Income and Program Participation (1999).

parent genetic households. Assuming divorce rates stay constant, the chances such a household will survive can only decline over time, a point borne out by snapshot data on children who are 15–17 years of age, among whom under 50 percent are living with two genetic parents.[9]

One important implication of the statistical normalcy of nongenetic childrearing arrangements—widely experienced but apparently still little known—is that studies showing high numbers of children "at risk" because they are not from households with two genetic parents regularly overlook that these numbers are approximately proportionate to the high numbers of children living in such households. For instance, much has been made of the fact that about half of sexual assaults are at the hands of men who live in households in which they are not genetic fathers (Gomes-Schwartz, Horowitz, and Cardarelli 1990), but since about half of all children will live in such households, the focus on stepfathers produces misleading evolutionary biological inferences (Stevens 2003, introduction).

9. In 1996, 50.3 percent of children ages 15–17 were living with "two biological or adoptive parents." The above is based on data gathered by the U.S. Census Bureau's Survey of Income and Program Participation: "Implemented by the U.S. Census Bureau since 1984, the Survey of Income and Program Participation (SIPP) is a continuous series of national longitudinal panels, with a sample size ranging from approximately 14,000 to 36,700 interviewed households. The duration of each panel ranges from 2 years to 4 years, with household interviews every 4 months" (U.S. Census Bureau, 2001, SIPPS Data Source Description). Indeed because the study is longitudinal, the data will more likely overstate the level of longstanding ties within genetic families, since those families that do not stay together are more likely to fall out of the survey and be underrepresented. Also, these tables collapse "adoptive" and "biological" parents into one category, rather than break out the approximately 3 percent of all families that are adoptive as I had done above.

For the past two decades forerunners of the socio-evolutionary method, Martin Daly and Margo Wilson, have urged readers to accept "(i) that genetic relationship is associated with the mitigation of conflict and violence in people, as in other creatures; and (ii) that evolutionary models predict and explain patterns of differential risk of family violence" (Daly and Wilson 1988). While able to offer some findings consistent with this in their research of homicide rates by genetic versus stepparents in Canada (Daly and Wilson 1988), their results have been widely disputed on methodological grounds as well as for their lack of generalizability. Similar, more recent studies with much better data sets in Sweden and Finland yielded different results. In Sweden, authors found that the main risk factor for children was not living with a stepparent, but living with just one parent: "Children with one stepparent and one genetic parent do not run a greater risk [of homicide] when compared with children living with two genetic parents" (Temrin, Buchmayer, and Enquist 2000, 944). And a study in Finland found that of the filicides between 1975 and 1994, 62 percent were committed by the genetic mother, 33 percent by the genetic father, and four percent by a stepfather (Vanamo et al. 2001, 202). Wilson and Daly are running into trouble not only in the literature on human families but also in the literature on nonhuman reproduction. For instance, a study co-authored by Daly acknowledges that quite frequently birds will be raised by adult birds who are not genetically related in species that can distinguish among its own versus other progeny (Rohwer, Heron, and Daly 1999).

Of course, there is an equally large literature in the social sciences purporting to show less violent but still adverse outcomes associated with single-parent families. A classic in this genre is McLanahan and Sandefur (1994). This research is fundamentally misguided and unhelpful. No researcher can "control for" the situations that render some dual genetic parent families intolerable and hence lead to their dissolution. Looking at these post-traumatic situations and comparing the results with those that stay together should take account of the underlying discord and its effects. If one does not consider the potential harm to children remaining in a conflict-ridden situation, one does no more than predict that it is better to be happy and stay together than it is to be miserable and end a custodial arrangement—a nice thought, but useless for making policy.

In fact, the Adoption and Safe Families Act of 1997[10] can be seen as a symptom of the problems attendant on the false belief that biological families are safe havens. According to Elizabeth Bartholet, the law was "designed to undo some of the damage that Congress perceived had been done by a 1980 federal law that required states to make reasonable efforts to preserve families before removing children on a temporary or perma-

---

10. Pub. L. No. 105-89, 111 State. 2115 (codified as amended in sections of 42 U.S.C).

nent basis" (1999).[11] Prior to this law, the ideology of families as warm fuzzy spaces that should be preserved meant children were legally required to remain in homes where biological parents had killed or tortured siblings (Bartholet 1999). If one were to take a cold look at what happens in the typical family household—the violence, jealousies, petty bickering, and so forth—one would expect a Congress mindful of its citizens' well-being to call for the family's abolition as soon as possible, and not to curry votes by giving speeches on the importance of the family to Western civilization, as occurred during the floor debates on the 1996 Defense of Marriage Act.

The U.S.-American Family in Law

Curiously, while the empirical evidence does not support the view of a two-parent genetic family as normal or even as especially adaptive, this model continues to dominate, albeit paradoxically, the authoritative juridical basis of the family. In one of the most striking exemplars of the copy defining the original, Antonin Scalia in *Michael H. v. Gerald D.* 491 U.S. 110 (1989) held that because "nature itself makes no provision for dual fatherhood" a custody case would be decided in favor of the husband and against the genetic father (115). In this case, because Gerald was married to Victoria's mother, Scalia awarded him sole paternal custody, even though Michael was acknowledged to be Victoria's genetic father and had actually developed a relationship with the girl, who was three when Gerald claimed custody.

Although Michael's relation conforms perfectly to the "genetic" idiom of paternity—a firm bond of the genetic father with his young progeny—the state proclaimed an entirely different view of the matter. The legal view of parenthood defined what counted as the natural family, and then the state used this so-called natural relation for providing guidance in shaping a result that in its details actually marginalized the genetic tie in the particular case—again, even while institutionalizing a nature-based view of parenthood, i.e., the single father of Scalia's nature authorizes, indeed requires, a single father at law. At the same time, Scalia asserted a principle that gives epistemological primacy to the state, not nature, in determining what counts as a family.[12]

---

11. For an expanded discussion of this law, see Freundlich (1999).

12. For the standards used to determine the constitutionality of laws used to revoke custody rights, see Wambaugh (1999), note 34. For a more complete discussion of how the U.S. courts have defined a putatively natural family that is not at all genetic, see Stevens (1999), chap. 5.

Genetic Matter: Rethinking Family Resemblances

Up to this point, I have been referring to "genetic" as opposed to "adoptive" parents. Such a distinction follows from idiomatic notions of children inheriting genes from two parents, producing hereditary links, and thus providing a template for the family, one that may be imitated in other contexts, to wit, adoption. However, not only do conventional genetic families fail to justify themselves on the grounds they are actually the natural organization for raising children, or even ones that are overwhelmingly popular, but the logic of Scalia and others using genetic analysis to fix the parental ties of those whose egg and sperm yielded DNA is itself unconvincing. The assumption underlying the notion that genetic contributions should yield custody rights is that a father's sperm contains something that is uniquely his and that by virtue of contributing this to the development of an embryo he gains certain rights, first to the embryo and then to the child. And the same holds for the woman who contributes DNA from her ova. Yet neither claim receives backing from the details of genetic transmission.

Not only do the genetic contributions from a particular inseminated egg contribute little to the individual distinctiveness of progeny beyond species specificity,[13] but the processes of inheritance also point to a much broader gene pool for the individual than one confined simply to the maternal ovum and the paternal sperm. These immediate conduits of genetic material—parental sperm and ova—contain DNA from hundreds of thousands of individuals going far back in time with the genes subject to random mutations, even during pregnancy. No particular parent single-handedly determines which portion of genetic matter actually will be part of the child's genome. Hence there is no scientific reason to single out the specific contributions of distinctly parental DNA as dispositive of a child's genetic identity, nor, in turn, to privilege the claims of individuals who convey genetic matter as possessing a special claim to the reproductive consequences of such genetic material, i.e., children.[14]

If genetic patterns alone were used to determine custody, then this would imply the potential to parcel custody rights to various individuals based on the specific proportions of one's DNA contributed to the child's genome, distinct not only from that of the other parent, but also from those of his or her ancestors. To be true to the logic of genetic prerogatives, one would need to trace out various recombinations and decide which ones most contributed to the distinctive characteristics of a particu-

13. Two good works on the subject are Lewontin, Rose, and Kamin (1984); Sarkar (1998).
14. For a discussion of ethically (in)defensible entitlements following from genetic ties, see Steiner (1994), 274–77.

lar child. In many cases, it might not be the genes mutated in one's parents' genomes, but genes, phenotypical or recessive, from mutations that developed several generations before the child was conceived. In short, the so-called genetic parents consist not only of one's immediate egg and sperm donors, but those relatives from different parts of one's genetic family tree. If because of the hazards of gene expression Jane turns out more like her great-uncle Joseph than her father, does that mean Joseph is her true "genetic parent"? Should Joseph have presumptive custody?

Moreover, not only do variations in DNA shuffle around among generations and within families, but the legal relevance of genetic similarities also seems doubtful. What is the logical basis of rights following strictly from the contents of one's genome, the shaping of which is beyond anyone's control, as are the contents therein? As grounds for any individual rights, including those of custody, DNA seems especially odd, since the individual does nothing to earn such rights. Classical Lockean theory awards property rights on the basis of laboring, a principle Locke himself applies to reproduction. Locke explains his way of thinking: God is King, not us earthly creatures, because God is "Maker of us all, which no Parents can pretend to be of their children," for to be a maker one would at least need a plan, or to put some hard work into the project. But, asks Locke, "What Father of a Thousand, when he begets a Child, thinks farther than the satisfying his present Appetite?" (1988, I. 53, 54). And, he continues, "for no body can deny but that the woman hath an equal share if not the greater, as nourishing the Child a long time in her own Body out of her own Substance it is fashioned, and from her it receives the Materials and Principles of its Constitution" (1988, I. 55). On Locke's analysis, awarding custody rights for conveying DNA would be like bestowing a Pulitzer Prize for delivering the newspaper.

Even if we accept the disputed view that genes encode our personalities in ways analogous to computers coding robots, we should not overlook the material semiotics of all sorts of symbols, not just those of DNA. Any armchair ethnologist can observe that individual variations depend more on the language, art, forms of technologies, and political institutions into which a human child is born than on the minute variations among individuals' DNA.[15] A child brought up in Athens in 500 B.C. would be more different from a genetically similar descendant there today than she would be from her Egyptian counterpart living in the same epoch. And although one can point to the role of genetics in transmitting a handful of rare diseases, 99 percent of all diseases, including cancers, have a pre-

15. For research debunking twin studies, see Duster (1990), Kamin (1974), Kamin and Eysenck (1981), Gould (1996).

ponderance of environmental etiologies, ranging from geographical location to wealth.[16]

Objections to genetic reductivism evoke especially strong responses from men, who, as actual or potential genetic fathers, may rely on mythical assumptions about gene transmission to claim custody rights. If the specific contributions of one person's DNA do not significantly shape progeny, then the weak claim to custody based on genetic similarity vanishes altogether. Moreover, even if paternal DNA could somehow be shown to significantly shape the individuality of the child, that fact alone provides no more reason to recognize the DNA transmitter's paternal rights than does my skill with English mean I can lay claim to owning my child's vocabulary. Gene bearers and language users alike convey information which they do not create or own, and to which they therefore have no individual rights (see also Steiner 1994, 274–77).

Rather than single out adoption as an intrusion into relations experienced as authentic by the transmission of DNA, we need to recognize that all families are adoptive ones, including those with discernible genetic links among their members. Once we recognize that the connotations of the family as an idea as well as a political practice emerge in the mutually determining discourses of law and myth, we can begin to attend to how these narratives stigmatize non-genetic families, the incoherence of the law in this area, and then press ahead with contemplating alternative rules.

ALTERNATIVE METHODS OF ADOPTION

Feminist Interventions

In the United States and, indeed, in all political societies, the family does not emerge from an unmediated nature, but rather, becomes defined through particular rules rooted in the membership practices of that political society. In recognition of the harms perpetuated by a Scalia-esque definition of the family, as well as observations about today's families, feminists have authored a range of proposals for alternative laws and practices to improve families. Underlying a variety of efforts is the belief that kinship rules create hierarchies of sex and sexuality, rather than passively accommodating them. The response to this is a range of legal proposals that would make family law, and in turn family life itself, more equitable, while also privileging the value of care within and toward families from the

---

16. For analyses of literature on the public health implications of the taxonomies being invented through the Human Genome Project, see Stevens (2002) and Stevens (2003). See also Duster (1990); Edlin (1982); Newman (1998).

point of view of the state, while removing the stigma from families that currently are "abnormal."[17]

Interestingly, such efforts are derided by "traditionalists" as social engineering or simply deviance.[18] And yet all families are socially engineered. Consider, for instance, the varying rules of endogamy and exogamy in political societies without bureaucratic states, the Catholic Church's bans on marriages through the seventh degree, the early twentieth-century eugenics programs, the 1965 Moynihan Report, and the contemporary policy prescriptions for a two-parent heterosexual family as a weapon in the war against the "culture of poverty." In light of these and many other formal and informal efforts to make the proper family, one can only wonder as to how advocates can center as normal and especially natural a form that obviously has taken so many shapes and that requires such tremendous work to reproduce, and unsuccessfully at that.[19] If the two-parent genetic unit cannot survive more than 50 percent of the time even when it is supposedly the cornerstone of this society, instituted by fiat in federal and state laws, and echoed in a range of important cultural activities—from religion to mass entertainment—then imagine how such an allegedly natural practice might fare without these.

Seeing that the present dichotomy between genetic and adoptive families is ill-conceived invites considering alternative kinship proposals. By making transparent the rules shaping the family and by institutionalizing practices that really do serve the interests of children—not myths about genes—a family policy may be possible that destabilizes the current dichotomy's stigmatization at the macro level, while improving the quality of life for children and their caretakers in individual homes. Methodologically this line of reasoning defies the typical postmodernist's suspicion of a liberated subject position that might be produced without harm to others, an anxiety especially provoked when it is the state being charged with authoring such changes. The hope here is that by instituting agnosticism about genetics, the state could avoid the treacherous terrain of hereditary discourse and follow a pragmatic policy of child-rearing. Politically, such a goal, one invited by lesbian feminist theorists since the early 1990s,[20] not only challenges Christian traditionalists, but also is at odds with main-

17. See Martha Fineman's excellent analyses in *The Illusion of Equality* (1991) and especially *The Neutered Mother, the Sexual Family, and Other Twentieth-Century Tragedies* (1995). See also Calhoun (2000); Jagger and Wright (2000); Robson (2000); Weston (1991); Lewin (1993).

18. Coming at the crest of the modern feminist movement in the United States, the classic text in this genre is Gilder (1973). Interestingly, Gilder's critique of feminists is incredibly defensive, premised on a masculine insecurity relative to what he describes as women's power in giving birth.

19. See Rainwater and Yancey (1975) and Wilson (1987).

20. See especially Duggan (1994) and Halley (1994).

stream gay rights organizations, including Lambda Legal Defense Fund and the Human Rights Campaign. These groups endorse the idea of having policies for same-sex couples that mimic those for different-sex couples, without fundamentally questioning the premises of this model or calling for broader changes in how the state should support the raising of children.

Before offering policy prescriptions that would eliminate the dichotomy between genetic and adoptive families, I want to turn first to earlier proposals by Martha Fineman, as well their modifications by Drucilla Cornell, as they both provide intriguing, radical alternatives to laws now governing parental custody. Fineman's *Neutered Mother* makes two bold suggestions: first, that the state back off from any involvement in marriage, and second, that instead the state recognize caregiving relations to the child as a legal status. Fineman refers to the "Mother/Child dyad" as a "caregiving family . . . entitled to special preferred treatment by the state." That is, rather than legislate sexual relations, the state should intervene only in the relations between the Mother (who does not have to be a woman) and the dependent child (1995, 146–47; 155; 172–73, note 36; 228; 230–31; 234–35). Under such conditions, Fineman says, "single mothers and their children and indeed all 'extended' families transcending generations would not be 'deviant' and forgotten or chastised forms that they are considered to be today because they do not include a male head of household. Family and sexuality would not be confluent; rather, the mother-child formation would be the 'natural' or core family unity—it would be the base entity around which social policy and legal rules are fashioned" (1995, 5).

In her *The Heart of Freedom* (1998) Cornell largely endorses Fineman's approach, but criticizes the connotations and denotations of Fineman's concept of motherhood (1998, 116). Also contrary to Fineman, Cornell believes that the state should use marriage to recognize sexual relations, including a polygamous one, but without stipulating the subject positions or who may occupy them (1998, 124–25).[21] According to Cornell, a group

21. There is a telling tension in Cornell's views on the relation between the sexual union and the caregiving one. Cornell's initial justification for insisting, against Fineman, on state recognition of sexual partnerships is that families are eroticized environments (1998, 115). Here she states, again, against Fineman, "it is one thing to argue that there should be no state-enforced confluence between sexuality and intimacy, and another to defend the proposition that the two *must* be separated in a new legally privileged baseline for the family" (1998), 116. But then later Cornell states that custodial units should be established in such a way as to make possible overlapping but analytically separate kinds of attachments: "[C]ustody would not be a given fact of [the] sexual unit. In other words, a man skittish about becoming a parent could choose to stay married to his partner and yet also choose not to share full custodial responsibility for his child, leaving his partner to take on custodial responsibility with another friend or, for that matter, a woman lover other than himself" (1998), 125. If Cornell wants to insist on her earlier statements about the eroticization of the family, then it is unrealistic to imagine a father in a household who is not somehow erotically engaged with a young child

of two or more individuals would contract among themselves to form a legally recognized family: "Custodial responsibility would remain for life; legal responsibility to the custodial children would continue regardless of the sexual lives of members of the custodial partnership or team" (1998, 125–26).[22] Finally, Cornell believes the state should provide income maintenance, child health care, and child care to all families (1998, 128).

While I appreciate Cornell's concern for wanting to make available to men an imaginary space she thinks Fineman's "Mother/Child" terminology limits, even if her definition is technically inclusive, Fineman's Mother/Child unit acknowledges a very important aspect of parenting often lost by analyses that treat paternity and maternity as equivalent. Grounding a jurisprudence of parental custody based on the mother invites attention, in particular, to the unique subject position of pregnancy. While this is not a point stressed by Fineman, I want to elaborate some reasons for why the law should treat the subject position of the pregnant mother as the one with the de facto status of "real parent" that should be the initial basis of de jure custody rights, though these may be alienated. The ontological difference of a nine-month pregnancy from the casual transmission of DNA from sperm warrants a conceptual acknowledgement Cornell fails to provide.

Cornell offers an internally inconsistent romanticization of genetic ties[23] and she fails to appreciate the material importance of pregnancy, in contrast with the largely useless nature of sperm.[24] As Locke points out, having shown the primacy of birth over sperm in reproduction, "as soon

---

also there, if only by his absent presence, and we should also expect to see the custodial group with a lifetime commitment to raising this child as similarly erotically engaged, despite the absence of any overt sexual behavior. Cornell does not acknowledge this. Also, the point of such a sexual relation without kinship commitments having state recognition can only be to circumscribe the scope of sexual access. This expectation of the state can only follow from assumptions about the requirements of monogamy that are unrelated to the condition of child-rearing (as in this hypothetical the man is uninvolved with this). Cornell gives no reason for singling out the potential erotic engagements of those engaged with child-rearing as requiring *legal recognition* of their sexual relationships, which is why Fineman's proposals—which do not include this provision—are more coherent.

22. Cornell emphasizes the contract is for life and can be broken only in "extraordinary circumstances, for example, sexual or physical abuse" (1998, 126).

23. "Heritage has a genetic component, but not only that. A break with the nation, culture, and language to one's birth which is inevitably imposed by an international adoption; these factors must be made available for symbolization" (Cornell 1998, 109). This claim is weak for two reasons. First, there is no evidence that one's place or parents of genetic origin mandate acquiring any particular culture. And second, there is a logical inconsistency in assuming otherwise: If genes are so important, then how can Cornell be so cavalier in her subsequent calls for custodial units separate from genetic ones?

24. This is not to say that Cornell seeks to limit birth mothers from visiting their children. She endorses this and the child's ability to find her genetic parents as well. However, Cornell's reasons for this are based on rather curious ideas about genes and belonging, as opposed to the view of maternity developed in this essay.

as the Father has done his part in the Act of Generation, that if it [the embryo] must be supposed to derive any thing from the Parents, it must certainly owe most to the mother" (I. 55). Birth mothers contribute intensive, constant, long-term labor to reproduction that fathers do not. However, Locke believes that fathers can make up for this by making sure to provide for their children economically and, equally importantly, taking a strong role in ensuring their education. Importantly, Locke offers no language at all to suggest he thinks women are incapable of providing these themselves—e.g., canards about only men being strong enough to earn money or smart enough to teach. Rather, he presents these masculine stereotypes of breadwinner and teacher as those compensatory to men's inability to give birth and their desire to reciprocate for the life they have been given.[25] While Locke himself makes these arguments to say that at minimum women have equal rights to parental authority to those of men, he seems to hint at more far-reaching implications, and surely we can extend those today. If Locke is right—that sperm itself does not give men any rights to the fetus—and if custody decisions must be made at birth, then the only person who has earned the prerogative to initiate these is the pregnant mother, a subject position inadequately represented in present law.

Cornell and other feminists who want to challenge the potentially restrictive sex-role implications that might follow from such an emphasis on the specificity of pregnancy would probably respond that although only birth mothers are pregnant, nothing about this act precludes establishing pregnancy's equivalences with other activities, say, contributing money or time in child-raising. Indeed Cornell makes just this point, turning around the Lockean position outlined above by using the fact of such compensations as evidence there is nothing so special about pregnancy (1998, 130). But are these apt comparisons? Is it sensible to consider pregnancy as just one more form of nurturance, one that is equivalent to, for instance, driving a child to soccer practice or saving money for her college education? The felicity of such analogies depends on whether we agree that the physical risks, excruciating pain, and uninterrupted dedication to the task of pregnancy can be equated with the cumulative labors invested in other life-sustaining enterprises, such as contributing food, shelter, and other goods and emotional attentions to an infant and child.

Pregnancy as Sui Generis

A further objection to equating pregnancy with financial support alone is that the equivalence seems to call forth the idea of blood money that of-

---

25. For a more general discussion of "pregnancy envy's" political implications, see Stevens (1999, 105 n. 11 and 269).

fends common sensibilities in other contexts. If we take offense at flesh as collateral for money (Shakespeare 1965), then perhaps we should also take offense at the Lockean offer of fathers paying for education and providing inheritances as a way of paying off the debt that sons owe their mothers, for in that situation a woman's flesh is literally being taken from her, in exchange for financial consideration given her child (as payment of debt for one's own birth) (Locke 1988, I. 55 and passim). Pregnancy involves one's entire body being at the beck and call of another human organism twenty-four hours a day for several months. And pregnancy entails a non-negligible risk of death. Some commentators have pointed out the relative safety of the abortion procedure in contrast to giving birth as a basis for invoking Good Samaritan laws as the grounds for abortion rights (Regan 1979, 1569–70). But analogies to hypothetical Good Samaritan laws for organ donors—suggesting that criminalizing abortion would be like requiring kidney transplants of unwilling donors—do not hold, for reasons that are somewhat revealing. Not only do current medical ethics not require such sacrifices, the norm is that they would not allow them, as pregnancies threaten the donor's life, require huge amounts of forbearance and hardship, and are physically intrusive. Our medical ethics guidelines seek to shelter individuals from such sacrifices and are especially cautious in the area of financial remuneration.[26] The point is not that a sexualized body should never be regarded in terms of labor power, one feminist critique of prostitution, but rather, that the very particular harms and risks expected of pregnant women are so enormous that no liberal society would allow this, that pregnancy itself would be rejected altogether by the same principle that liberals forbid slavery, even as a so-called choice—a practice with which women's reproductive choice activists have sometimes, quite aptly, analogized unwanted pregnancies. The very arguments distinguishing the condition of pregnancy for purposes of abortion rights arguments resonate in calls for acknowledging the condition of pregnancy as one that entails special legal recognition. While it is unconstitutional for states to allow even mutually consensual slavery, and it is

26. The U.S. National Organ Transplant Act prohibits "any person to knowingly acquire, receive, or otherwise transfer any human organ for valuable consideration for use in human transplantation," a requirement based on studies concluding that "society's moral values militate against regarding the body as a commodity . . ." (*Harvard Law Review* 1990, 1622–23), quoted in Jefferies (1998). The British Medical Association advises its members that the British Human Organ Transplants Act of 1989 requires that in "every case where the transplant of an organ is proposed between a living donor and a recipient who are not genetically related, the proposal must be referred to ULTRA. As an independent authority, its function is to consider cases where no genetic relationship exists or where such a claimed relationship cannot be established. When an organ becomes available the Authority will have to be satisfied that no payments have been made or will be proposed" (2001).

against all norms of medical ethics to expect one individual to put her life at risk to preserve another, there is no discussion of legislation to protect women from the potential harms of pregnancy.

The dangers of pregnancy notwithstanding, the U.S. Department of Health and Human Services has not invoked the Hippocratic Oath's maxim of "First Do No Harm" as grounds for prohibiting pregnancy, which suggests that this is an act that really is sui generis. Unlike Cornell, my own objection to Fineman's "Mother/Child" dyad is not based on its wrongly excluding people from the category, but on it wrongly including those as "mothers" who do not labor to bear children. Current laws wrongly instill a dichotomy between genetic and adoptive parents and also fail to distinguish the contributions of a woman's pregnancy to the life of her child, raising the question of new laws that would remedy these gaffes and lacunae.

Proposals

The objectives guiding the following proposals are as follows:

1. To provide children with resources and caretakers who can attend to their physical, emotional, and intellectual needs.
2. To make viable long-term relations between a child and a child's caregivers.
3. To allocate the privileges and responsibilities of child care equitably, and, as a corollary to this, to recognize the special relation of pregnant mothers to the children they bear.
4. To ensure that laws designed for the micro level resonate positively in broader social discourses.

The policies offered below in pursuit of these objectives are of course not immune to violation, just as current family laws may be disobeyed. However, because these alternatives are much more flexible than rules giving rise to our current child-rearing roles, they are far less likely to be broken. They are also conducive to inviting people to participate in forming families through a range of encounters, not just sexual ones, and therefore may enrich other relations by allowing for this potential to develop, while at the same time lessening the pressure on sexual ones. No single item below should be considered in isolation from the others.

1. The government should provide health services to everyone, including reproductive health services.
2. The government should make child-care services available to all parents.

3. Every child has one mother, the person who gave birth to him or her.[27]

4. Every child shall have one or more parents. For purposes of legal custody, a parent is someone, including a mother, who adopts a child alone or in a group of two or more.

5. The adoption is valid until the child is twenty-one years of age.

6. The mother is responsible for finding one or more parents to raise her child within three months of birth. She fulfills this responsibility either by (a) signing an enforceable contract with the state acknowledging that she is adopting the child by herself; or (b) by forming a larger group to legally adopt the child; or (c) by finding another adult or group that will sign this contract; or (d) by requesting that an officially sanctioned adoption agency perform these activities. No money other than incidental fees can be exchanged for the purpose of executing adoption contracts.

7. All adoption contracts will require minimum adult commitments to child care.

8. Marriage is a purely private activity, receiving no recognition as a legal status by any government agency.

Taken together, the above proposals would directly accomplish the rather mundane objectives mentioned, the goals of which differ not much if at all from those offered by mainstream and even conservative commentators on the family. One would be hard pressed to find the critic advocating a family policy designed to increase children's chances of being malnourished, unsafe, and stupid. The major difference between the present framework for family policies and the one used to develop the above recommendations is that the latter does not attempt to meet its objectives through mediated, confusing, and unfounded religious aims or genetic fantasies.

Were the Christian fundamentalists associated with the rhetoric of "family values" really concerned with the well-being of children, then the first policy they would direct attention to would not be ballot initiatives pre-

27. The above status seems to formalize not only discrimination against genetic fathers—it does, for reasons explained above—but it may appear also to disadvantage the parent in a lesbian relation who does not give birth. However, this is not the case for two reasons. First, the arrangement above precludes any state recognition of sexual arrangements altogether, so same-sex couples would have no different relation to the state in contrast with different-sex couples. Second, while the status of "mother" is held by only the person giving birth, the effect of this in the context of laws denying the status of "father" is to put all non-maternal parents on equal footing. Instead of the non–birth parent in a lesbian couple being inferior to the mother, the emphasis here is on providing juridical parity for parents, making the female non–birth parent in a lesbian relation legally identical to the male partner of in a different-sex relation where the mother maintains custody with the man who may be the one whose sperm inseminated the maternal egg.

cluding the possibility of same-sex marriages,[28] but a national health and child-care system that would ensure children and their caretakers would receive high-quality services. These Christians would argue vociferously against allocating health care on the basis of either employment status or marital ties to someone who has health care benefits, and the same would go for lesbian and gay groups pressing to change marriage law to make it more inclusive by invoking "family values" as well. It seems partial and parochial to press for domestic intimacies as the basis for the security presently afforded by marriage. One deserves such protections because one is human, not because one has the romantic affections of someone who has good benefits, a good apartment, or assets one may inherit if that person dies — the traditional arguments for why same-sex couples deserve marital recognition.[29]

Eliminating Fathers

Confining "mother" to the person who gives birth (not the egg donor, in cases where she is not pregnant) gives due weight to this key activity that allows a child to come into the world while appropriately diminishing the possibility of custodial privileges gained by the illogical privileging of genetic ties. Curtailing custodial privileges[30] (as well as obligations)[31] based on parental genomes affects two classes of people regarded as parents today: women whose eggs are carried by another woman would no longer have any claim to custody on this basis; and, more significantly, the claim

28. As of January 26, 2003, 37 states have laws prohibiting the recognition of same-sex married couples, even when these couples are legally formed elsewhere (Human Rights Campaign Foundation 2001). And President Bush has given his blessing to a Constitutional Amendment that would ban any state from recognizing same-sex marriages.

29. David Chambers writes: "A final criticism of the laws bearing on married persons is more fundamental: even if legal marriage would offer benefits to a broad range of same-sex couples, some might claim that all these advantages are illegitimate—illegitimate for both same-sex and opposite-sex couples—because they favor persons in two-person units over single persons and over persons living in groups of three or more, and because they favor persons linked to one other person in a sexual-romantic relationship over persons linked to another by friendship or other allegiances" (1996).

30. If, for reasons of superstition regarding their sperm and DNA, men do not want "their" children to be conceived without assurances of custody, they can either wear condoms or decide to have sex only with those women whom they trust to comply with these desires, a situation similar to that confronting women who are anxious about conception. If genetics companies may "own" someone else's DNA because the company's research created something of use, then surely mothers too come to possess the consequences of the sperm, especially as the use of it in the creation of a child is always an implied possibility and therefore a matter of presumptive consent when men ejaculate in women's vaginas. For a defense of paternal genetic prerogatives, see McCulley (1999).

31. If the state provides basic provisions for raising children such as health and child care, then there is little argument for pursuing child support payments from "fleeing inseminators," who, under current regimes, do not pay in any case. For an excellent discussion of the law and theory of paternal obligations for children of poor women, see Smith (2002).

to paternity based only on sex and DNA would play no legal role in custody decisions, including that of the mother to contract an adoption. In short, with "mother" as the legal term for the woman who gives birth and "parent" the legal term for those contracting to raise a child, the "father" as a subject position will be eliminated altogether, a consequence that radically reconfigures not only particular families, but, at least as significantly, refashions the gendered psychic life ordered by kinship rules and the law of the father.

While this call to eliminate the father is the change likely to provoke the most resistance, its implementation is the most logical of all the proposals above. As we saw above, as a matter of political anthropology, current marriage law exists to bring men into relation with children, even if these are not their genetic offspring.[32] That pregnant women must be secured by men in matrimony (from the Latin *matrix*, meaning womb) institutionalizes the paranoia of a masculinity anxious about men's inability to give birth, and therefore intent to influence reproduction by those who do give birth. Forcing men to earn the status of parent outside the realm of sexual access—managing to ejaculate during intercourse—promotes a new incentive system for becoming a parent.

Eliminating the "father" does not mean limiting men's participation in child raising; in fact, it suggests the opposite. By decoupling gender from parenting altogether—confining "mother"hood only to pregnancy and not to egg donors—all people should consider themselves on equal footing for this responsibility of parenting. Moreover, by removing the availability of family ties based on the crude act of ejaculation, men would have to actually work to earn this status, presently accomplished now either by copulation or by simply having the legal status of husband to the child's mother.[33] As far as same-sex couples are concerned, the absence of the sexed parental subject positions in the present heterosexual genetic family undercuts the search for, or avoidance of, the "real" parent. Assuming some sexual dyads may decide to adopt, gay male and lesbian couples will both be "parents," eliminating the possibility that the non-mother (if a mother exists in that couple) or the non-genetic parent will be either a copy and therefore inferior to a real father or a copy and therefore inferior to a real mother. Analytically and legally distinguishing the custodial relations that follow from conception—none—from those attendant on birth —mothers may adopt—recognizes the uniqueness of maternity as a condition that should legitimately engender the choice of whether to pursue custody. This, again, is a mother's choice and does not entail an es-

---

32. This is a basic anthropological point made most succinctly by Durkheim (1965) and elaborated most systematically by Lévi-Strauss (1969).

33. *Michael H. v. Gerald D.* 491 U.S. 110 (1989).

sentialist biological collapse of maternity with long-term child custody. Rather, maternity is recognized as a *sui generis* condition without a copy.

Obviously, idioms and hence intuitions about genetic and adoptive parents, as well as a discourse of "fathers" and "mothers" would persist in the immediate aftermath of legal changes, but eventually one can imagine that the "father" will be as meaningful a status as the Sultan, a subject position that just 100 years ago seemed as though it would persist for eternity as well. Once the Ottoman Empire was vanquished as a legal system, its titles of authority also disappeared.

Implementation

Cornell says parenting contracts should be for life. While such ties over life are definitely something to aim for, it seems very important to make sure the rules governing child rearing are narrowly tailored to the task. People can survive and flourish, even if their parental units break up after they are twenty-one; this may not true for children who are younger. I selected twenty-one as a possible threshold, because this is the age when most people in developed countries finish their formal education. The number is based on the belief that parents should commit to making education a financial possibility for their children. I am not sure that this is really right. Perhaps the state should guarantee funding for higher education, or perhaps the interest of the child in an education beyond high school does not outweigh the parents' desire to cease what may well be uncomfortable relations among each other or with the child by that time. That is, as a social value as well as a utilitarian one, we can imagine a calculus that gives heavy weight to family stability, whatever form that family takes, but does not ignore tensions that arise in any social setting, especially such a demanding one as the family, tensions that themselves make for an unhappy home. From a child's point of view, the need for the family to be stable and nurturing decreases over time. While of course one prefers those caring for children to be always on good terms, a child's survival depends less on this over time. Conceptually, then, there is a point at which considerations of parental discord trump the interest of the child. That point will depend on the particularities of the situation. None of this requires that families dissolve their emotional and other ties; it merely ends their legal responsibilities, and even here the agreements may be revisited with a new contract.

A uniform family law cannot accommodate these details—no laws do— but by taking account of such factors and being reasonable about what parents must commit to, parents may actually follow through on these obligations in a manner that many currently cannot. Again, parents who want to continue to support their children's education or training, not to mention assisting children in other ways, will not be prevented from doing so. By lowering the expectation of what parenting entails, we can perhaps develop realistic goals that give parents an incentive to stick it out rather than leave in despair.

The provisions of the contract should be substantial minimum commitments to provide for a child's physical, emotional, and intellectual needs. This requirement is more of a burden on the very poor than on the very rich, but it is much less of a burden than exists under current laws, which do not provide for health coverage or child care, and hence impose tremendous hardships on poor families. In any case, if a parental group cannot provide minimum care, then they should not be allowed custody. If Good Samaritan laws cannot require me to donate a healthy kidney, they certainly should not require a child to donate her entire future in exchange for a culture's myths about genetic prerogatives—the only basis an unfit parent would have for asserting the right to care for a child. If the state provides for health and child care, then it is fair to expect potential parents to live up to this minimum expectation regardless of class background.

Finally, Fineman's arguments for removing any state role in the recognition of intimate relations among adults should be heeded. If people want to establish long-term contractual commitments with each other based on their sexual or mutually caregiving affinities, they would be free to do so. However, there is no reason to expect this relation to receive special treatment from the state.

While I have tried to sharpen some contrasts now at play in family law between genetic and adoptive parents—to point out how they unfairly stigmatize certain kinds of families—I also want to emphasize some positive implications of the above proposals. A new model of family life, one that severs the raising of children from the traditional kinship group, would not only be good for children and parents, but for all adults. As Fineman has pointed out, currently people who seek intimate relations are faced with the confounding task of finding qualities in a romantic partner also suitable for a parent. Separating the two roles clearly removes some pressure from sexual relations. However, far more importantly, the legal norm that any two or more people can be parents together and form a family regardless of genetic or biological ties institutionalizes a potential connectedness among all of us. Not the person I am dating, but perhaps my colleague or the person who I met in line at the supermarket could be the perfect parent. Enlarging the scope of potential parenting partners, acknowledging a broader community as potentially family, can only deepen all our connections.

CHAPTER FOUR

Several Steps Behind: Gay and Lesbian Adoption

SARAH TOBIAS

Steve Lofton and Roger Croteau live in Portland, Oregon, with their five foster children, three of whom were placed in the family as infants by the State of Florida's Department of Children and Families. Although all three of the children placed in Florida entered the Lofton-Croteau family with developmental delays and special needs, they are now thriving in response to the love and attention they have consistently received from their foster parents. Bert, who is twelve years old, was HIV+ at birth, but no longer tests positive for HIV infection. Since he is under fourteen years of age, and healthy, the State of Florida now deems him eligible for adoption. Yet Steve and Rodger are unable to adopt their foster son—this despite their intense desire to do so. In Florida, the effects of Anita Bryant's 1977 "save our children" campaign, which misleadingly depicted gays and lesbians as dangerous to children, are still felt. Bryant's ugly cultural narrative has been translated into policy—with a cruel twist. Even though gay men and lesbians can foster children, they may not adopt them, as a Florida statute emphatically stipulates that "no person eligible to adopt . . . may adopt if that person is a homosexual."

In this paper I will use a narrative approach to ethics in order to explore the tensions between adoption by members of the lesbian and gay community and the heteronormative conception of the family. I will argue that our dominant moral narratives, especially those which valorize and normalize the married, heterosexual family, ultimately make it possible for policymakers to marginalize lesbian- and gay-headed families, rendering them profoundly vulnerable from a legal and political standpoint. Given that dominant moral narratives also reinforce stereotypes about traditional gender roles, and are deeply critical of single mothers, it is instructive for feminists who are trying to challenge these discourses to analyze the ways in which lesbian- and gay-headed families are morally and politically subordinated.

Adoption — Gay and Straight

When gay or lesbian couples decide to have children, they confront different issues from the majority of their heterosexual counterparts. Heterosexual couples can often choose to reproduce biologically or, if they are married, to adopt as a couple. When heterosexuals choose to reproduce, marriage defines legal parental status. If a woman gives birth in the context of a marriage, then her partner automatically acquires parental rights, even if he is not the child's biological father. In these circumstances, a man effectively undergoes a summary adoption—gaining legal paternity without formal procedure or expense.[1]

A married heterosexual couple can also become legal parents through the process of joint adoption. They can adopt through a private adoption agency, through a governmental agency, or through the process of open adoption (the latter involves independently finding a birth mother willing to consent to adoption). A home study is legally required by all states as well as the District of Columbia as part of the process for an agency or an open adoption.[2] This rigorous background investigation of both prospective parents includes a criminal records check, a check to ensure no prior history as a sexual abuser, and a sequence of in-depth interviews intended to expose each person's religion, medical, financial, and work history. A judge makes final decisions about adoptive placement, determining what will be in the child's best interest.

Non-married, heterosexual couples can become adoptive parents through the process of individual adoption.[3] The general contours of this process are the same as for married couples, except that only one partner may petition to adopt and is recognized as the legal parent thereafter. If the couple subsequently marries, parental rights can be extended to the other partner through the relatively straightforward process of stepparent adop-

---

1. In some states, the right to summary adoption is extended to relatives, such as aunts and uncles. In other words, extended family members may adopt children without undergoing the expensive, investigative procedures required when individuals or couples adopt a child from outside their family.

2. See the National Adoption Information Clearinghouse: http://naic.acf.hhs.gov/pubs/f_homstu.cfm.

3. In Utah, however, unmarried individuals are expressly denied the right to adopt.

tion. This process involves a very limited background check and then confirmation by a judge.

The cost of a private agency or open adoption can be anywhere from $4,000 to over $30,000, while a public agency or a stepparent adoption can cost up to $2,500.[4] A summary adoption has no price tag attached.

For heterosexual couples, then, adoption is a mechanism for creating a family, or for adding a new child to a pre-existing one. The process of adoption is designed to secure a legal relationship between parents and children—be this in the form of joint adoption, stepparent adoption, or summary adoption. Joint adoption and stepparent adoption, however, are almost exclusively available to legally married couples, and summary adoption is *only* available to legally married couples.[5]

When gay and lesbian couples decide to have children, the context of their lives dictates a different starting point.[6] If they wish to adopt, they must first of all confront a series of formal and informal prohibitions. Florida is not the only state that restricts the ability of gay men and lesbians to become adoptive parents. Mississippi also prohibits adoption by same-sex couples, and Utah gives priority to heterosexual married couples for adoption and foster placement. Other states allow individual gay men and lesbians to adopt in theory, but a judge can always intervene in practice to prevent placement—thinly veiled homophobia has frequently been used to deny gay men and lesbians the right to adopt. Even when states allow gay men and lesbians to adopt as individuals, they rarely extend this right to same-sex couples. Only seven states—California, Connecticut, Massachusetts, New York, New Jersey, Pennsylvania, and Vermont, along with the District of Columbia—enable joint adoption by gay and lesbian couples.

Given this context, the process of adoption is substantively different for gay men and lesbians than for heterosexuals. In the first place, adoption is not offered to gay men and lesbians on equal terms with heterosexuals.

4. See the National Adoption Information Clearinghouse: http://naic.acf.hhs.gov/pubs/s_cost.cfm.

5. Lower courts in the San Francisco bay area began granting joint adoption to unmarried couples in the mid 1980s, and appellate courts in Washington, D.C., and New York have granted unmarried couples the right to adopt jointly since the early 1990s (the most public of these cases was when Woody Allen and Mia Farrow jointly adopted a child in 1991). New Jersey became the first state to allow joint adoption by unmarried couples in 1997, when Jon Holden and Michael Galluccio won the right to adopt their son, Adam. The only unmarried couples who can legally adopt through the stepparent mechanism are registered domestic partners, living in California. This was made possible by the passage of AB 25, which has been effective since January 1, 2002.

6. This assumes that gay men and lesbians cannot marry and are therefore denied access to the rights and benefits associated with this legal status. As this chapter goes to press, in December 2003, the Massachusetts legislature is considering how to interpret the Massachusetts Supreme Court's directive that gay men and lesbians should be entitled to the benefits of marriage in that state.

For instance, heterosexuals are in no place denied the right to adopt based upon their sexual orientation. In the second place, to the extent that it is a mechanism for family formation, adoption, when it is an option, is a process that is fraught with insecurity. Regardless of the caliber of the potential parents, or the results of their home-study, or the considerable body of literature which reinforces the view that gay and lesbian parents make good parents, a homophobic judge may decide at the last minute that it would better serve a child's interest to be placed in a heterosexual family.

Adoption also plays a different role in gay and lesbian families from that in their heterosexual counterparts. In a gay or lesbian relationship, biological reproduction almost invariably results in only one member of a couple acquiring legal parental status.[7] For gay men, biological (and therefore legal) parentage is most likely to occur when a child (carried by a surrogate) is conceived from the sperm of one partner in a relationship; for lesbians, the birth mother is designated as the child's biological and legal parent.[8]

It follows from this that in the vast majority of two-parent lesbian and gay families, at least one parent has no biological relationship to his or her child. Indeed, from a legal perspective, most gay and lesbian biological parents are single parents whether they are in a committed, long-term relationship with a partner or not.

Second-Parent Adoption

Second-parent adoption originated in the mid 1980s as a way to ensure the integrity and security of lesbian and gay families. Unlike in a primary adoption, where an individual or a couple adopt a child whose biological parents have already surrendered their parental rights, in a second-parent adoption, the original legal and/or biological parent retains her/his rights, which are also extended to another person.

Second-parent adoption differs from stepparent adoption, a process with which it is often erroneously confused. Stepparent adoption, which except in California is only available to legally married couples, involves a relatively cursory state investigation of the potential stepparent. The state rarely conducts an examination of the home or inquires about the potential stepparent's employment or medical history. This type of adoption is

---

7. An extremely rare exception to this occurs when a lesbian birth mother uses her partner's egg for reproductive purposes. Under these circumstances, some courts have declared both women to be the legal parents of their child.

8. Here I refer to deliberately planned lesbian and gay families.

therefore relatively inexpensive—costing less than $2,500, as opposed to between $4,000 and $30,000+ for a private agency or open adoption.

By contrast, the prospective second parent must undergo all the same evaluation procedures as in a primary adoption. In other words, the second parent has to undergo an exceptionally detailed investigation involving a home-study and an intense interviewing process, along with inquiries about everything from medical and employment history to past relationships, religious beliefs, and child-rearing philosophy. This process is complex, time consuming, and very costly. Given that state statutes explicitly permit adoption by a second, same-sex partner only in California, Connecticut, and Vermont, there are also additional complications involved. As one observer notes:

> What is unique about the second-parent adoption is that unlike other forms of adoption, whose procedures are clearly spelled out in state adoption statutes . . . lesbian and gay couples wishing to build two-parent families through adoption must convince the judges hearing their cases that the proposed adoption is both in the best interest of their children and permissible under that state's law. (Dalton 2001, 211)

Although courts in almost 25 states have approved second-parent adoptions, more courts turn down applicants for this type of adoption than approve them.[9]

As a result of a second-parent adoption, the state recognizes both partners in a lesbian or gay relationship as parents. Thereafter, the state provides a variety of legal rights and benefits to children by way of their parents. For instance, either parent can claim a child as a dependent and hence acquire health insurance for their offspring. If tragedy strikes and one parent dies, then the state automatically recognizes the other parent as guardian to any surviving children of the relationship. Moreover, the child can acquire Social Security survivors benefits from both parents.

The fact that all of these rights and protections are not automatic, and that in many cases they are impossible to achieve without second-parent adoption, highlights the vulnerability of lesbian and gay families. Since summary adoption is always unavailable to lesbian and gay couples, and since stepparent adoption is only available to lesbian and gay couples in the state of California, second-parent adoption is a vital tool for enabling

---

9. In CT and VT, the state adoption law explicitly allows second-parent adoption by same-sex partners (in CA the state adoption law permits stepparent adoptions by same-sex partners). In IL, IN, MA, NJ, NY, PA, and Washington, D.C., the state Supreme Court or an intermediate appellate court has ruled that second-parent adoption by same-sex couples is permissible. Lower courts have ruled in favor of second-parent adoption by same-sex couples in AL, AK, DE, HI, IN, IA, LA, MD, MI, MN, NV, NM, OR, RI, TX, and WA. (Cahill, Ellen and Tobias, 2002, 81; National Center for Lesbian Rights, 2003).

gay and lesbian parents to maintain legal ties with their children. Yet it is far from universally available, and even in states where second-parent adoption is an option, its cost makes it inaccessible to low-income gay men and lesbians.

This is especially significant as, contrary to the prevailing myth, gay men and lesbians are not an affluent community. Using GSS data, a ground-breaking 1995 study found that gay men earn between 17 and 28 percent less than heterosexual men, and that lesbian couples earn less than heterosexual couples, because both partners in the relationship are women and hence are already economically marginalized (Badgett 2001). As Terry Boggis, who runs the Center Kids program at New York City's Lesbian, Gay, Bisexual, and Transgender Community Center so trenchantly observes:

> Queer parents are not *only* educated, comfortable, employed, dual-income, guppy (gay upwardly mobile professional) couples. We are also people who live in cars with our kids, and people who live in rural areas in economically stressed regions with little to look forward to in the way of work or education. . . . We are families on welfare, living in public housing. We are incarcerated, we are homeless. We are people whose desire to parent is every bit as strong as the middle-class candidate, but we lack health insurance sufficient to cover the most basic care, let alone sperm washing, intrauterine insemination, in-vitro, gamete intra-fallopian transfer (GIFT), and other sophisticated medical technologies, or midwifery, or the funds to cover legal counsel (a basic requirement in a society where our children can still be taken away from us based on our sexual orientation). (Boggis 2001, 176)

In practice, then, second-parent adoption serves as a mechanism to provide security to a very small proportion of lesbian- and gay-headed families—those families (usually white) who have the means to purchase the protections offered by second-parent adoption, and the luck to live in a second-parent adoption friendly state (or, alternatively, sufficient financial flexibility to move to one).

There is a narrative that shapes the availability of adoption. It is a narrative that prioritizes one particular family type—the heterosexual, patriarchal family—at the expense of all others. It a narrative with ethical import, because it makes claims about what is best or right. There is a politics that both accompanies and results from this. The accompanying politics is the politics of hegemony and disempowerment, whereby a certain powerful portion of the population refuses to acknowledge other, different families on equal terms. The resultant politics is a set of policies that disadvantages any family type that deviates from the heterosexual, married one. Accordingly, a variety of different families face unfair barriers and obstacles, including single parent families, unmarried families, and families that defy traditional gender roles.

Narrative Ethics

Among the premises of this argument are the claims that ethics is interpretative and narrative. These claims require explanation.[10]

To argue that ethics is interpretative is to suggest that moral knowledge, the knowledge we use to evaluate what is right and what is wrong, is locally attained and discursively constituted. In other words, our moral knowledge is not transcendentally acquired, and there are no self-evident moral truths. Our moral knowledge is necessarily limited, because our encounters with the world are partial and reflect our particular situations within a wider social context. Factors such as race, ethnicity, religion, class, and gender fundamentally shape what we know.

Accordingly, even at the individual level, moral knowledge is contingent and potentially shifting. For instance, a person who adheres to the teachings of the Roman Catholic Church might consider abortion to be the moral equivalent of murder. But a single mother of three who becomes pregnant after a vicious rape might revise her understanding of the morality of abortion, regardless of the tenets of her Roman Catholic faith. When considered interpersonally, moral knowledge takes on an even more amorphous character. For although two people may share an experience, they may also understand it very differently, and hold contrasting opinions about the morality of what ostensibly constitutes the same act.

Our moral evaluations are predicated on the meanings we give to particular actions and experiences. In other words, to suggest that moral knowledge is interpreted knowledge is to recognize its multi-leveled character. For instance, a dictionary definition of the verb "to know" reveals a series of incrementally different meanings that we do not always consider when contemplating the character of knowledge. Knowledge is defined both as awareness and as recognition. Yet it is possible to be aware of something, say, a history of childhood trauma, without the capacity to recognize or identify the precise contours of its impact upon oneself.

Furthermore, knowledge is also frequently defined in terms of personal experience, as well as in terms of public acknowledgment. As feminist critiques of the public/private distinction have revealed, however, there is a vast disparity between undergoing an experience and having one's account of experience authorized as knowledge. This partially explains the

10. A longer version of this argument appears in Tobias (2001).

controversy associated with the radical feminist assertion in the 1960s that "male power is exercised and reinforced through such 'personal' institutions as child rearing, housework, love, marriage, and all kinds of sexual practices, from rape through prostitution to sexual intercourse itself" (Jaggar 1983, 101).

When women articulated such self-perceptions during the process of consciousness-raising, they realized they were not alone in their experiences; that personally experienced harms were collectively shared; and that male dominance was structural, political, and unnervingly commonplace. The articulation of these commonalities enabled women to challenge the socially dominant interpretations constituting received knowledge. Until this time, women's perceptions of oppression were frequently individualized, privatized, and denied the social authorization that is often the corollary of public knowledge.

To claim that ethics is both interpretative and narrative is to assert that moral knowledge takes a storied form. Steven Winter has observed that the concepts of narrative and knowledge are etymologically related. Winter writes that "The word 'narrative' derives not only from the Latin *narrare* which means 'to tell'; but also from the Latin *gnarus* which means 'having knowledge or experience'" (Winter 1989). "Telling" is a mechanism we use to create knowledge from experience. Narratives are internal methods of cognitive organization, as well as a means of expressing our thoughts to others. When we create narratives, we frame our interpretations in particular ways that ultimately come to represent what we know.[11]

Central among our narratives are those concerning our moral experiences. Our moral knowledge is a form of narrative knowledge—that is, it consists of contingent stories about what constitutes right and wrong. When we make judgments we mediate between a multiplicity of moral stories that help us to discern the appropriate responses to the situation at hand. Because our narratives are patterned, we frequently make judgments according to the predictable priorities of specific moral narratives. Sometimes we refer to the claims emanating from broadly conceived, societally sanctioned stories, such as consequentialism, or some form of Kantian deontology.[12] At other times we make judgments in a very partic-

11. Lynne Henderson (1997) makes a similar point.
12. Crudely put, a deontologist tries to establish if an action is right or wrong by examining the agent's motivations for performing a particular act. A consequentialist evaluates an action's rectitude by examining its results—or the state of affairs it precipitates. In both evaluations, a certain kind of statement about truth or rectitude prevails, along with a claim that this type of evaluation process is appropriate for all moral dilemmas. For the purposes of my argument, a grand narrative is one that makes claims about universality and objective truth. There are many competing narratives of this sort. A dominant narrative is one that is widespread, socially authorized, and imbued with power—it may or may not make claims about universality or objective truth.

ularistic way, such as according to the priorities of the ethic of care. By making evaluations based upon storied knowledge, we can create new moral stories, or reinforce old ones.

Yet the creation of moral knowledge is not an individual endeavor. When we adjudicate between moral narratives, and when we create our own moral stories, we do so in the context of interpretational communities.[13]

The concept of interpretational community has two major implications for my argument. In the first place, our knowledge is shaped by the communities to which we belong. We all carry with us a set of epistemological "background assumptions" which derive from our situatedness and shape the stories, including the moral stories, that we tell. Furthermore, we all belong to a set of epistemological and experiential "communities" which overlap, conflict, and influence our understanding of morality.

In the second place, what we often recognize to be moral knowledge is actually socially authorized moral knowledge. In other words, we transform experience into what counts as knowledge by creating narratives within interpretational communities. However, an individual's location within a specific interpretational community fundamentally impacts his or her capacity to partake in the interpretative process—it is not the case "that all interpreters have equal and equivalent access to the rhetorical spaces where authoritative interpretations are made" (Code 1995, 231). Socially ascribed power impacts the creation of authoritative moral knowledge. Those with socially ascribed power confer more authority on the moral stories of some groups than on the moral stories of others.[14]

This understanding of the relationship of narrative, morality, and power corresponds, in many ways, with the approach to law that is articulated in the writings of critical race theorists and feminists who practice oppositional jurisprudence. Richard Delgado, for instance, notes how the creation of narrative is an important tool for those concerned with "community building," because "stories build consensus, a common culture of shared understandings, and deeper, more vital ethics." He notes, however, that the stories that comprise the law are partial ones, masquerading as objective and universal standards. Their authority derives from the socially ascribed power of those who enshrined their perspectives as legitimate, while discounting the views of others. Delgado asserts that:

> The "objective" approach is not inherently better or more fair. Rather, it is accepted because it embodies the sense of the stronger party, who centuries ago

13. My understanding of interpretational community owes more to Daniel Ortiz than to Stanley Fish.
14. Feminist epistemologists have recently begun to focus on the concept of interpretative community and its importance to the process of knowledge creation. I take their arguments further by addressing the issue of *moral* epistemology.

found himself in a position to dictate what permission meant. Allowing ourselves to be drawn into reflexive, predictable arguments about administrabil-
ity, fairness, stability, and ease of determination points us away from what really
counts: the way in which stronger parties have managed to inscribe their views
and interests into "external" culture, so that we are now enamored with that
way of judging action. First, we read our values and preferences into the culture; then we pretend to consult that culture meekly and humbly in order to
judge our own acts. A nice trick if you can get away with it. (Delgado 1992)

Delgado illustrates this claim in a discussion of date rape. He cites MacKinnon to show how "normal" sexuality has been constructed with reference to
gender stereotypes. Dominant social narratives imply that men desire sex
and are entitled to be sexually gratified by women. Meanwhile, sex itself is
seen as "ordinary and blameless" (Delgado 1992). This understanding of
sex—an understanding that reflects patriarchal priorities and reifies male
power—is enshrined in law.[15] Consequently, it is often very difficult to recognize that a women who complies with the "outward manifestations" of
consent is subjectively being coerced.

Although Delgado uses his discussion of date rape to reveal the biases in
North American law, I suggest that his arguments can be equally well applied to a critique of our dominant moral narratives. Date rape, for instance, is not merely a legal issue—it is also a moral one, relating to our
perceptions of right and wrong, as well as to our conceptions of justice. To
the extent that we base our understanding of justice on a contractual
model of consent, and yet ignore the way in which socially ascribed power
impacts our capacity to act as moral agents, we accede to a moral narrative
which simultaneously reinforces existing social hierarchies while cloaking
them behind a veneer of equality. That is to say, by beginning from the presumption that we can all enter contracts and consent to particular acts, we
endorse a rhetoric of equality that is frequently defied by our situatedness.
For when a person is disempowered by virtue of their race, class, gender,
or sexual orientation, their consent does not have the same meaning as the
consent of a person who talks and acts from a position of power. Yet this
difference, which is a difference in *moral significance,* is frequently camou-
flaged in narratives based on consent or contract, and in which the subjective moral understandings of the powerful elide rhetorically into the
objective moral standards of all. Carol Gilligan's research reinforces just

15. As scholars like Alexandra Wald have noted, when rape first entered the legal landscape, it was defined as a property crime of men against men. She notes, for instance, that
historically "[i]n English and American common law, proscriptions against rape existed, not
to protect women's interests, but to safeguard both the value of women to men and the stability of the marriage market." The fact that married women have traditionally been regarded
as property of husbands and fathers also explains the difficulties lawyers have encountered
in trying to classify marital rape as a crime (Wald 1997).

this point. Gilligan's account of the ethic of care reveals the existence of an alternative trajectory of moral development from the one that Kohlberg depicts as universal. The significance of her work on moral theory does not, therefore, derive from the fact that she "discovers" a particular type of "different voice" that is predominantly associated with women (for both the gendered nature of this claim and the characteristics that Gilligan ascribes to the ethic of care are subject to critique and refutation). Rather, it stems from her understanding that the ethic of justice is dominant yet partial, and effectively suppresses different moral voices, regardless of what these voices articulate.

Although Gilligan's work lacks an explicit analysis of the relationship between power and moral knowledge, her account of Kohlberg's analysis of moral development suggests why the ethic of justice has attained hegemonic status. For Kohlberg, moral development begins with a preconventional focus on individual needs, and then progresses to a conventional stage, where "judgment is based on the shared norms and values that sustain relationships, groups, communities and societies" (Gilligan 1982, 73). The final, postconventional phase involves attaining the capacity to reflect upon these norms, and to develop from them "a principled understanding of fairness that rests on the free-standing logic of equality and reciprocity" (Gilligan 1982, 27). Yet if norms and values in the conventional stage are not shared, and if certain moral interpretations are diminished or silenced because of where particular subjects are located within interpretational communities, then it is inevitable that the moral principles characterizing the postconventional stage of moral development will be partial and subjective ones.

HETERONORMATIVITY — A DOMINANT MORAL NARRATIVE

Building upon this framework, I argue that our dominant understandings of sexual orientation are heteronormative in character. Heteronormativity is a pervasive, socially constructed story which assumes that heterosexuality is the norm—meaning both normal, and normatively desirable, or good, and that sexuality itself can be dichotomously categorized along the axes of gay and straight. It is a story that is so entrenched that it renders heterosexuality "compulsory"—that is, heterosexuality is so deeply assumed that we rarely question "whether, in a different context or other things being equal . . . [we] would *choose* heterosexual coupling and marriage" (Rich 1986, 28). Because of this story's existence, we tend automatically to assume that people are heterosexual unless they have declared their sexuality otherwise. The heteronormative story is reiterated every time someone conducting an opinion poll or survey calls a household and asks to speak to a woman, and then, if she is unavailable, to her husband. This story is driven home every time an obstetrician/gynecologist routinely asks a woman what type of birth control she uses, without hesitating to think that she might be a lesbian with a sexual existence that can be separated from a reproductive one.

Both aspects of heteronormativity—that is, heteronormativity as normal and heteronormativity as normatively desirable—are apparent in dominant discourses about the family and the politics of adoption. The pervasiveness of heteronormativity accounts for the fact that gay and lesbian families are constantly marginalized. This marginalization is demonstrated every time a television commercial depicts a nuclear family composed of a father (gender-male) and a mother (gender-female) and one or more children. It is reinforced every Mother's Day or Father's Day that goes by without seeing depictions of lesbian or gay parents. The practice of marginalization is played out every time a non-biological gay or lesbian parent is not recognized as someone with the authority to sign a permission slip enabling his/her child to take a school trip, or when this same parent is prevented from visiting her/his sick child in hospital. Heteronormativity simultaneously exacerbates the way in which gay and lesbian families differ from straight ones, and obscures the fact that they have distinctive needs—such as the need to adopt their own children to provide them with basic supports.

Because of heteronormativity's existence, we regularly ignore the intersections between race, ethnicity, and sexual orientation—intersections that uniquely situate gay men and lesbians of color. For instance, African American lesbians report considerable difficulty with the process of creating a family through donor insemination or adoption. Lesbian-friendly fertility clinics that carry sperm from white donors frequently do not carry sperm from African American donors. Similarly, even when adoption agencies have worked with African Americans, as well as with gay and lesbian couples, it is rare for them to have worked with gay or lesbian African Americans (Cahill, Ellen, and Tobias 2002, 86–87).

The ethical dimension to heteronormativity is highly apparent in the discourses of those who would deny gay men and lesbians the right to adopt, as in the Lofton-Croteau case. Here the claim is that homosexuals are deviants, who live an immoral, hedonistic lifestyle. They will corrupt youth, this argument goes, and so should not be allowed to form families and especially to adopt children. In this spirit, groups such as the Family Research Council argue that "The evidence demonstrates incontrovertibly that the homosexual lifestyle is inconsistent with the proper raising of children. Homosexual relationships are characteristically unstable and are fundamentally incapable of providing children the security they need" (Dailey 2002).

One political consequence of heteronormativity is that law and family policy have been built around the norm of the married, heterosexual family. The most striking contemporary political manifestation of this can be found in welfare reform. The passage of PROWRA in 1996 fundamentally restructured welfare policy—making recipients work for their benefits, and limiting welfare receipt to five years. Yet PROWRA also included important provisions reinforcing heterosexual marriage. For instance, states may now prioritize married couples needing help—the state of West Virginia has added $100 to a family's monthly benefits if the parents are married (LeRoy 2001). Moreover, PROWRA set aside $50 million for abstinence-only education, teaching that sex outside of a heterosexual marriage is dangerous and bad (Cahill and Jones, 2001). PROWRA thereby shows how morality and politics are fundamentally entwined.

Challenging the Narrative — Reshaping Politics

This discussion is not meant to imply that either our narratives or the power structures creating them are categorical or monolithic. In fact, I wish to assert quite the opposite—both structures and narratives are diverse and overlapping. Although our dominant moral narratives reflect the power dynamics pervading society, these narratives are necessarily partial and frequently conflictual in and of themselves. Moreover, other, less authoritative, forms of moral knowledge exist alongside the hegemonic ones, affecting their content. In this sense, I argue that our dominant narratives are dialogic—that is, shaped though constant contact with otherness, and constantly being renegotiated (Bakhtin 1981).

To illustrate the way in which our narratives shift, we might consider the changing responses over time to gay and lesbian parents from both professionals and the public. For instance, homosexuality was once defined as a mental disorder by the American Psychological Association and American Psychiatric Association. In 1975 and 1980, respectively, these organizations changed their formal position on gay men and lesbians, with the American Psychiatric Association stating that, "homosexuality *per se* implies no impairment in judgment, stability, reliability, or general social or vocational capabilities" (cited in Patterson 1995). More recently, both organizations have come out in support of gay parenting—the American Psychological Association, together with the National Association of Social Workers, now emphasizes that "[C]hildren who retain regular and unrestricted contact with a gay or lesbian parent are as healthy psychologically or socially as children raised by heterosexual parents, and . . . the parenting skills of gay fathers and lesbian mothers are comparable to their heterosexual counterparts" (ACLU 2002). Indeed, a 2002 ABC News poll found that, for the first time, a plurality of the public expressed support for adoption by gay men and lesbians (Cahill, Ellen, and Tobias 2002, 86).

The shifting perspectives on gay and lesbian parenting are encouraging. They invite us to contemplate the emergence of a new, more representative set of dominant narratives, based on inclusion rather than exclusion, and reflecting people, not parodies.

Underlying my argument in this chapter are two assumptions that I have yet clearly to explicate. The first assumption is that it is possible to differentiate between better and worse moral narratives; the second is that it is possible to differentiate between better and worse feminist narratives.

I suggest that better moral narratives are more representative ones, reflecting the participation of as many groups as possible in the generation of socially authorized discourse on right and wrong. Yet in the process of creating and articulating moral narratives, we must be sensitive to power disparities and to the potential of incorporating oppressive tendencies into our moral conversations and conclusions. The best moral narratives, then, will not only be representative ones, but will also be stories which are attuned to the possibilities of oppression and which refuse to reinforce oppressive arrangements of power and stratification. This argument therefore recognizes that democratic participation can foster agency, and that exclusionary moral narratives can damage and deny.

What does representative mean in this context? My call to tell more representative stories is not an argument for the creation a singular, all-inclusive new story. For as I have already indicated, all narratives are necessarily partial ones. Rather, it is an argument for the creation of dominant social narratives (in the plural) that acknowledge and affirm our differences without denigrating them—narratives that are respectful of group identity as well as of individual integrity. In this sense, representation connotes an inclination to create dominant narratives that are not based upon exclusionary dichotomies, and that actively strive to recognize who we are and to welcome our diversity. My understanding of representation is the antithesis of the tendency to legitimate certain values and practices and to delegitimate others on the basis of a set of ascriptive characteristics assigned to a particular group.

Historically, for instance, dominant narratives about gender have been predicated on a series of polar oppositions—the characteristics typically associated with masculinity have been positively valued, while those associated with femininity have been negatively valued. Other dominant discourses have served to demean those who differ from the majority because of their skin color, ethnicity, or sexual orientation. Clearly, those who are devalued in the dominant discourses are also prevented from engaging in civic participation on the same terms as those who are validated in these narratives. The capacity for agency of those who are inappropriately represented is therefore diminished.

It follows from this that a good collectively based narrative is a reflective one, based upon reasonably accurate perceptions of selfhood rather than upon denigrating and negative stereotypes.

Implicit in this argument is the claim that despite the existence of multiple, conflicting feminist stories, there is an epistemological pattern that is identifiably "feminist" (which is *not* to claim that there is a single, universal, unchanging definition of feminism). Generally, feminist narratives are fashioned around some sort of recognition that women's subordination is problematic and should be redressed. Clearly, this acknowledgment also constitutes a moral evaluation—a judgment that the subordination of women is wrong. And to the extent that feminists find this evaluation compelling, it indicates that moral knowledge does not need to be contextualized in order to be authoritative (although moral knowledge may be *more* compelling when it is analyzed in contextual form).

A feminist approach to ethics (and there may be many conflicting approaches that fall into this category) is an oppositional one, revealing that many existing authoritative moral stories are neither objective nor neutral, even if they are societally privileged. Consequently, a feminist approach to ethics also demonstrates that existing moral standards are not necessarily ones that will lead to good judgments, where goodness is defined with reference to the priorities of particular feminist narratives (and may even be contested therein).

A better feminist narrative will be one that is most reflective of women's self-representations, and therefore one that refuses to objectify women or to treat them as monolithic or discrete. In many ways this corresponds with Lorraine Code's description of treating "a person as a *person,* in such a way as to take her sense of herself, carefully and respectfully into account." Code notes that such an endeavor entails grappling with individuals in all their complexity and recognizing that "this is always a delicate matter; it is extraordinarily so when a person's self-perceptions are fluctuating and evanescent to the extent that even a minimally coherent 'sense of herself' is intermittently (and according to no fixed pattern) difficult to discern" (Code 1995, 88–89). A feminist narrative that achieves this goal will be rich, complicated, and "compact." Moreover, since feminism reflects a resistance to women's subordination, a good feminist moral narrative will also be one that is empowering to women, without demeaning or subjugating others. For these reasons, a good feminist narrative would reject hetero-

SARAH TOBIAS

normativity—recognizing that this type of narrative is one that derogates rather than represents, thus creating inequity for lesbians and gay men.

Clearly, this argument also implies that our dominant narratives affect policy and institutional structures, and vice versa. If we forge a new and more representative set of dominant narratives, then we can also envisage the development of a politics and a set of institutions that neither exclude nor deny on the basis of heteronormativity. Yet how this politics should be structured is not clear cut.

As I have argued throughout this chapter, the dominance of the heteronormative conception of the married family simultaneously marginalizes gay and lesbian families and systematically disadvantages them.[16] One possible solution to this situation would entail divorcing public policies concerning the family from marriage. If the government supported caring relationships between adults and children, rather than just the married family, then single mothers, lesbians, and gay men would inevitably be beneficiaries. Under such circumstances, couples could embark upon joint adoption regardless of their marital status, ending marriage-based discrimination in the adoption process, and removing one of the biggest structural obstacles to creating secure lesbian and gay families. From the perspective of feminist narrative ethics, then, this approach would reflect the view that greater equality is attainable through an affirmation of diversity.

Another possible way to revise dominant narratives is to change the institutions they purport to describe. If marriage were legally available to gay men and lesbians, then heteronormative narratives surrounding marriage would no longer be hegemonic. For marriage, as feminists have accurately described it, is the ultimate hetero-patriarchal institution. Yet allowing gay men and lesbians to marry would challenge the definition of marriage as a union of a man and a woman with traditionally defined gender roles. In this sense, gay marriage is potentially as subversive of patriarchy as it is of heteronormativity. Allowing gay men and lesbians to marry would therefore eliminate the need for second-parent adoption, thus providing gay- and lesbian-headed families with the securities that married heterosexual ones take for granted.

Advocating for gay marriage *in conjunction* with increased government support for all family types might therefore be a more comprehensive way for feminists to challenge the current politics of exclusion. But accom-

16. Beyond the parameters of adoption, it should be noted that married families are entitled to 1049 federal rights and benefits—from the right to sponsor a spouse for immigration purposes to the right to file joint taxes—all of which are denied to gay and lesbian families. See http://www.marriageequalityny.org/.

110

plishing either goal would improve the security of lesbian- and gay-headed families, as well as fundamentally reshaping the role of adoption therein. Both political strategies would be compatible with a feminist narrative ethics that seeks to end the subordination of women by enhancing representation and embracing diversity.

CHAPTER FIVE

A Child of One's Own: A Moral Assessment of Property Concepts in Adoption

JANET FARRELL SMITH

A "child of one's own" in its positive sense signifies a close bonded connection between parent and child. Such an intimate and life-long tie has a particularity and special status by virtue of the moral imperative which calls forth a parent's commitment to the child. This sense of "one's own" need not signify what I shall criticize in this article, namely that:

a. the child is somehow one's natural property or possession and
b. the special status of being "one's own" derives from the fact that one biologically produced the child, and biological reproduction is prized as the primary, normal condition and foundation for parenting.

"one's own" has poor connotation

Both (a) and (b) place an adoptive child in a secondary status. Assumptions that children are natural property have been made in Western culture, law, and tradition. They still affect the moral psychology of parenting (as in the query commonly directed toward adoptive parents: "Is she your own or did you adopt her?"). These property-based assumptions, when intertwined with premises about what is "natural" have tended to work against egalitarian social practices and the equal worth of all children. A biologistic paradigm coupled with a property-based view of parental rights has historically tended toward the stigmatization and unequal status and worth of orphaned, foster, and adopted children.

What is important, I claim, is the equal worth of all children, that is, the egalitarian thesis that parents ought to be equally responsible for all their children, regardless of how they came to be in the family; moreover, I claim that the philosophical justification for parent-child responsibility is based on a moral commitment, not only biology. Good reasons can be produced for regarding all parenting as based on a uniform moral foundation. A moral foundation of commitment and responsibility is to be preferred to a biologically based "natural right" foundation where children are regarded implicitly or explicitly as a possession or property. Finally, this essay argues that society and the state ought to regard families of many kinds as valid. Neither society nor the state should valorize the biological tie as paradigmatic, normal, primary, and most desired.

My method analyzes the moral and philosophical dimension of property relations insofar as these affect adoptive children and parenting. Rather than assume essential or universal structures of the family, an adequate philosophical methodology takes socially specific cases revealing a broad diversity of cultural practices in defining kin, connection, and parent-child bonds. Thus, social practices tied to distinct historical periods, classes, and cultures illustrate my philosophical points.

Property concepts may be manifest on many levels, for example, psychological, social, or political levels. The moral implications of the psychological and social function of property concepts are my focus here. To begin, consider a preliminary sketch of varied ways that property relations overlap or affect personal human relations. First, parental rights and responsibilities have explicitly overlapped with property rights, as in the Ancient Roman Paterfamilias's right to sell, abandon, enslave, or even kill his child (Nicholas 1962, 183).

Second, analogies between property relations and parental relations still affect the implicit structures and meaning of parent-child relations. For example, the common view that a parent justifiably has "possession" or "custody" of a small child in ways that exclude others may be structurally parallel to custody of property (Smith 1983). Today in democratic societies, social-legal rules for parental rights rightly reject a property system. They frame the nature and justification of parental rights as distinct from property rules. Yet some theorists still see ways that parental rights are similar to or structurally analogous to property rights and responsibilities (Woodhouse 1992).

Third, the moral psychology of parent-child relations may manifest attitudes that are similar to or modeled on property relations. Take, for example, a possessive attitude toward one's children or the view that energy devoted to children is an investment like any other. The return will be productive children whose demonstrated achievements will one day reflect back positively on parental and familial status.

One purpose of my analysis is to distinguish the morally harmful from the relatively neutral modes of possession and property-like rights parents have over small children. My observations throughout apply to different forms of families, individual and communal, lesbian and gay families, as well as different modes of becoming parents of children: stepparent and extended families, open adoptive families, and numerous other kin structures. Methodologically, taking into account the diversity of concrete familial practices turns out to be especially crucial in moral and philosophical analysis of adoptive families.

Part 1 of this essay analyzes what is morally harmful in applying property concepts to children. Then I turn to arguments for a uniform moral foundation for parenting, both biological and adoptive in part 2. I conclude by affirming a moral grounding for parenting rights and duties based on commitment and responsibility. This means that demonstrated responsible action ought to be the basis for parenting, not appeal to a natural proprietary right grounded only on biological reproduction.

Moral Assessment of Property Concepts in Children

One way to focus on what is harmful, neutral, or beneficial in applying property concepts to persons is to consider a societal practice and highlight property themes. Here I focus on adoption in the societal treatment of children as way to consider what precisely is morally harmful or beneficial in treating persons as property.

Under a democratic and egalitarian framework, children can be affirmed as developing persons, even if they are not accorded full rights and duties under a legal concept of personhood, and even if they have not yet developed certain classic features of the moral concept of personhood, such as reflective deliberation or self-conscious awareness of their moral choices. Assuming such a democratic framework, let us accept the premise that children fall under the moral concept of personhood in the sense that they have inherent worth and deserve respect. Children's freedom, even if it stands only fully in the future, ought to be protected in the present. In brief, children have moral rights to equal worth and, in Joel Feinberg's phrase, to an "open future" (Feinberg 1980, 124).

The first moral argument against treating a child as property appeals to the *intrinsic* versus *instrumental* worth of a child. In affirming the moral personhood of the child, one affirms the theses that each child has intrinsic as opposed to merely instrumental worth and that each child has equal worth. The question arises: is the intrinsic value of the child, or moral worth of a child as a full person, incompatible with instrumental valuations of children? Philosophers have answered that simultaneous valuations are not incompatible as long as a person is not reduced to "mere" instrumental valuation (Kant 1956, 96).

Adoption raises complex challenges to this issue. Children without the protection of biological parents, who were abandoned or orphaned, have sometimes been denied their intrinsic worth as human beings. For example, they were "adopted" into situations which valued them solely for their labor, their instrumental value. Orphaned or abandoned children in the United States during the nineteenth century were regularly "bound out" to apprenticeships or indentured servitude as ways of gaining sources of labor and removing social problems from the street (Carp 1998; Grossberg 1985; Mason 1994). Social practices that "use" children as sources of cheap labor without regard for their well-being and development clearly denigrate the intrinsic value of a human being. Yet some of these children were valued for themselves, as well as for their instrumentality. Potential violation of intrinsic value is not the only moral wrong here. We need to look more realistically at the economic foundations of each society to see a more nuanced view.

A historically contextualized perspective emphasizes that children under whatever economic-historical era still have economic significance, for example, depending on their productive or consumer status of children in family structure. For example, in a pre-industrial household-based agrarian economy, typical of nineteenth-century America, all members of the family were valued for their productivity, including children who worked fields and did domestic labor alongside adults. Some social historians have argued that the category of "child" as a protected, distinct life-phase had not yet been historically established in the early nineteenth century (Zelizer 1985, 10–15). In addition, the practice of biological parents "binding out" their bloodline children to apprenticeships was not uncommon. However, adopted children were frequently worked harder and given fewer opportunities than blood children. (Zelizer 1985, 178). What is morally objectionable here is not the valuing of children's productive labor *per se*, because all persons were valued for their labor. Rather what is morally objectionable—beyond the egregious case of according an adoptive child no intrinsic worth—is the double standard for adoptive versus biological children. In cases such as these, the adopted child is accorded lesser rights, and the adoptive parent fewer duties. Such social practices entail a second-class status for the adoptive parent-child relationship and a second-class status for the adoptive child. This second-class status is not compatible with the equal intrinsic value of all children.

The second moral criticism of applying property concepts to children concerns the status of a child as a moral subject. To treat a child directly as property is morally wrong, because it reduces a subject to an object. It denies or disregards the consciousness of a subjective being in favor of using and disposing of this being as the owner/proprietor wills. According

adopted children treated diff/worse

to this criticism, objectification is the moral wrong at stake. (One form of objectifying treats persons directly as forms of property; others, indirectly, like property or similarly to property.) This argument assumes that "being property" entails "being subject to the will of the owner." To treat a child as subject to another's will is to treat them as an object and deny their subjecthood. And denying subjecthood means denying basic freedom of agency, that is, the capacity to develop the autonomy to be a freely choosing developing being. (Of course, the objectification criticism could also apply to many instances not involving property issues.) Each child is a moral subject in the sense that he or she has the potential for full human consciousness which others have the moral responsibility to help develop. Others, namely parents, have the responsibility to nurture the child toward a healthy self-concept of self-worth. Of course, this objection must be qualified, particularly in the case of children, because parents do need to control the bodies and behavior of young children; for example, for safety reasons we need to pick up a small child and move her against her will. Treatment may look "like" an object or possession. Yet the moral attitudes surrounding the care are what make the crucial difference. What is morally objectionable is the treatment of a child "merely" as an object, with no regard or respect for the child as a moral subject and potential adult subject. Reciprocity of conscious regard is possible, and morally required, even with infants and small children.

The third criticism of treating children as property maintains that a social system of property rules eclipses the ethical significance of the child as moral subject having intrinsic worth. This third criticism can be introduced by considering an objection by a hypothetical critic. What conception of property is assumed in the above moral criticisms? The preceding arguments may depend on the notion that property is a thing, an object, like a house or a physical object of some kind. However, suppose we discard the simplistic premise that property is an object, or thing (or a person's relation to an object), and espouse the theory that property consists in a bundle of rights (Becker 1980; Honore 1961). Then what is morally objectionable in saying that parental rights are a form of property rights? Or that they are "like" property rights?

On this bundle of rights theory of property, nothing need be implied about the "nature" of what falls within the purview of these rights. Moreover, some specified subset of rights, negating some property-like rights and allowing others, would seem to capture parental rights over their own children. For example, although a parent ought not have full liberty of transfer to the extent of monetary sale of his or her child, parents do have the right to determine where and with whom the child resides. Under a scheme of this sort, according to this analysis, property rights or some subset thereof need not entail lesser treatment. After all, our hypothetical critic might observe, some people treat their property with more care and attention than others treat children, so treating as property is not necessarily to devalue human significance or reduce a subject to an object.

The response to this objection is to emphasize that, on a general level, the intrinsic value of a child as a human being cannot be captured by a system of social rules concerning property and ownership. In brief, the human value of children exceeds the scope of property or ownership rules. This point, addressing the connections between ethical values and social systems, claims that the relevant ethical principles applied to children cannot be consistently maintained alongside treatment as property. While it is true that some parents are benevolent masters, others under legitimated proprietary power become possessive and controlling, denying their children's status as developing moral subjects. At least this is true under a notion that children fall under full ownership rules of property. Intrinsic value may more easily be reduced to mere instrumental value by legitimation of parental rights based on ownership rules. Put another way, the scope of ownership is too narrow to encompass ethical recognition of the child's moral personhood, intrinsic worth, or subject status as a developing person.

This argument can be elaborated. To value a child under a property regime or a system of proprietary rights means that what is "owned" is subject to the owner's will to dispose of it according to his choice. Even if ownership rights are curtailed, the fundamental meaning of ownership entails that what is "held" is subject to the will of the owner to control, manage, and transfer as he or she pleases. The crux of this third criticism can be summed up: the fundamental point of property ownership, which is to fulfill the will of the owner, is not, on a general level, consistent with the ethical demand that children be intrinsically valued. The imperative that children have intrinsic moral worth, and require to be treated as subjects, stands in contradiction to the prerogatives of full ownership rights. The child's well-being, best interests, opportunities for development and flourishing, have their own moral imperatives; they must be considered as worthy for the child's sake and not simply as a function of the "owner's" interests and will.

So from a moral point of view, control over the child accorded by parental rights cannot be equivalent to—or fully analogized to—property rights without stripping out the morally relevant features of the child as a moral person. By "moral person" I mean a conscious, developing human being with the potential to develop a set of aims, principles, and interests independent of the will of its owner qua parent. The property owner's right of transfer allows transfer at the will of the owner. This set of rights allows moral treatment and attitudes which may, under certain social conditions,

children need to be cared for by parents, but they have more value than just being property

ownership is not enough

negate the intrinsic worth of the child. For example, consider the sale of a child. Such sale is prohibited. In general, even if the right to sell X (market alienability of X) were prohibited, a property owner might still be able to transfer X at his will according to values he set for himself. He might set up transfer to maximize benefit to himself of various kinds without regard to the worth or destiny of X, whatever that is.

Now we may ask, analogously, if property rules governed children generally, what would be allowable. In general, even if the right to sell children (market alienability) were prohibited, a property owner might still be able to transfer at his will according to values he set for himself, planning to obtain benefit for himself without regard to the benefit or worth of the child. Suppose, for example, social rules allow birth parents to "give away" their children with lavish inducements or added compensation (Corbett 2002). Or, on the "buyer side," transfers of children allowed prospective parents to "shop for" children who met their specifications, like acquired products. Such social and ethical attitudes could flourish, even if transactions involving exchange of children in adoption fall short of monetary market exchanges, for example, exchanging financial resources or monies directly for children. Observers of adoptive social practices, in the twentieth and twenty-first centuries, have criticized each of these phenomena on moral grounds. The early twentieth-century progressive reform movement to regulate adoption was designed to overcome just such phenomena described above (Tiffin 1982).

My conclusion is that if social rules allow adoption to range too close to transfers of property, then we as a democratic society risk violating the ethical premises affirmed about children's moral status. To clarify the position argued here: in societies governed by the modern state, that is, developed industrial or post-industrial societies, two sorts of rules or systems are needed to protect parental control and familial unity and child well-being. First, a kind of control in the form of rules or rights over children which prevent unjustified others from "taking" children in unjustified ways. Second, a set of rules is required to protect children's well-being and development now and into the future. (Ideally these could be two dimensions of the same set of rules.)

In principle, the first type of such rules or rights could be modeled on property rights or simply subsumed under them. However, rule systems based on full property rights, I am arguing, when taken alone are ethically insufficient. They are also ethically harmful, because they are potentially degrading the personhood of the child. A second set of ethical values and guidelines is needed to set out the ideals and standards for treatment of children on the social level. Other moral criteria and values than property are required. Even under a modified and limited system of proprietary rights, such as a stewardship or trustee model, where the trustee (e.g., parent) is constrained to follow the dictates of a higher principle than their own will in managing and disposing of their "property," the ethical content of how children ought to be treated needs elaboration.

So far, these arguments stand on a general level, consistent with a variety of ethical theories, for example, framed in deontological or pluralist terms (Anderson 1993; Murray 1996), human flourishing (Radin 1996), and consequentialism (Sen 1992). Each of these ethical theories affirms, in its own way, the core value or irreducibility of a person's or human being's moral worth, and in particular a child's moral worth and potential for becoming a person with consciousness of his or her own agency. For example, an approach based on human flourishing stresses that we are morally required to support the child's potential for becoming a conscious, deliberative actor. To treat the developing child as an object (i.e., under the domination of parental will) negates this developing potential. To take another example, under a consequentialist approach, promoting the child's well-being involves developing his or her capabilities for full agency, that is, exercising at least a minimal degree of freedom and participating in the social and political world (Sen 1992, 4). These philosophical arguments also parallel constitutional affirmations that children "are 'persons' under our constitution," with valid constitutional protections (*Trimble v. Des Moines School District*, 393 U.S. 503, 511).

These arguments also imply that society as a whole has a responsibility to children. Society ought to be included among the ethical agents responsive to the moral worth of children and the equal moral worth in the case of orphaned, abandoned, foster, or adoptive children. In many cases the state is mandated to implement the standards of moral and equal treatments, as in removal for parents' neglect. But the state's legal action remains limited to what is justified by ethical imperatives of social responsibility toward children. Society also has ethical responsibilities toward families, and parents who care for children.

As a way of sorting out the harmful versus morally neutral elements of parental control, let us now reiterate our hypothetical critic's viewpoint supporting property or proprietary-like rights. Is the presence of a proprietary angle in a given parental right or interest always morally harmful? Not so, according to some views. Without the parental right to control custody, domicile, and a child's whereabouts, someone else could sweep in and take the child away without warning. Without the right to determine their child's medical treatment and educational course, parents could not exercise morally responsible child rearing. While these are not outright, direct instances of property rights, they are structurally analogous to control, disposition, and custody of property. They are limited rights of a proprietary nature over one's children in a sense similar to the rights of a proprietary character each person holds over himself or herself (control over one's custody, right to manage and direct one's self and person).

The above objection observes that proprietary parental rights over children are not always or necessarily morally harmful. Indeed parental proprietary rights may protect against unjustified state or societal intrusion. A limited degree of proprietary control is compatible with child well-being and responsible parental caretaking. A degree of proprietary control in parental rights may also be necessary for effective parenting, especially in societies where the state has enormous power. This point applies when parental caretaking is mostly individualized in particular families, as well as in communal caretaking by extended families. In other words, the proprietary element of controlling the whereabouts of one's children applies to many different kinds of families, not only individual one- or two-parent families, but communal, tribal families, clans, and even nations within nations. We may note that a communal village, functioning as caretaking parent, has a proprietary right against some outside agent sweeping in and taking "its own" children away. Indeed the pervasive forcible removal of Native American children sanctioned by the U.S. government throughout the nineteenth century has been evidenced in state boarding schools which took children away from their native clans and prohibited native language, customs, dress, and affiliation (see Smith 1996). Such historical patterns of taking children from communal clans are considered adequate justification for the 1978 Indian Child Welfare Act, which gives custody and adoption jurisdiction to native tribal courts over U.S. ones (Hollinger 1996).

Therefore, in most advanced industrial societies, including democracies, with the potential for state coercion, it is necessary to strike a balance between state power and familial control. In this case, parental control rights, or proprietary interests in aspects of the child's life, hold off unjustified state coercion and limit the state's proprietary interests in children.

We may concede that parental rights of a proprietary cast may actually help parents develop more intimate and nurturing ties with their children, especially if the threat of outside interference is unjustified state or societal coercion. Given a realistic analysis of the bureaucratic state, and social power of majority cultures, proprietary protections may support children's intrinsic, not merely instrumental, worth. Rights to control location and custody, and to manage and direct a child's education and health care, can be seen as having a proprietary character, even if they are not subsumed under per se, that is, literal, legal rules. Also, they are not subsumed under moral notions associated with full liberal notion of ownership and property. Prohibiting unjustified appropriation applies property concepts to children and, within limits, this has a morally legitimate grounding. However, along with this concession, another very important qualification must be made. We must also be clear that this proprietary character is observed at a very high theoretical level of discourse. Explicit appeal to property rules need not justify actual parental social privileges or legal rights, especially if such naming encourages possessive attitudes in the moral psychology of parenting.[1]

MORAL FOUNDATION FOR PARENTING

The question arises, is the moral foundation for adoptive parenting different from biological parenting? What justifies parental obligation to children? What justifies parental rights and authority over children? Does all parenting, whether it has its origin in biological production or adoption, rest on a uniform moral foundation? Or do we need a separate theory to ground the legitimacy of adoptive parenting? For example, if a "natural right" conjoined with a "property right" gives the moral foundation for biological parents rights, then adoptive parenting must be made out to rest on a separate and distinctive moral foundation. This latter move, I believe, is risky and leads to a marginal or compensatory view of both adoptive children and families.

A more egalitarian and just view of all kinds of families, especially including adoptive families, is more likely if we affirm a uniform moral foundation of being a parent. Yet, there are differences in ways adoptive and biological parents come to be parents. What moral significance lies in the differences? Two philosophical points help make sense of them.

First, consider the very helpful distinction between "becoming a parent" and "being a parent" made by Onora O'Neill (O'Neill 1979, 25). The moral responsibilities involved in "becoming a parent" involve the ability to provide responsibly for that child or make feasible plans for specific others to rear the child. The moral responsibilities for "being a parent" involve raising the child; for example, ensuring the child's well-being with consistent caretaking, providing for basic necessities, and developing the child's sense of self-worth (O'Neill 1979, 25). This distinction allows us to acknowledge the relevant differences in the moral structure of *becoming* a parent for adoptive and biological parents. The moral responsibilities in-

[handwritten marginal note: becoming a parent, more important than... being a parent is... more to it than just a parent]

1. In delineating four dimensions of genetic privacy, for example, legal theorist Anita Allen defines "proprietary privacy" as "concerns about the appropriation and ownership of interests in human personality" (Allen 1997, 33). However, the term "privacy" rather than "property" remains the focus in legislation. The social dangers of parental or adult proprietary rights and privileges over adoptive children's genetic information are delineated in my "Genetic Testing: A Cautionary Tale of Foster and Pre-Adoptive Children" (Smith 2002, 1–21).

volved in someone's becoming a parent would obviously differ for adoptive, foster, stepparent, and biological parents. For example, social responsibility demands that we screen adoptive parents to at least a minimal level in "becoming a parent" because we are dealing with an existing, living child who needs parents. This social responsibility becomes more evident in light of historical exploitation of adopted children. But this difference, alongside the obvious differences about biological production or genetic ties, does not entail a division between the moral analysis of "*being* a parent" for adoptive versus biological parents.

We may then affirm a moral uniformity in the moral foundation of being a parent. In other words, once one has become a parent, the moral foundation for *being a parent,* whether due to adoptive, kin care, or biological source, should rest on a uniform moral foundation. Rather than viewing adoptive parenting as an exception to the natural right and proprietary presumption—which is supposed to be, for example, biologically given or "instinctual" (Rousseau 1762, 96) or, in Locke's phrase, resting on "God's workmanship" (Leites 1979, 308)—we should see the practice of "being a parent" as similarly justified regardless of its origin. Rather than postulate a moral exceptionalism for the adoptive parenting, we should, on the view urged here, provide a uniform moral foundation for both biological and adoptive parents' moral responsibility to children. In short, all parents have the same basis for their moral obligations to their child or children; and this holds true regardless of how they came to be parents.

Second, being a parent amounts to a kind of role-responsibility, where parents take on a role of caretaking toward some particular child. A role-responsibility means that some particular person has a special set of responsibilities or heightened duties, toward some other particular person; for example, as parent I am responsible for my child in a way that some random person is not similarly responsible. All persons are responsible to a certain minimal level toward others, but persons with special duties due to role-responsibilities have extra duties. As a morally responsible person I might have a moral obligation to help a lost child find her parent, but not to take her home and raise her. Indeed, if someone else has already committed to this role-responsibility, then I am obligated not to take over rearing the child.

Contractual View of Adoptive Parenting

Does adoptive parenting take a contractual moral foundation whereas biological parenting is based on natural right? We may grant that on the surface adoptive parenting may appear more contractual. But, drawing on O'Neill's helpful distinction, we can see that this appearance is due to social differences in *becoming* a parent, not *being* a parent. The social hurdles entailed in "becoming" adoptive parents dictates that prospective parents must in the United States go through screening agencies and court procedures where the child is formally released to the new parent. These social facts highlight the operation of the so-called "private" versus "public" spheres in advanced industrial societies with predominantly nuclear parenting. In these, biological reproduction typically appears to be confined to the "private sphere," whereas adoptive family formation is sanctioned in formal social rituals that rise into visibility in the "public sphere" (Zainaldin 1979).

However, the impression that biological reproduction is "natural" and untouched by social-bureaucratic procedures remains too simple. The state supervises and oversees many aspects of biological reproduction. State laws uniformly demand birth certificates of public record, public acknowledgment of maternity and paternity, state-mandated medical and genetic newborn screening, vaccinations, and assignment of Social Security numbers to newborns. So the more visible prominence of social-legal transactions in adoption hides the social fact of state or public regulation of both biological and adoptive modes of "becoming" parents. The presumption that the biological mode is the norm and that adoption is a deviation from it tends to hide these factors. To be sure, there are private aspects of becoming a biological parent, for example, concerning the decision to become or remain pregnant; but likewise there are private aspects of becoming an adoptive parent, for example, the personal deliberation prospective parents go through on whether or how to handle the adoptive process. Hence the private-public contrast is not a solid basis for distinguishing adoptive and biological parenthood; each mode of becoming a parent has both private and public aspects.

From a moral point of view, it can be argued that the moral responsibilities of *being a parent* are not more contractually justified for adoptive parents than for biological ones. To theorize that adoptive parenting is contractual because of the lack of biological connection is to suppose what I have argued is a problematic assumption, namely, that the biological tie is primary and paradigmatic. This conceptualization risks valorizing the "natural" biological tie, and in turn puts adoptive parenting in second place. We can grant the differences in becoming a parent, without assuming a differential moral legitimation for being a parent.

In other words, I am arguing against what might be called an exceptionalist moral foundation for adoptive parenting, meaning that biological parenting serves as a primary normative type of parenting, whereas adoptive parenting, as an exception to that norm, must be given a separate grounding. Given that one has already become a parent, I am arguing that "being a parent," regardless of the way one became so, has a uniform moral foundation. A uniform moral foundation does not of course deny social or biological differences, but insists that these differences be seen in the light of equality of many kinds of parent-child relations.

This position need not deny differences on a descriptive level of specific responsibilities for adoptive as compared with biological parents. Two levels need to be distinguished. A general legitimation of parental rights and duties has a justificatory moral purpose: a legitimating argument for general social rules about which types of parties have rights and duties regarding child rearing. In contrast, on a descriptive level concerning specific circumstances in parenting, one might find differences perhaps with moral relevance as, for example, between adoptive and biological parenting. Adoptive parents, for instance, ought to make developmentally appropriate communications to the child about the adoption itself and the child's birth family. Biological parents might have analogous responsibilities for revelations about birth experiences, medical history, and the like. My position argues that these are specific differences and do not disturb a uniformity in the general moral legitimation of parental obligation.

There are many "differences" in modes of parenting and how persons came to be parents. Adoptive differences should be located on a level where multiple circumstances affect how persons came to be parents, as in, for example, gay and lesbian families, grandparents who parent their children's children, extended family multiple parents such as aunts and cousins, single or sole parents, gamete-donor parents, and so on. These differences will be relevant in responsibly attending to the child's development and can be acknowledged, socially respected, and psychologically accommodated. Yet it is questionable whether these differences will call forth a differential moral grounding for diverse forms of parenting. In brief, the mode by which someone "becomes" a parent need not affect the moral foundation of "being" one. On the level of moral theory, once the commitment is made to take on the responsibility for "being a parent," the moral foundation or legitimation for parental rights and duties should, in my view, be uniform.

It will be helpful to add a comment on the distinction between "natural" and "biological." Is biologically based parenthood capable of a more "instinctual" or a more physically close connection just because of the biological connection? As we've seen, it is tempting to view biological parenting as "instinctual." However, social research shows that biological ties do not necessarily correlate in every case with strong instincts to parent or to parent well. Indeed, many biological parents are bewildered by "instinct" and feel guilty when "instinct" fails them. In fact, much parenting appeals to the catchall category of "instinct," because in the demanding, complex duties of child rearing, rationality fails. *In medias res,* reasonableness frequently collapses, regardless of how the parent-child relation was formed. The fact is, "normal" parenting is felt as "natural" some of the time and felt as "non-natural" at other times, for example, when dealing with tantrums, crying, or colicky infants. Parental bewilderment, helplessness, and frustration occur, and are solved often by appeals to "instinct" or gut-level decisions, regardless of how the parent-child tie was formed or this particular human being came to be one's child. The fact is, all parenting can feel "natural" at some times and "non-natural" at others. The prospect of a rebellious adolescent challenging parental authority is just as daunting to the sympathy and equanimity of a biological parent as to an adoptive one. Parenting simultaneously requires strong intuitions about one's child, sound deliberations, and altruistic motivations. Or all *good* parenting does. Parenting, regardless of its source, requires the highest forms of the moral emotions of forbearance, patience, empathy, and compassion for others.

PHILOSOPHICAL ARGUMENTS AGAINST A CONTRACTUAL ANALYSIS

On a more theoretical level, there are sound philosophical reasons to reject a contrast between biological parenting as "natural" or non-contractual and adoptive parenting as contractual. First, such a contrast plays into the mistaken view that biological parenting as we know it is always a given or fundamentally "natural," whereas adoptive parenting is socially formed by artifice. However, all parenting is a socially constructed moral and political phenomenon, whether it arises from a biological origin or some other source. Historical examples across class and culture amply demonstrate that child-rearing practices have varied considerably between cultures; there is no reason to think that the current norm of the biologically based nuclear family is more natural than other family forms.

"Natural bonds" of emotional closeness and intimacy are supposed on a biological model of healthy parenting to arise from a biological connection. However, the association of "natural" with biological ties is not an essential or universal form of family, according to many family historians. Natural bond views coincided with the evolution of the bourgeois family in the historical era of the mid-nineteenth century in both America and England (Barber 1955; Grossberg 1985; Stone 1975). This historically specific form coincided with the "bonds of true womanhood" ideology stressing the moral role of women as nurturers of their biologically produced children (Cott 1977; Sklar 1973; Welter 1982).

Numerous historical, class, and anthropological examples show that biological production is not always linked to close emotional bonds. Aristocratic parents in eighteenth-century France considered close affective ties to be the role of servants who performed the caretaking of their biological children. Not only was it uncommon to see close emotional ties between aristocratic biological parent and child, it could have been down-classing. The children's duties as heirs to estates and class status overshadowed intimacy. To take another example, in seventeenth-century French peasant farming communities, the rearing of young children was done primarily by teenage girls or elder women left behind in the villages, while their biological progenitors were often out working the fields (Berkner 1973; Poster 1978). The whole village, rather than biological parents, formed close bonds with children communally, a social practice that can be observed in many cultures. Moreover, "natural" ties can be socially recognized apart from biological connection as, for example, in kin structures in elder Native American peoples. Certain highly respected elder women take on certain children (not biologically related) to rear and bond with, nurturing them to special roles in native social structure (Evans-Pritchard 1959). Contemporary psychological studies show that adoptive parents are just as, if not more, "attached" or "bonded" to their adoptive children as biological parents (Hoopes 1982; Bowlby 1969).

Second, the putative opposition between "natural" parenting and contractual elements in adoptive parenting is overstated. From a historical viewpoint, so-called "natural" parenting involved contractual relations about and over one's children, for example, many so-called "natural" parents indentured or bound out their children to other families through the seventeenth to nineteenth centuries in Colonial America or in England. Families in poverty or those who could not care for children used the indenture system as a kind of temporary foster care without releasing their parental status (Carp 1998, 183). In contemporary times, rights of biological parents include contractual relations over children's sport or theatrical performances. Parents have the right to sign contracts for their children's performing on stage for entertainment. Informed consent to a child's medical treatment is a contract between the parent and the medical professional. Moreover, "natural" parents have sued physicians for "wrongful birth," signifying their prior contractual relation with the physician.

Third, on a philosophical analysis, following O'Neill's distinction between becoming a parent and being the caretaking parent, each prospective parent (set of parents) makes a conscious or non-conscious commitment at some point to "being a parent," that is, takes on the task of rearing a particular child. In contemporary democratic societies, where most child rearing is carried out by individual (nuclear) families, even biological parents take this step transitioning from "becoming a (biological) parent" to "being a (rearing) parent." For example, they decide not to terminate a pregnancy but go forward with the birth and then decide (implicitly or explicitly) not to give the child to someone else, but to retain the birthed child

as their responsibility to rear.[2] Temporizing decisions may be made by biological parents by placing the infant one has just borne with a relative or
in a foster home. Or, a permanent decision may be made to release one's
parental rights and responsibilities to someone else through legal adoption. Or, one may abandon the decision itself (to responsibly become a parent or responsibly assign the care to another) by abandoning the child on
the street. Social forces, particularly harsh in certain societies, may constrain such choices. The morally relevant observation is that, at some point,
every parent makes some kind of commitment in the transition from becoming a parent to being a parent; that is, either they assume what I call
the role-responsibility of caretaking parent or they do not.

Fourth, there is the difficulty of ascertaining the parties to the contract.
Are these parents and child? Parents and state? Some contract theorists
have postulated that parents' care over the youthful child is based on contractual agreement, exchanged for the child caring for the parent in old
age. (Others question whether an empirical version of such a contract now
operates in Asian cultures only for male heirs, to the extreme detriment of
female progeny who are often abandoned or discarded.) Hobbes gave a
consent theory of parental authority; that is, the child consents to parental
domination. Since children by definition lack full rationality to form
contract, child-parent contract would seem very odd and subject to the
now-classic criticisms that liberal contract theory neglects the facts of dependency by presupposing the adult autonomy of every party to the contractual agreement. If the contract is posited between state and parents,
then the moral responsibility for the child's well-being is parsed into the
private sphere. In other words, child well-being is covered by the assumption that parents hold "natural duties" toward their "natural" children
(Rawls 1971). (One is left to presume that "natural" means biological progeny.) This premise can be challenged by the above distinction between
"bearing" and "rearing" or between "becoming" versus "being" a committed parent. To some critics, these assumptions leave the well-being of children too vulnerable to the vicissitudes of adult political power.

In contrast, the responsibility theory proposed here allocates ethical responsibility for child well-being to the whole democratic society as well as
parental role-responsibility in particular caretakers. Then, the state's action in constraining parental neglect is justified by an ethical grounding in
social responsibility. The state is not a contractual negotiator or determinant of ethical standards for treating children. It is merely an executor of
a prior higher moral-political principle, namely the democratic equal per-

2. Crises usually make these conscious decisions. Obviously, in non-critical circumstances
in contemporary America the majority of biological progenitors of children take on the task
of rearing them without anyone asking the question, "Do you wish to rear this child?"

sonhood and future citizenship of all children. In summary, the critique or impression that adoptive parenting is more "contractual" than biological parenting relies on social differences in "becoming a parent," not on moral differences in "being a parent." We may concede that society or the state enters more heavily into adoptive child transfer from birth to adoptive parent. Yet the moral foundation of parental rights should remain uniform across multiple ways of becoming a parent and diverse forms of families. Finally, the presumption that biological parenting is natural, whereas adoptive parenting is contractual, leans hard on the deeper presumption that the biological way of becoming a parent, since it is "natural," leads to good and committed parenting. Clearly this is not always the case.

Consider the case of Phillip B, whose natural parents, daunted by his disability of Down syndrome, placed him in an institution for the mentally retarded, virtually lost all emotional and social contact with him, and refused to approve heart surgery recommended by physicians (*Guardianship of Phillip B, a Minor*, 188 California Reporter 781 Ct. App. 1983). Also, they prohibited Phillip's being taken out of the institution on weekends to a home care program with a loving family, the Haights, who toilet-trained him, gave him adequate nutrition to grow, and taught him reading skills at age five. The biological parents undertook no nurturing activities toward "their own" child, even lost contact with him, but barred other willing nurturing figures from contact or guardianship. They asserted only their right to control the status, location, and personnel involved in the caretaking of their own child.

If their rights were justified by solely by a proprietary natural right—that is, this child is ours to do with what we choose—then Phillip's biological parents' decision would have been justified. However, on a responsibility and commitment foundation for parental rights, they ought to lose their parental proprietary right to exclude the Haight family claim to nurture Phillip. In fact, when the Haights appealed to legally adopt Phillip, the court judgment did not terminate the biological parental rights but awarded guardianship to the Haights who with Phillip's wishes, formally adopted him at age eighteen, his age of majority (Mnookin and Weisberg 2000, 779).

Thus, poor, neglectful, and abusive parenting can nullify the commitment to being a responsible caretaking parent. (One cannot nullify the historical fact of having become a parent who "bore the child," that is, the birth parents.) If, by one's actions or oaths, one does not meet a threshold of adequate nurture, one nullifies one's responsibility and commitment to a child. Hence, the moral foundation of parental right to this child is nullified. The "natural right" justified by the simple fact that the child is "mine" does not go far enough to support a legitimated parental right to that child.

The case of Phillip B. illustrates several points. The mere fact of being the parents or being "natural" (in the sense of biological) parents does not imply good parenting. Nor does this fact alone, especially under certain circumstances, legitimate parental rights. Rather, a standard of care ensuring a child's well-being is needed in addition. Parents may nullify their responsibility and commitment by failing to give adequate care, as when Phillip's parents refused necessary medical and emotional care. By failing to meet the threshold of committed parenting, as demonstrated in their actions, they forfeited their rights to determine Phillip's care when the Court awarded custody to the Haights as foster parents.[3]

Sound reasons support a principle of moral uniformity in legitimating parental rights. We should aim for a theoretical consistency in the way we give moral legitimacy of parental rights, that is, consistency among different forms or sources of parenting. This method of consistency is preferable to one which postulates separate justifications of parental rights depending how one came to be a parent, whether biological, foster, stepparent, or adoptive. For example, the argument that because X bore and begat a child, that X has a natural right to do what they will with this child (whereas others who did not bear or beget do not have such a right) is not an adequate justification, especially in light of actions which fall below a threshold of adequate care, as in the case of Phillip B. In any case, biological parenting under this interpretation is no more and no less "contractual" than adoptive parenting. If we mean by "contractual" that one who accepts "being a parent" basically affirms an agreement to be responsibly committed to this particular child, then both biological and adoptive and other forms are grounded on some kind of agreement to that moral role.[4] Accordingly, biological parenting is no less subject to moral standards just

3. Whether the court should have terminated parental rights can be debated separately. The issue rests on the pervasive assumption that biological parents are and ought to be the caretakers of children they directly reproduce. Nothing said in this essay undermines that social assumption. If parental rights were too easily terminated, then that social structure might be weakened. Obviously, social and ethical controversy, beyond the scope of this article, surrounds this complex issue. A responsibility-based moral foundation for parental rights is fully compatible with the assumption that biological parents have the responsibility to care for their children, unless, as O'Neill remarks, they make a feasible plan for other responsible adults to care for the child.

4. On a rudimentary level, we may concede that some would detect promise or agreement as the core meaning of both commitment, affirmed here, and contract theory, criticized here. Granting the core emphasis on agreement does not mean that the responsibility theory slides into the contract model in moral or political theory as the foundation of parenting. To some readers, the meaning of the phrases "committing to care for a child" and "contracting to care for a child" may seem synonymous. However, in my analysis, contract, based on rational self-interest, lacks a key element of emotional commitment and intimacy. See Anderson (1993) on values pertaining to market or contractual relations, in contrast to values pertaining to personal relations. A model of contracting on a theoretical level suffers deficiencies noted here and elaborated by critics such as Okin (1984).

because the child is naturally "mine" or "ours." In sum, there are good
moral and political reasons to affirm a morally uniform foundation for "being a parent." There are additional reasons, as I hope to have shown, to
reject a contractualist grounding and prefer a commitment and responsibility grounding for adoptive parenting.[5] These two lines of argument lend
support to a moral egalitarianism in the types of parent-child bonds.

To sum up the argument, affirming parental rights of a proprietary nature in general risks legitimating parental actions that are less than optimal to a child's moral personhood and well-being. There is a moral danger
in assuming that the proprietary "ours" rests on so-called "natural" biological or genetic ties. The danger in taking what is perceived as "biological" as paradigmatic is that adoptive ties appear as merely substitutes and
not "real." Or that adoptive ties are secondary compensations for the ideal
norm. These are all good reasons to become more aware of the proprietary
background and to utilize or discard it as we see fit. We may appeal to ethical criteria outlined in part 1, that maintain: the child has intrinsic value,
not merely instrumental value; is to be treated as a developing subject and
not an object; is to be regarded as having his/her own intrinsic ends, and
is not a means to the parent's ends. These values may guide the formation
of humane and egalitarian recognition of diverse kinds of families.

The desire to call a child "one's own" may signify belonging, connection,
and commitment rather than possessiveness and proprietary exclusion.
Parental rights need not be framed as proprietary or exclusive rights based
on biological ties. Rather, parental rights may be construed as preliminary
or necessary social conditions to responsible rearing of children. If lack of
commitment and responsibility is demonstrated, for example, neglect,
then these rights may be curtailed or even terminated. On the ethical level,
a theory of commitment and responsibility, combined with a notion of

5. For theoretical consistency, we should note that various types of theories could satisfy
a demand for uniformity in legitimating parental rights. Under a property model, "natural
property right" over a biological child could be conferred by natural law or divine power; and
a social property right over an adoptive child could be conferred by social power or the state.
Each justification appeals to property, so satisfies a principle of uniformity. Yet my argument
strategy takes an additional theoretical step of criticizing both property and contract legitimations of parenting.

Because the property assumptions fail to encompass the ethical imperatives for children's
treatment, such legitimations would in my view be deficient. To address another criticism: Egalitarian social treatment is not necessarily ruled out by various legitimizing theories criticized
here. That is, it is theoretically possible that egalitarian social conditions would be compatible
with non-uniformity, for example, differential justifications for biological versus adoptive
parental rights. However, because of the history of children as property, and the stigma associated with children not under the protection of permanent legal parents (orphans, abandoned children, street children, foster children, children waiting to be adopted—that is,
children who are not "held" in a proprietary way by adults), strong doubts could be raised
about this possibility.

parental role responsibility, makes up the justification of parental rights and obligations. Of course, a principle of social responsibility stands behind each of these, with all of us, collectively, having responsibility to ensure fair social rules that support the well-being of all children equally. These ethical principles combined with just social rules help to ensure the well-being of all families.

FAMILIAL RELATIONSHIPS AND PERSONAL IDENTITIES

CHAPTER SIX

Family Resemblances: Adoption, Personal Identity, and Genetic Essentialism

CHARLOTTE WITT

Recent developments in reproductive technology, increasing numbers of gay and lesbian parents, and growing numbers of families formed through adoption pose new questions concerning the definition of the family and what families ought to look like. In our culture, according to the standard view of the family, there must be a genetic tie among its members, even though the parents in a family are normally not biologically related to one another.[1] For us, therefore, what is meant by describing the family as a biological unit is that in ideal families the children are biologically, or genetically, related to their parents. The biological view of the family undergirds both family law and social policy on family issues—to the detriment of families not united by biology. Even though many families in our culture—stepfamilies, "blended" families, adoptive families—do not fit the pattern of the biological family, it nonetheless functions as an ideal.[2] It is important to emphasize at the outset that there is nothing inevitable about our culture's idealization of families based on genetic ties between

ideal fam in modern society

1. The range of this paper is limited both historically and culturally. By "family" and the "standard view of the family," I mean the view that is reflected in the legal code and social policies of the United States at the end of the twentieth century. This view might not adequately represent what all Americans assume about the family, but it is an influential view, and as such is worth addressing. In other cultures, and in our culture at other times, family structures vary widely.

2. For an important discussion of this topic, see Bartholet (1993) and reviews by Cahn (1994) and Dowd (1994). The thesis that families ought to be united by a biological or genetic tie between parent and child is a key element in legal arguments against gay marriages. See, for example, the argument in *Baker v. Vermont*, "Hence, the Legislature is justified," the State concludes, "in using the marriage statutes to send a public message that procreation and child rearing are intertwined" (*Baker v. Vermont* 18).

135

parents and their children; it is as much a socially constructed form of life as are other kinds of families—stepfamilies, "blended" families, adoptive families.

Remarkably, the idealization of the biological family receives support, both tacit and explicit, from feminist theorists and from the adoption community. The biological view of the family is prevalent in feminist ethics and theorizing about the family. Feminists, who privilege the maternal relationship and emphasize its gestational and bodily aspects, at the same time privilege a biological view of family relationships.[3] And, in a related development, feminist theorizing about the self, and personal identity, often endorses a relational view of the self, based upon the mother-child relationship, which is again assumed to be biological (Moody Adams 1999; Meyers 1997).

Further, recent adoption literature, in its stress upon the importance of the birth mother, and on the adopted child's family and culture of origin, echoes and reinforces the idea of biology as a crucial or definitive feature of the family.[4] Of course feminist philosophers and adoption advocates approach the question of the nature of the family from different perspectives, and with different arguments and interests. For many feminist philosophers, the elevation of the mother-child tie as the natural origin of, and model for, ethical behavior was motivated by the desire to bring women's lives and experiences into the domain of ethics for the first time. For adoption advocates, in contrast, the biological or traditional family serves as a ghostly Platonic model of perfection to be emulated in various ways.

It is important to note some dissenting voices. Feminist and progressive legal scholars have used recent developments in reproductive technologies and new family configurations to illuminate and to criticize the normative assumption that biology is the best basis for the family (Bartholet 1993). Others have exposed the social meaning of the genetic tie, and have explored the cultural conditions within which that assumption has served and continues to serve racist and patriarchal goals. For example, as Dorothy Roberts explains, "the institution of slavery made the genetic tie to a slave mother critical to determining a child's social status, yet legally insignificant to the relationship between male slaveowners and

---

3. Fineman (1995) argues explicitly on feminist grounds that the mother-child relationship (conceived as a biological one) should be the basic unit of society, replacing the patriarchal family.

4. In both feminist ethics and in writing about adoption, there are practical reasons and theoretical concerns, which I accept, for stressing the role of biological/birth mothers. For example, advocates of open adoption might list both practical advantages (medical history) and ethical concerns (paternalism toward adult adoptees) in making a general argument for the importance of open access to the birth mother and family of origin. And feminist ethicists are certainly correct in their attempts to develop the ethical aspects of women's lives, like being a mother, which have been overlooked in traditional ethical theories.

their mulatto children" (Roberts 1995, 209). And, within feminist thinking, there is a long history of criticism of the traditional family and, in particular, the assumed superiority of its biological basis (Firestone 2003). There is good reason, therefore, for feminist philosophers writing about adoption to be skeptical about social and legal policies that simply assume and endorse the superiority of the biological family. And there is good reason as well to reconsider those feminist theories that reinforce the superiority of biological relationships in constituting family ties.

The biological view of the family that I have been discussing concerns primarily the role and superiority of biology in determining parenthood, or as the basis for parental rights. There is a second strand to the argument from biology concerning the family, which concerns the role of biology in constituting personal identity. Genetic essentialism means that a person's identity is determined by his or her genetic endowment. So, except in the case of an open adoption, an adopted child will have a defective sense of identity, which can be mitigated only if she is reconnected with her family of biological origin. Even in the case of an open adoption, the thesis of genetic essentialism casts doubt on the ability of an adopted child to fully identify as part of his or her adoptive family. There are two claims here: the first, that personal identity is determined in a substantive way by one's genes; and the second, that one's self-understanding requires a relationship with the source of one's genetic endowment, the birth family. While these claims are independent of one another, they are nonetheless related in the following way. If you thought that personal identity is substantially determined by genetic endowment, then you might also think that a relationship with the birth family would be central to an adequate self-understanding on the part of the adopted child. Alternatively, in the case of open adoption, you might think that the child would identify as part of the birth family rather than the adoptive family. On the other hand, if it turned out that one's personal identity is not substantially determined by one's genes, then the grounds on which self-understanding is enhanced by contact with the birth family would not turn on a biological or genetic notion of personal identity but would rest on other grounds.[5] Below, I discuss one way in which knowledge of a child's birth family might be important in consideration of family resemblances and personal identity.

Genetic essentialism, if true, would provide a justification for our culture's understanding of the family, which considers the biological family to be better than families formed in other ways. For, it is reasonable to suppose that if genetic essentialism were true, the identity and hence the self-

(margin annotations: "Genetic Essentialism"; "two main claims")

---

5. There are many other reasons for thinking that a relationship with a child's birth family is a good idea. First, for an adult adoptee it is a simple matter of right that access to records be open. For young children, depending upon the circumstances, these relationships can be useful in a number of ways.

understanding of adopted children would be either blocked or defective. This would contribute to the evaluation of the biological basis of the family as better than, or more important than, other ways of creating families. Biologically based families would be better for children, and this would be one reason for favoring them, for thinking that normal families in the statistical sense really are better than families formed through adoption.

In section 1 I argue against genetic essentialism, using as my starting point Kripke's metaphysical doctrine of the necessity of origins (Kripke 1980). This is the idea that originating in a particular sperm and egg is a necessary property of individual human beings.[6] Even if the necessity of origins were true, it would not entail genetic essentialism, because what is at issue for adoptees is their identity as persons—and to be a person requires self-understanding. This is not to deny that certain biological facts about us can play an important role in our self-understanding, like the fact of being a female rather than a male. However, if personal identity requires self-understanding, and self-understanding requires achieving understanding of oneself in a particular context and set of relations, and in the light of facts about people generally, including, but not limited to biological facts, then non-adopted and adopted children would face fundamentally the same challenges and have fundamentally the same set of resources in forging a sense of self. It might seem, therefore, that once we understand personal identity as mediated by self-understanding, then genetic essentialism is vanquished.

While at a very high level of generality that may be right, it is not the whole story. For one thing, we know that adopted children do seem to face some unique problems in forging a sense of self.[7] One common experience in adoptive families, which I examine in this paper, is the discussion of family resemblances. Adopted children puzzle over who they look like in a way that non-adopted children normally do not. And since many family resemblances are inherited, biological, genetic, or at least thought to be so, they appear to reconnect personal identity to genetic inheritance, to sperm and egg. In "normal" biological families, when we attribute a family resemblance, we do so in order to create or endorse a family bond, which we often assume is based in a genetic connection among family members. Although not all family resemblances are thought to have a biological basis, those connected with racial and ethnic differences certainly are. It is in the realm of family resemblances, therefore, that an adopted

---

6. There is a large literature on Kripke's work that I cannot address here. One problem that might be worth mentioning is that of identical twins who originate in the very same sperm and egg and yet are two individuals.

7. There is a large literature on this topic. Cherie Register's *Are Those Kids Yours? American Families with Children Adopted from Other Countries* (1990) includes a discussion of identity and family resemblance in the context of international adoption.

child's self-understanding might seem to be more problematic or more difficult to achieve than that of a child living in its biological family.

The issue of family resemblances raises the following kinds of questions.
Why is the question of whom I look like (or act like or think like) important to my sense of self?[8] And what is the value for self-understanding, of
finding in my family someone who looks like me? The context of adoption
allows us to unravel what are, in many (and perhaps most) cases, overlapping strands of the self. For many of us, our genetic endowment, our identity as members of a family, and whom we look like, coincide or overlap,
and so it is difficult to ask questions about how these aspects of the self are
related to one another. It is easy to assume that genetic endowment, family resemblance, and self-understanding are inextricably intertwined.
Adoption allows us, indeed forces us, to separate out each strand, and lets
us raise questions about how they influence one another.

I end by considering how the issue of family resemblances might contribute to the debate among feminist philosophers concerning relational
and individualistic conceptions of the self.[9] The importance of family resemblances, which are relational properties, for personal identity provides
new support for a relational view of the self. Unlike the biological mother-
child relationship favored in feminist writing, however, the relational properties that constitute family resemblances do not privilege the maternal
relationship. Instead, this discussion can be read as supporting an "eclectic" approach to relational theories of the self that "might appeal to the
identity-constituting properties of a variety of personal and associational
relationships—including those in families, friendships, and even the associational ties of communities and groups organized around various professional and personal interests" (Moody Adams 1999, 256).

THE METAPHYSICAL DOCTRINE OF ORIGINS

One of Kripke's most interesting proposals concerning the identity of
individual human beings is that our origins are essential to us, and, in particular, that each of us originates in the combination of a particular sperm
and egg:

> How could a person originating from different parents, from a totally differ-
> ent sperm and egg, be *this very woman*? One can imagine, *given* the woman,
> that various things in her life could have changed: that she should have be-

8. Family resemblances are relational properties, ranging widely from physical appearance, to character traits, and even to intelligence. On the assumption that intelligence is genetically inherited, see Wriggins (1997).

9. For an excellent discussion, see Moody Adams (1999).

come a pauper; that her royal blood should have been unknown, and so on. . . . It seems to me that anything coming from a different origin would not be this object. (Kripke 1980, 113)

Kripke asks us to contrast the necessity of a woman's origins, the particular sperm and egg, with what we could imagine about the life history and events of her life. The idea is that while our genetic origins are necessary to our identity, we could imagine our life history altering significantly, even as we remain the very same person. So, for example, an adopted child necessarily originates from the very same sperm and egg that she in fact came from, but she might have remained with her birth family (had circumstances been different) or been adopted by a family other than the one that did in fact adopt her (again, had circumstances been different). Our life stories are filled with contingency and circumstance, but our genetic origins are fixed and necessary. Surely, it is what is fixed and necessary about us that is central to our identities, rather than the vicissitudes of our lives and fortunes. But if this is so, except in cases of fully open adoptions, an adopted child might well be missing knowledge of the basic ingredients in his or her identity and hence will have a defective sense of self. In this context, adoption and the adoptive family fall on the side of contingency, while a child's biological origins fall on the side of necessity. Kripke's doctrine of the necessity of origins supports genetic essentialism by articulating a principled contrast between what about our identity is fixed and necessary, and what is contingent.

It is useful to distinguish between personal identity and the identity of individual members of natural kinds, like human beings and tigers. For Kripke's metaphysical doctrine of origins only supports genetic essentialism on the assumption that to be a person is the same as to be a human being or an individual member of a natural kind. But, ever since Locke, philosophers have distinguished between persons (who have legal and ethical standing) and human beings (biological organisms). Persons are beings that have some degree of self-understanding, and hence for persons which person one is depends in large measure on how one understands oneself. For this reason, the relevance of any biological facts or genetic facts to the identity of persons, as opposed to the identity of biological organisms, must be mediated by the person's self-understanding.[10] What writers about family and adoption find problematic is not the necessity of the biological origins of human beings, but rather the child's self-understanding or sense of self. In making this distinction, I am not claiming that facts about us could not enter into our self-understandings; they surely do.

10. In the quotation, Kripke does not recognize this distinction referring to the woman as a "person" and as an "individual." The question of how the person is related to the biological organism is beyond the scope of this paper.

But the facts in question might be biological or fixed, or they might be part of the contingencies of our lives, like choosing to become a philosopher or a painter. Kripke's distinction between the necessity of our biological origins and the contingency of our life experiences does not coordinate in any useful or systematic way with the important and trivial features of how we understand ourselves as persons. The contingent fact of adoption might be much more significant to a person's identity than a genetic predisposition to develop flat feet. For an adopted child, the process of creating a narrative of the self may well require knowledge of biological or genetic origins (as far as these are available)[11] and not because these are thought to determine any particular characteristic of the adopted child, but in order to complete the narrative of the self. In Drucilla Cornell's words, "once we accept that even a primordial sense of self is not just given to us, but is a complicated lifelong process of imagining and projecting ourselves over time, we can see how important it is to have access to one's family history [sic] if one feels the need to have it" (Cornell 1998, 109).

FAMILY RESEMBLANCES AND PERSONAL IDENTITY

I have argued that personal identity, because it requires some degree of self-understanding, is not directly and simply constituted by any of our properties, whether they are necessary and genetic, or contingent and social. Which properties are most important to a person's self-understanding can vary from person to person. One set of properties, which are often at issue in adoptive families, concerns family resemblances. These seem to be properties that are both genetic and ingredients in a person's self-understanding; hence, they seem to resurrect the claim of genetic essentialism and with it to support the superiority of biological families.

Family resemblances are part of a family's mythology, and they serve various purposes: bonding family members, explaining behavior, assigning blame. Family resemblances attribute relational properties to individual family members. A family resemblance is not simply a matter of having blue eyes, but having blue eyes like Aunty Ginny; not simply being moody, but being moody like Mom. Family resemblances are used liberally and inexactly to refer to appearance, mannerisms, character traits, and habits—both positive and negative. Family resemblances are relational properties which are biological/social hybrids; they exist only as part of a family mythology and hence are social, but the myth tells a story of genetic in-

---

11. In some cases, such as the recent adoptions from China, information is simply not available; in others the birth parents are dead or missing.

heritance, and hence they are biological. What is important in the context of adoption, however, is that the attribution of family resemblances, insofar as they are thought to be inherited via the gene, are not available to children in relation to their adoptive families.[12]

When a child is adopted from a different racial group or ethnicity from the parents, the question of family resemblances becomes magnified to encompass ethnic or racial similarities and differences. "She looks like me," my daughter will say of another child from Vietnam, even if that child does not look very much like her. What she means is that, like her, this child has black hair and brown eyes which are almond shaped. The topic of who looks like whom is a very familiar one in adopted families, especially those which are racially mixed. One strategy in these cases is to be certain that the child is surrounded by others who "look like her," so that she does not feel entirely isolated and strange looking in her community. But this strategy does not address the problem of family resemblances, which concerns resemblances within families, and not among members of an ethnic group. My daughter's Vietnamese-American friends, who live in their biological families, face the problem of not looking like the majority of people in their community, but they are connected to various members of their families by family resemblances.

It is worthwhile to pause a moment here to reflect upon what it means to say either that a child "looks like" another family member or that a child "looks like" others in her community. What I want to emphasize is that these judgments are not straightforwardly descriptive or observational. They are complex judgments made within a community, and they reflect community norms. For example, my daughter discovered at age 5, from her British friends, that she did not look like the rest of the family and that she ought to do so. She explained to me that she needed a Chinese family and not a British one, an idea whose precise articulation reveals its cultural context and its origin. Another example is that some Vietnamese acquaintances have asked me whether my daughter is Vietnamese, because to their eyes, and in their cultural context, "she looks Chinese." The cultural embeddedness of both attributions of family resemblances, and ethnic judgments, with the complex norms that govern their use and vary from context to context, make this aspect of identity particularly challenging, complex, and fluid.

Because family resemblances are relational properties, which are commonly believed to hold among genetically related family members, the importance of family resemblances to our self-understanding as members of a family connects the question of genetic endowment directly to personal identity. Or so it might seem. It is useful to distinguish between the heri-

12. Of course, this would not be the case for an adoption within a biological family.

tability of a characteristic and the means by which it is heritable. For a characteristic or trait to be heritable, there must be some way to ensure that offspring resemble their parents with respect to that feature. One vehicle for heritability is the genetic mode of transmission, which coordinates features with different genes or gene complexes in a population. Another vehicle for transmission could be parents teaching their children to have a certain characteristic, like moodiness, thriftiness, or a wacky sense of humor.[13] Depending upon the constitution and history of the adoptive family, the language of family resemblances is available to them, at least in relation to those characteristics that are "passed on" but not written in the genes. Still, since the dominant myth of family resemblances assumes heritability via genes, the project of self-understanding as a member of a family will often be more complex for adoptees than for other children.

The issue of family resemblances raises another complex question of personal identity for an adopted child, which is how to relate to and understand her biological family of origin, some of whose members she undoubtedly resembles. Curiosity about family resemblances might propel a child to want contact with her birth family as part of the development of her sense of self. Alternatively, in an open adoption, family resemblances might complicate or enrich the child's negotiation of her identity. Family resemblances make the process of self-understanding more complex and challenging for an adopted child than for a child in a biological family. The challenge posed by family resemblances has two sides—the problem of not "looking like" members of one's family, and the problem of "looking like" the members of another family, the birth family.

Of course, the importance of family resemblances in the development of a sense of self for adopted children will vary from situation to situation as will the child's ability to negotiate the issue. And, family resemblances which are heritable via the gene are just one ingredient in a child's self-understanding; many important family resemblances are passed on in other ways. Recall further that we can think of the self in an eclectic way, as enmeshed in many kinds of relationships that are important to personal identity; family resemblances are just one piece in this mosaic. Without wanting to minimize the challenge for either parents or children, it seems fair to suggest that the issue of family resemblances, in itself, does not justify the evaluation of biological families as superior to other families. Therefore, based on the problem of self-understanding faced by adoptive children who are not biologically related to their parents, we can conclude that the evaluation of the biological family as superior to the adoptive family is not justified in terms of the issue of family resemblance.

Even if the existence of family resemblances, and their contribution to

13. For a discussion of these topics, see Sober (1994).

a child's self-understanding as a member of a family and ethnic group, ultimately fails to provide justification for social and legal policies favoring biological families, the discussion has highlighted an interesting set of relational properties that are important for the self-understanding of persons as members of families. I close with a brief discussion of family resemblances and relational theories of the self.

FAMILY RESEMBLANCES AND RELATIONAL THEORIES OF THE SELF

Let me begin by clarifying what is meant by a theory of the self or of personal identity. It is useful to distinguish two kinds of questions concerning personal identity. First, we might ask an ontological question. What is it to be a self or a person, as opposed, say, to a biological organism? Second, we can ask a causal question. What causes, or caused, a person to be the person that she is? I take it that both relational and individualist theories of the self are intended as replies to the first question, the ontological question, and not the causal questions. What distinguishes relational theories of the self from individualistic theories is that the preferred answer to the question of what is it to be a person or a self includes relational and/or contextual properties.

I said earlier that what it is to be a person or a self necessarily requires self-understanding, and that was the reason that genetic essentialism failed as an argument in favor of the superiority of biological families. But, the fact that persons are self-conscious or self-understanding does not in itself discriminate between relational and individualistic conceptions of the self; it is compatible with both. For example, persons could be those beings that understand themselves to be rational, autonomous choosers, which is an individualistic conception of the self. Or persons could be those beings that understand themselves as enmeshed in social relationships and, as constituted by them, a relational conception of the self.

The existence of family resemblances, which emerged in our discussion of genetic essentialism and adoption, is relevant to the debate within feminism concerning relational and individual theories of the self. Roughly, relational theories of the self, which have been advocated by feminist philosophers and others, hold (1) that personal identity cannot be extricated from a web of contingent facts about the social, psychological, and historical circumstances of the self and/or (2) that selves are relational beings. Further, feminist relational theories of the self have privileged the mother-child relationship as central to personal identity. Although the relational view of the self originated in developmental psychology (the object relations theory of Chodorow, taken up by Gilligan and others), the relational theory of the self has played a central role in feminist moral and political theory. In these contexts, it is advocated as an alternative to individualistic theories of the self, which view the self atomistically as an individual that is not constituted by its contingent psychological, social, and historical context.

The experience of adoption contributes to this debate within feminist theory, for the existence and importance of family resemblances to personal identity, ironically enough, can only really be grasped in their absence. It is only through the experience of adopted children and their families who engage with the issue that we can see this class of relational properties emerge as constitutive of personal identity. In general, therefore, the discussion of family resemblances can be seen as supporting relational theories of the self.

The importance of family resemblances does not, however, support those feminist relational theories of the self that privilege the mother-child relationship. For family resemblances arise in a web of family relationships; they can skip generations; they can extend sideways across the family tree. For this reason, family resemblances fit best with an "eclectic" relational theory of the self in which many different kinds of relational properties might be important ingredients of the self. And, as we move from a privileged relational theory of the self to an eclectic relational theory, the significance of each element lessens and becomes variable. In the context of adoption, this means that the significance of family resemblances to a particular child's sense of self can vary from individual to individual—as it surely does.

CHAPTER SEVEN

Being Adopted and Being a Philosopher: Exploring Identity and the "Desire to Know" Differently

KIMBERLY LEIGHTON

Ever since I can remember, I have been someone who identified herself as adopted. I have, in fact, always had a difficult time answering the common questions of when and how I was told about my adoption, as my memories of and stories about being *myself* have always included my being *adopted*. It was as if coming into my own self-knowledge included, and perhaps was even constituted in relationship to, the knowledge that my parents were not always my parents and that I was born, as I later came to think, before they knew that I existed. My claiming of "being adopted" as an *identity* has thus included claiming the contingency and ambiguity such a grammatically awkward statement involves. The meaning of my *self*, of who I was, I thought, could always have been different. That my parents were my parents was accidental, while the fact that they *could* be (and hence might *not* have been) my parents was determinative to who I was. While being raised by my parents from infancy certainly affected many aspects of my identity-formation, including my understandings of myself through religion, class, race, and ethnicity, my identity *as adopted* was produced by the fact that these identifications could have been different. They were, in short, constitutively arbitrary.[1]

1. As this essay reflects the support and suggestions of many, I want to thank the following people for their thoughtful responses to earlier drafts: Charlotte Witt, Sally Haslanger, Ann Ferguson, Allison Hopper, and Rachel Brooks. I offer a loving thank you to Julie Vandivere for helping me create the space in which to finish. I would also like to acknowledge Bella Brodzki, who first encouraged me to write about adoption, and Lyndy Pye, whose creative presence continues to help me find "the words to say it." My deep appreciation also goes to those whose lives are forever intimately bound with mine: to all of my family I say, "Thank

Being adopted for me, then, has not been an identification with an unknown lost family; it has not been a marking of myself as scarred or damaged or as having less knowledge than others who are born into their families. Instead, being adopted has been an identity of *possibility;* it has been a way to make sense of the tensions produced by being *both at once* the product of one's environment *and* someone whose meaning always exceeds that environment.[2] It has been a way to understand family as both a place from which one comes and a place for which one is always looking. Being an adopted self has encouraged me to imagine the self as both known and unknown, as born as well as produced, in short, as more than *either* natured *or* nurtured.

Crucial to my sense of the *possibility* of adopted identity, I think, have been the ways in which I have been able to approach "being adopted" as a position from which to investigate the problem of identity *in general*. While having been adopted left the meaning of my identity open, it was not the case that the act(s) of adoption left me without an identity, left me missing something, or in a position in which something was hidden from me. My concern with my identity has thus not been defined by attempts at resolving some particular "identity issues" or overcoming some senses of loss or inadequacy. But rather, because adoption involves social, cultural, and historical events, and because taking having-been-adopted as the basis for an identity necessarily evokes the idea that social practices are *intimately* involved in one's own identity, my concern with *my* identity as adopted has propelled me to think about the ways in which identity in general is more than either essence or construct. Thus, my philosophical investigations of *my* identity as adopted have engendered certain aporias which, I have come to believe, are not specific to having been adopted.

There is an intended slippage throughout this paper, then, between my narrative descriptions of my experiences of and struggles with claiming for myself an identity as adopted and my use of "adopted identity" as a term applied to the *problem* of identity in general. Thus, like the meaning of my

you." This essay is dedicated to the memory of Skip Whitney, whose life made so much of mine more possible.

2. I hope that this essay will make clear that the notion of "possibility" as I am exploring it here is not a kind of pure freedom entailing the idea that one could "re-invent" oneself. I am also not suggesting that having a sense of one's identity as arbitrary means that one can simply change it, nor am I proposing that adoption offers a way to see identity as constructed and therefore not real. What I *am* offering is that as a paradigm (or metaphor) for identity, "being adopted" opens up a space of non-identity (or non-identicalness) between the self as a subject and the self as an object such that one *cares* about the processes (social, historical, cultural, political, and relational) through which one has come to be. It is through this relation of care, or what I want to call "desiring knowing" (but do not explore as such in this work), that one can undertake (the pleasures and pursuits of) self-knowing in a way that engenders a recognition of self-difference (i.e., that the self one is [and can be] is not identical to the knowledge[s] of it).

identity as adopted, I want to encourage the multivalent potential of "adopted identity" as I want the phrase to suggest the possibility of claiming an identity based on the *history* of the production of one's identity, that is, that one was (literally) adopted, *and* the idea that identities are neither born nor made but are *adopted*.

While the difference between the notions of born and adopted in this context may be obvious, it is the difference between made and adopted that is critical. While both ideas refer to the notion that identity (itself) and individual identities do not come from some essence of self but are instead the products of social, cultural, and historical forces, the notion of an adopted identity, as I am exploring it, also refers to the *historicity* of an identity. I am here exploiting the double meaning of adopted as both to have been adopted (as someone else's) and to adopt (as one's own). Connoting two different sets of practices (and, importantly, two different *temporal* locations of self), these different meanings of adopted together generate a liminal space where the subject is positioned as that which is subjected to/by social practices *and* that which is the subject of such practices (in both senses, as content and agent). Such dual positioning, I claim, entails both a sense of opacity about the ways in which the subject submits to adopting an identity, and a sense of agency in terms of which the subject is involved in her own identity. Thus, as *adopted*, an identity *is* the position from which one attempts to understand one's own history. An adopted identity is both essential to who one is and historically produced at the same time.[3] How identity, when considered as adopted as such, at once cannot be known in some transparent sense, but yet can be evoked, claimed, and articulated, is the question of this essay.

While such paradox-producing notions regarding adopted identity did not give rise to an overtly problematic childhood or an overly rebellious adolescence, they did perhaps direct me toward the path of becoming a philosopher. Philosophy as a discourse of Truth has interested me not in terms of what it provides arguments for, but in terms of the tensions within such arguments which cannot be erased. Philosophy's concerns with truth, objectivity, knowledge, and certainty have called to me as a scholar, as such concerns also suggest notions (and, perhaps, fears) of falsity, relativism, fiction, and uncertainty. There has been an interesting tension for me, sometimes acknowledged and sometimes only recognized through feelings of

3. As such, I want to propose that an adopted identity is (necessarily) incompatible with a notion of complete self-transparency. While this incompatibility gestures toward the constitutive presence of social and historical forces in the production of identities, it also allows for an assumption of an ontological position which, though not outside of such constitutive forces, is not thoroughly available as (an object) explained by them. This chapter is part of a larger project that explores the relationship between such (ontological) opacity and the notion of possibility that adopted identity implies.

anxiety and even melancholy, between my knowing myself as adopted and my encountering philosophical texts.

I think my reaction to much philosophy, and especially to *writing* philosophically, has involved assuming the position of the outlaw, the one on the margins who critiques the normative discourse of philosophy, who names the ways in which such discourse might contribute to the marginalization of the other. What has been so difficult in writing this essay, then, has been the complexity not only of including the personal within the philosophical, but of working with the different voices that each of those styles demands. Finding a way to be (in the space writing offers) both an adopted self and a philosopher has been the task of this essay, the unexpected journey it has taken me on. Negotiating the tensions between these two voices or author(iz)ing positions has involved reckoning with not only my insecurities as a writer but also my insecurities as a *knower*.

I have imagined, for example, that part of the reason I was asked to contribute to this collection was due to the place I hold within the adoption triangle. As such, I wanted to write an essay which would counter philosophy's obsession with knowledge and clarity with my own (foundational) position of contingency and ambiguity. I wanted to present a critique of the traditional demands for epistemological certainty as clearly oppressive in their denial of difference. But, the truth is, I have always *wanted to know*. My identity as adopted has always involved a "desire to know . . ." such that my *being* adopted, my experience of myself as an adopted person, has been defined by and in relation to this desire.[4]

While my "desire to know" has been of personal import to me, the concept of *knowing* is key to the cultural signification of adoption as well. As the practices of adoption in the United States over the last fifty years have changed, shifting from closed to open, and the social attitudes about adoption have moved from those of shame to acceptance or even celebration, the issue of "knowing" (through such metonyms as "finding" or "search-

---

4. Importantly, I want to leave my "desire to know . . ." open and undefined. This essay, in its meanderings both personal and philosophical, is an attempt to present in a legible way stories through which I know (and have experienced) myself as adopted. As should become clear, there is no real object that I desire to know, nor is there some essence of being adopted that I am trying to convey. Instead, I am claiming that my desire to know is (1) part of what being adopted means to me, its notion of possibility, that is, that there is something to be engaged with that is always there to be desired, a kind of moreness, (2) connected to the very ways in which it has been mis-recognized, and (3) (re-)produced through the failed attempts to erase it.

I put the "desire to know" in quotation marks because, while I am claiming it as *my* desire, it is also an important trope in the signification of adoption. My use of the phrase is thus also a citation of this trope. As I note later in this paper, when I tell people that I am adopted, I am almost always addressed with others' curiosity about what I know. I am presenting my desire to know within the context of how I have been addressed as a knower in order to suggest both the ways in which this address has placed me in a certain position as a knower (and as a kind of legitimate subject) and the ways in which I have resisted this address.

ing," for example) continues to be an important part of how sense is made of adoption. I have, for example, almost always been addressed by questions about what I *know* when I tell people that I am adopted. "How long have you known?" "When did your parents tell you?" "What do you know about your biological family?" "Do you know why you were given up?" is the usual litany of responses. Interestingly, the last or seemingly most important question is always the same and involves not only *what* I know, but what I *want* to know: "Have you ever searched?" "Do you want to know . . . ?" Sometimes the question really does have a sense of an ellipsis in it, as if what I might want to know cannot itself be named. No matter the time and place, my identity claim as *adopted* is almost always addressed within the context of *self-knowledge*. My claiming of adopted as an ontological position, or one about *being*, is re-inscribed in such dialogues as an epistemological claim, or one that is essentially about *knowing*.

This reinscription not only shifts the weight of my claim, but importantly it raises an issue about the status of knowledge in relation to identity. Rather than merely asking me what I know, such interrogations address both the object of knowing and the *subject* of knowing. The questions (and perhaps the questioners themselves) assume not only that there is something to know and that such information is important, but that I *can* know it and it is important to *me* to know. While both the issues of knowing and of desiring to know circulate in the cultural imagination about adoption, what I want to begin to unpack here is how the figuration of desiring self-knowledge can itself be productive of a certain kind of self. How my desire to know has been made sense of, how it has been possible and impossible to articulate, involves how *I* have been interpellated as such a self or subject (who is able to claim an identity). What I want to suggest here is that the ways in which the "desire to know" has been denied, recognized, and mis-recognized in terms of adoption reveal the ways in which the *what* of self-knowledge is intimately tied up with the *who* of self-knowledge. This project is thus driven by the following questions: if I am going to claim my desire to know as fundamental to my identity as adopted, and, further, if my identity as adopted is somehow a different kind of identity, do I need to present my desire to know differently? How can I know my desire to know in a way which allows me to claim being adopted as an identity? And how might philosophy's claims about knowing and my experiences of being adopted come together to make such a presentation possible?

Issues of knowing and desire were paramount to me as a child. I was the adopted child who both knew and accepted herself as adopted, and yet always included in that narrative a desire to search. Importantly, the first *lie* I remember telling was a denial of this desire. It occurred when I was six. My cousin had told her mother, who, of course, then told my mother, that I said that when I was eighteen I would search for my birth mother. I sensed that admitting to this desire (and to its articulation to someone in my mother's family) was impossible and regretted having, in a rather bragging kind of way, spoken my intentions out loud. Despite my saying "no" to my mother when she asked me about my cousin's story, the fantasy of "knowing" or of "finding" was an important part of my imagination about being an adult, a grown up Kim Leighton. My parents were always concerned that I should not feel adopted, which for them meant feeling abandoned or inadequate or accepting as true the cultural stereotypes associated with the trope of "illegitimacy." While having been adopted was not something I should be ashamed of, they assured me, I also sensed that being *someone who wanted to know* was a dangerous way to be.

I now believe that making public my desire to know by speaking my intention to search, while it exhibited my six-year-old senses of curiosity, will, and even determination, it also, more poignantly, exhibited me as adopted. The reason I think I lied, perhaps, was because I sensed that not only was I not supposed to *feel* adopted, but I was also not supposed to really *be* adopted. I lied out of *shame,* perhaps—not the shame of being adopted, but the shame felt from breaking some implicit rule. My parents (with the best of intentions, I do feel) considered me just the same as my cousins who were not adopted, and, as such, I was never referred to as adopted, nor was I ever (that I knew of) treated differently. My brother and I got the same gifts from our grandparents that my cousins did. We were seemingly loved and teased in the same ways that they were. I grew up feeling that what people liked, loved, and found annoying about me had nothing to do with my being adopted. And in many ways, of course, this was good.

While the sensitivity my family felt about my being adopted meant that I was seemingly treated the same as those children who were not adopted in my extended family, I also felt an unspoken imperative present in such practices, a commandment which was not addressed to my aunts, uncles, etc.: they were who they were (i.e., not adopted), but I had to *be the same as* they were (i.e., not adopted). My being *like* them was in some ways an achievement. Most clearly, my following this command of likeness took the form of limiting which family language games I could (and could not) participate in. Obviously, I could not talk about being adopted—I could not refer to myself as adopted or discuss how it felt to be such. I could definitely not refer to my parents as "adoptive" nor could I muse aloud about my birth family or wonder about whom I looked like. In addition to being silent during some conversations, it was also important not to make logical mistakes which would raise the specter of adoption. I could not, for instance, compare myself to members of family in ways that didn't make ready sense. I could be "just like" my father or grandmother in a general kind of way, or in a way which could (if necessary) be explained as a product of socialization. I could have my father's "gift of gab," for instance, or my grandmother's stubbornness. But I could not say I had their legs, their eyes, or some other particular feature that seemed too close to the body.

My silence around my body and its relation to the bodies of others not only left unspoken the fact of my adoption, but moreover, it helped invest in the narrative that I was just like those who were not adopted. The markings of my bodily identity could, without being talked about, be "read" *as if* they had the same meanings, the same (imagined) history as those bodies of my relatives. I do not mean to suggest that bodily markings are in some sense real, that they reflect some natural meaning (or identity) which exists pre-culturally and is then expressed through language. The notion of bodies as meaningful containers of signs of relation, I am suggesting, is a notion constituted (in part) by spoken language games of family resemblance and silent language games based on assumptions and on habits of association.[5]

While it is not my project here to do a philosophical analysis of the relationship between the cultural constructions and meanings of the body and the politics of the family, it is important to note that the two themes here of "being just like" the non-adopted and being silent about the body or the bodily are key to understanding the issues I am raising about the desire to know.[6] I was silent about my body so that my body could be considered as part of the body of my family, so that it could reflect (constitutively) the *identity* that such inclusion engendered. This practice of making a body seem to be naturally part of the family was not particular to my own family, *per se*. I was able to be silent about my body, able to live without its difference always already being "spoken," in part, because my adoption, like many others during the 1950s and 1960s, was (probably) conducted in a way such that no such "difference" would (seem to) exist.

The dominant ideology regarding adoption at the time during which I was adopted involved policies which, when implemented, would in fact limit anyone's *ability to know* that a child was adopted. This was done in terms of both hiding actual information which pertained to the difference of the child and the process by which he or she was begotten—sealing records, changing birth certificates, etc.—and "hiding" those bodily mark-

5. To see how Wittgensteinian philosophical tools might offer a way to analyze the production of (essentialized) family likeness, see Charlotte Witt's essay in this collection.

6. I am making a slight distinction here between *body* and *bodily:* by "body" I mean the physical fleshiness of a person and by "bodily" I mean the ways in which that flesh is perceived, understood, and read as meaningful. So, for example, how the body is thought to represent or contain family-relatedness is part of how it is bodily. It is part of my larger project to find a way to discuss the ways in which bodies are conceptualized (and experienced through such conceptualization) without falling into a kind of idealism. By expanding the grammar of the body into the bodi*ly* I am trying to create a space of *action* which both affects the subject and, once (necessarily) taken up by the subject, affects the world.

ings by which a child's difference might stand out. In order to clear the child (and the family) from the stigma(s) of adoption, it was thought that child's physical appearance should "match" that of the adopted family. While most clearly (and complicatedly) about racial likeness, the policy of matching included other features thought to be tokens important to (creating) family likeness. As contained in the euphemism of "background," such issues as class, education, and interests could become themselves morphological, or thought of as having some connection to the bodily identity and identification of the family (Modell and Dambacher 1997).[7]

So, while my family's sensitivity was in many ways helpful, it did promote the idea that being adopted was not something to be talked about, let alone something that could be claimed as an important part of *my* identity. I was "a Leighton." And that was that. I was not different, it seemed, and there was nothing "to know." Therefore, to articulate a desire to know was as illogical as it was improper, and my musings about my desire to know were, like my musings about my body, something to be silent about—something to wonder about alone. To articulate them and make my desire known, it seems, was to disown my identity as a Leighton, a rejection that was as painful as it was *impossible.*[8]

The manipulation of difference—especially through the figurations of the body—as a means of creating *identity* is not unique to the practices of adoption. "[A]s consciously constructed and scripted kinship," write Judith Modell and Naomi Dambacher, "adoption reveals fundamental prem-

---

7. "The refinement of matching attempted to render adoption invisible. The adoptive family could fade into the woodwork, as it were. No one had to know about the origins of the family, not even the child himself/herself. For the sake of the child, adoption was kept secret and the 'fictive' quality of the relationship covered over by the real—that is, perceptible—surface resemblances between members. . . . During the two post-War decades, adoption practices locked a genealogical model of kinship to historically situated class and race distinctions" (Modell and Dambacher 1997, 17).

8. The choice of verb here is very difficult for me both theoretically and personally. To write that I was *given* an identity feels very painful. I grew up watching a lot of television, particularly shows of the Norman Lear variety. In one episode of *All in the Family,* Mike, the son-in-law, argues that he doesn't want to have a child biologically, because there are so many needy children "out there" who need families. Archie is furious and, as usual, dumbfounded. While watching the show at age ten or so, I thought that I was one of those children, that I was taken in because I didn't have a family, that there was a sense of doing something good for me by *giving* me a name.

There is a sense of an impossible choice present in my dilemma: either I spoke my desire or I had an identity. More than simply having a name, having an identity in this sense means having an ontology, *being* an X. On the one hand, it was through my "successful" subjection (my successfully becoming a person capable of having her own feelings, ideas, sense of self) that I could have my desire to know, while on the other hand, articulating my "desire to know" was an act that would subvert the very means through which I gained a sense of being in the world. Not only did it feel in some way "ungrateful" to want to know, but it felt like I would lose my access to knowing by speaking my desire. To give up *being* for *knowing* was not a fair trade. In *The Psychic Life of Power: Theories in Subjection,* Judith Butler explores this kind of impossible choice as itself constitutive of modern subjectivity (Butler 1997).

KIMBERLY LEIGHTON

ises about birth, blood, and contract, which themselves reflect ideologies that in Western societies enshrine the dichotomies nature and culture, fictive and real" (Modell and Dambacher 1997, 7). To construct any collective identity as if it is unified—for example, culturally, politically, historically, or ethnically— can involve practices that deny the importance of difference, or that even place the marker or sign of difference onto others who are then considered outside the main group. Such formations of unity also often rely on a notion of sameness based on something naturally given rather than socially or legally constructed. This sameness gives the cohesion and unity of the group that is formed a kind of facticity that is beyond questioning. Borrowing a term from Theodor Adorno, Iris Marion Young refers to the means through which a kind of *ontological* sameness as a kind of *being* is created as the "logic of identity." "The logic of identity," she writes, "tends to conceptualize entities in terms of substance rather than process or relation; substance is the self-same entity that underlies change, that can be identified, counted, measured" (Young 1990, 98–99).

Hence, the logic of identity engenders the possibility of having a nature, a something which can be one's essence. Such an essence, this logic contends, can then be transmitted to others, assuring that, like property itself, the property that is the identity will continue on. This construction of identity as a kind of natural essence that is *transferred* through practices of inheritance—both reproductive and legal—but is not *constituted* by them is not dissimilar to the kind of "as-if-the-same" construction involved in a traditional, historically "closed" adoption such as mine. According to anthropologist Barbara Yngvesson, "the family" is constituted as a location and source of identity through the simultaneous denial of and re-inscription of the "natural." Regarding traditional closed adoption, she writes:

American adoption laws circumvented the common law "repugnancy" to "creating children by act" with a kind of legal sleight-of-hand in which the *filius nullius* [the concept of the child as "nobody's child," a child without filiation] could be incorporated into the new (adoptive) family by erasing the old (biological) family; this "old" family then became the covert model for the new one, in the "biological" space made available through the law's erasure of "original" blood ties. In this way the "blood institution" (Shalev 1989: 11) that is central to the concept of family in Anglo-American culture and law was simultaneously eradicated and affirmed. (1997, 43)

As simulacrum, the adoptive family is reproduced as "natural" through the denial of bodily details and traces in the family, who "passes" as if it were not produced by law. As the same as the natural family, the adoptive family can transfer the essence of its own identity to its kin. In order to have an identity, then, a requisite for cultural participation, I not only had to be a Leighton, but I had to be "born" and not adopted, that is, without ambiguous or fabricated or otherwise un-natural origins. I had to perform not only the language games of my particular family but also the language game that is *identity*. Being able to take on my name meant being someone who could trace her heritage, who could trace, through the logic of the patronym, her family's lineage. The cost of not being marked as adopted (i.e., as not a bastard in some important historical and epistemological senses) involved adopting a model of identity that celebrates sameness, is founded on nature, and believes in essences.[9] In such adoptions where the fact of adoption is erased, being adopted thus involves not only being treated just like those who were not adopted, but moreover, it involves denying taking or claiming "being adopted" as an identity.

It is not only the institutional practices of the State and the family which perform such "sleight-of-hand" acts—acts which, as Modell and Dambacher describe, make possible "[t]he slide from appearance to essence" (1997, 24).[10] Part of the ongoing construction of the fiction of naturalness in general and the natural essence that is the morphological connection of the family, in particular, its *identity*, depends on the constant reiteration of the logic of identity through the everyday.[11] *Having* an identity thus entails being addressed as a certain kind of subject who both *is* and *knows* her identity in particular (normative) ways. I, like most adoptees (as well as others who come from non-traditional families), have had to face the awkwardness involved in doing the 7th-grade family tree, or filling out medical histories at the doctor's office, or simply being told "you look just like your parents." Such instances evidence the assumption and expectation of the ability to perform an identity in a certain truthful, non-ambiguous way. Other everyday practices show how such expectations of identity involve "disciplinary" practices. Many times in my life, for instance, people have responded to my telling them that I was adopted by saying, "No, you're not. You *couldn't* be. You look (are, act, etc.) just like your Dad." Such denials indicate not only the assumption that I am like them (biologically related to my family), but an additional assumption that likeness

9. While I am supportive of any adoptee's desire to know, I do question how the "right to know" is formulated in a way that reifies the notion of the naturalness of identity. Adoptees are necessarily in a position from which they can claim that family—its importance in one's life and sense of self—is not decided by blood. It seems critically important to me not to sacrifice this knowledge in order to accomplish political and legal change.

10. They continue: "The slide from appearance to essence is characteristic of American adoption policy and stems from a deeper tendency of western culture: utilizing biology as the way of 'constituting and conceiving human character, human nature, and human behavior' (Schneider 1984: 175). What a person looks like signifies what a person *is* and becomes an indicator of 'biology,' in an American scheme" (Modell and Dambacher 1997, 24).

11. This ability to have an essence that is something connected to others and independent of them is crucial to the conceptualization of individualism. For an analysis of the discursive formation of the Individual, see *Only Paradoxes to Offer: French Feminists and the Rights of Man* (Scott 1996).

comes from a kind of biological essence, a kind of naturalness. Together these assumptions eradicate the possibility (in a most literal way) of my claiming a position of difference. This position of impossibility, in which my difference could not be articulated because of the assumptions of others, continued throughout much of my life. I was constantly addressed as not adopted, and such acts of interpellation, such readings of being just like the non-adopted, not only rendered my adoption invisible, but made my responses to such addresses impossible. How could I answer their address as someone they seemingly could not recognize?

In middle school, I simply decided to fake it, drawing my family tree as if I was not adopted. Because I knew that the assignment assumed this tree was a tree of biological lineage, a tree of "begetting," I knew that what I wrote was not exactly true.[12] I remember having deliberated about how to proceed with the assignment, and that I had made a choice to take the path of least resistance. (This was not an issue I brought home for discussion, mind you.) I also remember that my humanities teacher wrote under the A-minus that she gave me that I was "lucky" to have so much information about my family, as I managed to include in the project facts about several generations of my parents' families. Simultaneously her comments were directed at me and yet completely missed me. She did not know that I knew this "lineage" was a fabrication, that I had, in a sense, plagiarized, having copied down another's family tree as my own, having chosen to write what I could claim to know rather than expose that what was critical to who I was consisted of what I *didn't* know (and in some sense that I couldn't know it). I wonder now what she thought was the import of such knowledge, such that I was "lucky." What did she think it gave me?

Later, in high school, I confronted my own feelings of forgery and complicity, of passing as a "lucky" one, and the assumptions of such institutional practices, by deliberately writing on all requests regarding medical information and "family history" (which were surprisingly many) in big

12. Even if the assignment was articulated as a tracing of cultural heritage, my argument is that because it involved the assumption that one individual had one tree, that there was a way to know and to trace one's production through a reproducible line of facts, it still would have caused me as adopted to feel uncomfortable. (It would have left no room for me to be what I am calling an adopted knower.) Knowing that there were whole parts of me that I was leaving out, huge things about me that I didn't know and hence couldn't include in such a tree, suggested to me that any version I did of my family tree was a construction and that such narratives of identity were themselves constructs. In other words, what was problematic wasn't just that the assignment assumed we were all from families constructed through biology; more critically, the assignment assumed that becoming (a self, a person, etc.) was a product of a traceable (knowable) lineage, that how one was produced could be evidenced such that what mattered about the being of a self was what could be known. Because this knowability became evidenced through the metonym of the body, the assignment importantly collapsed together the facticity of being born, or biological reproduction, the social-epistemological requirements for recognition, or socio-political reproduction.

bold letters on a diagonal across the page: "ADOPTED." I was old enough to fill out such forms by myself, and so without the presence of my parents' imagined gaze, I took this step of marking myself as not the same as biologically reproduced subjects. Interestingly, this self-ascription or marking was usually met with a kind of lacuna: upon learning of my adoption almost all medical personnel would not (and still often don't) ask *any* family history questions, either about my adopted or about my biological families, skipping right along to the individual history portion of the inquisition. They read "ADOPTED" as indicative, it seems, of the position of someone incapable of answering such questions. Perhaps they assume that if I knew my biological medical history, I would have not have made such a statement, and would have just simply checked off the appropriate diseases and filled in the corresponding lines left blank next to "relationship."[13]

While the demands of a "matching" ideology in traditional adoptions— including the legacies of shame and secrecy—made it rather impossible to speak my "desire to know" earlier in my life, the new age of "openness" regarding adoption has had its own issues that make such an articulation of desire difficult to perform. Similar for me in both paradigms is the tendency of being read as just like the non-adopted, so that my "desire to know" is still understood (and misrecognized) as normative, that is, as being what "normal" subjects would (or wouldn't) do. Being "just like" the non-adopted or "as if" not adopted while growing up meant that my desire to know could only be like those "normal" subjects as well. While adoption itself has recently become a more public phenomenon, the greater access to information and more open discussions of adoption have made it more possible to talk about my desire to know, but not necessarily more likely to have such desire understood. What is still at issue in both of these contexts is the need to address what we think the presence or absence of such information means, what it gives or takes away from one's notion of having an identity.

Just as I could not answer "when were you told you were adopted?" I am unsure if I could answer the question, "why did you search for your birth mother?" Unlike the ubiquitous questions I have been posed (how old were you? what do you know? etc.), the question of *why* has never been asked. Its inarticulation makes me nervous, as I often feel when I start telling my story that there are unspoken assumptions about the meaning of my

13. Interestingly, this metaphor of the form (as a site of truths about the self) raises the complexity of taking "adopted" as an identity in a culture which doesn't really have different words for relations that are biological (or kin) and relations that are social/cultural (or created through family practices). The biological becomes the truth of identity on the form as what is relevant in such documents is specifically the kin relationships. So while I could check off "cancer" on such intakes (as my birth mother's mother died of multiple cancers), I couldn't really, in truth, check off "grandmother." My grandmothers died of pneumonia and strokes. But checking off vascular disease or lung disease didn't seem "true" either.

search, including misunderstandings about the desire to search, the meaning of the body, and the understanding of and importance of identity. Two common notions evoked reflect what is at stake in such a misrecognition. First, many people often express their belief that it is "natural" to want to know.[14] And second, they extend this claim of naturalness to (or perhaps even base it on) their own imaginings of what *they* would want to know if they were adopted. The tropes involved here are something like, "Of course, it's natural to be curious" and "Well, if I were adopted *I* would *definitely* want to know."

In both of these tropes we begin to see that what is involved in claims of self-knowledge, in claims about "desiring to know . . ." oneself, is not only the establishment of the object of knowledge, but also of the subject of knowledge. More than being about *what* is known, responses to my "coming out" as adopted almost always invoke articulations about desiring knowing, articulations which assert a *who* who is desiring. While I used to think this was just an interest in what *I* desired to know, that it was natural to be curious about *me*, more recently I have begun to consider how others' articulations regarding their own desires to know reflect an insecurity (or anxiety) that adoption invokes in *general*. This insecurity opens up a way to see how the fantasy involved in knowing (or, conversely, in not having *reason* to desire to know, not having reason to not know or even to doubt oneself) elides into a kind of being (one doesn't have to know, one just is an X). It is through such fantasy that the self is established as having a coherent, natural, and unquestionable identity, and as capable of being a *legitimate* knower.

While I am no longer quiet about being adopted, especially when I am mis-read as biologically related to my family, I am still uncertain how to speak about my adopted identity: either my being adopted is "forgotten" or I am constructed as the "lucky" one.[15] Having, as an adult, searched for and found my birth mother, I am cautious about how I respond to the re-

14. When some members of my extended (adoptive) family found out that I had searched for and found my birth mother, they addressed my (adoptive) brother upon seeing him in terms of my search. They asked him not if but when he was going to search, expecting without doubt that he would want to. I wonder about this expectation of his desire, about how they were reading it in relation to mine, and how they were constructing us as siblings. Interestingly, their address involves reading what some might consider to be cultural as natural: in their eyes my brother would also want to search because we were both raised by the same people or because we were both adoptees.

15. Even among friends who know that I am adopted, it is a common experience for me to listen to others talk about their families and their relationships with and attitudes toward them without their realizing that their experiences and so on are very much based on their (assumptions about) being from a biologically constructed family. This is most common, of course, around body talk, including "looking like" and disease discourse. It is often uncomfortable and even a bit hurtful when such exchanges turn toward a kind of celebration of (the morphology of) a kind of bodily likeness. I liken this to a kind of "family romance" and have

sponses of others when they learn of my successful search story, for I have often felt like it was easy to have my desire to know (and my understanding of what I now know or what I found) appropriated and misread. Similar to the false identification I felt when I passed as not adopted, I often feel uncomfortable when people respond to my story with a kind of empathy about what it means to be adopted and how great it must be to know my birth mother.

Thus it seems that haunting the articulation of the desire to know, when recognized within an identity discourse—that is, the logic of identity—is a kind of ontological uncertainty, an uncertainty relieved by the presumption of an epistemological power. That such knowing is less about the information known and more about the (cultural) legibility or legitimacy its having offers (and its absence denies) the knowing subject became more apparent to me when, several years ago, after mentioning to a colleague that my birth mother was coming to visit, I was invited to tell my story to a local group of adoptive parents.[16] It was the first time that I had ever presented my narrative of adoption in a public forum, and I did not know what to expect. At first, the audience was quite interested in my experience of being adopted—when was I told, how did that make me feel, was I teased by others—but later their interest shifted as the parents became very engaged with my story of searching for and finding the woman who gave birth to me. After outlining the details of my search, many of the parents began to offer their own stories of what they did *not* know about their children. It became apparent to me that this *not knowing* was of crucial importance to them. Several parents lamented that they did not or even could not know the details of their children's backgrounds. They wished they could have names, dates, places, stories—an infinite list of items regarding information they seemed to think critical to their children's identities.

At this point in my presentation I began to become uncomfortable as it seemed that such lack of knowledge was a lack more crucial to these parents than to their children. I was being constructed by the audience as "lucky" (again), as full of information, as somehow more whole than their

---

seen it particularly arise when friends (who do not have children) discuss their (biological) nephews and nieces.

16. While I am relying here on an actual event that I participated in, I also readily admit that my reading of this event is wholly my own. I am using this event to draw out some of the complex and often unspoken assumptions about the meaning of "information" regarding the family and the individual. I do not mean in any way to assert that the interpretations I make of the adoptive parents' concerns and articulations are true of either all adoptive parents or even those parents in the room with me. As I hope is clear in this project, I think it is important to use experiences of the everyday as a means of analyzing the ways in which subjects are constituted and performed. My understanding of the Truth of identity as an impossibility, however, also extends to the meanings of those events of the everyday. In short, my interpretations of the desire to know as presented by the adoptive parents should themselves be considered as speculative, though perhaps instructive as well.

children, or maybe more whole than they. As a group, the parents seemed to suggest that not knowing all of the details of one's past, of one's life, made one less than a whole person.

I wondered, sympathetically, if the parents weren't transposing their anxieties as both parents and as adoptive parents onto their children, though I also wondered, resentfully—transposing my own anxieties, perhaps—whether *my* parents felt this way when they were raising me. I began to wonder what it was they thought such "information" would give them. It was during my presentation and the audience's response that I really considered not what I did know about my birth family, but how such knowing did not solve all of the identity issues that I had. Rather than resolving my questions about "who I am," finding a new family complicated my identity, problematized some of my relationships, and encouraged all kinds of re-definition of my family and its identity. Knowledge of my birth family has indeed made the *impossibility* of definitively answering the question "who am I?" ever more clear.[17]

17. Since both giving this presentation and beginning the arduous journey of writing this essay, the dynamics of my family have changed considerably, changes which reflect the ongoing impossibility of finding a true self or "becoming whole"—illusions promoted in certain adoption literature. While the death of a close family member engenders huge and painful shifts within the identity and identifications of a family, the (sudden and unexpected) death of my birth mother's husband Skip has caused shifts I did not expect. In particular, as he was not my father, but was the father of my birth mother's other three children, I have felt more of a "bastard" than I ever felt when he was alive. (This word, in fact, continued to present itself to my mind at his funeral. It never had before. This was in part due to his unquestioning acceptance of me into their lives.) This feeling of being a bastard after he died was a reversal of what might have been expected, viz. that when he was alive I would have felt more acutely the sense of being somehow an outsider, not his, put up for adoption, without a father, illegitimate. It is my alienation from my half-siblings' grief that has engendered, in part, my feelings of otherness. This alienation includes both my inability to talk about the man who died as "my father" and my discomfort and inability to talk about anyone as "my father" when I am with them. Since my relationship to these siblings is based more on a kind of biological essentialism than anything else (the sibling issue has been *the* most complicated part of searching/finding) in that it is based on the fact that we (problematically) "share the same mother," I am left without a father when I am with them. And my fatherlessness is, in this moment, of course, so very different from theirs. Perhaps there is a way to approach this feeling of being a bastard that can help me reach them in their grief.

The connection, of course, lies in our profound and distinct losses. While meeting and building a relationship with my birth mother has enriched my life in innumerable ways, her husband's death brought home to me the permanence of my loss of her as my mother. Feeling the differences in (the grammar of) our grief over Skip's death continues to underscore how, after relinquishing me for adoption, my birth mother went on to make a life without me. Perhaps as a kind of substitution I turned to feeling "bastardly" in relation to Skip's death as a way to present my feelings of being "motherless" in the sense that a bastard is fatherless (a condition for which there is no corollary term). I also wonder if the "bastard feeling" is not a part of the difficulty I have had in mourning a man who was not my father but whom I loved. There is no name for who he was in my life, as I discovered when I tried to get time off from work for the services, and as I acutely felt when meeting strangers at the funeral (who kept crying as they said, "I'm so sorry about your Dad"). I tell this story in part to show the complexity not only of the family relationships within the context of adoption, but also of the

Anxious and slightly frustrated in the face of my audience's implied assumptions (and misunderstandings) about the status of knowledge in the context of adopted families, I asked the group if any of them were themselves adopted. No hands went up. I then asked if any of them had in the last ten years or so (all were between 35 and 50, I thought) found out something new about their own families and histories, something they had never known or even something that contradicted what they had believed to be the case, maybe even something startling. Many of them groaned in response, raising their hands, rolling their eyes as they considered the changes in what they knew about who they and their loved ones were. I suggested to them to consider in relation to their adopted children's histories how such "knowledge" in and of their *non*-adoptive (i.e., biological or natural) families circulated, changed, was revised so that a true definitive narrative of their family and identity was itself an ideal, if not a fiction.

To underscore the complexity of their desire to know, of our (Western modern) culture's imperative regarding the knowledge of the self and the failure to meet such an idealization, I offered a story from my own search for and failure to find the (imagined) truth of my identity. Like other agencies in other states, the Catholic organization through which I was placed offered me "non-identifying information" when I presented myself to them at the age of 19. Among other details, the social worker there offered that I had been named "Mary Kathleen."[18] The parents in the room were audibly moved when I relayed my knowledge of my (non-identifying original) name. To know the name, the original name of their child seemed so important to them, as it had been to me.

I finally met my birth mother when I was 27, so for over eight years, I carried that name around as a secret and magical key which carried me back toward a past that had been hidden and forward toward a future that might have existed. The name was an important part of my imagining a

complexity of the shifting terms with which we make sense of such relationships. That the term "bastard" could appear for me in the context of death suggests that its force continues in my life as an adoptee, while it also suggests that its meaning as shifting and unpredictable might be malleable in some creative way.

18. Ironically, perhaps, my name was not considered to be "identifying information." There is much political sedimentation in the meaning of this performative, as it says that the name given to me is always-already unavailable for my identification. While the rules for non-identifying information are constructed to protect the other parties involved, calling my given name non-identifying raises questions about how much cultural force is needed in order for a name to be considered a means of identification, to be an effective interpellation, and how included in such force is the power of the patronym. My "name" was non-identifying, that is, not able to give or lend identity, because it lacked a "sir-name." Although this lack of any last name sites both the lack of my birth mother's name and my birth father's name, the history of adoption in the United States as a means for white middle-class young unmarried women to hide their pregnancies suggests that the weight of these absent last names in terms of their abilities to identify was not the same. It is here that the intersection of non-identifying and illegitimate needs to be unpacked.

life I did not have. It was a gift, a shining ring, the stone of which represented the truth of who I was, a secret true me, the self whom I would have been had I not been adopted. I would have been, I thought, a Mary Kathleen not a Kimberly Jean.

After several conversations and meetings with my birth mother, I raised the issue of "the name." In a casual voice, perhaps unaware of the investment I had made in those two words, she responded, saying "Oh, I had forgotten about that." The audience gasped. It seemed this was almost as "bad" as saying that she had forgotten the actual date of my birthday. I asked my birth mother why she chose that name, and her response both silenced and relieved me: "I'm not sure. I think I had an aunt named Mary and a friend at the birthing home named Kathy. I thought it was a pure sounding name. Something to give you as a good-bye, knowing that you certainly wouldn't keep it." There was a pause. She continued in a voice hesitant and sensitive: "But, I never would have named you that, though, if I was going to keep you. It was a name to leave you with . . ." The emphasis here, as I heard her words, was on the leaving not on the with.

There was now a tension in the room with the adoptive parents, and I felt like I had done something wrong. Something really wrong. I had not only perhaps broken some unspoken rules (of hierarchy) about the relationship between adoptees and the people who adopt them, but I had also broken a key rule about the role of the speaker in such a forum. As I re-read this event now, I think that on a meta-level I was asked to speak to the group about how I had searched for and found my birth mother, a metonymic object that stands in for my *self*. I was to present to the audience my "desire to know" my history, my genealogy, my self, and the means by which I satisfied that desire. My narrative was to legitimate the parents' "need to know" (to show them that it was the same as mine, not something odd about them as adoptive parents) by showing them how I had constructed my own need to know as natural, as morally right, as justified by the happy ending.

As I had presented my search narrative to the audience, replacing the simplicity of a "happy ending" with a kind of aporia, however, I had challenged the demand in Western culture to present oneself as an object of knowledge to oneself and to others, to satisfy the demands of such knowing by rendering myself as an object free of ambiguity. I had, in short, aroused but resisted the demands of the logic of identity. My narrative of searching and finding did not end with self-knowledge in a traditional sense, but instead left open (in an uncloseable or aporetic way) what the meaning of the knowledge I found was.

While the adoptive parents' desire to know seems to be very different from the refusal of the desire to know within the paradigm of matching and silence, there is something they have in common in terms of the production of identity. Both contexts involve knowledge (about the child, the families, the bodies, etc.) being thought to provide the *force* of identity. In the paradigm of *silence,* this knowledge was produced through an erasure of details that might contradict what could be read or seen about the body; whereas in the paradigm of *openness,* it is not the bodily details per se that are at issue, but the power they seem to hold as unknown. The adoptive parents' desire to know involved making the unknown of their children known; like the desire to erase bodily excess in "matching," their desire to know involved, I think, a desire to erase the *otherness* that haunts the construction of identity. Again, as Iris Marion Young has pointed out, difference when seen as *otherness* is a threat to the construction of identity. She writes:

> Through the logic of identity thought seeks to bring everything under control, to eliminate uncertainty and unpredictability, to spiritualize the bodily fact of sensuous immersion in a world that outruns the subject, to eliminate otherness. Such a subject is conceived as a pure transcendental origin: it has no foundation outside itself, it is self-generating and autonomous. (1990, 98–99)

Such otherness, it seems, might be acceptable when the identity in question is *not* one produced through adoption; it might in fact be merely difference. But the passion involved in the parents' desire to know involved more than just getting more information, more details or stories they could offer their children. It seemed they wanted to know such information because they wanted to eradicate the uncertainty to the establishment of identity that *not* having it (themselves) evoked. The issue of truth here is complicated, for clearly these adoptive parents wanted to know their children's bio-genealogical information *not* because such knowledge was the truth of their children's identities, that is, their "true natures," such that the parents and their particular cultural values and practices could not compete, could not affect their children's senses of self. Rather, having such information would give the adoptive parents, in some way, the *power* invested in such knowledge, power that seems to deepen (and to threaten) when such knowledge is absent.

Aware of the ever-changing narratives of family definition and the uncertainty present in any intimate organization, the parents in my audience implicitly were still appealing to an ideal of self-knowledge, to the possibility of knowing with certainty the origins of individuals.[19] Despite their

19. I am uncertain of their class positions, but it was my reading that most if not all of those present were middle to upper-middle class and were white. As the organization through which I was invited to speak brought together those parents who specifically adopted internationally, many of the parents present had adopted non-white children and most if not all had adopted children from "under-developed" or "Third World" countries. It is outside of

own uncertainties of their own families, these parents still believed in (or were strongly imagining) both the possibility of such knowing and the importance of it. They were, in terms of their desire to know, citing the ideal knower of the Western political and epistemological subject, an agent capable of knowing his own self-origins. Despite their obvious care about and investments in the families they were making, these parents were treating knowledge about the "others" (and the otherness) in their families in a way similar to the ways in which Western philosophers have considered knowledge—its status and power—for several hundred years: as discernible, knowable, capable of certainty, and of, paradoxically, providing the answers to one's identity. My intuition is that rather than having the bodily (itself, in some sense) be the morphological substance through which identity is established and transmitted, this example suggests that *knowledge* of the bodily can itself when *known* be that which is the morphological "source" of identity. While it is not exactly *sameness* that is at issue, there is something about knowing without impediment, some romance with information about the body, especially when raised to the level of some kind of science (via genetics, for example), giving it the status of Truth, that will supplement the adoptive family, allowing it a sense of normative identity. In other words, what is known is still thought to be able to render identity, but rather than it being the facts themselves that evidence identity, it is the *having* of them that—as unified, transparent, unambiguous, etc.—engenders identity.

So I learned that the parents' desire to know was not the same as my desire to know. I had, in the telling of my tale, not only presented my desire as different, but I had questioned the purpose of their desire. I had put into relief the issue of the naturalness of the desire to know, making it a desire more connected to the cultural, the social, and even the political. There is a paradox of sorts involved in the desire to know within the logic of identity, especially in the context of knowing the self through family. The desire to know as natural, as something "anyone" would want to know seems to be about connection, about relation, about one's intimate ties to others. As such, what is known could never be complete. If how one becomes "who one is" is linked to the lives of others and the meanings of their lives, then an *ad infinitum* quickly develops. But what if according to the logic of identity, identity doesn't *become*, it *is*? How does the notion that an identity *is*, has *being*, is *substance* affect what we consider to be relevant information about our identities, especially in terms of the family?

I do not want to go too far, but I think that there is, borrowing from

---

the scope of this essay to analyze the complexity of such adoptions, but it is important to admit that I am making the suggestion that it was in part due to the parents' positions as "First World," white, middle-class American citizens, that they were seemingly easily able to assume the position of hegemonic epistemological subjects.

Naomi Scheman, a paranoid logic at work in the construction of identity as a substance (Scheman 1997). There is a way that information about the self, when constructed as knowledge, has to be patrolled for otherness, such that its status as identity-knowledge can be secured. There is a tension, for instance, in the adoptive parents' desire to know the "facts" of their children's lives. On the one hand, they want to know of this information as that which reflects their children's connections to others—other people, cultures, languages, ethnicities, and even other names. But if they want these details to be facts, then the details, once known, must become finite and complete. As knowledge they have about their children, the facts can be used within the construction of the new life, the adopted identity of the child. I wonder if having such information doesn't make their children's identities less adopted, less about being adopted (which the parents were not), less a different kind of identity than they themselves believe they have. And yet, when asked, the parents knew that there was no way that information about themselves and their identities was constant, secured, without change or ambiguity.

In order to construct the fantasy of identity, it seems we want to believe that self-knowledge is possible, that we can in fact not only know the facts about someone else's identity, but that we can know them about our own. That such a fantasy involves the fantasy of self-transparency is suggested by the other common response to my speaking my adopted identity. "Oh, if I were adopted, I would definitely want to know. . . ." The (non-adopted) person who says that she would definitely want to know is referring to her experience as a non-adopted person, it would seem, as she asserts that she would not want to be without the knowledge that she has. She could not imagine not knowing. The exact predicate here, *what* it is that must be known, is necessarily left incomplete or even unstated. The ellipsis involved in "I would definitely want to know . . ." is not my shorthand. It is in the statement itself, suggesting that what it is that is being known is less important than the act of knowing (imagined or otherwise). This inability to imagine not knowing . . . would seem to indicate that for such an interlocutor, the content of this knowing is so important to her identity that she could not imagine (being) herself without it.

But how do we make sense then of her imagining herself as adopted? The second part of the trope is, "I would definitely want to know," but the first part is, "If I were adopted." Those who "would definitely want to know" are imagining that they would in some sense be the same person with the same desires and needs around their identities, even though in their thought experiment, they are imagining themselves in a very different life. In other words, these subjects at once assert a sameness over time of their desires and of the I who would want (to know), and simultaneously raise the specter of having totally different familial, cultural, and class positions.

While the notion of identity we have been exploring maintains a self-sameness between (and among) family members, the desire to know suggests that this establishment of self-sameness transcends the familial. Such an articulation of the desire to know both relies upon and constitutes a notion of identity as *self*-sameness over time that is foundational to the status of the individual subject. What this suggests is that the desire to know (one's family), paradoxically, can be a desire which asserts, constructs, and even confirms one's autonomy (from family). The naturalizing of the desire to know, then, I want to suggest, recites and perhaps re-enacts the paradigm of identity as autonomous, particularly as it posits the existence of the self as *knowing* his way through his own identity—a movement which reduces the complexity of relatedness to the singularity of identity.

The desire to know for both the adoptive parents and for the interlocutor who imagines herself as adopted, as I have explored it thus far, involves a desire for certainty. As both parties invoke the model of identity as substance, they construct knowledge of that identity as finite and suggest that the *having* of such knowledge itself performs a legitimate identity. The *desire,* in fact, is a desire which exhibits the subject's (desire to be able to know with) certainty, and thus is a desire which asserts the existence of the subject (and his identity) as *real.* The exhibition of such desire to know functions as (or becomes metonymical with, perhaps) the idea that such a desire to know *can* be satisfied (by the subject itself). According to historian and social critic Michel Foucault, knowing oneself was a requirement for modern subjectivity. In the modern era, he writes, "one of the main moral obligations for any subject is to know oneself, to tell the truth about oneself, and to constitute oneself as an object of knowledge both for other people and for oneself" (Foucault 1997, 177).

That the *exhibition* of such self-knowledge is part of this moral obligation means that the obligation is doubly required: To satisfy this moral obligation is both the *work* of the subject and *evidence* or proof of one's subjectivity. In other words, to be recognized as a subject it is required that one have such self-mastery and that one performs it for others. I think that the exhibition of the "desire to know" in this sense performs one's *status* as subject and thus attempts to secure one's position as (socially and politically) intelligible. Critically, then, there is a paradox here, for, as "desire," this exhibition of the desire to know is necessarily a performance that at once entails both the *capacity* for knowledge and the *absence* of knowledge. Being through *desire,* even if a desire for knowing, opens up a space of vulnerability. Working through this dialectic of vulnerability, of certainty *and* lack, is the heart of my project in developing a notion of adopted identity.

Intelligibility—that is, the erasure of the desire to know *as desire,* as that which alludes to lack—comes at a cost. In one sense, the cost is a kind of schism in the subject, a kind of impossible position. In another sense, the cost is a limiting of relations (and their meanings) with others. Discussing the ways in which philosophy, having shaped the standards of knowledge, has affected this schism in the subject, Naomi Scheman highlights how the maintenance of epistemological certainty might result in a kind of *splitting*. As the subject has to secure his own certainty through a process of estrangement from that which is uncertain—such as the body, relations to others, the unknowable of the self—those parts of him which thus impinge his claiming of what Scheman calls "epistemic authority" must be denied. This denial, she explains, engenders a subject (both the individual subject and the subject of philosophy) severely divided. This division leads to a kind of paranoia, as a subject (who can pass as authorized, who can pass as bodiless) feels he must choose between the legitimate status of epistemic authorization and the illegitimate status of being too closely associated (or identified) with the body. Scheman writes:

> Such a self, privileged by its estrangement from its own body, from the "external" world, and from other people, will, in a culture that defines such estrangements as normal, express the paranoia of such a stance not only through oppression, but, more benignly, through the problems that are taken as the most fundamental, even if not the most practically pressing: the problems of philosophy.... Such problems are literally and unsurprisingly unsolvable *so long as the subject's very identity is constituted by those estrangements*. A subject whose authority is defined by his location on one side of a gulf cannot authoritatively theorize that gulf away (1997, 356–57, italics mine).

My project here is to approach the "desire to know" within the narrative of adoption in a way which does not re-invest in such a paranoid logic, and which would allow for an articulation of such desire without disciplining the subject according to the norms of epistemic authority. As the paranoia of which Scheman writes seems to come from the very dichotomies by which Western philosophy is compelled, any attempt to develop a philosophical subject who escapes the costs of such paranoia must also escape the logic of "splitting" endemic to it. For an adopted subject to resist the dangers of such paranoid logic, I contend, the desire to know must not be a desire that strives for resolution, for unity, for oneness, given that such (imaginary) singularities will demand the splitting off of what is inconsistent, incoherent, and unable to be assimilated. As such, I want to suggest a way to explore the *moreness* (or surplus) of adopted *identity* as a means to achieve a way to articulate a kind of (aporetic) self-knowing without paranoia.

Naming my own desire to know is thus risky business. I have come to believe that *being* adopted (rather than only recognizing that one was adopted), demands always recognizing that the complexities of "who one is" are produced by and negotiated through multiple social practices and relationships. As these practices are always changing, always in discursive flux, and depend upon repetition for their production, so too *who one is* is always in process, in relationship with others, and in need of re-signification. Being adopted (as an identity) thus involves appreciating the fact that identities in general are socially constructed and that the appearance of solidity, of substance or essence, is itself an effect of such construction. What I also want to suggest is not only that identity is a "socially constructed (and constitutive)" category but that the claiming of "adopted" as an identity *requires* the recognition of this constructedness.

While I believe this to be true, I also recognize the *force* the desire to know—to fill in the gaps, to flesh out my story, and yes, even to "see my face in the face of another"—has had in my life. There has been an *affective* or emotional place constituted where the trope of "being adopted" as the story of my *identity* and the trope of "being adopted" as the story of my *body* intersect. It is in this intersection between the narratives of identity and of body (which are, perhaps, the limits of the metaphor of adoption) that my desire to know becomes both announced and felt. As a liminal space, however, I cannot claim (to know) that this is its place of origin. My philosophical and political explorations of what being adopted, being a subject means to me have produced this desire to know as a kind of epistemological excess: I neither believe that the self is transparent to itself, such that its desires can be explained, nor that the subject can be an object of knowledge (for itself or for others) such that its status as in-process and relational is limited. As I cannot explain (away) this desire as socially or biologically caused, it is a kind of remainder which points to a moreness of my self. As such it is neither a desire for certainty, for knowing my own essence, or truth, nor is it an abandonment of the search for authority. It is a felt desire, particular to me and my history, but not an explicable desire based on some discernible feeling of lack. It is a desire not to know my self as an object of knowledge, but to experience my self as a subject outside of the limits of knowing with certainty. It is a desire to be a subject who has authority without abandoning as foundational to that authority the pleasures of uncertainty.

In order to be able to speak my desire to know, I have to articulate that desire as not a desire for privileged, normative, intelligible identity. In one sense, of course, this is impossible. My desire to know (differently) has necessarily been produced in relationship to this desire for (legitimate) recognition. My relationship to my desire to know, in fact, has shifted in my life in relation to how I have desired, received, and resisted social and cultural recognition and/or legitimacy. What I have tried to present here in the space that is engendered by exploring adoption philosophically is how, having been interpellated as an epistemologically legitimate subject, that is, a subject who *can* claim the status or privileged position of (self-)knower,

I have been *un*-able to claim a position as adopted. My recognition as someone who can know herself has come, in fact, from the *mis*-recognition of me as *not* adopted. These (repeated) acts of misrecognition have, throughout my life, made the articulation of my *desire to know*—its specificity, its difference—quite difficult. Even when my claim of being adopted as an identity position seems to have been recognized, the ways in which my desire to know have been understood suggest that my *difference* as adopted has not really been appreciated.

This essay, then, is a (partial) account of those practices that have denied my difference. It is also, however, an articulation of what has not only resisted such denials, but has desired *through* them. I cannot argue, in short, that the ways in which I have been addressed as not-adopted, the ways in which I have "passed" as someone who would never have been referred to as a "bastard," are not part of the very reason I have been able to claim my desire to know. But neither can I deny that my sense of difference, of possibility, of *being adopted by* rather than *born into* my family and its identity didn't give me the strength to resist the seductions of such an offer of legitimacy. In other words, if being adopted did encourage me to become a philosopher, as some might want to think, it is not because philosophy offered me the position of being-in-the-know that I lacked as an adoptee. Philosophy, as a field engaged with such questions as what is knowledge, what is identity, and what is desire, has instead been a location where my *ambivalence* as a knower can be explored, where my desire to know *as desire* can find home. If I am to speak that desire in this home, then I cannot, like the logic of identity might demand, separate from it the means by which it has become known to me.

To have an adopted identity—which is for me an identity based on the desire to know—is thus to include in that very identity the ways in which it has been denied. To be adopted, then, involves including in *being* those processes of *becoming* which not only affirm who we are, which not only give us the means with which we can assume an identity, but which also make the articulation of an identity impossible. As adopted, then, identity evokes both the past through which our identities have been assigned, addressed, and determined, as well as the present through which we claim imperfect positions of knowing ourselves. By exploring the trope of identity *in general* through the metaphor of adopted identity *in particular*, it is my aim to transcend the dualistic framework of lack and certainty that drives the subject toward both the need for epistemic authority and the dis-ease that is paranoid logic. Approaching identity as adopted engenders the possibility, I want to claim, for locating a positionality of the subject in relation to her own desire to know (herself). By re-placing or shifting the emphasis in the desire to know from *knowing* to *desiring*, it is my hope that we can engender (1) subject positions that involve both a recognition of and resistance to the (limiting and oppressive) aspects of identity-ascription and their corollary authorizations of epistemic privilege, *and* (2) a recognition of and movement toward the personal ways in which a subject is concerned with knowing her processes of being and becoming. By reading the trope of identity as necessarily impossible to (thoroughly) know, I am not claiming that it is necessary to give up on identity. Instead, I am offering a way to re-read identity as *adopted* in order to highlight that identities, as objects of our desire, can be seen as both locations of subjection and places of potential freedom.

CHAPTER EIGHT

Real (M)othering: The Metaphysics of Maternity in Children's Literature

SHELLEY PARK

MY REALITY

"You are not my REAL mother!" she screams from behind a locked bathroom door. She is seven. Although all adoptive mothers anticipate this moment, I'm not ready for this yet. What is a real mother? Am I one? What would it mean to claim this? And how do I defend my status as real without implying that her birth mom is somehow unreal, or at any rate less real than I am? Clearly, my daughter's current metaphysical schema will not readily permit the notion of multiple mothers. One of us must, according to her, be an imposter—someone who, like Descartes's evil genius, has subjected her to an illusory construction of reality.

As I sit in a stupor outside the locked door, contemplating the metaphysics of maternity, my younger daughter saunters over and plops herself in my lap. "You're MY real mother," she confidently claims while giving me a big hug. I'm not sure whether she says this to comfort me or to further annoy her sister. Probably both. And although the hug does help, her possessive metaphysical claim further confounds me.

Because we have one daughter by adoption and one by birth (as well as a set of grandparents and numerous cousins that our children have adopted), we have been tremendously vigilant about avoiding any privileging of biological connectedness over social relatedness. Hence it comes as a shock to hear both of my daughters proclaiming the metaphysical primacy of blood relations. Certainly, I have never used the phrase "real mom" to describe either myself or my eldest daughter's birth mom. Nor have I ever used (or even thought) the phrase "real daughter" to privilege my birth daughter over my adopted daughter. Yet here these phrases are in my home, functioning to exclude and include, to marginalize and privilege, to separate and bind together. This essay emerges from my efforts to sort out for myself and for and with my daughters what is meant by the phrase "real mother." I am also engaged in attempting to transform this concept in ways that would make the metaphysics of maternity both more fluid and more inclusive.

A fluid metaphysics of motherhood would allow that maternal status is not static. As I will examine below, traditional conceptions of motherhood have assumed that genetic, gestational, and social mothering are indivisible and thus that motherhood is a stable concept and institution. Such a conception of motherhood ignores the historical realities of genetic families divided by poverty, war, and slavery. It is further contested by the now multiple forms of family created by adoption, divorce and remarriage, and new reproductive technologies such as surrogacy and in vitro fertilization. Thus, we need a conception of family in general and motherhood in particular that allows for change over time.

An inclusive metaphysics of motherhood would permit a child to have more than one real mother (and more than two real parents), an option preferable to the metaphysics presupposed by most cultural, social, and legal narratives surrounding parental status, including the private adoption narrative. As Uma Narayan (1999) notes, the private adoption narrative takes an "all or nothing" approach (85). The gestational mother has all parental claims prior to giving the child for adoption, and no parental claims after a statutory change-of-mind period has passed. The adoptive parents have no parental claims prior to the cessation of the gestational mother's rights and all parental claims thereafter. In contrast to this "all or nothing" approach, Narayan advocates a custody approach that "potentially allows for a wider range of parental relationships to be preserved." Such a reformed approach, she argues, would be preferable for gestational mothers who wish neither to assume full responsibility for a child nor to surrender all ties to that child. Such reform would also have "the virtue of privileging a child's interests above those of competing parents, treating children more as ends-in-themselves than as objects of property-like disputes between contending parents" (85).

Like Narayan, I am interested in developing a child-centered perspective on parent-child, and especially mother-child, connections in the sense of developing an account of parental status that best serves the "interests of the child." I believe, as does Narayan, that a child is best served by "maintain[ing] as many . . . parental connections with adults who wish to maintain these bonds as is . . . feasible in any given case." This is not to say that a child is always best served by having multiple, diverse, parents. It is, however, to say that this option should not be "arbitrarily foreclosed" (85).

It is not my project here, however, to debate legal policy or even informal custodial arrangements. My project here is rather to interrogate the social constructions of motherhood as these are taught to children and propose in their place an alternative metaphysics of motherhood that would permit my daughter and other children to recognize multiple mothers without having to feel divided loyalties. While this might be more easily achieved within a reformed legal environment, it can also be achieved, I argue, by a child who develops the ability to conceptually and ethically reposition herself in regard to (m)others. Thus, my project is child-centered not merely in terms of its concern for a child's well-being, but also in two additional senses. First, my emphasis here is on a child's potential to bring multiple (m)others into being *for herself.* Rather than trying to define what it means to be a mother politically, morally, legally, or socially, I attempt here to understand (and prescribe) a particular psychic configuration in a child's attitudes toward her parents. In examining what it means for a child to accept or reject some person as her "real mother," I am exploring what it means for a mother to be real-for-a-child. In this sense, whether or not I am my daughter's "real mother" is a separate question from whether I have or ought to have legal custody of her. It is also a separate question from whether or not I participate in certain forms of motherwork—although as I will suggest here, certain forms of motherwork may contribute to my becoming real to my child.

Secondly, my account aims to be child-centered insofar as I am interested not only in the well-being of a child, but in how that child's well-being can be secured, in part, *through the child's own agency.* As Robinson, Nelson, and Nelson (1997) note, within the sentimental family, the power to name reality typically accrues to parents, rather than children (91). This does violence to a child's ability to develop a sense of herself as a moral agent, as a person "with the power to shape reality" (95). This essay is, in large part, about respecting and nurturing a child's potential to shape her own familial reality.

More specifically, as my title suggests, this essay is about respecting and nurturing a child's potential to bring real (m)others into being-for-herself. I focus here primarily on children's relation to mothers for several reasons. First, the experiential context from which this essay emerges is one in which maternal, not paternal, reality is the issue. I suspect that this context is a common one for *adopted* children. At least in our current Western context, birth mothers are often known—or locatable—in ways that birth fathers may not be. It is also a common context for *young* children who often come to first understand adoption in terms of being birthed by one woman and "given up to" to "chosen by" another (usually married) woman. Additionally, the depictions of family that *all* children are exposed to at an early age often focus primarily, or even exclusively, on mother-child relations.

Although it is not my position that an emotional or social division of labor demarcates mothers from fathers, prevalent cultural meanings of "mothering" do assume this. Thus, outside of certain feminist contexts, the still widely held assumption is that mothers are (and should be) the primary emotional and physical caregivers, while fathers are (and should be) the primary breadwinners. In other words, "mothering" and "fathering" are still widely used to denote different functional and normative roles. Sometimes, although not often, it is allowed that the functional role of mother may be occupied by a man. But the role itself remains gendered, as illustrated by the ways in which prevailing social norms for "good mother" parallel the norms for "good woman" (i.e., loving, kind, emotionally responsive, sensitive to the needs of others, giving of herself, and so on). Since my project here involves examining the social construction of motherhood, I speak specifically about mothering, rather than using the more generic "parenting." Ultimately, however, my interest is in helping children resist conservative narratives of mothering in order to see their mothers— *and others*—as real. My hope, although I do not argue for this here, is that children who can learn to see mothers as real persons with independent interests (despite these culturally defined meanings of "mother") could also learn to see fathers and others as real.

I begin by examining the social and cultural meanings of motherhood as transmitted to, and potentially resisted by, children. Since my adopted daughter's notion that she must have one and only one mother is not gleaned from complex understandings of social policy or judicial decision-making, but derives rather from the social constructions of motherhood embodied in children's popular culture, I take children's literature as my point of departure.

Critical legal theorist Barbara Bennett Woodhouse (1995) suggests that stories written about and for children "provide a window on children's experience" from which we may draw conclusions about meaning (5). To be sure, the perspective on children's experience provided by children's literature is not transparent. Children's literature is, after all, written *by* adults. Thus to read such literature from a child's point of view requires that we imagine what the text means to its child reader, rather than focusing exclusively on what the author may have intended. Thus, I attempt to focus not merely on what these texts say, but also on what they "fail to say, and what they suggest by innuendo" (Rosenau 1992, 36–37). The meanings I am concerned to glean from these texts originate not in their production but in their reception by the reader (37). Sometimes, of course, children may uncritically digest the adult-centered narratives proposed by authors. At other times, however, children, including even very young children, may develop "counternarratives" as they read (or listen to) these stories (Cloud 1992, 6). In imagining what the texts here examined might mean to children, I am aided by the counternarratives offered me, both implicitly and explicitly by my own children.[1]

The specific stories I will use here as examples of narratives (and potential counternarratives) of "real motherhood" include *Are You My Mother?*, *A Mother for Choco, Stellaluna, Horton Hatches the Egg,* and *The Velveteen Rabbit.* Three of these stories are classic parables that enjoy continued wide readership. Two are more recent publications, also much loved by children and parents. These stories exemplify constructions of motherhood common in children's literature, much of which functions as a series of (sometimes competing) parables of family relationships and children's belonging.

The first two stories take up alternate sides of the nature-nurture debate over children's needs and parental rights. *Are You My Mother?* depicts motherhood as a biological identity, assuming that a child's birth mother is, and always will be, a child's real mother. In direct opposition to this claim, *A Mother for Choco* portrays real motherhood as a social identity. From an adopted child's perspective these two frameworks are irreconcilable; loyalty to either script requires the child to be disloyal to someone in their life. Hence, as I suggest below, neither script's notion of "real" mother is adequate and the adopted child—indeed any child with multiple mothers—needs to learn to deconstruct the nature/culture dichotomy that gives rise to these notions.[2]

Stellaluna and *Horton Hatches the Egg* provide more complex narratives that help deconstruct the natural mother/social mother dichotomy, by deconstructing motherhood as a unified process. Taken together, they also illustrate the competing claims to motherhood that inform discussions about adoption, as well as non-adoptive custody disputes.[3] In these conversations, the notion of "real mother" is a contested notion that requires evaluation of several facets of maternal fitness. Here as in black feminist

1. Of course, insofar as readers participate in the attribution of meaning to a text, there may be as many different meanings as there are readers. Thus, while I suspect the meanings I examine here are not uncommon readings for the young, adopted child, I do not purport to provide the definitive readings of these texts. Nonetheless, I hope that my readings may be suggestive and useful to others whose children struggle with the concept of "real mother."
2. Although my focus here is on adoption, the adopted child's struggles regarding mother identification, as generated by the nature/nurture dichotomy, may share certain similarities with the struggles of children borne of divorce and remarriage, children with lesbian parents, and children birthed with the aid of new reproductive technologies (e.g., in vitro fertilization) and relationships (e.g., "surrogate" mother contracts).
3. Stanworth (1990) notes how new reproductive technologies, such as in vitro fertilization and "surrogate" mothering serve to "deconstruct motherhood as a unified biological process," but this deconstruction was begun by the separation of nurture from nature embedded in (formal and informal) adoptive relationships, long before new reproductive technologies emerged. Moreover, as stories such as *Horton* illustrate, even the separation of genetic and gestational mothering was imaginable prior to its becoming technologically possible.

literature on "othermothering,"[4] we are invited to consider not only birth mothers but also others as mothers. However, serious questions arise in these narratives concerning how "other" a mothering figure can be while still claiming fitness as a "real mother." In defining "real mother" as an issue of maternal fitness, these stories, I suggest, erect a good mother/bad mother dichotomy, different from the nature/nurture dichotomy, but still problematic.

In the final section of this essay, I explore the notion forwarded in *The Velveteen Rabbit* that reality, in the sense that I am advocating, is a function of being loved. Together with feminist accounts of ontology and epistemology, this notion can be used as an entry into a useful notion of real motherhood, perceived here as an existential and fluid process that allows for multiple real mothers, constructed in relation to, rather than opposition to, each other.

MOTHERS AND NON-MOTHERS: THE NATURE/ CULTURE DICHOTOMY

My eldest daughter's insistence that I am not her "real" mother stems originally from two sources: first, that she was not borne to me, and second, that she does not look like me. The notion of family belonging as a factor of birth and genetic mirroring reflects a traditional kinship narrative. This narrative has had a profound effect on adoptive relationships which, until recently, were governed by the principle that such relationships should mimic, to the greatest extent possible, the relationships of the biological kinship unit. Thus, until the open adoption movement of recent decades, placement of children practiced racial and ethnic matching, adoption records were closed, and adoptive parents were advised to raise their adopted children "as if" they were their own flesh and blood. Often this practice of secrecy surrounding adoption extended to keeping a child's origins secret from the adopted child as well. As remains current practice, birth certificates sealed this biological fiction by recording a child's adoptive parents as their birth parents (Modell 1994).

Opposition to the practice of closed adoptions has been led largely by the adult children of adoption seeking access to information about their birth parents. In some cases, adopted children may seek their birth parents because of special circumstances that may arise, such as a health crisis that requires family medical history. In most cases, however, adopted children's search for their birth families—and especially their birth mothers—stems from desires related to felt gaps in their identity formation. In

4. See, e.g., Collins (1991), hooks (1984).

order to know adequately who they are, adopted children often feel the need to know their stories of origin and the source of their unique appearance, talents, and/or difficulties.[5]

The notion that family membership is a function of biological origins and genetic inheritance is a theme both accepted and contested in children's literature. In the 1960 story *Are You My Mother?* (a book in the Beginner Books series still widely reproduced and distributed), a baby bird hatches from his egg while his mother is off in search of worms for him. Looking up, down, and all around, in search of his mother, but not finding her, the newborn bird leaves his nest and goes off in search of his mother. Along the way, he encounters many creatures—chickens, dogs, cats, and cows, as well as cars, planes, and boats—asking each in turn, "Are you my mother?" Each creature encountered responds negatively, highlighting the differences between themselves and the baby bird. ("How could I be your mother?" said the cow. "I am a cow.") In the end, however, a friendly, if frightening, earth-moving machine returns him to his nest where he is happily united with his "natural" (i.e., species) mother.

In direct contrast to the privileging of biological connection in *Are You My Mother?*, the 1992 story, *A Mother for Choco* tells the story of a little bird who lives all alone, wishes he had a mother, and eventually finds a mother bear. Like the baby bird in the earlier adventure, Choco encounters all kinds of creatures who have, at best, a marginal family resemblance to him—e.g., a giraffe who is yellow, penguins who have wings, a walrus that has big, round cheeks—and who uniformly reject his need for a mother.

> "Oh, Mrs. Walrus!" he cried. "You have big, round cheeks just like me. Are you my mother?" "Now look," grumped Mrs. Walrus. "I don't have striped feet like you, so don't bother me!" (Kasza 1992)

Dismayed by his inability to find anyone who looks just like him, Choco cries, eliciting a maternal response from nearby Mrs. Bear who comforts him with hugs, kisses, singing, dancing, and apple pie and adopts him into her family—a family already including a baby alligator, pig, and hippo. The moral of this story is clear: when Choco quits looking for someone that looks like him and begins thinking instead about all the things that his mommy would do, if he had one, he finally finds the mother he needs.

The contrasting depictions of mothers as natural versus social creatures found in these stories parallels two traditional lines of thought about motherhood. Both of these lines of thought are, however, oversimplified and ultimately unsatisfactory. The first line of thought assumes motherhood to

5. Whether this information would be necessary for adequate identity formation in another socio-historical moment is an open question. But the felt need for such information is extremely common among contemporary Western adoptees.

be a "natural" state, assuming that genetic, gestational, and social mothering are one and the same. Thus, a woman's biological connection to her offspring automatically gives her the rights and responsibilities of a mother. It is this conception of motherhood as a natural and unified process that makes it difficult for many persons, including many children, to understand why a pregnant women could decide not to mother, choosing instead to abort her fetus, or to abandon her child. Like the mother bird with her nesting and worm-gathering instinct, adult women are supposed to have a natural bond with their offspring that guarantees they will have both the desire and the ability to engage in responsible mothering activities. As the phrase "maternal instinct" connotes, motherwork is viewed as a natural, not a learned, ability or skill.

If we assume that biological and social mothering are one and the same, questions concerning children's identity formation and sense of belongingness within the family are rendered unproblematic. Like the baby bird, children who remain in their family of biological origin can easily "see themselves" in their parents. They look like, and, it is often assumed, act like their parents due to genetic connections. Hence, their "fit" in the family unit is uninterrogated. Idiosyncratic differences may be tolerated to a greater or lesser degree, but the homogeneity of the family unit is largely taken for granted.

As Elizabeth Bartholet (1993) notes, because these assumptions underlie the tale *Are You My Mother?*, the story is profoundly anti-adoption. In contrast, *A Mother for Choco* is a positive tale of adoption. Not only does its underlying metaphysics of maternity depict real motherhood in terms of motherwork, rather than biological connection, its happy depiction of the non-homogenous family opens the possibility of building genuine relations between those who are different in significant ways. A much loved story of adoptive parents—especially those who have, like myself, adopted transracially—*A Mother for Choco* depicts families as chosen, not given, and mothering as an activity that can be successfully extended to children in need, regardless of those children's "natural" origins.

A Mother for Choco thus seems a radical departure from the dominant ideology surrounding motherhood that for centuries has deemed a woman's destiny to be a function of her biology. And indeed, it is. Nonetheless, as Fineman (1995) notes, "in examining discourses about motherhood . . . underlying symbols and values are more uniformly shared than differences in discourse would superficially indicate" (220). On the surface, *A Mother for Choco* embraces an understanding of motherhood that combines norms of choice and caregiving in ways compatible with feminist values. However, a closer reading of the story reveals a conservative counternarrative in tension with those feminist values. The singing, dancing Mrs. Bear bakes an apple pie as a token of her caregiving. This act, in combination with a textual failure to develop Mrs. Bear's character in even minimal ways, gives rise to a stereotypical depiction of the caregiving mother as perpetually happy and instinctively nurturing. This stereotype of mothering could be potentially undermined here by including in the narrative a depiction of Choco's birth mother relinquishing her child as an act of care. By omitting such story elements from the narrative, however, *A Mother for Choco's* redefinition of motherhood falls short of radicalizing the concept. Instead, its redefinition of motherhood as the act of nurturing ultimately channels a potentially radical idea "into set categories approved by the existing conceptual system," thus "domesticating" a rhetoric of motherhood by choice into a rhetoric of mothering as caregiving (219–20).[6] This is problematic for both mothers and children.

My initial response to my elder daughter's insistence that I wasn't her real mother was to try to undermine her claim by way of pointing out all the maternal activities I had been engaged in both for and with her. After all, who had fed, diapered, and bathed her as an infant? Who had walked the floors with her each night when she had colic? Who encouraged her to take her first steps, say her first words, and make her first friends? Who has played, sung, and danced with her? Who has consoled her when she is hurt and applauded her many achievements? In short, who has lived with her and cared for her since she was three days old?[7] Downplaying the role of biology and focusing on social aspects of mothering also seemed a satisfactory solution to avoiding my younger daughter's one-upmanship in the form of a claim to biological connection with me that her sister lacked. Seeking to reconnect sisters, as well as adoptive daughter and mother, it was expedient to force a redefinition of mother that made me equally real to both of them, and made them equally real to me. I thus positioned myself as Mrs. Bear. Strangely, however, only my younger, biological daughter was receptive to my bear hugs.

To understand why my adopted daughter resisted my attempts to redefine mothering as a social activity, I had to read the social mothering narrative from her own, rather than my own, perspective. When I did so, I recognized that from an adopted child's perspective, *A Mother for Choco* oversimplifies the concepts of mothering and family in important ways.

First, a child's birth mother is notably absent from this narrative of social mothering.[8] "Choco was a little bird, who lived all alone." Why? Where

6. Fineman (1995) is concerned to examine the images of mothering in poverty discourse. Her general point about the domestication of the rhetoric of motherhood holds for my purposes as well, however.

7. This response, whether or not verbalized, is a common response of adoptive parents to their children's first "real parents" question. See Engle (1995) for a similar narrative.

8. The erasure of children's birth mothers in parables of adoptive families, as well as other forms of blended families, is commonplace in children's fiction. See, for example, con-

did he come from? And how did he manage to survive at all in the absence of any nurturing creature? From a child's perspective, the narrative erasure of the birth mother is both implausible and ethically suspect. The erasure of Choco's bird mother, combined with the notion that a non-bird is his real mother, negates the possibility of genuine competing grounds for claims to motherhood. By positioning myself within this narrative context, I had implicitly devalued my daughter's own narrative context, a context within which her birth mother figured prominently as a key to her own identity.

Secondly, *A Mother for Choco* falsifies the experience of the adopted child, by suggesting that the child voluntarily chooses her adopted family. In reality, adopted children rarely exercise any influence over such decisions. Women who adopt in an important sense choose motherhood; moreover, they exercise the right to accept or reject any particular child offered them for adoption.[9] Adopted children, on the other hand, are "placed" within a home deemed suitable for them. Indeed, my daughter's anger could be explained, in part, as stemming from *her* inability to choose her home and family, and by virtue of this, her inability to know what has been lost to her.[10] While no child is able to choose the circumstances into which they are born, a special sense of frustration and loss attends the experience of adopted children insofar as they know that choices *were* available; they were simply unable to intervene.

Finally, *A Mother for Choco* devalues the fears and anxieties that may be related to an adopted child's sense of difference within her adopted family. This adoption parable minimizes the potential impact on children of the truly heterogeneous family. Can bears, alligators, hippos, pigs, and birds truly live together harmoniously? Can they all eat the same meals? Enjoy the same games? Speak the same verbal, emotional, or physical language? Real family relationships are complex; even in the most homogeneous families tensions may arise. These tensions are exacerbated as the family becomes more heterogeneous. In families where racial or ability dif-

---

temporary stories such as *Susan and Gordon Adopt a Baby, The Day We Met You, Through Moon and Stars and Night Skies, Horace,* and *Murmel, Murmel, Murmel,* as well as classic fairy tales such as *Cinderella* and *Snow White.*

9. Unlike biological mothers, adoptive mothers (and fathers) must undergo lengthy interviews and house visits and complete substantial paperwork related to their desire and ability to "have" a child. Throughout this often lengthy and invasive process, a would-be mother has significant opportunity to reflect on her reasons for wanting a child in her life and significant opportunity, even after a child is placed in her home, to change her mind.

10. This also explains, in part, why adopted children may direct rage disproportionately at their mothers. It is the sense of loss for a birth mother, rather than a birth father, that is most significantly felt. This is generally true for both young girls and young boys, once they have learned that babies grow in mother's tummies. As children age, however, and struggle with identity formation, the tension may become most pronounced between mothers and daughters.

ferences exist, for example, ordinary sibling rivalries may become intensified and, as I have often noted, motherwork becomes more intense.

From my daughter's perspective, however, the situation is no doubt more anxiety-provoking than even this suggests. Her experience is the experience not of a truly heterogeneous family, but is perhaps the experience of being a bird among bears. It is the experience thus of being "other" among those who are (or at least appear) "alike"; related to this, it is the experience of being small and vulnerable.[11] Under such circumstances, it is less surprising that she should resist my overtures of comfort. Even a well-intentioned bear hug may appear risky to receive; in order to refrain from crushing her spirit or her potential to fly, I must ensure that I am not *over*bearing.

REAL MOTHERS AND OTHER MOTHERS: THE GOOD
MOTHER/BAD MOTHER DICHOTOMY

"My REAL mother wouldn't make me do this!" She is doing her homework. More accurately, she is supposed to be doing her homework. She hates homework; she especially hates having to write vocabulary definitions. She has difficulty sitting still and difficulty concentrating. She is hungry. She needs a glass of water. She wants to phone a friend. She wants to watch TV. Her sister is watching TV, as her homework is long completed.

I am tired. Tired of the nightly homework wars. Tired of being unfavorably compared to her "real" mother. "You can do this. Just sit down and concentrate," is the best response I can conjure up. Of course, concentrating is precisely what she seems unable to do. "I want to live with my birth mom! She'd be nicer to me!" she retorts. "Sit back in that chair and finish your vocabulary definitions!" I respond, still refusing to take the bait, but raising my voice enough to live up to her accusation of my unkindness.

Later, as I tuck her into bed, trying to recoup my losses, I patiently explain to her that I am quite certain that her birth mother would also want her to do her homework. "All mothers want their children to do well at school, so that they can grow up to be whatever they would like to be." At my request, my daughter's birth mom sends a letter confirming my hypothesis and urging our child to do her homework. In separate correspondence, however, she reveals that she too had childhood difficulties in school. I begin to wonder if I am mistaken in believing that my eldest daughter can succeed in school simply by internalizing the work ethic on which I was raised. I wonder also about the value our family places on academic success—a success that has come more or less easily to myself, my partner, and my youngest daughter, but that is a struggle for my eldest child. Perhaps, because of her similar experiences, my daughter's birth mother would be better able to empathize with our child's struggles.

In the contemporary children's story *Stellaluna*, a young bat, lost by her biological mother during an encounter with an eagle, is adopted by a fam-

11. For an adoption parable more sensitive to this experience of being "different," see Keller (1991).

ily of birds. There she is well cared for, but has difficulty assimilating to her new environment—an environment which requires eating worms and insects, sleeping upright, and giving up her nocturnal ways. Although her bird siblings are open to learning bat skills, Mama bird is less flexible. Coming home one day to find all of her children hanging upside down, mother bird panics, sending all of the baby birds back to the nest, but stopping Stellaluna:

> "You are teaching my children to do bad things. I will not let you back into the nest unless you promise to obey all the rules of this house."
> Stellaluna promised. She ate bugs without making faces. She slept in the nest at night. And she didn't hang by her feet. She behaved as a good bird should (Cannon 1993).

Importantly, Mama bird does care for Stellaluna. Yet she does so in ways that are inappropriate, indicating her failure to understand that Stellaluna's needs may differ from those of her bird-siblings. In contrast, Stellaluna's "real" mother understands her offspring's needs; thus the story ends happily, when bat mother and child are reunited.

Like *Are You My Mother?*, *Stellaluna* is a story that ultimately resolves the question "who is the real mother?" by identifying the biological mother as real. Unlike the earlier story, however, the resolution of this question results from a more complex narrative that depicts Stellaluna's bat mother as possessing caregiving and relational skills relevant to mothering—skills that Stellaluna's "other" (bird) mother lacks.[12]

Unlike the essentialist narrative in *Are You My Mother?* that reduces motherhood to biological connection, here biology and identity are depicted as instrumental rather than intrinsic to mothering. Biological identity is important insofar as it gives rise to similar needs and experiences, which in turn ground empathy. The story opens the possibility, however, of empathic connection across difference. While Mama bird, having no previous experience with bats, seems unwilling to accommodate Stellaluna's difference, the baby birds are more playful and willing to try new things. Even after Stellaluna is reunited with her natural mother, she and the younger birds continue to explore one another's worlds, learning both the possibilities and the limitations of their boundary crossings.

By deconstructing the notion of the "bad" child, this story is comforting for children and educational for parents. It teaches us that children's nonconformist behavior may be neither good nor bad, but simply an expression of their needs and abilities. It suggests that parents need to be flexible;

12. From the beginning, we are assured that Stellaluna's biological mother is a good mother, who "loved her soft tiny baby," crooning to her and clutching her to her breast each evening, as she went in search of food.

children's active resistance to and/or inability to follow household rules may indicate a difficulty with the rules rather than a difficulty with the child. Unfortunately, the story deconstructs the good child/bad child dichotomy by erecting the good mother/bad mother dichotomy. This dichotomy also features prominently in the Dr. Seuss classic, *Horton Hatches the Egg*.

In *Horton Hatches the Egg*, Horton the elephant is charged with caring for the egg of a Lazy-Mayzie bird who flies south to frolic for the winter. Horton suffers many trials and much ridicule for his troubles, but is ultimately rewarded when an elephant-bird that hatches from the egg identifies him (and not Lazy-Mayzie) as her mother. In contrast to *Stellaluna*, *Horton* advances the notion that real mothering can transcend significant differences. Although it requires extraordinary care and Horton is belittled, ostracized, and exoticized for it, Horton learns the skills necessary to faithfully nurture the egg that he promised to care for. In exchange for his willingness to become bird-like, the hatchling emerges with elephant traits. As the bird with "ears and a tail and a trunk just like his" flies toward Horton, an astonished crowd cheers in approval.

As Mahoney (1995) suggests in discussing legal rights to frozen embryos, and *Horton* exemplifies, such cases are "not . . . about who *is* a [natural] parent," but are instead about "who has a right to become, or not become a parent" (41).[13] The crowd surrounding Horton cheers precisely because Horton has earned the right to become a parent. As the book concludes:

> And it should be, it *should* be, it SHOULD be like that.
> Because Horton was faithful. He sat and he sat. (Seuss 1940)

This seems right. And yet the obvious distinction between good and bad mothers underlying the Horton parable is troubling. Unlike Stellaluna's loving, caring, genetic mother, the elephant-bird's genetic mother is, as her name clearly indicates, a lazy, neglectful, untrustworthy, irresponsible "other" with no legitimate claim to her offspring. After all, she abandoned her maternal responsibilities for no apparent reason other than the desire for an extended vacation, and she broke her promise to Horton that she would "be back in no time at all."[14] Horton, the gestational/social mother,

13. Mahoney suggests that frozen embryo cases are unique in this sense. Custody cases, she claims, are about who *is* a parent. However, it is part of my argument here and below to suggest that custody disputes should be treated somewhat analogously.

14. As Marlee Kline (1995) notes in her discussion of the construction of First Nation women as "bad mothers," judges (and others) blame mothers for their difficulties without seeing the roots of those difficulties in colonialist and imperialist practices. Lazy-Mayzie is here constructed in a way that makes it appear that there is no good reason for her to abandon her child. It is an interesting exercise to have children try to imaginatively flesh out the

on the other hand, is self-sacrificing to a fault, willing to give up his friends, his natural environment, his freedom, and ultimately "his" child as well.

"But it's MINE!" screamed the bird, when she heard the egg crack.
(The work was all done. Now she wanted it back.)
"It's my egg!" she sputtered. "You stole it from me!
Get off of my nest and get out of my tree!"
Poor Horton backed down
With a sad, heavy heart.
(Seuss 1940)

Indeed, like the "real" mother in the story of Solomon, it is his willingness to give up the child that proves, in part, his status as the mother.

On a surface level, the story of Horton is both funny and heartwarming. Yet, from a foster or adopted child's perspective, this tale has a disturbing underlying message. It suggests that those who grant temporary or permanent custody of their offspring do not care about them, while simultaneously raising the fearful hope that their birth mother may return for them. It also raises completely unrealistic expectations regarding their adoptive parents.[15] Am I, like Horton, willing to suppress all of my wants, desires, and abilities for my children? At what price do I become real? Frankly, sometimes, like so-called Lazy-Mayzie, I too feel I need a vacation.

In her essay, "A Different Reality," Caroline Whitbeck (1984) develops a feminist ontology that "has at its core a conception of the self-other *relation* that is significantly different from the self-other *opposition* that underlies much of so-called 'Western thought'"(51). The self-other opposition, she argues, is closely aligned with other dualistic oppositions such as culture-nature, productive-reproductive, knower-known, lover-beloved, and theory-practice. These dualisms, she suggests, are rooted in the hierarchical practices of patriarchy and the competitive practices of individualism that ignore human vulnerability and human development. They can be undone, however, by engendering practices that entail the "(mutual) realization of people," practices exemplified by the rearing and education of children.

At the core of Whitbeck's proposal for an interactive model of reality is

---

contexts that may explain Mayzie's behavior. Certainly, adopted children need to be encouraged to see their birth mother's actions *in context* in order to resist patriarchal, classist, racist, and/or colonialist thinking. This is an important site of political struggle for adoptive parents, who have a somewhat unique opportunity here to enable children to critique ideologies of motherhood. See also Marie Ashe's (1995) discussion of the construction of bad mothers. As she notes, even mothers whose behavior is clearly (and inexcusably) abusive need to have their behavior understood within the context that helps to produce such behavior.

15. As Kline (1995) says, "women are designated as caregivers and the caring is never sufficient" (Kline 1995, 152).

a "self-other relation that is assumed to be a relation between beings who are in some respects analogous" (62). In such relationships, we do not see the other as opposite, although we may be distinct and different in some respects (60). Horton's elephant-bird metaphorically captures this self-other relation in ways readily understandable by children, by depicting Horton and "his" hatchling as similar enough to mutually recognize one another despite their equally obvious differences. This mutual recognition is made possible by Horton's responsible maternal practices.

While the self-other dualism between Horton and the hatchling is transcended, however, the self-other dualism between Horton and Mayzie is not. Starkly contrasted as responsible (good) and lazy (bad) mothers, Horton and Mayzie have no basis for mutual recognition. The result is that the hatchling must choose one and only one mother, rendering the self-other relation in this story a dyadic one. As Whitbeck notes, however, the dyadic relation of self and other may undermine a truly interactive model of reality. The relation sought "is better expressed as a self-others relation, because relationships, past and present, realized and sought, are constitutive of the self, and so the actions of a person reflect the more-or-less successful attempt to respond to the whole configuration of relationships" (62).

In adoptive relationships, a complex configuration of relationships is essential to a child's developing identity. Thus maternal practices must be aimed at ensuring children acquire the "virtues necessary to engage in the key practices of mutual recognition" with a variety of others (67). However, as Whitbeck suggests, following Jean Baker Miller (1976), developing these skills in others doesn't entail self-sacrifice of those engaged in this practice (68). The erasure of self is as destructive to self-other relations as is the erasure of others. In my own case, this means that I would be ill-advised to be as self-sacrificing as Horton. Instead, I must engage in maternal practices that enable my daughter to see both of her mothers—in addition to a variety of others—as real, even when we don't live up to the socially constructed ideal of "good" mothers.

BECOMING REAL: TO LOVE AND BE LOVED

"Mom, when I said I hated you earlier, I didn't really mean it. Sometimes words just come out of my mouth before my brain thinks." This is comforting. I am glad to hear she doesn't hate me; I am also glad for her developing ability to engage in candid self-observation. I reassure her that I know she doesn't mean such things, at the same time gently cautioning her that, just like her, I am capable of having my feelings hurt. "I don't want to hurt your feelings, Mom, but I really want to live with my real mom." Here it is again. I'm not hurt this time; the words aren't spoken in anger. Yet, it is not a straightforward statement of desire, either. It is a test and I'm not sure how to respond, because I'm not sure precisely what the question is. Would I give her up? (No.) Would I let her

go visit her birth mom for a weekend or a few weeks? (Yes, but this is not solely my deci-
sion.) Will I allow her to love her birth mom without retracting my own love for her?
(Yes.)

 I decide to choose the last question, as it is the easiest to answer. "I know that you miss
your birth mom and you would like to spend more time with her. That's OK. I know you
love me too." "I do love you, but you're not my real mom," she explains. I try a different
angle. "Am I fictional?" I inquire playfully. She giggles. So do I. And on this evening,
she initiates the bear hug.

In the classic children's story *The Velveteen Rabbit,* a young boy loves a
stuffed bunny into being real. The bunny, who loves the boy very much,
nonetheless yearns to be like real rabbits. Having encountered real rabbits
on an outing with the boy and having been made to feel inadequate because of his obvious stitching and inability to hop, he inquires of his friend
the skin-horse, how he might become real. The skin-horse, the nursery stable philosopher of the story, explains:

> Real isn't how you are made. . . . It's a thing that happens to you. When a child
> loves you for a long, long time, not just to play with, but REALLY loves you,
> then you become Real. . . . It doesn't happen all at once. . . . You become. It
> takes a long time. That's why it doesn't often happen to people who break eas-
> ily or have sharp edges, or who have to be carefully kept. (Williams 1995)

On the basis of this theory, reality is a function of being seen lovingly by
another. As Marilyn Frye (1983) reminds us, love is too often equated with
servitude (73). This is not the sort of love I have in mind, nor is it the sort
of love that the boy has for the bunny. From an adult's perspective, a stuffed
toy is just an object to be put on a shelf and admired or to be exploited for
one's own enjoyment until it is no longer good for either. Certainly, this is
the point of view of the boy's nanny, who throws the threadbare bunny in
a cupboard, and the boy's doctor, who demands the bunny be thrown into
the trash because it may carry scarlet fever germs. From the child's point
of view, however, the bunny is, or more accurately becomes, beloved. The
boy imagines the bunny as having its own desires and powers, as a being
capable of exploration and adventure, indeed, as a being capable of independent existence. And in perceiving the bunny as real, he makes it so.[16]

 The loving eye (Frye 1983) both recognizes and enables the other's independence, both sees the other as real and contributes to the other's reality. Such recognition is rarely immediate; it requires, as the skin-horse
suggests, considerable time and patience. Indeed, as Lugones and Spel-

16. In this story, the stuffed bunny becomes real (i.e., a live biological bunny) with the intervening help of a magic fairy. I have omitted this part of the story here, as it is the bunny's
becoming real-for-the-boy that is of interest. The boy accomplishes this without intervening
assistance.

man (1983) suggest, receiving recognition from another, especially where that other is significantly different from yourself, may require one to "be patient to the point of tears." One also needs to learn to accept criticism from the other(s) whose recognition we seek (26). This is why those who are brittle, sharp-edged, or fragile may never become real.

If we take seriously the notion that reality, in the sense of reality-for-others, is a function of being seen lovingly, it follows that a real mother is one whose child does not see her primarily with reference to his interests. A primary task for a mother who would be real-for-her-child is, thus, to nurture non-arrogating perception in her child.[17] The arrogant perceiver sees the world as revolving around him. As Frye notes, his vision organizes everything as either "for him" or "against him" (67). Accordingly, the child who sees with an arrogant eye will see a "real" mother as one who serves him and his wishes exclusively and expediently; any blood-relative or guardian who does not is cast as a non-mother or "bad" mother. The sad irony here is that a real mother, on this conception, fails to be a real person; she is merely an appendage of the perceiver who cannot imagine her as having separate interests from his own.

As Maria Lugones (1989) suggests, a child needs to learn the skills of a "world-traveler," in order to see others, including his own mother, through "loving eyes."

> As a child, I was taught to perceive arrogantly. . . . I also learned to graft my mother's substance to my own. . . . I thought that to love her was consistent with my abusing her (using, taking for granted, and demanding her services in a far reaching way that, since four other people engaged in the same grafting of her substance onto themselves, left her little of herself to herself). . . . (276–77)

> To love my mother was not possible for me while I retained a sense that it was fine for me and others to see her arrogantly. Loving my mother also required that I see with her eyes, that I go into my mother's world, that I see both of us as we are constructed in her world, that I witness her own sense of herself from within her world. (280)

Traveling, as an adult, with her mother to her mother's "world," Lugones finally sees her mother as "a creative being" (290). Thus seeing her, Lugones is able to identify with her, to see her in Whitbeck's terms as an "anal-

---

17. This form of motherwork doesn't replace the form of maternal work that Ruddick (1989) refers to as "preservative love" (the maternal work necessary to preserve a child's physical survival), as exemplified by the birds, bats, and elephants of children's stories who incubate eggs, gather worms, insects, and fruit, and worry about their children hanging upside down. It is better depicted as a form of what Ruddick terms nurturance and/or training, although she does not directly address this form of motherwork in her discussions of such.

ogous being," thus overcoming the self-other divide that previously separated them.

Lugones suggests that world-traveling must be a mutual activity in order for both self and other to become real. Distinguishing her notion of loving perception from Frye's notion that loving requires seeing the other as an independent being, Lugones claims that she and her mother cannot love one another in this independence:

> We are fully dependent on each other for the possibility of being understood and without this understanding, we are not intelligible, we do not make sense, we are not solid, visible, integrated; we are lacking. So traveling to each other's "worlds" would enable us to *be* through *loving* each other. (280)

I am skeptical that the mutuality demanded by Lugones and by Whitbeck is always possible, although it certainly is desirable. Thus, I think that we need to countenance the possibility that in daughter-mother (or daughter-mothers) relationships, as in any self-other (or self-others) relationships, loving may not occur in all directions. You may be more willing or able to travel to my world than I am willing or able to travel to yours (or vice versa). When this happens, as I think it frequently does,[18] you know and love me better than I know and love you. Thus, I become more real (or become real more rapidly and/or fully), in the context of this particular relationship, than do you.[19] In extreme cases of asymmetrical loving, I may be real, while you are not real at all.[20]

There is a ring of paradox to this claim. Ordinarily, we speak of someone as a "real friend" for example, when we feel they know us and love us well. On the account I am suggesting, someone may possess these epistemic and moral virtues while failing to be a real friend; their reality does

18. Consider the relationship of parents to an autistic child or of adult children to a parent stricken with Alzheimer's. Consider also the relationships of friends and lovers to those who are alcoholic, drug-addicted, or just plain abusive. These and other asymmetrical loving relationships are not uncommon.

19. As Lugones notes, "knowing can be done in greater or less depth, as can the loving" (Lugones 1989, 284). If reality is a function of being seen lovingly, then reality too admits of degrees.

20. Our reality here is always within a given context. Someone may be very real, as so-and-so's friend, or mother, or lover, yet fail to be real within another relational context (e.g., as a secretary to a CEO). There is no such thing on this account as unsituated reality. To say that reality is situated is not, however, to say that it is merely a matter of perspective. Within a given relational context, we can say truly or falsely of people that they are (more or less) real.

I agree with Haslanger (1996) that "a change in my thinking, *by itself,* cannot make my body, my friends, or my neighborhood go out of existence, nor thankfully can a change in anyone else's" (Haslanger 1996, 85). However, my thinking (or failures to think) in conjunction with the actions (or omissions) intimately linked with such thinking, can bring (or fail to bring) someone or something into existence insofar as that being is defined in terms of its relation to me. "Mother" and "daughter" are examples of such relationally defined entities that depend on the embodied thinking of the participants to such a relation.

not depend on their own actions so much as it depends on ours. Thus, if we fail to possess the virtues necessary for mutual recognition to occur, they cannot become real. To reduce this air of paradox, however, we need to note that when we speak of someone as a "real friend," what we ordinarily mean is that they are a *good* friend; they do the sorts of things that we expect of friends. If, however, I do not reciprocate—I fail to travel to your "world," by listening to your stories, visiting your home, meeting your family and friends, discovering your hopes and fears and dreams, and responding to your needs as appropriate—then, as Lugones suggests, I am alone in your presence (289). You are not real at all. Like the woman who remains in an abusive relationship, your acts of self-sacrifice, while marked as virtuous within the phallocratic moral scheme, result in a literal sacrifice of the (your) self.

This asymmetry of loving is common in mother-child relationships and is one reason that some feminists have rejected motherhood as both an institution and a practice.[21] Certainly, in mother-infant relations, caregiving is largely non-reciprocal, because abilities to know and to love and to act based on this knowing and loving are radically unequal.[22] Even with older (minor) children, non-mutuality may occur as children may know considerably less about our (work, social, and emotional) "worlds" than we do about theirs. This is because a mother's worlds, of necessity (even if she is not a particularly virtuous mother), include much of her children's world(s) in ways that the children's world(s) do not encompass their mother's.[23] In some cases, of course, the child's world and the mother's world are virtually identical—especially in cases where the mother lives in and through the child's world. But in these cases the mother is apt to be self-sacrificing. Hence, here as in other cases, mothers are less real to their children than their children are to them.

To note these reasons for asymmetry in mother-child relationships, how-

21. See, for example, J. Allen (1984). Rejections of the institution and practice of motherhood are also related, of course, to the ways in which motherwork supports and reproduces patriarchy, capitalism, racism, and other forms of oppression. I don't think this is necessary, although I admit that it is frequently the case.

22. While mother-infant relations are largely non-reciprocal relations, it is important to note that infants can and do initiate relationship and, in limited ways, attempt to know their mother. See Whitbeck (1989) regarding this point.

23. This claim assumes that a mother is also a legal guardian, i.e., that the children live with her and that she is charged with understanding and meeting at least their basic physical, emotional, and other developmental needs. Where mothers are not legal guardians (e.g., birth mothers whose children have been adopted or divorced mothers whose children live with their fathers), the situation is more complex. Even non-custodial mothers may, however, be privy to more information about their children's lives than their children are privy to about their mothers, assuming parents speak with one another about their children. Also children are less likely to self-censor themselves than (most) adults; hence even non-custodial parents will often know more about their children's emotional lives than their children know about theirs.

ever, is key to learning how to become a *real* mother to our children. As hooks (1984) notes, children of post-industrial cultures are rarely exposed to the occupational world of parents and other adults (143). Similar points apply to the non-work worlds typically inhabited by adults only. Contemporary Western parents frequently isolate ("shelter") their children from the adult worlds of politics, finances, law, culture, sex, and even spirituality. (In many churches, for example, children are ushered into nurseries or Sunday school while the adults participate in more solemn rituals; similar practices of adult-child segregation may also take place at weddings and especially funerals.) Under such circumstances, it should come as no surprise that our children may know little about us. To be real to our children, we must resist such isolationary practices.

In many cultures, parents are also reluctant to reveal their emotional lives to their children, with unfortunate results. As a mother claims in Amy Tan's novel *The Joy Luck Club:*

> For all these years, I kept my mouth closed so that selfish desires would not fall out. And because I remained quiet for so long, now my daughter does not hear me. . . . All these years, I kept my true nature hidden, running along like a small shadow so nobody could catch me. And because I moved so secretly, now my daughter does not see me. (67)

In contrast, the mother in Tan's later novel *The Kitchen God's Wife* does share her stories with her daughter. Here reciprocal caring is achieved.

These points apply to making non-custodial, as well as custodial, mothers real. On the account of maternal reality I am advancing here, my reality as a mother is not in opposition to my child's recognition of her birth mother as also real. Indeed, the motherwork necessary to develop non-arrogating perception in my (our) child provides the foundation for a child's ability to bring multiple others into reality. My (our) daughter cannot do this alone, however.[24] To know and thus love her birth mother well, her birth mother must also be revealed to her. This may occur through her birth mother's self-revelations if her birth mother is willing and able to tell her stories, share her life and dreams, and so on with our daughter. In many cases, however, as in my own, a birth mother may be reluctant to become real. The reasons for this may be several: she may feel that I do not wish her real to our daughter, she may feel that persons in her current household do not wish her real to our daughter, or she may, herself, be unready to be real to our daughter. In order to understand her reasons and

24. It is difficult to know whether to use the phrase "my daughter" or "our daughter" here. On the one hand, "my daughter" sounds possessive, which is not my intent. On the other hand, "our daughter" indicates, on the view I am advancing, that her birth mother has made her real (i.e., sees her with a loving eye), a fact about which I am uncertain.

respect them, I must also travel to her "world(s)" as best I can, even if only imaginatively. And I must teach my daughter to also become such an imaginative traveler.

In either case, a non-dyadic self-other relationship is necessary in order to bring multiple mothers into reality for our daughter. In the case of open adoptive (surrogate, foster, or other complex family) relationships, two (or more) mothers must mutually collaborate and co-operate in order to help a child adopt a metaphysics of maternity that permits that child to freely countenance multiple mothers. This requires that the mothers see their child lovingly, but also that they see one another lovingly. In cases where the possibility of open relations, and thus mutuality, is foreclosed by law or by the choice, death, or disability of one or more parents, it remains imperative that the custodial parent(s), in loving their child and recognizing the complexity of that child's identity, cast a loving eye also toward the child's birth (or other) mother, thus seeing her too as a being analogous to, albeit different from, themselves. It is only under such circumstances that a child can freely, and without fear, bring multiple mothers into being-for-herself.

SOME MATERNAL WORRIES

In this essay, I have suggested that we need, and in particular that children need, a concept of "real mother" that is more fluid and inclusive than that typically offered children in the literature that they read, while they develop this notion. Traditional (patriarchal) conceptions of mothers that reduce them to their biological capacity to procreate or, alternatively, that stereotype them as self-sacrificing caregivers, set up false oppositional dichotomies of "natural" versus "social" mothers and/or "good" versus "bad" mothers. These conceptions of mothers as found in children's literature and elsewhere have been rightly criticized by feminists as oppressive to women. Here I have tried to suggest that such notions may also be oppressive to children, leaving them without the rich array of genuine family relationships that might otherwise be available to them. I have thus advocated that we assist children in deconstructing these patriarchal notions of motherhood, as part of the process of nurturing a child's positive potential to bring multiple (m)others into being-for-herself.

A child's ability to do this—especially if that child is adopted or a member of another type of nontraditional family unit—is, I believe, an important component of a child's ability to secure her own (psychological) well-being. Nonetheless, one might worry whether the view of maternal reality I have advocated here *is* good for children.

Indeed, a primary worry about my account may be that the analysis of "real mother" I have offered is idealized and thus very difficult to achieve. Is the position I am advocating based on a moral-metaphysical framework that is alien to children? Does it therefore prioritize adult capacities in relationships over what children are normally capable of? Might my view therefore have the result, contrary to my intentions, that many children have no real mother? These are serious interrelated worries. As it is my intention here to open the possibility of a child having multiple real mothers, it would indeed be a serious flaw in my proposal if it rendered it impossible for children to have any mother at all. I do not think this is a general result of the view that I have proposed, however, for the following reasons.

First, I do not think that the position advanced here *is* alien to children *as a potential practice*. Certainly, the ability to *articulate* this view of maternal reality may require some degree of philosophical sophistication—in the same way that the ability to articulate the principles of grammar may require some degree of literary sophistication. But just as children can learn to speak grammatically without having the ability to analyze sentence structure, children can, I believe, learn to recognize and respect others without having the ability to analyze the philosophical foundations of their practice.

Certainly, young children's play indicates the early capacity for imaginative world travel that brings others into reality-for-themselves. Like the young boy who makes the velveteen rabbit real by loving it, most children's worlds are rich with companions and possibilities. Indeed, it is the adult world that instructs them that the dolls and animals they cherish "are just toys," and that the friends whom we can neither see nor hear "are just imaginary." We also teach them that animals "are just pets (or meat)" that unknown others "are just strangers," and that people who can't distinguish between fantasy and reality "are just crazy." Once they have internalized *our* truths about reality, we then criticize them for their self-centeredness, wondering why they insist on believing that the whole world should bend to their wishes. Often, it is we, however, who have diminished their world by teaching them to see with an arrogant eye.

As this suggests, the difficulty in achieving the metaphysical/moral maturity required for bringing others into being-for-ourselves may be a result of a particular sort of social acculturation prevalent in, although not exclusive to, the post-industrial, Western world. Given this social conditioning, it is true that many children may fail to reach the level of epistemic and moral maturity I prescribe here. As I have earlier suggested, our children are often kept isolated from both the joys and struggles of the adult worlds of work, politics, and spirituality. We also isolate them frequently from our intellectual and emotional worlds. This makes it difficult for our children to travel to our world(s). In this sense, the position I advocate here is, indeed, difficult for children to achieve. This should not, however, be interpreted as an incapacity unique to children *as children*. To present barriers to children's epistemic and moral development and then conclude, having examined children under such non-optimal conditions, that they are incapable of such development is to undermine children's agency formation in ways similar to the ways in which women's epistemic and moral agency has been historically undermined (cf. Frye 1983, 46–47). As Hughes (1996) notes, and we would do well here to remember, philosophers have often denied autonomy to women on the same grounds it has been denied to children: lack of rationality, capriciousness, and vulnerability (Hughes 1996, 16).

This is not to imply that the experiences and abilities of women and children are homogeneous. To be sure, some degree of cognitive and emotional development, and linked to this, some degree of neurophysiological development, may be necessary to achieving the position I here advocate. Thus, it is true that infants, children with delayed cognitive development, and children with particular types of chronic neurological, perceptual, or emotional impairment may not have (and in some cases may never have) real mothers in the sense I have explored in this essay. However, this regrettable fact is a function of their adverse circumstance and not of my theory. And the fact that we find this regrettable indicates that we do indeed hold that the ability to recognize (m)others in ways that make them real is an ability conducive to one's own psychological well-being.

Finally, while I acknowledge that some children, such as those described above, lack the epistemic and moral potential necessary to create mothers real-for-themselves, my view does not entail that they thereby lack mothers of any sort. Such children may have (and in an ideal world, all would have) one or more women (or men) in their lives who love them and care for them. And these adults may be considered parents by the persons and institutions (e.g., other family members, neighbors, friends, teachers, and courts of law) that confer reality, in alternative senses, on them. As I indicated at the outset, my project here is not to define what it means to be a mother politically, morally, legally, or socially. It is rather the more limited project of understanding and nurturing a child's capacity to bring her mother into reality.

I conclude, then, by answering the questions with which I began this essay: What is a real mother? A real mother can be defined many ways. However, a real mother-for-a-child is someone whose child has acquired the skills of loving perception and thus who can see her as real, even when that mother does not "fit" the notion of "good mother" as this is defined by the phallocratic conceptual scheme. Am I one? Yes and no; I am in the process of becoming. To claim this is not to set up an unattainable ideal that I may never reach. It is simply to note that becoming a real mother, in the sense that I have been investigating here, is an existential process, not an essential state that can be defined by some set of necessary and sufficient conditions.[25] How do I defend my status as real without implying that my daughter's birth mother is unreal or less real than I? I don't (any longer) defend my status, but instead attempt to develop for my child and myself a network of real relationships in which she can be beloved and learn to love in return. Because I love her, I want her to have all the mothers she needs and this requires that she develop the epistemic and moral virtues necessary to bring us into being.

25. In this sense, becoming a real mother is a process akin to the development of self, as discussed by Ferguson (1989).

CHAPTER NINE

Accidents and Contingencies of Love

SONGSUK HAHN

with Response by Harry Frankfurt

In "Autonomy, Necessity, and Love," Harry Frankfurt raises love to the status of being necessary and unconditional (Frankfurt 1999, 129–41). There is a great deal of idealization in his position, which is not readily apparent because he typically draws on more or less standard cases; his favorite paradigm being the love of one's children. But it is important that an account of love cover cases falling outside the norm, otherwise, we may miss the extent to which certain well-scripted feelings and normalizing beliefs in the more standard cases are masking the complexities, instabilities, and darker variations of love.

If love is based, in part, on certain expectations and social roles, then cases of adoption, in particular, would seem to present a realistic challenge to Frankfurt's idealizations. Since expected behaviors appropriate to adoption are not as clearly defined as they are for kin-families, different social expectations would seem to set actual experience at odds with Frankfurt's abstract assurances about the unconditionality of love. I take it as undeniable that adoptive parents love their children with all the necessity and wholeheartedness of biological kin, notwithstanding residual differences having to do with the lack of the blood tie. And that anyone who questions this, or whether an account of love should cover such cases, does not understand what it means to be a parent.

My aim in this paper is not to refute or deny Frankfurt's concept of love, but to resituate this static concept in a concrete context in order to bring out its complex dynamism. My reconstructive critique will try to take some of the abstract purity out of his concept, by stretching its meaning over a wider field, to include nonstandard cases falling outside the norm. This

SONGSUK HAHN

will require me to take a somewhat extended detour through some concrete empirical details surrounding adoption. But I will frame these empirical details more generally within Frankfurt's larger theoretical framework about freedom and free will as it relates to love. My interest is not in the details, *per se*, but to how they alert us to a special class of destabilizing features of love, most salient in adoptive families, but equally present in their kin counterparts.

I apologize in advance if some of the intuitions that I will be drawing on seem to spring from an autobiographical orientation. Taking a frank look at adoption from within the practice is intended to deliver authentic insights from the inside, not to assume a confessional tone. The fact that Frankfurt himself was adopted at birth, and grew up during the closed adoption system, makes his intuitions about love particularly relevant to this context. Such experiences must clearly have an impact on a philosopher's views about love, even one from mainstream analytic philosophy.

VOLUNTARISM VERSUS NONREDUCTIONISM

Frankfurt's account of love can best be characterized, I think, by framing it quite generally within a debate between voluntarist and nonreductionist accounts of love.[1] Call the view voluntarism, which claims, roughly, that there can be no basis for love, where love is not accompanied by personal relationships or substantive interactions. On this view, bare relations with persons, whom one has never met nor had any substantive interactions with, are ruled out as a source of love. By contrast, Frankfurt's "nonreductionism," as I'll call it, claims that love has an unreducible, unconditioned source. He writes, "The claims that are made upon us by our ideals or by our children, or by whatever we may love disinterestedly and without conditions, are as unconditional and as unyielding as those of morality and reason" (Frankfurt 1999, 136). Bare reasons, taken in abstraction from substantive interactions and relationships, are what are of significance to love. The idea that love just consists in a bare relation of loving and caring, rather than in any beneficial consequences, has respectable origins in Aristotle's conception of philia, as wishing for what is good for another person as an end in itself and for its own sake apart from

1. This general way of framing the issues, in terms of a contrast between voluntarism and nonreductionism, is influenced by Samuel Scheffler, who generates the contrast specifically in connection with moral obligations and responsibilities in "Relationships and Responsibilities" (Scheffler 1997). The further contrast that I draw upon here, between substantive and bare relationships, is made by Lionel McPherson, who builds on Scheffler's initiating discussion in "The Moral Significance of Bare Reasons," in "Special Concern and the Reach of Moral Principle" (McPherson, PhD diss., Harvard 1999). Thanks to McPherson for initially suggesting adoption as a good test case for these two accounts.

any advantages or pleasure that might result (*Nicomachean Ethics* 1166a2–5). I can't give reasons for why I love my children, Frankfurt writes, "they are important to me just because I love my children very much" (Frankfurt 1999, 140).

From the irreducible, unconditional ground of love, it follows correctly on Frankfurt's view that love is not entailed by any judgment or appreciation of the value of its object (Frankfurt 1999, 129). This thought has deep origins in Kant's thought that persons have an intrinsic dignity, rather than a conditional value, and, accordingly, our love and respect for them ought to have a basis in what they are essentially, not contingently. To be loved for yourself alone is to be loved as a special and irreplaceable object, exalted above all price, admitting of no comparisons or equivalents. Whereas, if something has a value, then it admits of comparison with other objects, implying that something weighing of equal value could be put in its place (Maclean 1994). That Frankfurt's attitude is the preferable one to take is confirmed in complaints by children, who are loved for irrelevant, extraneous reasons having to do with their dessert or merit: "I just want to be loved for myself alone," is their refrain; "I would hope you would still love me even if I became a heroin addict or a corporate lawyer!" That the opposite attitude is an undesirable attitude to take toward persons is confirmed in the chilling links between surrogate parenthood, property exchanges, and commerce.

One criticism of nonreductionism arises particularly over this idea that a bare relation of loving is what is of significance to love, regardless of the value of the love object. On issues of worth and value, so this type of criticism goes, Frankfurt remains conspicuously silent (Wolf 2001). It is an open question, on his view, whether love reliably tracks value and merit. We desire to be loved as unique persons, with distinct and individual traits of our own. Yet, by Frankfurt's own lights, one can acknowledge that a person has an intrinsic value, which ought to be desired for its own sake, yet this is no guarantee that one will actually desire that particular person (Frankfurt 1999, 158). Despite our recognizing a person's intrinsic value, that person simply may not be very likable. This would explain why we do not fall in love with everyone. Anything that can apply promiscuously to each and everyone can't reflect anything significant about one as an individual. We don't indiscriminately value everything and everyone; we don't love everyone since not everyone is equally lovable. Some people aren't even likable. This might explain how some parents can love their children, based on a bare relation of loving, but not *like* them very much, based on their value.

Frankfurt's reply to this objection is clear. He does not dismiss the value of the love object as irrelevant in all respects. While love relations may not be not based on the value of the love object, this does not mean that we don't have *reason* to value the relationship. Value is what enables love; and the enabling conditions that generate love for a person just will be relations that the person has reason to value. Certainly, Frankfurt doesn't advocate that we neglect our substantive personal relationships in order to cultivate bare feelings of love. After all, where there is a bare relationship to a loved one, there is commonly a valuable personal relationship. But the coexistence of the valuable personal relationship tends to run interference with the bare relation of loving in determining *what* you love. Value and a valuable relationship are only what make it possible to make yourself vulnerable to loving, Frankfurt insists; the enabling conditions are not *what* you love. What is of significance, rather, is the caring itself. While the value of the loved one may provide the enabling conditions that make it possible to love, insofar as that value waxes and wanes, it is not enough to hold it in the grip of the kind of necessity that Frankfurt has in mind.

Enter adoption as a test case for deciding whether love is based on a bare relation of loving or grounded in reasons referring to the value of the loved one. Prima facie, considerations about adoption would seem to support the claim that love is conditional on the value of a substantive relationship, since the reasons for adoptive parents choosing to take a custodial role, and the circumstances that give rise to caring, clearly can't be a bare biological or causal relation. But Frankfurt's claim that love is based on a bare relation need not imply that this must be a bare *biological* relation. Only a conventional bias in favor of biology would necessarily tie love to being the biological child of X, genetic similarity, or the fact that the parents originally caused the child to come into being. Frankfurt's nonreductionism is meant to be perfectly general and to cover cases of love between equals not related by blood.

Far from being refuted by the case of adoption, Frankfurt's nonreductionism has the advantage over voluntarism in being able to explain a lot of otherwise inexplicable phenomena surrounding adoption practice. For example, bare relations as a source of caring can explain how the mother, mentioned by Aristotle, whose children are separated from her and do not know her, can still love them and wish for their well-being for their own sake (*Nicomachean Ethics* 1159A27–33). Although the mother has little more in common with her children than the original moment of birth before severance, she can still love them and feel deeply invested in them. Bare relations also have the advantage of being able to explain why children adopted at birth can feel a strong essential bond to their anonymous birth parents, with whom they stand in nothing more than a bare biological relation. A newborn baby can't grieve over the loss of a substantive relationship, much less conjure up the lost parent in imagination. Yet, a bare relation of loving, which arises at the beginning of life, can explain why many adoptees devote many frustrating years to searching, in order to retrieve this bare, but vital, connection to their anonymous birth parents, whom they have never known. Whether their searches are based on an irrational belief in the importance of the biological tie is irrelevant here, since Frankfurt thinks love is non-rational.

Furthermore, Frankfurt's nonreductionism is flexible enough to cover more complex cases of separation at birth. My own intuitions about such cases split, since in my case, emotional claims and custodial rights of both birth and adoptive parents collided.[2] A bare biological relation to a father, with whom I shared no significant past, could not override competing claims made by my adoptive parents, who raised me since birth. But the fact that a certain man is my father can never have a negligible significance for me. If repeatedly destructive interactions and thwarted expectations were to lead me to abdicate all sense of obligation and responsibility toward him, certainly I could factor him out of my future deliberations and preferences. But I can't simply opt out of loving him. He has some enduring claim upon me, which has its unconditioned source not in my personal history, but in the social and historical relations into which I was born. Voluntarism can't explain the intuitively felt grip that this fundamental fact will always have on me; whereas, Frankfurt's nonreductionism provides an elegantly simple and passionately persuasive explanation of how primal human attachments, based on nothing more than a bare relation of loving, can bind in a way that seem unavoidable and necessary.

FRANKFURT'S LOVE TEST

But if love is something desirable for its own sake, not for its beneficial consequences, then it belongs to a category of goods, which is notoriously hard to describe. If the irreducible nature of love rules out all conditional goods as relevant factors to love, then this makes love wholly distinct from all other conditional goods. But how could one test Frankfurt's claim that love is unconditional, if the unconditional element coexists with other conditional elements? In this regard, we may look to the precedent that Kant set in testing for the presence of pure virtuous willing, done for its own sake, in his prime example of an unconditioned good, the good will. Kant bypasses standard cases of actions done willingly because the motive is mixed up with other attractive incentives. He directs our attention, instead, to special, even atypical, cases of willing, in which the will struggles to over-

---

2. My birth mother had grounds for contesting the legitimacy of the foreign adoption, after I had been sent abroad, since she had never been consulted. Later, in 1994, in order to guard against just such challenges, the U.S. Immigration and Naturalization Services implemented a law requiring that both parents be consulted and authorize a foreign child's being adopted into the United States.

come opposing incentives. We are asked then to test whether virtuous willing persists, in the absence of other attractive incentives.[3]

Analogously, to isolate the unconditional element in love, our strategy must be to go to atypical cases outside the mainstream: cases in which love is faced with the threat of adverse conditions, corrupting influences, and defeating conditions, which throw up temptations to transgress on one's love. We must bypass standard cases of love, in which there is no struggle or opposing incentives, since there is no way to distinguish actions done from selfless feelings from actions done from selfish inclinations. The feelings get mixed up, and it is hard to know which feeling one is feeling just by feeling it.

One proof of the unconditionality of love, then, is to see if it passes the following love test: strip away the valued personal relationship and leave over the bare relation as the sole basis for love. Then test for whether love endures, based only on recognizing the intrinsic value of loving, rather than any beneficial consequences.

This is the hypothetical love test, I believe, behind Frankfurt's hyperbolic claim: "I would love my children even if they were worthless."[4] The idea is not that he would love them *in virtue* of those aspects in which they were worthless. Rather, that if he were deprived of all attractive incentives for loving them, leaving over only a bare relation of loving, some residual love would remain, since the worth of his children was never a chilling factor in determining what he loves. A demanding love test, to be sure, but no harsher than God's test of his worthless children, the fallen sinners of his own creation. The test of Job's love (strictly speaking, "unconditional obedience") was to strip away any and all worthwhile incentives of being the beneficiary of his blessed acceptance, then to see if it would persist in the face of opposing incentives. The proof lay in the unwavering constancy of his love, in the absence of all value and the presence of extreme adversity: he was deprived of all his valuable worldly goods and his children, subjected to pests, locusts, and boils—a test so harsh that it could only be inspired by Satan. Frankfurt's love test has to be just as harsh because the stakes are just as high. What is at stake is the wish not to be deceived by the beguiling appearance of love, but to get to its authentic essence.

---

3. For a discussion of this aspect of Kant's strategy, see Wood (1999), 21–23, 35ff.

4. Although Frankfurt has never said this in print, he means it. He has said it, in one form or another, on numerous occasions in public discussions. Once, during a talk at Columbia University, Nov. 4, 1993; again at his Lovejoy Lecture at Johns Hopkins, Feb. 11, 1997; another time at "Contours of Agency: The Philosophy of Harry Frankfurt," Wake Forest University, Winston-Salem, NC, Nov. 5–6, 1999; and he said as much at an APA panel on love, with speaker David Velleman and commentator Tom Hill, Philadelphia, Dec. 1997. "One can love someone without any inherent value, someone unworthy of love." He means it.

"WE GOT THE WRONG CHILD!"

Now, moral saints from the Bible may pass Frankfurt's love test. But the test fails spectacularly in real live cases of adopters, who feel less bound by the social taboos that might inhibit biological parents from disavowing their love for their blood kin. Their oral testimonies serve to inject some tragic realism into Frankfurt's idealized picture. Listen to the way some adopters talk about their incorrigibly bad child: "We got the wrong child." This, said by parents pushed to their limits by an unhealthy, emotionally disturbed adolescent, when they had requested a healthy one. The factors that can contribute to personality mismatches are also present in blood-kin, such as learning disabilities, hyperactivity, genetically inherited alcoholism, attention-deficit disorders, inherited behavior disorders, neurophysical impairment, even undiagnosed schizophrenia. But dump into the mix additional pre-existing conditions, of which the parents were unaware at the time of adoption, such as background pathologies, early traumatic experiences, a history of psychological and physical abuse, lies about the age and health of the child, and so on, and this can add to the stress and tension of family life, pushing it to the breaking point where some parents will miserably fail the love test. One adoptive father, driven to despair by a gross personality mismatch, said, "Don't feel weird about taking [your child] back and trying somebody else." Another father, forced to disclose his true feelings as an outlet for uncontrolled rage and frustration that had been building up for years said, "The blackest part of my whole life is having that kid and everything that it's done to our family."[5]

These frank testimonies are a fair test of the limits of Frankfurt's account, because they are the result of stripping away certain normalizing, scripted attitudes and beliefs about love that introduce idealizing distortions. Stripped down to a bare relation, minus the myth of enchanted parenthood, these parents confess that loving their child unconditionally, for better or for worse, is no longer practically feasible. Their love was conditional upon attributing to the child a capacity to improve the condition of the parents' life, in that the child's continued participation in family life would largely fulfill mutual expectations through countless positive interactions and substantive experiences. In their disclaimers, these parents imply their child was an accident, an error, a mistake. They convey the wish that the adoption had never taken place; regret that they could not reverse the decision; in effect, wishing their child out of existence. But more, abdicating a commitment to love in a way that is not possible if love exercises a binding, unconditional authority.

5. Some of these oral testimonies are from "The Genetic Influence" in *Adoption Crisis: The Truth behind Adoption and Foster Care* (McKelvey and Stevens 1994, 139).

These disclaimers would seem to point to a disturbing asymmetry between adoptive and biological kin. The biological and adoptive situation are not the same, and biological parents are not commonly faced, as an acceptable option to be exercised, to disown their child, which signals a total abdication of love. Kinship ties represent important cultural values, which are furthered and reinforced in kin families by cultural scripts and positive institutional supports. In kin families, returning a child to an institution, adoption agency, or foster care because of "bad fit," "disvalue," "unfitness as an object of love" is an option only to be exercised in jokes around the dinner table: "You must have been adopted to be so stupid!" "Ma, send him back. It isn't working out. He's *gotta go*!" Mock threats, like, "We would stop loving you if you became an investment banker,"[6] are harmless because of the value placed on an enduring, unbreakable commitment to kin, which is largely voluntary rather than imposed by law or social pressures, and which it would be preposterous to opt out of. Whereas, the incidence of adopted children being sent back, and the special elements of unpredictability, contingency, and loss surrounding their lives, make their fears of losing their parents' love more justifiable than the insecurities and growing pains that ordinarily all children face.[7]

This asymmetry between adoptive and biological kin is not meant to imply that there is more fragility and dissolubility in the tie to adopted children. I don't mean to stigmatize adoption or engage in recriminations against a whole group of people. Certainly these philosophical reflections aren't meant to have implications for policy or practice. Abdications are no more of a problem for adoptive families than biological families, though the lack of any psychological literature on the subject or an archive of national statistics makes it difficult to gauge the true extent of this phenomena in kin families. But we know that abdications occur in the family of the mainstream in a bewildering variety of forms: biological fathers desert and abandon their children; divorcées relinquish their custodial rights. Many fathers are geographically distant from their offspring, emotionally absent, negligent, and even unknown to their illegitimate kin.[8] Total abdication usually gets expressed in the courts in material terms, where

6. Barbara Herman's seriously funny remark to her son (from a conversation).

7. Biological children, too, fear losing their parents' love. In the normal course of growing up, they ask extraordinary questions like, "Dad, could you ever give us away?" "Could you ever let us be taken away?" But these questions take on a uniquely charged significance to the child who was once taken away or abandoned than to the child who only conjures up the stolen child fantasy in her wild imagination. The original abandonment of the child provides her with ample evidence that her fear of a repetition of that original trauma is not entirely unjustified. Although no exact figures exist, the incidence of Black children being returned to foster care is significant enough to lead some African American organizations to cite this phenomenon in their opposition to biracial adoption.

8. The *Washington Post* reported that 35 percent of children live apart from their biological fathers. "Close, but no Cigar" (*Washington Post*, June 18, 2000).

parents disinherit their children of their property rights. But in the most celebrated case of a father abdicating his biological child, Lear disinherits Cordelia in both material and emotional terms: "Here I disclaim all my paternal care,/ Propinquity and property of blood,/ And as a stranger to my heart and me/ Hold thee from this forever."[9] That acts of repudiation also occur in kin families is undeniable once this fact is remanded to our attention. That we lose track of this fact is due, in large part, to social pressures to conform our perceptions to ideology about what the ideal family should be like.

What adds to the fragility of the tie, in both adoptive and biological cases, is the fact that it is a purely accidental and contingent matter that any particular child is the focus of a parent's love. A biological mother might never have had children, Kripke observes, much less be free to decide to have this particular child. To the extent that a mother's interests in giving birth to children in the first place are personal, rather than a priori, Frankfurt adds, even the most selfless parent's love is determined by contingencies. Since love is necessary yet directed at an accidentally determined object, Frankfurt admits paradoxically, "It goes without saying that love is a contingent matter" (Frankfurt 1999). The accidents and contingencies of love are probably more of a problem for adoptive families, since children adopted as a result of parents pursuing their personal interests are even more a product of forces alien and external to themselves.[10] The strains and tensions, which adoptive families have in common with their mainstream counterparts, are further exacerbated by the lack of social conventions and institutional supports that serve to minimize the accidents and abdications within kin families. But insofar as love, in either case, is directed at a contingently determined object, abdications show that it can be directed at the "wrong" object.

The common thread linking these living testimonies, adoptive and kin, is that love does not have a stable enough structure to withstand the pressure of Frankfurt's love test. In the abdications we have considered so far, what parents believe when they love unconditionally should not be at too far a distance from what they *say*. Parents who abdicate ownership, or sign a baby away, may *say* they still love their child unconditionally; and they very well may in their hearts. But while such declarations are admirable and safe enough to make in the abstract, there is a sense that unconditional love is not just a feeling, but a commitment to love that issues in action.

9. *King Lear* (1970), 1.1.113–16.
10. It is not uncommon for adopters to have to make a snap decision, based only on a grainy, passport-sized photo of a child from overseas. The basis for picking a child from a cast of hundreds in an orphanage is not unlike the basis for picking a kitten in a pet store: "I chose him because he was the lively, healthy one, who seemed especially responsive to me!" (What if he had been listless and sluggish that day?)

What parents say should be further implied in what they *do*. But their acts of repudiation, verbal and behavioral, are in conflict with Frankfurt's high-minded assurances about the unconditionality of love. What they say is in contradiction with what is implied in what they do. For the very act of disowning a child, or premeditating the absence of a concrete future relationship in which one will benefit that child, seriously calls into question whether the imperatives deriving from that love carry unconditional authority. A relation of caring, Aristotle said, is inseparable from a concrete and effective desire to benefit the beloved. We call a love that is severed from urges to benefit the child in a serious and effective way "hypocrisy." Children of divorce intuitively hear the hypocrisy in their father's assurances of love, as he packs his things and moves out of their life. If you can relinquish your child, or even find yourself seriously contemplating doing so, as heart-wrenching as this may be, then there is a sense in which the authority of your love is not unconditionally binding.

Frankfurt's reply to this criticism is clear. Whether or not love persists through various fluctuations in fortune is irrelevant to his account. He himself concedes that love may fade over the course of time, disappear, or reappear (Frankfurt 1999, 136). He insists that his account aims only to give an analysis of the unconditional, a priori ground of love, which, by itself, is not meant to carry with it any empirical predictions or practical guarantees about whether that love will last. In his theory, he claims, the issue of ground is independent from the issue of limits.

But the issues of ground and limit are difficult to hold apart in practice. If love has an a priori ground, then this is something it has in common with Kant's pure will. In this connection, it is significant that what the pure will wills is determined entirely a priori and, as such, ought to be immune to the empirical fluctuations and contingencies of fortune. The parallel thought is that if love springs from an unconditioned source, then similarly it must have built into it something to guard against the corrupting influences, defeating conditions, and contrary incentives that throw up temptations to betray one's love. There are signs in Frankfurt's own theory that the two issues can't be held apart. What makes love worth having, on his view, beyond abstract, formal considerations about a priori grounds, is that love is less like a blind impulse or fleeting feeling, and has more to do with more or less stable motivational structures that derive from the essential character of one's will (Frankfurt 1999, 132, 135, 137). Since love is part of one's stable, volitional nature, hence, one's very identity as a person, if one were to transgress on that love, one would be manifesting a disrespect for what one is essentially as a person.

There is something disturbing about the thought that while your father loves you now, this is subject to change later, so far as you are grown tiresome, old, and useless (and vice versa). The significance of his love would be diminished by the thought that it is subject to the fickleness of the human heart. The characteristics of irreducibility, irreplaceability, and particularity don't have any value in connection with love by themselves as abstract, theoretical ideals, but only if they are connected meaningfully to things that we value in ordinary practice, such as continuity, persistence, and bindingness. Thus, if Frankfurt's concept of love can't capture some of the continuity, bindingness, and persistence that we ordinarily think should attach to genuine love, then we would have to wonder why this kind of love would be worth wanting in the first place. The idea that love derives its significance from its durability and dependability is something so deeply embedded in our ordinary concept of unconditional love that giving up on it would mean giving up the concept altogether.

Once we face the facts to which repudiations call our attention, we must agree that they point to richer, darker, more complex determinations that are relevant to our understanding of the concept of love. If we think that genuine love should last longer than love of the conditional, fickle variety, even in the presence of defeating incentives that detract from the loved one's value, then abdications call for a restructuring of our very concept of love.

Notice that abdications do not call for a wholesale rejection of Frankfurt's concept. Certainly, his notion of disinterested, selfless love is not refuted in cases of abdication that imply selfless conduct that is designed to benefit the child. The teenage birth mother, for instance, who surrenders her child, not entirely for her own self-interest, continues to love the child in her heart, as shown by her grief reaction and the severity of depression following relinquishment. Nor is Frankfurt refuted even by selfish abdications, which are not like falling out of love, negligently, or akratically failing to love. Repudiating a child can't ensure that a father's love for the child is then conveniently extinguished. In such cases, one senses a profound sadness and regret in the parent; a sense of having profoundly failed the child and oneself; regrets about how life could have been, and will be, without the child. One can never wholly escape the influence or significance of that love, by simply speaking the child out of existence. Lear, for instance, may try to opt out of loving Cordelia, as if she had never been born. In a moment of blind hurt and rage, he may disavow his commitment to love her. He may foolishly prefer the articulate appearance of love over its silent essence. But no matter how deeply hurtful, incorrigibly bad, and even incomprehensible one's children are to one, Frankfurt is right in insisting that at the deepest levels we can't help loving what we love.

My revision, rather, is meant to preserve his insight, while restructuring Frankfurt's classically simple concept in a way that will bring out these richer determinations without being reducible to his initial meaning. Once we distinguish the emotion of unconditional love itself from those that attend the behavior of abdication, we are set to see that the emotions that go with abdication are juxtaposed and in conflict with those of unconditional love. In disowning a child emotionally and materially, the father actively dissociates himself from any future desire to benefit the child or be moved by appeals to love. But while he can sever or repudiate such ties, he can never escape their influence or deprive those ties of all significance.[11] Just as he can choose not to act on what he has a desire to do if he has a destructive addiction, compulsion, or phobia, he can fail to act on his desire to love. But as with almost irresistible urges and addictions, this doesn't conveniently extinguish the desire. Try as he might, he can't eliminate his love from his heart. He does not now love the child less, or even to a lesser degree (even if it were possible to will himself to do so). Frankfurt is therefore right in insisting that unconditional love plays a vital and ineliminable role in caring and loving.

But this simple element only precedes what is complex. For the put-upon father actively chooses not to act on his desire to love, or to allow it to figure in his future deliberations and preferences. From this point on, he acts as if his child had never been born. By no longer identifying himself wholeheartedly with his first-order desire to love, his commitment to love is now irrevocably altered. Thus, his desire to love unconditionally can't be the sole determining factor here. For his desire to love unconditionally leads to loving and almost irresistible urges to benefit the child, even to the point of destroying himself. But the subsequent feelings that go with abdication annul his desire to love and to benefit the now dead child. Since both feelings differ in directing behavior, they collide and paralyze each other, until one wins out. In real abdications, we get an intolerably unstable soup of feelings, which takes us far from Frankfurt's idealized, stable picture of love.

These abdications exhibit a pathology that is symptomatic of a more general psychological phenomenon. It is a familiar fact that we can feel conflicting desires toward one and the same object at the same time. No doubt, love has a much more complicated structure than the simple paradigm of children would suggest. The special contingencies and instabilities surrounding this paradigm are symptomatic of something inherently paradoxical and unstable about the structure of love in general. They alert us to a class of destabilizing features, which are also present in love between social equals, who can afford a disinterested, reciprocal affection for one another. We see the same witches' brew of feelings in a once-married cou-

11. To have repudiated a personal tie, Scheffler observes, is not the same as never having had it. "One is, in other words, forever the person who has rejected or repudiated those bonds; one cannot make oneself into a person who lacked them from the outset" (Scheffler 1997, 204).

ple who still love each other but who can't stand being in the same room together. The resultant unstable equilibrium of love and hate is in unrest and never settles into a stable result. This frank look at what real marriages are like, for better or for worse, should take us just as far from an idealized, romanticized picture of marriage.

The reason that abdications don't call for a wholesale rejection of Frankfurt's view is that the specific revision they call for can be made from within his own hierarchical model of desires. In his account of human psychology, there are hierarchical structures that can account for a conflict between our action-governing desires (Frankfurt 1988). At the lowest level of desire, the basis for love is non-rational and motivational. In this sense, we don't have a reason to love, thus what or whom we love is not under our voluntary control. This would have disturbing implications for freedom, if it weren't for the fact that Frankfurt thinks we can develop a higher-order desire or volition, over which we do have voluntary control. We can step back from our first-order desires, in order for our actions not to be wholly driven by our destructive impulses (e.g., compulsions, addictions, and obsessive neuroses). The distinguishing mark of a person, as opposed to a wanton, he thinks, consists precisely in this ability to resolve to step back from your involuntary first-order desires and to form the kind of action-governing desires that you want to have.

Now, my claim that unconditional love is not the exclusive factor, but only one of the relevant desires, can be recast specifically in terms of this freedom with which we may move away from our first-order desire to love to a higher-order desire not to want to love. If love were to stay at the lower level, we could never escape its gripping captivity. But the abdicating father is not just passively overwhelmed by his love. His volitional capacity to love is not a permanent or static feature of his psychology, but something discovered and achieved through long struggle. A father's biological contribution to causing his child to come into being does not always prevail, as we well know, and he must actively choose to take on the sociological role as father. He must form a higher-order desire to identify with his role as father and the supreme effort it involves. The volitional attitudes that he maintains toward his lower-level motivational tendencies are up to him. Whether he identifies himself with loving his children will depend on what kind of father he wants to want to be. At best, he wants to be the kind of man who loves his children unconditionally, but sometimes not, depending on the circumstances. Loving a child to the point where it destroys him and his family may just not be what he wants. Torn by conflict, he has this ability to step back and form a higher, second-order desire that his first-order desire to love no longer be effective in action. His desire not to want to love eventually assumes greater importance and overrides his first-order desire to love. The gripping necessity of his desire to love recedes, just as do other gripping compulsions and destructive addictions, when the needs and imperatives associated with the dominant part of his will become more insistent.

It does not over-intellectualize the business of love to say that fathers possess this psychic complexity, then, to articulate the psychological structures that make this possible. What explains the deep pull of Frankfurt's intuitions about love, I think, is that they are backed by a powerful human psychology and rigorous theoretical apparatus about free will, which can make sense of the complex psychological structures operative in everyday examples. For instance, if one can be a "wanton" with respect to one's second-order desires (Watson 1982, 108), then the deadbeat dad may not care which of his second-order desires wins out. What's disturbing and destabilizing to love is the ease with which the wanton moves away from his first-order desire to love unselfishly, to a higher-order desire not to identify with that love and the effort it costs him. Since his higher-order desires are not taken from an evaluative system subject to reasons, then whether he identifies and commits to his lower-order desire to love is subject to the vagaries of his motivational system. In order to act on his love, with constancy and predictability, the wanton dad would have to overcome his volitional incapacity to love. But we know it takes lavish effort, sometimes even forceful interventions, to make deadbeat dads do the right thing, even by their blood kin. It's not my place, of course, to moralize about whether paternal love has moral significance, which should entail moral duties and responsibilities. But what I can say from my place in the argument is that his motivational system may not be enough to enforce an alignment of his higher-order desires with selfless desires. And without an objective evaluative system, grounded stably in reasons, to enforce in the hierarchy of desires an exclusive emphasis on selfless, unconditional conduct, derelict dads are unstably related to their desires to love.

LOVE AND FREEDOM

This ability to abdicate what we love should be reassuring in the matter of love, as perverse as this may sound, because of the positive contribution it makes to our freedom. So far, I've only considered disturbing cases in which this flexibility in freely determining which desires you will act on is destabilizing to love. But this flexibility is positively reinforcing to love in successful cases. Without this freedom to move away from our first-order desires to love, to higher-order commitments, the nonreductionist would be vulnerable to the following voluntarist's objection. To the extent that our love relations are based on necessary bare relations, independent of our choices, such relations are not up to us to determine. If a mother can't help but be selflessly devoted to her child, if she can't help loving what she loves, then her experience of being held hostage to the necessary, gripping captivity of love hampers and constrains her freedom. If her love originates from an unconscious, maternal instinct, driving unerringly forward toward a blind goal, then her love is unfree and virtually compulsive. Put this together with the metaphysical fact that a parent's love-interests are determined accidentally, and this should raise our anxieties that the bare fact of caring leads to indiscriminate loving. Moreover, what makes bare relations particularly troubling to the voluntarist is that they seem to threaten our capacity for self-determination; our very capacity to determine who, in social terms, we are. If whom we love and are loved by defines in part who we are, though this is not up to us to determine, then who we are is not up to us either (Scheffler 1997, 203).

If the voluntarist's objection were true, we would have to wonder why this kind of love would be worth wanting in the first place. If the source of a mother's affection doesn't lie in her voluntary act, then she is unfree with respect to her affects. Yet, we desire a love that is elicited freely with the willing consent of a free agent. The worth of this kind of love would be further diminished by the thought that it is of an underived origin, over which she has no ultimate control. No wonder, then, as rebellious adolescents, we were already cynical about adults who assured us they would always love us no matter what. We were right to shrilly complain: "Well, if you would love me even if I were worthless, then it's not *me* you love at all. It could be me, it could be anyone. This is all about YOU! Something of *me* gets lost in this picture." Thus, to the extent that the bare love relations into which we were born, adopted, or thrown were fixed independently of our choice, the nonreductionist has to explain why such a love would be worth wanting, without doing violence to our compatibilist intuitions.

What specifically needs revision, then, to meet the voluntarist's objection, is Frankfurt's claim that love-attachments have a special status different from other first-order desires (Frankfurt 1999, 137). Frankfurt's aim is only to identify the unconditional source which gives rise to love in the first place. But the derelict dad is living proof that we can't guarantee the subsequent fixity of his commitment to that love. Since his subsequent commitment to love derives from a conditional source, not the unconditional source that gave rise to that love, there is no predicting it will remain constant and true. The nonreductionist, therefore, needs to add that we are related no differently to love than to our other first-order drives, desires, addictions, compulsions, and passions—for good or for bad. Frankfurt needs to leave us this room to freely repudiate love relations that are destructive, degrading, and demeaning to our identity.

Love can be very bad for someone. It can come in the wrong degree, at the wrong time, and be directed at the wrong object. In an obsessively neurotic love, the irresistible, compulsive force to love may be alien to the desires the neurotic prefers to be moved by. Hopeless love doesn't enhance the neurotic lover, but rather erodes her self-confidence and well-being, her very core sense of who she is. If her desire to love is frustrated, if she can't get out of it what she wants, then like an unhealthy addiction or compulsion, she can avoid frustration by ceasing to want to love. She need not surrender herself to an abasing enslavement to love, just as she need not wantonly submit to a debilitating heroin addiction. While still recognizing that, at the lowest level, her love-passions do not stem exclusively from her choices, nevertheless her volitions derive from the character of her will. Her neurotic love doesn't count as genuine love on Frankfurt's account, if she doesn't identify in a cool, reflective moment with that aspect of her will which leads her to love obsessively. Since wanting to love is a configuration of her will, she can choose to identify with it or abdicate it. With the help of therapeutic intervention, she may realize that loving is outweighed by countervailing considerations about her emotional health and well-being. By betraying a destructive love, which undermines rather than reinforces her well-being and identity as a person, she shows she is free with respect to loving and manifests a respect for herself.

The important point, for our purposes, is that this flexibility in freely determining which desires you will act on can be either destabilizing or reinforcing to love. If we have this freedom to step back from our destructive passions when love leads us astray, then the same freedom to step back from our healthier passions gives us a sense in which they are not compulsory at higher levels. In successful love, love is a gripping, compulsive force that moves us to act in ways we can actively identify with and are pleased to endorse. Although our love interests are contingently determined, and to that extent are not up to us, they still belong to the stable volitional structure of our will. If love in our social relations determines in part our social identity, and we care deeply about whether our social identity is influenced by our choices, then it is clear that we need this higher-order capacity to want to love, to freely commit to it. To the extent that we choose to want to love, and are free to decide how much worth it is to have in our life, our passions and love-attachments are not a necessary form of servitude to love, demeaning to our freedom and self-control, as the voluntarist would have it. Our volitional capacity to love is something with which we actively identify and endorse and is a positive source of identity. Once these social ties are in place, it is as difficult for us to sever them, and betray whom we love, as it is to betray who we are.

Is Love Conditional upon Sameness?

So far, I have focused on special, atypical cases of love in crisis, because the love test required that an unconditionally loving heart exhibit its distinctive nature when threatened by opposing incentives. These atypical experiences outside the norm would seem to point, in the starkest and most dramatic terms, to something inherently unstable about the experience of love in general. Hopefully, these nonstandard cases have gone some way in loosening up our intuitions about the false choice we are rigidly presented with on nonreductionist and voluntarist accounts: between the concept of love as either irreducibly unconditioned or reducible to a substantive relationship—all or nothing. Not all love possesses the critically unstable structure of love in crisis, however, and in what follows, I wish to round out this picture, by filling in some further limiting conditions and contingencies that arise in more everyday cases of successful love.

In successful adoptions involving well-adjusted adoptees (whatever that means), loving entails identification, therefore, sameness. Something loosely called "fit" and personality "matches" are factors in determining the suitability of the adopted child for affection, as much as the suitability of the adoptive parent for parenting. Caseworkers, social workers, and lawyers try to match the physical traits of the baby to the adoptive family, when possible, in the belief that physical dissimilarities, especially racial ones, can hamper identification and physical bonding. The positive value of the adopted child gets scrutinized and assessed in terms of personality "fit," where fit seems to be loosely determined as much by the value that the child brings to the family as by the prospective adopters' fitness for parenting. By contrast, judgments about the disvalue of the child are expressed in terms of problems assimilating into the new family, caused by racial and physical dissimilarities, personality and temperamental clashes, and psychological and style differences. The working assumption in many adoptive families, especially in the absence of biological and genetic sameness, is that sameness is of value in establishing a strong bond, and the child should aspire to be more "like" the adoptive parents. What binds parents to their adopted child, in many instances, whether or not they are prepared to acknowledge it, is this continued perception of sameness and identity.

One might think that in its healthier variety, love seeks out difference and diversity. But the demand for sameness and avoidance of difference is thought to play an important role in mitigating the effects of racism in different-race adoptions. A premium placed on sameness is at the basis for demands from the National Association of Black Social Workers and leaders of Native American groups, that African American and other minority children be placed in racial and cultural settings similar to their original group. Both leading groups opposed transracial adoption in the early 1970s, on the grounds that White parents, no matter how liberal and well meaning, would lack the skills, insights, and experience necessary to help Black and Indian children survive in an inherently racist society (Simon and Alstein 2000, 41). Adoptees may wish to distance themselves from their original group, for a variety reasons; but they can't forget where they come from, since discrimination will always serve as a painful reminder. Racial sameness, it was thought, could make the difference between knowing "that" your child has endured a painful experience of discrimination, and a deeper kind of empathy that springs from having been subjected to the singularly vicious experience yourself: "That's *exactly* how I felt the first time it happened to me."

Moreover, this criterion of sameness is not a fetish peculiar to the adoption literature. The desire for sameness, seen dramatically amplified in biracial and even inracial adoptions, also appears in a milder form among kin families. Sameness is a common desideratum running throughout the classical, philosophical literature on love and friendship. Plato's maxim in the *Republic,* for instance, is that "philoi have all things in common, so far as possible."[12] The themes of reciprocity and sameness appear in Aristotle, as providing a basis for love between social equals. In the perfect friendship, Aristotle said, there must be a strong similarity or fundamental sameness (in moral constitution) between friends, and this similarity or fundamental sameness must be intuitively felt by each of them.[13]

This preoccupation with sameness is especially revealed in the way some biological parents talk as if their love were conditional on their perception of biological continuity. The premium some parents place on the blood tie is salient in remarks like, "I love you; you're my flesh and blood." Or said in anger, "I love him (in spite of himself); he's my blood." Biological identity is similarly appealed to as the authoritative basis for love in the most canonical expression of an adoptive parent's love: "I love you *just like* you were my own." The same sentiment gets variously paraphrased: "I love you *as if* you were my own." "I love you *like* my own flesh and blood." "Even though you're not blood-related, I love you *just the same as if* I was your real grandmother." This time, said in anger and frustration, "What are you crying for? We've given you a wonderful home and life. We've loved you *like* our own."[14]

What is striking in this collection of metaphors and similes is the use of the make-believe devices "as if" and "just like" to create the pretense that there is an exact sameness between adopted and biological children. Use

12. *Republic* 424A, cf. 449c. cf. Vlastos (1981, 12).
13. Aristotle, *Nicomachean Ethics* 1156b7–8. On this issue, see Cooper (1980).
14. From "The Adoption Triad: Loss and Healing," in *Adoption Crisis* (McKelvey and Stevens 1994, 163, 151).

of these fictional constructions implies that love is conditional on this mythical sameness. The etymology of the word "metaphor" is telling here. The term derives from two Greek words: "meta," meaning "across," and "phora," meaning "to carry." Literally "to carry across." One must travel across a vast distance, in order to engraft upon one another two things that are, and yet are not, the same in certain respects. Thus, a transracially adopted child is "carried across" the racial, biological, genetic, and cultural gap and transplanted into a foreign family, and the graft is delicately carried out abroad with the bridging device "as if." These devices perpetuate an artifice, a kind of benign deception, a nonserious lie that is clearly not intended to fool anyone. When Madonna sings, "*Like* a Virgin," nobody is really fooled into thinking she's *really* a virgin. In transracial adoptions, no one is meant to be fooled into thinking that the two things being identified are related by blood, since this would be a biological and historical impossibility. Even when the graft takes in the immediate family, sometimes it's rejected by the extended family. Rather, the remark, "I love you *just like* my own," expresses the mother's wish that the sheer force of her unconditional and unbounded love will have the remarkable ability to transfer the child's parentage across the distance created by the biological and racial gap.

"WE THINK OF YOU AS WHITE"

The need to indulge in this suspension of disbelief, in order to ensure a thread of family continuity, is most salient in cases where parents withhold information from their children about their birth and origins.[15] Reasons for and against protecting a child from disclosure are particular to the case. Withholding this information, one could argue, lays a child's trust open to betrayal later in life by a startling revelation about the basic facts of his life, for which he was unprepared. In one of the most extreme cases of this, disclosure might devastate a child of the Lebensborn program, who thereby would learn of his ties to the Nazis' experiment in master race building and racial purification. Upon full disclosure, the shock and disbelief a Lebensborn child might experience as an adult could leave him wonder-

15. This phenomenon was especially prevalent in same-race adoptions in Korea in the 1930s. According to Kirk, parents may be motivated to conceal the truth because of a common value system in local and regional life, which define negative attitudes toward adoptive kinship, and the prejudices about it, in very similar terms. Kirk (1981), 24. The attitudes toward differences in parenthood by birth and adoption, much of them based on irrationality, social prejudice, and stigma, get echoed in the attitudes and sentiments of other people in their community. The attitudes of the larger community toward adoption are that, while acceptable in times of crisis (war, economic hardship, etc.), it is an inferior, less than desirable, even stigmatizing alternative to the "enchantment" of natural parenthood (Kirk 1981, 41).

ing what else the people involved had been doing that they were prepared to lie to him about, if all along they had lied to him about the basic facts about his birth and origins. But the matter of disclosure is complex. By contrast, a child of the Kindertransport might benefit from disclosure, as painful as that process might be, in order to help remember who put her on the transport and why.[16] Frankfurt himself, whose mother revealed to him at age 36 that he was adopted, reports having this reaction: "I wasn't shocked or disbelieving at all. The fact is, I had no trouble believing it. And I was not at all shocked; rather, I was exhilarated. I had always wanted to have a different family. Also, I never thought of my adoptive parents—then or now—as having lied to me. That way of construing the situation simply never occurred to me; and it still doesn't seem to me like an authentic characterization of it."

Whether right or wrong, disclosure is inevitable in interracial adoptions. Yet, sometimes adopters who value heredity try to mask the racial differences by assimilating the child to their racial and ethnic identity. One Anglo adoptive parent said of her half-Black half-Hispanic daughter, "My child didn't have the perfect childhood, but she is loved and she is *very much like us*" (McKelvey and Stevens 1994, 146). Read: there are differences in her racial and biological identity, but we think of her as White. This attempt at denial and self-reassurance is consistent with my own experiences of being a full-blooded Korean adopted from Seoul. I was assured many times by my adoptive mother that, "We think of you as White." She even urged my older sister, also Korean, to undergo an operation to get her eyes "fixed." The compliment implied in her assurances was that being White was the positive standard that we should aspire to because there was safety in the appearance of "passing."[17]

There is something peculiarly unstable about a love made conditional on a continued perception of sameness, in the face of salient differences. Sameness, along with other conditional factors, is ruled out as a relevant factor to love on Frankfurt's account by the irreducible nature of love. What is specifically unstable about a love made conditional upon sameness is similar to what is falsely flattering in the compliment, "We think of you as White" (also said to me by well-meaning friends). The implication was that the value of my own race, east Asian, was derivative on how closely assimilable it was to the dominant race. Certainly, passing as White wasn't a

16. "The Jewish Kindertransport from Germany to England, 1938–39," Göpfert, 47.
17. A recent study of the racial identity of adult Korean and Black adoptees is revealing. Among the Korean respondents, 60 percent of which were racially pure Korean, only 30 percent described themselves as Korean and 20 percent described themselves as White. Of the Black respondents, only 32 percent identified themselves as Black, and 68 percent described themselves as "mixed" (Black/White). From *A Comparison of the Experiences of Adult Korean and Black Transracial Adoptees* (2000), 124–25.

means to fuller acculturation into American life, growing up, as I did, in predominantly Black Detroit City. Furthermore, it implied that I could hope to achieve only a pretty good facsimile of being White, since racial physiognomy makes it impossible for me to become anything more than a secondary citizen of the primary race.[18] And if passing was an incoherent experience for a person such as myself, with a specific knowledge of her racial and ethnic identity, imagine the dissociation of living an "as if" life in an ambiguous person of mixed or unknown race.

Similarly, a child living "as if" she were born to the parents who raised her is like the incoherent experience of passing. A love made conditional on the likeness to love between blood kin implies that there is some built-in deficiency in the adopted child's own lineage and heritage. Moreover, that there is some lingering deprivation in the adoptive parent. For in "carrying across" to the adopted child the affection that a mother would feel for a biologically related child, despite the incongruities, the mother relates to the child through the felt absence of the biological child. What mother could assuage her sense of deprivation with a surrogate love, if its value were secondary to the primary biological relation, when she might have had the real thing? Similarly, the falseness of "passing" can't assuage an adoptee's sense of being deprived of all that she was entitled to as her birthright: her country, culture, native language, parents, siblings, grandparents, blood-related kin, ancestors, long lines of lineage, genetic history, genealogical history, social heritage, a common biological-social past, even her name.[19] In short—this is her essential, not adopted identity (at least in the Republic of Korea, a Confucian society, where bloodlines and family heritage are defining characteristics in establishing a person's essential identity). You can hear the same point being made in the streets of Detroit: "You can't forget where you come from."

But the fact that many adoptive parents engage in this fiction indicates a refusal to accept that a superabundance of unconditional love can't conquer the all too apparent racial, biological, and genetic differences. The mother's need to cope with her deprivation by misconstructing the past sometimes takes precedence over her sensitivity to the child's deprivation. According to the sociologist David Kirk, the greater the deprivation the adopters have suffered (e.g., multiple miscarriages, premature death of a birth child, involuntary childlessness, years of infertility, etc.) the greater

18. You hear a resignation and defeat in the testimonies of first and second generation immigrants and a clear admission by racial minorities living in this country that there are inherent and insurmountable barriers to acceptance. "No matter how fluent I am in the language, no matter how assimilated I am, no matter how long I live in this country, I will always be a second-class citizen. I'll never be fully accepted here because I don't look white" (Wu and Song 2000).

19. Minimally, the right to a name and a nationality was guaranteed in 1989 by the United Nations Convention on the Rights of Children.

the likelihood they will cope by rejecting the differences.[20] In some cases, the attempt to assimilate the child to the parent's race expresses a desire to make the replacement child take the place of the child she could not have, or had but lost. The belief that a surrogate blood tie will give her the immediate relatedness of blood helps her assuage the pains of her own deprivation, though it tends to hamper further integration of the replacement child into the family.

"WE CHOSE YOU"

The need to take the sting out of the contingency of love is more pressing in adoptive families, since adopted children are even more a product of arbitrary circumstances external to themselves. If the concept of unconditional love should be relevant and reassuring to anyone, it should be to adoptees, as an antidote to the precariousness of their fate. But matters only get worse when adoptive parents try to deflect worries about the arbitrariness of their love-interests, by telling their adopted child "We chose you" stories. These narratives try to provide a child with a unique genealogy that is meant to convert what was otherwise an arbitrary, contingent happening into a felicitous choice. Whereas birth parents had to take whatever they got, somewhere in the adopted child's interrupted genealogy, a pair of loving benefactors made a voluntary, nonarbitrary choice. "My child is *especially* lovable because . . ." and they run through a catalogue of contingent circumstances, varying somewhat in detail and credibility: he was rescued from a life of abuse by an alcoholic father; she was found abandoned in a box on a busy street in Beijing; she was saved from a life of malnutrition and misogyny in Korea; he was found floating down the Nile in a basket (Moses); he was left to die hanging upside down by his pierced ankles from a tree on a hillside (Oedipus); and so on and so forth.

But far from deflecting the threat of arbitrariness, "We chose you" narratives should rather heighten our worries about the accidents and contingencies of love. To attach value to purely contingent circumstances both dehumanizes and exalts the child with a bogus value. "I rescued you from

20. Kirk suggests that the birth mother's memory of her deprivation and sorrow may play some role in refusing to acknowledge differences. Acknowledgment of differences, he argues, has the best chance of furthering the child's integration and attachment to the adoptive family, because it facilitates greater empathy with the child's circumstances. Not to acknowledge the differences, he argues, makes the mother less equipped to empathize with the child's confusion over differences. Children adopted into families who acknowledge the differences, and deal with them openly, are more likely to fare better because acknowledging difference involves trust, risk, flexibility, and courage. Trust breeds integration and greater empathy, opens communication, and facilitates bonding. Kirk (1981), 39–40.

the gutter" stories, a variant on such narratives, dehumanize the child because they are often filled with squalid details, illicit circumstances, stains of illegitimacy, factual errors, half-truths, improbable distortions, concocted details, fudged dates, unimaginable horrors, and gaping omissions. At the same time, to overcompensate for the social stigma that adopted children are somehow inferior to biological children, these narratives exalt the child with a bogus value. Even physical defects and handicaps sometimes get converted into trophies of uniqueness and specialness. Basing a child's sense of value on purely contingent marks or circumstances distorts his sense of authentic identity and serves as a negative reminder of the pain and deprivation surrounding his origins. The "specialness" surrounding his birth and origins is on the flipside of rejection. For being "chosen" in light of a dubious specialness, over which he had no control, coincided with the original gesture of rejection.

Moreover, the genealogical "specialness" and uniqueness that the child is supposed to enjoy only gives him a sense of the vast distance he has to travel across just to be regarded as "normal," where there is no patronizing need to overcome the distance by concocting a fiction that makes him "especially special." Being special isn't a unique prerogative of adopted children. Children who grow up in stable and loving homes are made to feel special, too. Any additional need to explain the child's value in terms of contingent circumstances beyond his control points to an uneasy asymmetry between adoption and the unreflective blood attachment. In biology, love is not mediated by a cool reflective choice to attach oneself to one's child. The blood attachment is immediate and unthinking, for which any critical reflection or choice would involve "one thought too many." Giving a child a *reason* for thinking he's special involves one thought too many. Children just are special. This thought returns us to the tautologous truth in Frankfurt's remark: "I can't give reasons for why I love my children. They are important to me just because I love my children very much."

This essay was intended as both a tribute and a challenge to the deepest, most vulnerable point of Harry Frankfurt's philosophy: a tribute to his understanding of love, which rests on convictions so deep and unshakable that they could not have been taken over secondhand from shallow sources. They had to have sprung directly from the deepest, most originary source of all: an unconditionally loving heart. As well as a challenge to whether his idealized account of love, which lends itself to articulation in high-minded, socially acceptable terms, can do justice to certain elements of instability, contingency, and risk in love. The idealized elements in such high-minded accounts are traceable, I believe, to an inability to tolerate the thought that loving someone, as well as being loved by them, involves an unstable mix of contradictory feelings, which can threaten you to the very core of your being. It is fitting, therefore, to end this critical tribute with the most classic paradigm of a father who made himself vulnerable to loving, to the point where the ambivalence of that love destroyed him.

Lear's unconditional love for Cordelia was conditional upon proof of being loved back unconditionally. What starts the slide toward instability in the opening act is Lear's shameless and self-congratulatory desire for proof of Cordelia's love. What starts the dynamic movement that sets Lear and Cordelia's feelings against each other, to the point where the union of them destroys them both, is the need for a stable expression of love. Love requires a stable and continuing representation, but there are dangers and risks associated with articulating one's love in determinate terms. A willingness and ability to profess one's love in public is classically associated with the false appearance of love, not its unconditioned essence. When Lear foolishly insists on testing the articulability and comprehensibility of love, this violation sets into motion an unstoppable chain of causes, which lead, adventitiously and senselessly, to the death of the very object of his love. A desire that entails the destruction of the very object upon which the lover depends for proof of being loved back is an inherently unstable desire. For minimally, the beloved must remain alive in order to give back a continuing expression of the love upon which the lover so vitally depends. A love that is so profound that it must destroy its own object is headed precipitously on a path leading back to self-destruction.

In the end, nothing can be said of such a love, with such an impossibly unstable structure that it eludes conceptualization and articulation. We must therefore commend the father, who loves his child so, that he would sacrifice his begotten love of her for a forbidden expression of it, even one so tragically disfigured. But we must caution the father, be he Lear or Frankfurt, who professes his love for his children in such dangerously determinate terms. Love is not boastful. Love is not proud. Love keeps silent.[21]

21. I wish to thank Susan Wolf, Meredith Williams, David Kim McCreight, and the editors of this volume, Sally Haslanger and Charlotte Witt, for their help, direct and indirect, in writing this paper. Most of all, I wish to thank Harry Frankfurt, for discussing this material with me in New York over food, and for setting the bar so high for how exciting philosophy should be.

RESPONSE TO SONGSUK HAHN

Harry Frankfurt

There are a number of quite wonderful things in Songsuk Hahn's essay—insights deep, penetrating, and resonant. There is also quite a bit of criticism of my way of understanding love. Needless to say, I don't mind her arguing that I am wrong about this or that. Criticism comes with the territory. But she goes much further than merely claiming that my view of love is flawed. According to her, it is "high minded." That really hurts. Let me see what I can do to defend myself.

In my work on love, I define a set of characteristics and declare that—regardless of the extent to which my usage corresponds or fails to correspond to the ordinary—I will refer to as "love" all and only conditions that have those characteristics. The phenomenon of love that I address is not properly identifiable apart from my characterization of it. Accordingly, when I maintain that love must be necessary and unconditional, I am not suggesting that I have discovered these characteristics to belong to the essence of what people generally think of as love. Nor am I proposing a standard—high minded or crass—for evaluating instances of love or for measuring their authenticity. I am merely stipulating what I intend to talk about. This is, to be sure, rather peremptory; but it is not merely arbitrary. What justifies it, I believe, is that the set of characteristics I define is philosophically significant and that it is in fact integral to some more or less paradigmatic instances of love—in particular, the love of parents for their infants—as the term "love" is commonly employed.

Perhaps it may be true, as Hahn speculates, that my view of love—as not necessarily linked to any judgment or appreciation of the value of its object—does somehow have "deep origins in Kant's thought that persons have an intrinsic dignity, rather than a conditional value, and, accordingly our love and respect for them ought to have a basis in what they are essentially, not contingently." But be that as it may, it is certainly not my position that we ought to love people either for what they are essentially or for some value that they inherently or unconditionally possess. I do not know what my children are essentially, nor do I love them for any intrinsic value or dignity that they may be supposed to have. In fact, I don't love my children for anything else either. I just love them.

In saying that my love for my children is unconditional, I do not mean that nothing can change it. Love is a contingent state of affairs, into which or out of which we are moved by natural causes. There cannot be a love that is somehow immune to causal influence. Thus, to say that I love my children unconditionally cannot sensibly be meant to convey that my love is invulnerable to circumstance and that I will always love my children no matter what.

The assertion that love is unconditional means just that the beloved is loved for its own sake rather than for its utility or for the sake of any other of its characteristics. Asserting this says nothing whatever about the strength of the love; nor does it amount to a commitment to act in any particular way. Loving consists partly in being constrained to take the fact that the beloved has certain interests as a reason for supporting those interests. Being constrained to do that does not entail anything at all concerning how powerful or how decisive the reasons generated by love are. We love some people and other things a great deal; some we love not so much. Our reasons for supporting the interests of what we love are, correspondingly, stronger or less strong. It follows that the reasons we derive from loving some person unconditionally may not be strong enough to resist being overridden by reasons that we derive from loving someone or something else that we love more.

Loving unconditionally is not a matter, then, of loving in a way that is unnaturally outside the scope of causes. It is simply a matter of loving without reasons. Someone who loves unconditionally employs no criteria for loving and sets no conditions on his love. It is not the case that he is determined to love as he does only so long as various requirements are met.

To be sure, something may cause his love to cease or to diminish. Something may even cause him to try to free himself from the grip of love. Thus, his love may be altered under certain conditions; and under certain conditions he himself may seek to alter it. But this is another matter. The fact that love is dependent upon conditions does not mean that the lover has made it conditional.

PART III

CONSTRUCTIONS OF RACE
AND CONSTRUCTIONS OF FAMILY

CHAPTER TEN

Abuse and Neglect, Foster Drift, and the Adoption Alternative

ELIZABETH BARTHOLET

THE LEFT-RIGHT COALITION: AN UNHOLY ALLIANCE?

The Puzzle

Our society's response to child abuse and neglect is something of a puzzle, however much tradition may lie behind it. While there is evidence indicating that it would be cost-effective to support families up front to prevent problems from developing (Daro 1988, 149–98; Schorr 1997, 4, 40–47; Schorr 1998, 270–73), we wait until families have deteriorated and children have been damaged. We then pour money into investigating abuse and neglect charges, into family preservation services, and into foster and institutional care for children. We know that at this point our efforts will be largely ineffective. We know that many of these children will grow up permanently damaged by their lives at home and in institutional care, damaged in ways that will result in huge future costs to society in terms of unemployment, substance abuse, crime, and future child abuse (Bartholet 1999, 95–97). We say we care about children, and much of our child welfare law indicates that the best interest of the child is our guiding principle. Yet we wait until children have been subjected to severe forms of abuse and neglect to address their concerns, and we then make it our primary goal to keep children within the families that have mistreated them. We choose to define children victimized by abuse and neglect as "at risk of removal," when we know that removing children from their parent will often be their only salvation.

Why is that family preservation policies have had such ongoing appeal? Why have there been so few voices advocating for children's right to grow

[handwritten marginal note: What we preach is not actually what we practice]

up in loving, nurturing homes and their related right to be removed from homes that don't fit that description?

Left and Right Perspectives

Left-leaning political groups tend to see poor and minority race families and communities as their constituency. They are committed to fighting class and race injustice and see child abuse and neglect as the end product of such injustice. They tend to see the removal of children from troubled families for placement in more privileged foster or adoptive homes as one of the ultimate forms of exploitation. They also know that issues involving child abuse, child removal, and family preservation are politically potent. They can be used as rallying cries to unite and energize the politically powerless and to appeal to the politically powerful. Political passions can be roused by describing adoption as a form of child purchase or theft and by equating transracial adoption with racial genocide. Comparisons can be drawn to the days of slavery when black children were put up on the auction block for whites to buy. The threat that children will be victimized by abuse and neglect can be used to gouge money out of a reluctant political majority: those too stingy and short-sighted to invest appropriately in supportive social programs may react viscerally at the thought of a small child being tortured and untie the purse strings for programs that sound in child protection terms. Abuse and neglect can thus be the vehicle for getting some level of support for the poor, so long as family preservation reigns supreme.

Right-leaning political groups tend to be true believers in family autonomy. They want to limit government's intrusion on individual freedom, and they want to keep government expenses down. Their members don't like the idea of government interfering with their own parenting rights and are not inclined to assert responsibility for other people's children (Bernard 1992, 92, 156–59, voicing feminist concerns that conservatives support family preservation precisely because it's consonant with conservative values). On the other hand, no one likes to see children suffer abuse or neglect, and everyone knows that there are long-term social costs involved when children do. Responding to child maltreatment with family preservation services has a lot of appeal.

Individuals and groups across the spectrum who do focus on children's interests tend at the same time to share many of the above values and political concerns. They worry about dealing with child maltreatment in a way that will have a discriminatory impact on poor people and on people from racial minority groups. They believe that limiting state intervention in the family helps protect individual freedom and societal diversity in ways

224

that are important to the entire society. They also think that state intervention in too many cases may do more harm than good to the children involved, given the limited resources now devoted to CPS agencies, and the related risk that they may do little more than disrupt parenting relationships without actually improving children's situations.

Politics at Work

Our history with family preservation shows these politics at work. Time and again, left and right have agreed that the proper way to respond to perceived crises in child abuse and neglect, and in the child welfare system, is to devote increased efforts to keeping children in their families of origin or, if that is impossible, then in their extended families, or their racial or ethnic groups, or their local communities (Costin et al. 1996, 118–32); "In the family preservation approach, liberal welfare professionals found common ground with the religious right" (Costin et al. 1996, 121). The result has been to channel at least some increased funding and social services to those families, groups, and communities.

Thus in the 1970s there was an agreement across the political spectrum on the nature of the foster care crisis and on the appropriate direction for change. Foster care was seen as damaging to children, given children's needs for continuity in nurturing relationships; and it was seen as unduly expensive. It was a time of fiscal constraint, with limited funding being made available for services to families. There was broad agreement that the appropriate solution was to make more efforts to keep more children at home. Left and right support enabled passage of the 1980 Adoption Assistance Act, which provided significant federal funding for state child welfare operations, and which required that as a condition for receiving this funding states respond to child maltreatment in the first instance with social services designed to support the family, rather than by removing the child and terminating parental rights.

There was also broad political support for the proposition that if children had to be removed from their biological parents, they should be placed with kin as a first preference, and if not with kin then within their racial group and their local community. From the late 1970s on, kinship preference policies have become increasingly prevalent, with roughly one-third of all foster children in kinship care today. During the same period race-matching policies have required public agencies to place children in same-race foster and adoptive homes if at all possible, placing across racial lines only as a last resort, if at all. Foster care policies developed during this period have favored selecting foster families from the same community as the child's family of origin. Adoption policies developed that give preference to foster parents who have established a relationship with their foster child; in many communities today adoptions by foster parents account for more than half the adoptions out of the foster care system.

All these preference policies have helped channel funding and social services to impoverished families and communities during a period when general welfare and social service funding was being cut back. The children removed from families on grounds of abuse and neglect come disproportionately from the poorest families and communities in our society; they come disproportionately from racial minority groups. Accordingly, when money is devoted to family preservation services, money is channeled to these families, communities, and racial groups. When foster and adoptive stipends are paid to abused children's kin, neighbors, and racial look-alikes, these stipends are going disproportionately to the relatively poor and to racial minority members. The services and stipends may seem far from generous. But they compare well to what exists in their absence. Foster parents are paid stipends that are significantly more generous than typical welfare stipends. Adoptive parents of "special needs" or "hard-to-place" children are entitled to adoption subsidies that roughly match foster stipends; and most children adopted from the foster care system qualify for these subsidies either by reason of mental or physical disability or simply by reason of their minority race status.

The Intensive Family Preservation Services (IFPS) programs that became popular during this same period are a product of the same politics. IFPS was promoted by liberals as a way to do better by poor families and children without spending money. The idea was to work intensively for a relatively short period of time, devoting human and other resources to helping the family address its problems. IFPS was sold on the basis of a claim that it would keep children out of foster care; the reduction in foster care costs was supposed to more than pay for a few weeks of intensive services. Success was judged in the early days solely in terms of whether or not the programs succeeded in keeping children from being removed from their homes, without regard to whether they were still being abused or neglected, or any other measures of the children's well-being. This focus seems odd if IFPS is understood as a child welfare program, since the issue of well-being would obviously seem central. Also, since the primary goal of IFPS was to keep children from being removed, it seemed predictable that the very existence of the programs would be likely to reduce the number of removal decisions (Bartholet 1999, 114–21). But this focus makes total sense if IFPS is looked at as political deal-making with respect to the allocation of scarce resources for poor people's services. If the foster care savings more than paid the costs of the family preservation services, then fiscal conservatives, social-welfare oriented liberals, and family values traditionalists could unite in celebration.

In 1993 The Family Preservation and Support Services Act was pushed through by child welfare groups in cooperation with others to provide significant new funding for family preservation (Bartholet 1999, 43 and chap. 1, n. 19). One observer describes the dynamics of the ad hoc committee convened in connection with this effort by the Clinton Administration.

> The ad hoc committee was, however, decidedly less interested in specific child abuse and neglect services. Child abuse and neglect emerge from the committee's deliberations only as indicators of a need for family preservation services. . . . [F]amily preservation was firmly established as the future paradigm for serving families at risk of child abuse. (Costin et al. 1996, 129)

Similar politics are at work in connection with new proposals promoted as child welfare reforms. Liberals press for subsidized guardianship as a long-term option for children who cannot return home. This would mean transforming kinship or other foster parents into permanent guardians who would be paid the equivalent of foster stipends but would be freed from the kind of monitoring that is supposed to go with foster parenting. The selling pitch includes the obvious money savings that would result from the elimination of monitoring.

Liberals press for the transformation of much of the current child protective systems into a new "community partnership" system. The idea is to divert most of the abuse and neglect cases now dealt with by the formal state system to an informal, community-based system. Funds that have supported centralized government agencies would be freed up to support community-based agencies, and those agencies would devote their new resources to supporting families rather than treating parents as perpetrators. These kinds of new program proposals seem likely, if implemented, to significantly increase the resources for poor and minority communities in the form of family preservation services, foster, adoptive, and guardianship stipends, funding for community organizations, and employment opportunities working for these organizations. But it's not so clear that they will reduce child abuse and neglect.

With welfare reform, the appeal of this kind of political deal-making increases. The AFDC program—Aid for Families with Dependent Children —has functioned as the most significant family preservation and family support program this nation has ever had. In 1996 Congress changed it in order to move many parents off the welfare rolls. Many states had passed legislation along similar lines. As welfare stipends are reduced or cut off, the pressure increases to find other ways to channel support to the poor. It's no surprise that at child welfare conferences in recent years, talk of the impact of welfare reform has sometimes been coupled with talk of the potential support to be found in *child welfare* programs. It's no surprise that the 1997 Adoption and Safe Families Act, which received support across the political spectrum in Congress, provides new funding for family preservation, kinship care, and other traditions from our past, even as it seems to push in new directions.

Who Represents the Children?

There's no problem with political deal-making, so long as the important interests are being represented and served. But it's not clear that children's interests are being represented, or served. Once children are identified as victims of serious abuse or neglect, it is likely that their interests would be better served by a system that placed a much higher priority on moving them out of the homes in which they have been victimized and placing them promptly in permanent adoptive homes, with parents selected primarily on the basis of their ability to provide a loving and safe environment.

People talk of a children's rights movement. But the brutal truth is that children are economically and politically powerless. They are dependent on adults, and adult political groups have generally not taken up their cause. *they need even more help than others*

LESSONS FROM THE BATTERED WOMEN'S MOVEMENT

Women, in contrast, have developed the kind of political and economic strength that powers social reform. As a result they have, in the last few decades, transformed our society's understanding of the problem of violence against women and radically changed our policies for dealing with such violence.

In the not too distant past, a woman's power situation in the family had many parallels with the child's situation. Women were subject to men, as children were subject to their parents. Men who battered women were protected, as were abusive parents, first by doctrines of legal right, and later by doctrines of family autonomy and privacy. Women were only marginally more free to leave the family than were children, bound as they were by economic dependence and social convention. Societal efforts to intervene in marital affairs favored a therapeutic approach, with the goal being preservation of the marriage and family.

Starting in the 1970s, the battered women's movement set out to challenge this state of affairs. Women's advocates argued that if men were abusing their mates and making the home more like hell than haven, this should not be understood as a private family affair. They argued that society was responsible for women's dependent state and should accordingly take responsibility for their protection. They argued that criminal laws used to deter men from assaulting strangers on public streets, and to punish those who committed such assaults, should be applied to men who beat on women in the privacy of the home. Women's advocates were suspicious of social workers and therapists, and suspicious of mediation and treatment as approaches to achieving marital harmony. They worried that such soft approaches would reinforce the status quo and leave women at risk for continued victimization. They put their faith in police, prosecutors, and power. They argued that women had a right to be liberated from the men who abused them. They challenged the assumption that all marriages can and should be preserved, and argued that instead women should be empowered to escape abusive relationships. They pressed for legal and policy changes that would give women the ability to throw men out of the marital home and keep them out, and they promoted the creation of a shelter system that would give women the ability to leave the marital home safely.

need to do this same kind of thing for children

Women's advocates have successfully pushed for many policy changes in this new direction over the past couple of decades. They have gotten changes in the criminal law so that men can be held criminally responsible for marital rape. They have gotten mandatory policies in many jurisdictions, designed to force police to arrest men for assaults against their mates. They have gotten new prosecutorial policies designed to increase the likelihood that male batterers will be criminally convicted and punished. Battered women's shelters have been created so that women will have a place to go to escape abuse, where they can be kept safe from their mates and where they can be given support in constructing a new life on their own. Women's advocates have also persuaded legislatures to authorize, and courts to issue, protective orders designed to keep male abusers out of women's homes and lives. New "stalking" laws have been enacted to deter and punish men who refuse to leave women alone. Some jurisdictions have created special units which coordinate law enforcement activities with shelter and other supportive efforts in order to better protect and empower women (Buzawa and Buzawa 1996; Schneider 2000).

Research so far provides no definitive evidence that women are better off as a result of this new direction. This is not surprising, since the policies are relatively new, and social science in this area is complicated. Even when mandatory arrest policies exist they may not be enforced, and if enforced they may not be followed up by effective prosecution and punishment.[1] Indeed, for all the progress women's advocates have made, it is

---

1. Many think the evidence on mandatory arrest policies indicates that they have significant deterrent effect, while others think the case not proven. The research so far indicates that the impact depends on the socio-economic circumstances of the perpetrator: men with

clear that they have only begun to change the traditional pattern of official unresponsiveness to male battering. So there is no way yet that research
could tell us much about what the impact of systematic policies penalizing
male batterers and protecting their victims would be.

But there has been little dispute within the battered women's movement, or more generally, that these steps in the direction of punishing
male perpetrators and liberating their female victims are a move in the
right direction for women. Women's advocates don't feel they need to wait
for more definitive research, or that they can afford to. Doubts about the
strategy are voiced only at the periphery. There is dispute, for example,
about whether "no-drop" prosecution policies, which mandate the prosecution of male perpetrators whether or not their victims want to press
charges, are consistent with the new emphasis on women's empowerment.
There is doubt about the relative efficacy of certain criminal penalties, as
compared, for example, to employer sanctions for employees who batter.
But there is no doubt about the fundamental direction of the movement
(Buzawa and Buzawa 1996; Schneider 2000; Jones 1994). No one argues
that the appropriate response to wife battering is to redouble efforts to
keep the wife in the home and her marriage intact.

"Domestic violence" is the phrase commonly used to describe the problem that the battered women's movement has taken on. But the fact is that
women have not mounted a generalized challenge to violence in the
home. They have focused their efforts on violence against *women,* largely
ignoring violence and other forms of maltreatment involving *children.* The
battered women's movement tends to pay attention to children only when,
as is often the case, the man's violence is directed against both a woman
and her child, or when children witness violence against their mothers. In
these circumstances the movement has challenged men's rights to abuse
power, and to parent, while at the same time trying to protect women's
rights to parent. Thus women's advocates have argued that when families
separate or divorce, male batterers should be denied custody in favor of
their wives and their visitation rights should be limited if not extinguished;
they have argued that when children are abused by their fathers, or their
mother's boyfriends, the state should punish the actively abusive male. But
women's advocates have opposed removing children from the mother's
custody solely on the grounds of her failure to protect them against abuse,
and even in cases when the mother is directly responsible for abuse.

So while women's advocates have radically changed attitudes and policies concerning violence against women, their movement has left the

more to lose seem to be deterred, while those with less to lose—the unemployed, for example—seem less concerned with the threat of arrest. But those who see little to lose from a simple arrest would more likely be deterred if they knew that arrest would be followed by prompt
prosecution, conviction, and punishment.

world of child maltreatment relatively untouched. Here attitudes remain largely mired in the past. Parents who abuse and neglect children are treated largely as victims in need of services and treatment, not perpetrators in need of incapacitation and deterrence. Families are to be preserved, not separated. Children victimized by their parents are described as children "at risk of removal," rather than children in need of liberation. Many new child welfare programs designed to address abuse and neglect place renewed emphasis on the old values. These programs encourage social workers to focus on family strengths, as opposed to family dysfunction, and to see all parents as capable of providing good parenting so long as they are given appropriate support. While women press for criminalization of male violence against women, "Community Partnership" advocates argue that we should avoid stigmatizing parents as perpetrators by investigating them for maltreatment or listing their names on child abuse registries.

Women's reluctance to directly address child abuse and neglect is understandable. Women are the primary custodians for children in our society. This is particularly true in poor and racial minority groups, where single parenting is the norm, and where abuse and neglect rates are highest. Not surprisingly, women are disproportionately responsible, as compared to men, for child maltreatment, and are responsible for three-fourths of all fatal and very serious injuries, although men are disproportionately responsible for certain forms of physical abuse and sexual abuse.[2] Even when men commit physical acts of abuse, a woman will often be in some sense responsible, in that the child was formally in her custody and she failed to provide protection. Advancement of children's interests in being protected against abuse and neglect may easily be seen as in conflict with women's own interests as parents.

Child maltreatment and woman battering are not, of course, exact equivalents. There are differences other than power politics that might ex-

[handwritten margin note: two imp. issues at odds, the needs of one the focal point of the other]

2. A recent and important national survey of child maltreatment found that 65 percent of the maltreated children had been maltreated by a female, whereas 54 percent had been maltreated by a male. Of children who were maltreated by their birth parents, the majority (75 percent) were maltreated by their mothers and a sizable minority (46 percent) were maltreated by their fathers (some children were maltreated by both parents). Children were more often neglected by female perpetrators (87 percent by female versus 43 percent by males), and children were more often abused by males (67 percent by males versus 40 percent by females) (U.S. Department of Health and Human Services, Administration for Children and Families, Administration on Children, Youth, and Families, National Center on Child Abuse and Neglect, "Executive Summary of the Third National Incidence Study of Child Abuse and Neglect (NIS-3)" (Washington, D.C., September 1996), 13. See also U.S. Department of Health and Human Services, Administration for Children and Families, Administration on Children, Youth, and Families, National Center on Child Abuse and Neglect, "The Third National Incidence Study of Child Abuse and Neglect, Final Report (NIS-3)" (Washington, D.C., September 1996), 6–10, 6–11.

plain the differences in our social attitudes and policies. Children are *necessarily* dependent. We can't expect them to make new lives for themselves by simply separating them from their abusers and finding them shelter and employment. If the state takes them from their parents, then the state will have to figure out what to do with them.

But in the end the parallels seem more powerful than the differences. For the state to provide real help to any given battered woman, it will usually have to play a variety of supportive roles over a significant period of time. At the same time, if the state steps in to remove a child from one set of parents, it can step out again. The state doesn't have assume the parenting role on an ongoing basis, as it does when it keeps children in long-term foster or institutional care. It can instead transfer the child to a new set of adoptive parents, giving them full parenting responsibility.

Richard Gelles, Research Director of the Center for the Study of Youth Policy, at the University of Pennsylvania School of Social Work, argues that people commit unspeakable acts against weaker members of their families in large part because they can get away with it (Gelles and Strauss 1988, 20–25). They can get away with it because it happens behind closed doors, and because they suffer none of the penalties that would apply if they committed comparable acts upon nonfamily members. We need to change this reality for children just as we do for women.

POLITICS FOR THE FUTURE

The traditional left-right deal-making in child welfare matters doesn't seem to have served either side's interests very well. The left has gotten some increased resources for impoverished families and communities but they are still far too limited. Even in the face of children threatened with abusive treatment, the right is far more ready to write requirements for family support services onto paper then it is to fund them.

The right may have thought that it was managing to promote family values without having to spend much money, but it seems to have made a poor bargain. Intervention after the fact of child maltreatment is costly. Family preservation services and related treatment programs, foster care, and group homes are expensive, as are the court costs related to removing a child and monitoring the CPS system's compliance with the law during a child's life in foster care (Daro 1988, 149–98; Schorr 1997, 4, 40–47; Schorr 1998, 270–73). Direct government expenditures for child welfare amounted to about $11.2 billion in 1995, including investigations, casework services, foster care, and adoption assistance. Per capita costs of foster care placements, group homes, and residential treatment centers taken together approach $22,000 per year (Lerner et al. 1998, 7; Courtney 1998,

88, 94). Long-term costs are even more significant. Studies link child maltreatment with an increased risk of low academic achievement, drug use, teen pregnancy, juvenile delinquency, and adult criminality. The cost consequences include mental health and substance abuse treatment programs, police and court interventions, correctional facilities, public assistance programs, and lost productivity. Child abuse and neglect are problems not just for the children who suffer, but also for the society that will pay the costs of their foster and institutional care, and of their future unemployment, drug use, criminal activity, and maltreatment of the next generation.

New political understandings and alignments may be in the works. Left and right have joined forces in recent years to pass laws to promote policies that seem to place a new priority on ensuring that children grow up in loving, nurturing families. The Multiethnic Placement Act has eliminated—at least on paper—racial barriers to foster and adoptive placement. While the Adoption and Safe Families Act has some significant flaws and gaps; there's no denying that it represents a new spirit at work in Congress. Throughout the country there seems to be widespread support for making child welfare policies more truly child-centered.

Children have no voice and no vote. The challenge is to figure out how nonetheless to ensure that their interests count (Minow and Weissbourd 1993, 1 [analyzing why social movements for children generally fail]; Minow 1995, 267, 295 [left and right support for family autonomy]). Liberals should recognize that children deserve protection as much as the other powerless and exploited groups whose interests they have promoted. Conservatives should recognize that policies which do more to support families and prevent child maltreatment are more truly cost-effective than the programs of the day.

CHAPTER ELEVEN

Feminism, Race, and Adoption Policy

DOROTHY ROBERTS

Most of the children awaiting adoption in the nation's public child welfare agencies are African American. This racial disparity reflects a general inequity in the U.S. child welfare system. Black children make up two-fifths of the foster care population, although they represent less than one-fifth of the nation's children (Administration for Children and Families 2003). The color of child welfare is most apparent in big cities where there are sizeable Black and foster care populations. In Chicago, for example, almost all of children in foster care are Black (Pardo 1999, 7). The racial imbalance in New York City's foster care population is equally mind-boggling: out of 42,000 children in the system at the end of 1997, only 1300 were white (Guggenheim 2000, 1718 n. 11). Black children in New York were 10 times as likely as white children to be in state protective custody. Spend a day at any urban dependency court and you will see a starkly segregated operation. If you came with no preconceptions about the purpose of the child welfare system, you would have to conclude that it is an institution designed to monitor, regulate, and punish poor Black families.

Most commentary regarding race and adoption concerns transracial adoption—the politics and ethics of white adults adopting Black children. Too little attention has been paid to why so many Black children are available for adoption in the first place. State agencies treat child maltreatment in Black homes in an especially aggressive fashion. They are far more likely

I presented an earlier version of this essay as a lecture in the Voices of Public Intellectuals series at Radcliffe Institute for Advanced Study, Cambridge, MA, on February 11, 2002. I elaborate my arguments about race and the child welfare system in *Shattered Bonds: The Color of Child Welfare* (New York: Basic Books/Civitas 2000).

to place Black children who come to their attention in foster care instead offering their families less traumatic assistance. According to federal statistics, Black children in the child welfare system are placed in foster care at twice the rate for white children (U.S. Dept. HHS 1997). A national study of child protective services by the U.S. Department of Health and Human Services reported that "[m]inority children, and in particular African American children, are more likely to be in foster care placement than receive in-home services, even when they have the same problems and characteristics as white children" (U.S. Dept. HHS 1997, Executive Summary, 3).

Most white children who enter the system are permitted to stay with their families, avoiding the emotional damage and physical risks of foster care placement, while most Black children are taken away from theirs. Foster care is the main "service" state agencies provide to Black children brought to their attention. Once removed from their homes, Black children remain in foster care longer, are moved more often, receive fewer services, and are less likely to be either returned home or adopted than any other children (Courtney and Wong 1996; Jones 1997). Thus, the over-representation of Black children in the adoption market stems largely from the child welfare system's inferior treatment of Black families.

The new politics of child welfare threatens to increase the racial imbalance in the population of children awaiting adoption. In the last several years, federal and state policy has shifted away from preserving families toward "freeing" children in foster care for adoption by terminating parental rights. Most notably, the Adoption and Safe Families Act (ASFA), passed by Congress in 1997, implements a preference for adoption through a set of mandates and incentives to state child welfare departments. The new law establishes swifter timetables for terminating the rights of birth parents with children in foster care and offers financial incentives to states to move more children from foster care into adoptive homes. It also weakens the chances of family preservation by encouraging agencies to make concurrent efforts to place foster children with adoptive parents while trying to reunite them with their families. Thus, federal child welfare policy places foster children on a "fast track" to adoption as a strategy for curing the ills of the child welfare system, especially reducing the enormous foster care population.

Welfare reform, by throwing many families deeper into poverty, heightens the risk that some children will be removed from struggling families and placed in foster care. The rejection of public aid to poor families in favor of private solutions to poverty—low-wage work, marriage, and child support—mirror the appeal to adoption to fix the public foster care system. The overlap of ASFA and the Personal Responsibility and Work Opportunity Reconciliation Act of 1996 marked the first time in U.S. history that "states have a federal mandate to protect children from abuse and neglect but no corresponding mandate to provide basic economic support to poor families" (Courtney 1998, 100).

In addition, tougher treatment of juvenile offenders, imposed most harshly on African American youth, is increasing the numbers incarcerated in juvenile detention facilities and adult prisons. These political trends are converging to address the deprivation of poor Black children by placing them in one form of state custody or another—the innocent ones to be moved via foster care into more nurturing, adoptive homes; the guilty to be locked up in detention centers and prisons. Child welfare policy conforms to the current political climate, which embraces punitive responses to the seemingly intractable plight of America's isolated and impoverished inner cities.

Feminists should be alarmed and activated by the racial disparity in the child welfare system. Feminists should be concerned about the role of race in determining which families are subject to state interventions and, consequently, which children become available for adoption. Feminism should also direct our response to the disparity. Concern about the over-representation of Black children in foster care has generated very different solutions. Today's popular answer is to expedite termination of these children's ties to their mothers and to move them more swiftly into adoptive homes. Quite a different approach would be to devote more resources to supporting their families to reunite them more quickly with their parents or to avoid removing them from their homes—and the need for adoption—in the first place. Feminism's reinterpretation of private problems as political issues, its ambition to emancipate and improve the lives of all women, and its commitment to taking women's voices seriously—especially the voices of the most disadvantaged women—shed critical light on these thorny questions of child welfare.

Feminism and Systemic Inequities

Feminist theory has highlighted the political dimension of intimate relationships and sought to restructure them in more just and equitable ways. So we should start out by recognizing that the very interpretation of child maltreatment is a political question. Which harms to children are detected, identified as abuse or neglect, and punished is determined by inequities based on race, class, and gender. The U.S. child welfare system is and always has been designed to deal with the problems of poor families. The child welfare system hides the systemic reasons for poor families' hardships by attributing them to parental deficits and pathologies that require therapeutic remedies rather than social change. The harms caused to children by uncaring, substance-abusing, mentally unstable, absentee parents in middle-class and affluent families usually go unheeded. Those privileged children might spend years in psychotherapy, but they won't spend a day in foster care.

Newspaper headlines about grievous child beatings, usually involving a tragic death, lead many people to believe that most of the children in the system are victims of serious physical abuse. But most cases of child maltreatment stem from parental neglect. Nationwide, there are twice as many neglected children as children who are physically abused (Administration for Children and Families 2000). When child protection agencies find that children have been neglected, it usually has to do with being poor. Most neglect cases involve poor parents whose behavior was a consequence of economic desperation as much as lack of caring for their children.

Poverty itself creates dangers for children—poor nutrition, serious health problems, hazardous housing, inadequate heat and utilities, neighborhood crime. Children are often removed from poor parents when parental carelessness increases the likelihood that these hazards will result in actual harm (Pelton 1989, 146). Indigent parents do not have the resources wealthier parents have to avoid the harmful effects of their negligence. Nor can they afford to pay professionals to cover up their mistakes. Affluent parents with a drug habit, for example, can check themselves into a fancy drug treatment center and hire a nanny to care for their children. No one suggests that their children should be taken away from them and placed for adoption.

Parental conduct or home conditions that appear innocent when the parents are middle class are often considered to be neglectful when the parents are poor. Several studies have found that mandatory reporters are more like to label poor children "abused" than children from more affluent homes with similar injuries. An investigation of suspected cases of child abuse referred by Boston hospitals, for example, discovered that removal of the child from the family was associated with Medicaid eligibility and not the severity of abuse (Katz et al. 1986). A recent study of missed cases of abusive head trauma found that doctors failed to diagnose the abuse twice as often when the child was white (Jenny et al. 1999). Another study of Philadelphia hospital records reported that African American and Latino toddlers hospitalized for fractures between 1994 and 2000 were over five times more likely to be evaluated for child abuse, and over three times more likely to be reported to child protective services, than Caucasian children with comparable injuries (Lane et al. 2002).

Because Black children are disproportionately poor, we would expect a corresponding racial disparity in the child welfare caseload. The Illinois Department of Children and Family Services prepares a multi-colored map that shows the distribution of abuse and neglect cases in Chicago. Neighborhoods with the highest concentration of cases form an L-shaped pattern colored in red. There is another map of Chicago with the same color coding that shows levels of poverty across the city. The poorest neighborhoods in the city form an identical red L-shaped pattern. A third map shows the distribution of ethnic groups in Chicago. The red-colored section marking the city's segregated Black neighborhoods is virtually a perfect match (Testa 2000). In Chicago, there is a geographical overlap of child maltreatment cases, poverty, and Black families.

There is a persistent and striking gap in the economic status of Blacks and whites that shows up in unemployment, poverty, and income (Dawson 1994, 15–34). The strength of the economy in the late 1990s didn't erase the racial gap in child poverty or improve the situation of Black children at the very bottom (Terry 2000). Despite recent declines, the U.S. child poverty rate is still exceptionally high by international standards, extreme poverty is actually growing, and Black children still lag far behind. State disruption of Black families reflects this gulf between the material welfare of Black and white children in America.

But racial differences in child poverty rates don't tell the entire story. Race also influences child welfare decision making through strong and deeply embedded stereotypes about Black family dysfunction. Some caseworkers and judges view Black parents as less reformable than white parents, less willing and able to respond to treatment child protection agencies prescribe. A popular mythology promoted over centuries portrays Black women as unfit to bear and raise children (Roberts 1997, 3–21). The sexually licentious Jezebel, the family-demolishing Matriarch, the devious Welfare Queen, the depraved pregnant crack addict, accompanied by her equally monstrous crack baby—all paint a picture of a dangerous motherhood that must be regulated and punished. Unmarried Black women represent the ultimate irresponsible mother—a woman who raises her children without the supervision of a man.

This is precisely how officials explained to Florida researchers Donna Bishop and Charles Frazier why they send Black delinquents to juvenile detention while referring white delinquents to informal alternatives for the same offenses (Bishop and Frazier 1996, 407–8). Many juvenile justice authorities think that Black children come from female-headed households that are ill equipped to handle a troubled child. Because they perceive Black single mothers as incapable of providing adequate supervision of their children, they believe they are justified in placing these children under state control. "Inadequate family correlates with race and ethnicity. It makes sense to put delinquent kids from these circumstances in residential facilities," a juvenile court judge told Bishop and Frazier. "Detention decisions are decided on the basis of whether the home can control and supervise a child," explained a prosecutor. "So minorities don't go home because, unfortunately, their families are less able to control the kids." Another prosecutor's racial (and patriarchal) views were more blunt: "In black families who the dad is, is unknown, while in white families—even when divorced—dad is married or something else. The choices are limited because the black family is a multigenerational non-fathered family. You can't send the kid off to live with dad."

The racial disparity in the child welfare system also reflects a political choice to address the startling rates of Black child poverty by punishing parents instead of tackling poverty's societal roots. It is no accident that child welfare philosophy became increasingly punitive as Black children made up a greater and greater share of the caseloads. In the past several decades, the number of children receiving child welfare services has declined dramatically, while the foster care population has skyrocketed (U.S. Dept. HHS 1997). As the child welfare system began to serve fewer white children and more Black children, state and federal governments spent more money on out-of-home care and less on in-home services. This mirrors perfectly the metamorphosis of welfare once the welfare rights movement succeeded in making ADFC available to Black families in the 1960s. As welfare became increasingly associated with Black mothers, it became increasingly burdened with behavior modification rules and work requirements until the federal entitlement was abolished altogether in the 1997. Both systems responded to their growing Black clientele by reducing their services to families while intensifying their punitive functions.

The child welfare system not only reflects an inequitable social order; it also helps to maintain it. It assumes a nuclear family norm that gives women the responsibility of caregiving while denying them adequate government support and vilifying those who do not depend on husbands (Fineman 1995; Kittay 1999). Mothers who are unable to rely on a male breadwinner or their own income to raise their children must pay a high price for state support. Feminist scholars have described how this model produces a welfare state that provides stingy benefits to poor mothers that are stigmatized and encumbered by behavioral regulations (Gordon 1994; Mink 1998). Less explored by feminist scholars is the role of the public child welfare system in caregiving by poor mothers. Like welfare, the child welfare system is a significant means of public support of poor children, especially poor Black children. The child welfare system also exacts an onerous price: it requires poor mothers to relinquish custody of their children in exchange for state support needed to care for them (Roberts 2001). Involvement in the child welfare system entails intensive supervision by child protection agencies, which often includes losing legal custody of children to the state. This state intrusion is typically viewed as necessary to protect maltreated children from parental harm. But, as I discussed above, the need for this intervention is usually linked to poverty and racial injustice. It is this systemic inequality, in the welfare of children and in the state's approach to caregiving, that produces the excessive supply of adoptable children in foster care.

The overrepresentation of Black children in this population represents massive state supervision and dissolution of families. This interference with families helps to maintain the disadvantaged status of Black people in the United States. The child welfare system not only inflicts general harms disproportionately on Black families. It also inflicts a particular harm—a racial harm—on Black people as a group.

Excessive state interference in Black family life damages Black people's sense of personal and community identity. Family and community disintegration weakens Blacks' collective ability to overcome institutionalized discrimination and work toward greater political and economic strength. Family integrity is crucial to group welfare because of the role parents and other relatives play in transmitting survival skills, values, and self-esteem to the next generation. Families are a principal form of "oppositional enclaves" that are essential to democracy, to use Jane Mansbridge's term (Mansbridge 1996, 58). Placing large numbers of children in state custody—even if some are ultimately transferred to adoptive homes—interferes with the group's ability to form healthy connections among its members and to participate fully in the democratic process. The system's racial disparity also reinforces the quintessential racist stereotype: that Black people are incapable of governing themselves and need state supervision.

The impact of state disruption and supervision of families is intensified when it is concentrated in inner-city neighborhoods. In 1997, one in ten children in Central Harlem had been taken from their parents and placed in foster care (Center for an Urban Future 1998, 6). In Chicago, almost all child protection cases are clustered in two zip code areas, which are almost exclusively African American. The spatial concentration of child welfare supervision creates an environment in which state custody of children is a realistic expectation, if not the norm. Everyone in the neighborhood has either experienced state intrusion in their family or knows someone who has (Sengupta 2000). Parents are either being monitored by caseworkers or live with the fear that they may soon be investigated. Children have been traumatized by removal from their homes and placement in foster care or know that their parents are subject to the state's higher authority.

I don't think we have even started to imagine, much less measure, the extent of community damage caused by the child welfare system. Social scientists are just beginning to investigate the harm caused to Black communities by locking up the large portions of young Black men and women in the nation's prisons (Garland 2001; Mauer and Chesney-Lind 2002). They have recently focused attention, for example, on the corrosive impact high

Black incarceration rates have on Black communities' civic life. Excessive state supervision of families inflicts a similar collateral damage on Black communities.

TAKING WOMEN'S VOICES SERIOUSLY

Feminism takes the child welfare system's political impact seriously. It also takes women's voices seriously. Yet in the public debate about the ills of foster care and the cure the one voice that is noticeably absent is that of mothers involved with child protective services. Newspaper stories mistakenly call *all* of the half million children in foster care "orphans of the living"—even though most still have ties to families who care for them. In promoting his "Contract with America," the precursor to welfare reform, Republican Speaker of the House Newt Gingrich proposed opening orphanages to house the children of women who could no longer count on government aid. As *The Nation* columnist Katha Pollitt pointed out, calling children in foster care "orphans" teaches the public to view their parents "as being, in effect, dead" (Pollitt 1994).

In a more equitable system, there would be fewer children in need of adoptive homes and policies promoting their adoption would be commendable. But the current campaign to increase adoptions makes devaluation of foster children's families and the rejection of family preservation efforts its central components. Adoption is no longer presented as a remedy for a minority of unsalvageable families but as a viable option—indeed, the preferred option—for all children in foster care. Black mothers' bonds with their children, in particular, are portrayed as a barrier to adoption, and extinguishing them seen as the critical first step in the adoption process. Congressional and media discussion of ASFA linked family preservation policies to white middle-class couples' difficulties in adopting Black children in foster care. For example, a *U.S. News and World Report* article titled "Adoption Gridlock" began with the story of a white North Carolina physician and his wife who resorted to adopting two Romanian orphans after several American agencies rejected their offer to adopt a Black child (Spake 1998). This article and others implied that the emphasis on reuniting Black children with their birth families unfairly prevented white couples from adopting American children. Terminating parental rights faster and abolishing race-matching policies were linked as a strategy for increasing adoptions of Black children by white families. Supporting this strategy is the myth that the foster care problem can be solved by moving more Black children from their families into white adoptive homes.

We are left with the impression that the parents involved in the foster care system have all abandoned their children. But I have heard from mothers across the country who defy this image. Far from abandoning their children, they devote every waking moment to winning them back. Many poor Black mothers fight desperately against a wealthy and powerful bureaucracy without resources and without adequate legal representation to regain custody of their children. If they give up, it is often because they are worn down by pointless and burdensome requirements and the constant assaults on their dignity.

Take for example Jornell, the founder of Mothers Organizing Systems for Equal Services in Chicago, whose one-month-old baby was held at the hospital when she brought him there for stomach problems and was still in foster care four years later. Jornell was suspected of overmedicating her baby because she was a recovered addict who lived in public housing. Jornell not only devoted her energies to being reunited with her son, but also began organizing other mothers in Chicago who felt that state authorities had unjustly separated them from their children. "I live for this now. I have no other life, I have no other purpose," Jornell told me at one of the group's meetings. "My life is an ongoing battle to hold on to my child" (Roberts 2000, 3). Or Devon, who cared for her four nieces and nephews since they were toddlers, until they were abruptly placed in a distant foster home because her apartment didn't meet the room requirements for licensed care. "Until my last dying breath, I'll continue to fight for my children," Devon told me. "All I can do is fight to let the kids know I didn't give up on them" (Roberts 2000, 13).

Or the desperate voice mail message I received at my office from Michelle: "I got your number from a friend. She said that you're a professor and can help me. I'm not sure really if you can help me or not. I've had a lot of people say they can and it has not helped. Please give me a call— if it's at night, if it's in the morning. I need to speak to you. My children are my life and it's been a year that they have been in the system. And now they're trying to take my baby who's only five weeks old. And they don't really have a reason why except they have my other two. He has nothing to do with why I lost them. He wasn't even here. I really need somebody who can help me. Please call me."

Feminists cannot dismiss these mothers' perspective on the child welfare system. Rather these voices must play a significant part in our analysis of the systemic reasons for the racial disparity in foster care and in our proposals to eradicate it.

BATTERED WOMEN AND ADOPTION POLICY

Does my argument about a feminist analysis of child welfare policy contradict the feminist analysis of intimate abuse against women? Harvard law professor Elizabeth Bartholet argues that the demand by the battered women's movement that the state "punish male perpetrators and liberat[e] their female victims" supports a similarly coercive approach to child abuse and neglect (Bartholet 1999). An initial problem with this analogy is that there is a significant difference between the typical case of battery and the typical case of child maltreatment. As I have described, most children in foster care were removed from their homes because of neglect related to poverty. It is misleading to compare a wife batterer to a mother who leaves her children unattended or fails to feed them properly. Feminists don't advocate imprisoning husbands who fail to support their wives. I do not mean to discount the very serious harm that children can suffer as a result of parental neglect. But parental neglect that comes to the attention of child protective services is usually harder to extricate from poverty and other unequal social conditions than men's battery of their intimate partners.

More important, feminists have critiqued the political implications of both intimate violence and coercive state intervention. Feminist analysis situates private violence within a broader context of inequitable social structures, including male domination but also barriers created by poverty, racism, and anti-immigrant policies, that trap many women in violent homes. Feminists of color especially have tied domestic violence to a continuum of social violence that, in the words of scholar-activist Angela Davis, "extends from the sweatshops through the prisons, to shelters, and into bedrooms at home" (Davis 2000). We know that the state can inflict injuries on our bodies, families, and communities at least as damaging as the fists of any man. We are cautious about participating in a regime that is eager to incarcerate huge numbers of minority men, but won't allocate similar resources to programs and services that would make women less vulnerable to violence (Richie 2000).

A new wave of feminist researchers who have examined state interventions, such as mandatory arrest and no-drop policies, are now questioning the emphasis on criminal remedies for domestic violence. These aggressive measures have not only led to the arrest of a disproportionate number of low-income and minority men, but they have failed to protect low-income and minority women. One study shows that mandatory arrest in Milwaukee, while decreasing violence by employed, married, and white men, actually increased repeat violence by unemployed, unmarried, and African American men (Sherman et al. 1992, 139). The author concluded that the policy prevented thousands of acts of violence against white women at the price of many more acts of violence against African American women. Given the history of police brutality against Blacks, many Black women are reluctant to turn to law enforcement to protect them (Crenshaw 1991). Some scholars point out that the criminal justice ap-

proach can intensify state control of women (Mills 1999). Mandatory arrest policies increase the arrest of women for domestic violence, usually because they acted in self-defense. Battered women have been forced to
testify against their will. A judge held a battered woman in contempt of
court because she violated a restraining order by contacting the abuser (Simon 2002). N.Y.U. professor Linda Mills warns, "feminists should reflect
on the abusive character of the state power they have unleashed upon the
women they seek to protect" (Mills 1999, 613).

It makes no sense to split women into two camps for purposes of evaluating coercive state intervention—guilty women whose children are victims of maternal abuse versus innocent women who are victims of male
abuse. The very same women who risk losing their children to child protective services are the ones who are hurt most by a unidimensional criminal approach to domestic violence. The most clear-cut example of this
overlap is the practice of some child welfare departments of taking custody
of battered women's children on grounds that the mothers abused them
by allowing them to witness violence or by allowing them to reside in a
home where violence takes place (*Nicholson v. Scoppetta* 2001). The child
welfare system blames and punishes battered mothers for exposing their
children to violence, just as it blames and punishes mothers for other family problems that may be beyond their control. State intervention in battered women's lives often replicates the terror they suffered at the hands
of their intimate partner and may make it harder for them to take steps to
counter it.

More fundamentally, it is the public's mistrust of poor women, especially
women of color, and its unwillingness to put money directly in their hands
that underlie the emphasis on coercive state intervention to address both
violence against women and child maltreatment. A social welfare system
that improved women's economic status would enable them to discard
violent partners and to take better care of their children. Feminists
shouldn't be fighting for increased state separation of mothers and children as part of a campaign against domestic violence. We should be fighting for affordable housing and generous supports for struggling mothers
as a more effective and just strategy to reduce both battery of women and
neglect of children.

It is not my impression, however, that there is a vociferous women's
movement rallying on behalf of poor Black mothers whose children are in
state custody. If there is a contradiction at work, it isn't in women's opposition to violence against women but not to violence against children. I see
a greater contradiction in feminists' silence surrounding the massive state
disruption of women's bonds with their children. Grappling with the
racism in the child welfare system is difficult for many women, even femi-

nists. It raises in a very personal way the power differences among women. Perhaps the most important development in contemporary feminist thought is its recognition that women are different in terms of race, ethnic background, class, religion, and sexual orientation. The critique of gender essentialism in feminist theory has inspired an ongoing reconstruction of feminism that includes this diversity of women's experiences. But facing the awful history and reality of racism that helps to create differences in power and privilege is much harder. This is especially true in the realm of child welfare where a privileged group of women stands to benefit from devastating state intrusion in the lives of the least privileged women. *Let's face it: the continuing supply of adoptable children for middle-class women depends on the persistence of deplorable social conditions and requires severing the ties between the most vulnerable mothers and children* (Solinger 2001).

The scene that best illustrates this point in my mind is the playground in the Cambridge Common that I passed everyday during a fellowship at Harvard University a number of years ago (Roberts 1997, 275–76). The diverse group of adults and children playing in the park appeared at first to represent an idyllic multicultural mix that one rarely finds outside a university community. But on closer inspection I discovered a disturbing pattern. It seemed as if all the minority children had white mothers—in many cases, the result of transracial adoptions. Many of the white children, on the other hand, were tended by minority women—not their mothers, but nannies hired by their white mothers. Despite the impression of racial harmony the scene conveyed, it really showed the clear demarcation between the status of white and minority women and their claims to children. Women have been complicit in silencing the voices of poor mothers with children in foster care—voices that are inconvenient to plans to create a new family, voices that complicate a simple picture of a benevolent government saving innocent children, voices that force us to deal with our own participation in an unjust system and that demand that we work to change it.

Some well-meaning feminists may think that the best way to help the thousands of Black children in foster care is to terminate their mothers' rights and place them in "better" adoptive homes. They do not see themselves as racists who are bent on destroying Black families. They may even endorse stronger programs to provide social supports for America's struggling families. But they believe child protective services must intervene immediately to save Black children from their current crisis. Bartholet, for example, recognizes that child welfare policy has a racially imbalanced effect, but sees family preservation as more damaging to Black children. "Keeping them in their families and their kinship and racial groups when they won't get decent care in those situations may alleviate guilt," Bartholet argues, "but it isn't going to help groups who are at the bottom of the socioeconomic ladder to climb that ladder. It is simply going to victimize a new generation" (Bartholet 1999, 6).

Instead Bartholet calls for intensified state intervention into poor Black families to protect children from parental harm as well as efforts to move these children from their communities to more privileged adoptive homes. This approach appeals to whites only to pity Black mothers involved in the child welfare system but not to respect their autonomy, their claims of discrimination, or their bonds with their children. It demands an especially pernicious type of white benevolence toward Black people—a benevolence that depends on loss of Black family integrity in favor of white supervision of their children. It sets up adoption as the only realistic way to persuade whites to care for Black children: White Americans cannot be expected to endorse programs that would improve the welfare of Black children living within their own families and communities. White compassion for Black children depends on Black children "belonging" to them, to use Bartholet's term. This, it seems to me, is a particularly selfish way to approach child welfare that perpetuates rather than challenges America's racial hierarchy.

Feminism's political critique of private problems, its commitment to improving the lives of the most disadvantaged women, and its method of listening to their voices should yield a radically different response. Feminists should reject the emphasis on adoption to cure the ills of foster care and insist on fundamental change in our approach to child welfare. The racial disparity in the foster care population should cause us to reconsider the state's current response to child maltreatment. The price of present policies that rely on child removal and adoption rather than family support falls unjustly on Black families. A policy that matches an individual child's need for a home and an individual woman's desire to be a mother, while ignoring the societal inequities and injustices that brought them together, is decidedly unfeminist. Feminists should see the racial disparities in adoption as a powerful reason to radically transform the child welfare system into one that generously and non-coercively supports families.

CHAPTER TWELVE

Racial Randomization: Imagining
Nondiscrimination in Adoption

HAWLEY FOGG-DAVIS

[handwritten note: private vs. public adoption & where race fits in]

In the novel *Edgar Allan,* a white middle-class American family adopts a black boy and then returns him to the adoption agency, unable to cope with the racist pressures of their community. Edgar Allan's white adoptive brother observes, "The funny things were nothing you could get upset about, really. But every once in a while a crazy kind of look from people in a passing car, or a little extra room around our blankets at the beach. That sort of thing. I guess people were just startled by seeing the five of us playing with the one of E.A. [Edgar Allan], and behaving as though we all belonged together" (Neufeld 1969, 43).

Race-based assumptions about which persons belong together in families run deep in our social ontology. Transracial adoption (TRA) has the potential to challenge both the normative weight of same-race family structure and the flawed assumption that strong and meaningful family bonds require a genetic tie. Supporters of TRA argue that race-matching policies violate the Fourteenth Amendment rights of prospective adopters not to be subject to state-sponsored racial discrimination. Those opposed to TRA maintain that race matching is a constitutionally permissible form of group preservation. With the exception of legal scholar Richard Banks, neither side of the debate has defended the Fourteenth Amendment rights of prospective adoptive children to be chosen without state-sponsored racial bias (Banks 1998). Moral inquiry into adoption policy should be expanded to address the full range of racial discrimination in adoption.

A comprehensive application of equal-protection law in adoption would prevent prospective adopters from selecting children based on racial classification. While Banks recommends implementation of such a policy, I

247

[handwritten note: you cannot use race as a factor in public adoption, but the same is not true of private]

present "racial randomization" as a thought experiment designed to refine our moral intuitions about nondiscrimination. These moral intuitions are crucial, because they guide social workers and prospective adopters in their interpretation of adoption policies. The 1994 Multiethnic Placement Act (MEPA), as amended in 1996, prohibits federally funded adoption agencies from using the race of prospective adopters or children to delay or deny a placement decision. MEPA aims to guard against state-sponsored invidious racial discrimination, but social workers and prospective adopters should be cognizant that a child's racial ascription will affect how others treat her and thus how she views herself. A fine line divides racial awareness and racial discrimination, a division that categorical legal language cannot hold by itself. We need an additional set of moral arguments that prompt us to reflect on the personal dimensions of racial meaning that all of us bring to the public event of adoption.

The thought experiment of racial randomization aims to accomplish this goal by supplementing the legal principle of nondiscrimination with a broad-based moral principle of nondiscrimination that challenges the widespread assumption that we are morally justified in racial selectivity in family configuration. The resistance that racial randomization is likely to provoke, even as a hypothetical, exposes the tenacity of de facto racial segregation in the American family. It reveals the limits of a colorblind approach to curbing aversive racism.[1]

Despite increased numbers of interracial marriage and partnerships, most U.S. families continue to be racially homogeneous. Biologism, the idea that adoptive families should resemble biologically based families, transfers the presumption of racially exclusive family structure to the adoption world and is illustrated by the low numbers of TRA. Rita J. Simon and Rhonda Roorda estimate that 1999 adoptions involving white parents and black children may be as low as 1.2 percent of all U.S. adoptions (Simon and Roorda 2000). Race-based aversion is widespread in today's adoption system. In 1994, black children comprised an estimated 52.3 percent of all U.S. children awaiting adoption, up from 50.3 percent in 1993. White children comprised about 42.6 percent of all children awaiting adoption in 1994, down from 47.6 percent in 1993.[2] Most adopters are white (about 67 percent) (Smolowe 1995, 50). Blacks adopt at higher rates than their

1. I borrow the term "aversive racism" from Joel Kovel, who defines it as a reluctance expressed by whites about engaging in any form of intimacy with blacks. Kovel contrasts aversive racism with dominative racism, which describes a violent reaction to the perceived threat of blacks (Kovel 1970). For an overview of different kinds of racism in socio-psychological studies, see Kleinpenning and Hagendoorn (1993).

2. Adoption Exhibit 19A, Race/Ethnicity of Children Awaiting Adoption (Question 21), VCIS Survey 1990 to 1994 Qualified Reporting States Totals and National Estimates, http://www.acf.dhhs.gov/programs/cb/stats/vcis/iv19a.htm.

white counterparts, controlling for socioeconomic class, and also adopt informally at much higher rates than whites (Stack 1974). But even so, there are not enough black adopters to adopt all, or even most, of the black children in need of adoption (Bowen 1987–88, 493). White adopters generally request healthy domestic white infants (or DWIs or HWIs, as they are sometimes referred to in adoption world vernacular), and many are willing to spend large amounts of money and personal energy to achieve that goal (Fein 1998, 1). When whites discover the short supply of healthy white infants, they are more likely to adopt children of Colombian, Korean, and American Indian ancestry than to adopt African American children (Courtney 1997, 757). As one researcher points out, "The lack of demand for African American children is demonstrated by the fact that 'there is no independent market for black babies'" (Kossoudji 1989, cited in Courtney 1997, 757).

The scant attention given to the race-based decisions of prospective adopters is connected to strong cultural attachments concerning the idea of privacy—attachments that are grounded in judicial constructions of the U.S. Constitution. This cultural attachment does not mean, however, that familial privacy has been consistently applied in practice. Antimiscegenation laws were constitutional until 1967 (*Loving v. Virginia*, 388 U.S. 1, 1967). And up until 2003, antisodomy laws that selectively targeted gays and lesbians were constitutionally protected (*Lawrence and Garner v. Texas*, 539 U.S. 558, 2003). Moreover, in most states the legal institution of marriage continues to be closed to any relationship other than one between one man and one woman. Adoption is a legal and social practice that involves both state-sponsored public decision-making and the privacy of familial association. As a matter of family law, adoption falls within the police powers of individual states. In order to formalize or legalize an adoption, a court must transfer parental rights from the original parents to the adopters, administer changes to the adopted child's birth certificate, and legalize any name changes. This state involvement is limited to the placement process, during which the state is entrusted to promote the best interests of individual children in need of permanent homes.

But adoption is more than just the moment of legal placement. Placement decisions initiate a long-term and intimate association of family life—an association we typically regard as private. The necessary involvement of the state in the construction of adoptive families attenuates, but does not destroy, the constitutionally sanctioned privacy we expect in the formation of families. None of this is to say that adoptive families are not "real families" or that once placement has occurred these families do not deserve the same privacy rights accorded to other families. Rather, the case study of TRA shows that private race-based preferences and race-based social aversion are interlocked.

RACIAL RANDOMIZATION

Adoption is a unique social institution. Unlike traditional biological reproduction, adoption requires that government coordinate the interests of three parties: the original parent(s), the child, and the adopters. Hence the catch-phrase "adoptive triangle" or "adoption triad." This state involvement is a form of state action and is therefore arguably subject to the Fourteenth Amendment's ban on state-sponsored racial discrimination. Richard Banks calls the racial classification of children by adoption agencies "facilitative accommodation":

> When engaged in by public agencies, facilitative accommodation, like race matching is an instance of race-based state action. In both cases, adoption agencies racially classify children. Through race matching, the state mandates the placement of children with parents on the basis of race. Through facilitative accommodation, the state's racial classification promotes the race-based decision-making of prospective adoptive parents by framing the choice of a child in terms of race, encouraging parents to consider children based on the ascribed characteristic of race rather than individually. In both cases, a court, in finalizing the adoption, validates the actions of the adoption agency. (Banks 1998, 881)

The invidious consequence of facilitative accommodation is that "most black children in need of adoption are categorically denied, on the basis of their race, the opportunity to be considered individually for adoption by the majority of prospective adoptive parents" (Banks 1998, 881). In Banks's view, public adoption agencies should stop classifying children based on race to safeguard the equal-protection rights of children in need of adoption. He calls this policy proposal "strict nonaccommodation."

Although our arguments share a constitutional basis, Banks and I differ quite dramatically in the scope of our application. Strict nonaccommodation is an actual policy proposal, whereas racial randomization is a thought experiment designed to motivate adoption practitioners and prospective adopters to question their own racial biases and expectations about what a proper family looks like. Banks wants to implement strict nonaccommodation within the current adoption system, whereas racial randomization imagines a new adoption system with the purpose of attitudinal reform. He would exempt black prospective adopters from strict nonaccommodation. In contrast, the hypothetical of racial randomization applies to all would-be adopters.

Imagine an adoption system consisting solely of centralized public adoption agencies within individual states. This system is the only option available to those who wish to become adoptive parents. In this adoption system, applicants must undergo a screening process during which each is informed of the agency's policy of discounting race as a permissible preference in being matched with a child who needs a home. If an applicant agrees to this policy, he or she continues the screening process for a minimum level of parental fitness. If all goes well, then he or she is approved to become an adoptive parent. In the randomization process, some white applicants will be matched with black children, and some black applicants will be matched with white children, while some from both groups will end up adopting children of the same racial classification as their own.[3] Whites are statistically likely to be matched with a black child through a system of racial randomization. And it is probable that a small number of white children will be placed with black parents.

The adoption of white children by black parents would be a beneficial consequence of racial randomization, because it would highlight the unilateral racial aspect of TRA. It would call into question the racist presumption that interracial care is unidirectional in family life, that whites should adopt black children but black adults should only care for white children as domestic workers (Carby 1996). Kim McLarin, a writer and the black mother of a light-skinned biracial daughter, recounts the refusal of whites to see her as the biological mother of a "white"-looking child. Remembering a visit to a white pediatrician, McLarin writes,

> The doctor took one look at Samantha and exclaimed: "Wow! She's so light!" I explained that my husband is white, but it didn't seem to help. The doctor commented on Sam's skin color so often that I finally asked what was on her mind. "I'm thinking albino," she said. The doctor, who is white, claimed that she had seen the offspring of many interracial couples, but never a child this fair. "They're usually darker, coffee-with-cream color. Some of them are this light at birth, but by 72 hours you can tell they have a black parent." To prove her point, she held her arm next to Samantha's stomach. "I mean, this could be my child!" (McLarin 1998, 58)

The pediatrician did not challenge Ms. McLarin's parenting ability in any direct way. Yet what are we to make of her disbelief that contrasting skin tones could represent a mother and daughter? The pediatrician's lapse in professional decorum is linked to deep-seated stereotypes of black neediness and white superiority. The possibility that racial randomization would match some black parents with white children forces us to confront some of the race-based expectations we collectively hold about which people belong together in a family.

3. I focus on blacks and whites because white-black TRA has been the most controversial form of TRA.

STRICT NONACCOMMODATION: "WHITES ONLY"

Banks's policy of strict nonaccommodation would in principle exempt black prospective adopters, who would be free to exercise race-based preferences in the selection of adoptive children.[4] Banks brackets the racial attitudes of black adopters for two reasons. First, the same-race adoptive preferences of blacks have a negligible effect on our social terrain, while those of whites will exacerbate existing racial inequalities. Second, the adoption of black children by blacks advances the social good of cultural pluralism, while the adoption of white children by whites does not.

Banks is right to be particularly concerned about revising the racial attitudes of whites in the adoption system. Whites constitute the majority of adopters, and their same-race adoptive choices are routinely overlooked, as public attention turns to highly publicized cases of "reverse discrimination" in which whites' efforts to adopt black children are thwarted.[5] But one can be concerned with revising the racial attitudes of white adopters and still find reasons to include black adopters in hypothetical racial randomization. As discussed earlier, one reason to include blacks in racial randomization is the social utility gained by the otherwise unlikely outcome of some blacks adopting white children. If blacks typically choose black children when they adopt, then TRAs involving black parents and white or other nonblack children are likely to only occur under randomization. Such adoptions challenge racist stereotypes about the direction of interracial care.

Banks defends his exemption of blacks from strict nonaccommodation on grounds of cultural pluralism. He believes that "our society has an important interest in maintaining cultural diversity." To further this social goal, blacks and other racial minorities are justified in using racial preferences in adoption to promote their cultural presence in the society (Banks 1998, 944). He tries to avoid collapsing the idea of race into culture, but ultimately cannot divorce his cultural defense of same-race black preferences from cultural nationalist and pluralist arguments that draw a causal connection between racial ascription and cultural practices. While race

4. Banks qualifies this position by stating that such an exemption might be too controversial to implement. As a "practical solution," he would ban all race-based adoptive choice (Banks 1998, 944). Nonetheless, his theoretical reasons for exempting blacks from racial randomization deserve attention.

5. The 1995 Hollywood movie "Losing Isaiah" exemplifies the popular framing of TRA as an instance of reverse discrimination against whites seeking to adopt black children. In the movie, Jessica Lange plays a white woman who runs into legal obstacles when she and her white husband try to adopt a black child born with cocaine in his system. "Losing Isaiah" sparked renewed discussion of TRA in the popular media. See also Johnson (1999), A18.

and culture may practically coincide, we cannot say that a causal relationship exists between them. And even if same-race adoption by blacks could be shown to further cultural pluralism, there is no guarantee that cultural pluralism would challenge racism. As Lawrence Blum points out, an explicit principle of antiracism is necessary for positive social interaction and education among racial groups (Blum 1997, 7).

Moreover, using cultural pluralism to promote black same-race adoption treats black children as the means to furthering adult conceptions of a black cultural community. This symbolic manipulation violates the idea that black children should navigate their own racial self-identification and cultural practices as they grow up. While the goal of placing more black children in adoptive homes, regardless of racial makeup, certainly furthers the individual welfare of children, thus contributing to social welfare more generally, exempting blacks from racial randomization can only be defended by conflating racial ascription and cultural practice.

Granted, Banks's policy of strict nonaccommodation would not force black prospective adopters to choose black children. Under strict nonaccommodation, blacks would be free to adopt nonblack children. Banks is confident, however, that most blacks will want to adopt black children when given the opportunity. Are the same-race preferences of black adopters less pernicious than the same-race preferences of white adopters? One could argue that the relatively small number of black adopters and the high number of black children awaiting adoption means that black adopters' preferences for black children are not likely to deprive a white child of an adoptive home. By contrast, when whites avoid adopting a black child, opting to wait for a white child or pursue independent adoption, they effectively deprive a black child of an adoptive home.

Without question, numbers matter. The overarching goal of finding adoptive homes for as many adoptable children as possible should be at the heart of adoption policy and practice. But children's welfare requires more than just finding them homes. Those who craft and implement adoption policy should also be concerned with decreasing aversive racism by encouraging TRA that flows in all directions. Blacks should be encouraged to adopt white children, not only because TRA benefits the members of their own adoptive family, but also to show others that blacks can successfully parent white children. Some might question black parents' ability to teach a white child how to be white. But if such instruction entails instilling a false sense of racial superiority in a child who happens to be born with a white skin, then it is a lesson best left untaught. What's more, the racial fissure between a white child and his or her black adoptive parents may stimulate critical thinking about the social and cultural meaning of whiteness.

IMAGINING COMPREHENSIVE CHANGE

Banks's limited policy of strict nonaccommodation does not strike hard enough against the perpetuation of race-based social aversion via adoption. His policy prescription is not likely to affect the majority of prospective adopters in today's growing trend toward independent adoption, where adoption brokers and lawyers have supplanted agencies as key adoption intermediaries. The kind of public agency-mediated adoptions that would be subject to Banks's policy of strict nonaccommodation accounts for a small percentage of adoptions. Increasingly, brokers and lawyers arrange and help to formalize independent adoptions. These independent adoption intermediaries would be unaffected by Banks's antidiscrimination policy, which only applies to public adoption agencies. So even if Banks were to include prospective black adopters in strict nonaccommodation, the policy's effect would be limited to those adopting through public agencies. Independent adoptions also fall outside the jurisdiction of MEPA.

Independent adoption has blossomed alongside a booming economic market in reproductive technology. Market efficiency depends on the satisfaction of consumer demand, and this consumer-like attitude has seeped into the adoption world, as couples and individuals pay hefty sums to "shop" for children with specific characteristics. Jane Radin warns that "market rhetoric could create a commodified self-conception in everyone, as the result of commodifying every attribute that differentiates us and that other people value in us, and could destroy personhood as we know it" (Radin 1987, 1926).[6] To guard against this threat, Radin urges us to take a position of market inalienability, by which she means that human reproductive tissue and other aspects of our personhood may be separated from us but not traded for money. Although today's adoption system is not an explicit economic market, the ability of adopters to choose children according to racial classification and other attributes does encourage a consumer-like mindset that few question. The thought experiment of racial randomization brings this underlying consumerism to the fore. If we agree that consumerism is misapplied in adoption, what can be done to address this problem?

Mary Lyndon Shanley does not express an opinion on racial randomization, but she supports the proposition that adoption is best conceived as a publicly mediated event free of consumerism:

---

6. Elizabeth Anderson takes a similar position, arguing against commercial surrogacy on the grounds that it "constitutes an unconscionable commodification of children and of women's reproductive capacities" (Anderson 1990, 71). In Anderson's view, this commodification violates the Kantian imperative to treat persons as ends rather than as means.

Placing a public agency between the original family and the adoptive family reflects the notion that the original family entrusts the child to the public (to the state as *parens patriae*) and that the public (in the form of the agency and its rules) accepts responsibility for the welfare of the child. Another family then assumes *specific* responsibility for the welfare of the child. (Shanley 2001, 41)

A civic-minded approach to adoption would, in my opinion, reject consumer-like racial preferences for children. The privatization of adoption opens the door for prospective adopters—those who are wealthy enough to afford high broker and attorney fees—to discriminate on the basis of many descriptors, including race, because lawyers are committed to fulfilling the wishes of their clients, the adopters.[7] Unlike the social workers who facilitate agency adoptions, private lawyers have no stated professional responsibility to furthering social welfare.

Americans often turn to the law, and the Constitution in particular, to resolve individual conflicts and social problems. But is law the best vehicle for addressing racial discrimination in adoption? Equal-protection law has been a powerful tool, both strategically and symbolically, for those who feel socially excluded and stigmatized on the basis of race. But civil rights law cannot and should not force people of different races to live together in families. To accomplish broader social change that includes altering the social norm of racial homogeneity within families, we need a broad-based principle of nondiscrimination that goes beyond legal claims. The thought experiment of racial randomization is based in the constitutional principle of equal-protection law: a state must not treat citizens differently because of their racial classification unless it has a compelling reason for doing so—one that is narrowly tailored to accomplish a legitimate governmental purpose. I draw on equal-protection law not because I think that racial randomization should be implemented as policy, but because this legal definition of equal protection resonates with our moral intuitions about racial justice. This intuition tells us that black children should not be denied an adoptive home based on their racial ascription. But hypothetical racial randomization does not stop there. It pushes us to imagine nondiscrimination as a comprehensive moral principle applied to all aspects and stages of adoption.

OBJECTIONS TO RACIAL RANDOMIZATION

Again, racial randomization is not meant as a blueprint for crafting actual adoption policy. The thought experiment aims instead to challenge

---

7. There has recently been some controversy over which party, the original mother or the adopters, is the client, and whether a conflict of interest arises when lawyers mediate between original mothers and adopters.

the social norm of same-race family structure, which is often transferred to adoption policy and practice. Racial classification is not a morally justifiable basis for building a family, biological or adoptive. Race-based social aversion is a formidable obstacle, but it is by no means immovable. I now turn to some of the strongest objections to racial randomization—objections that can excavate some of our ingrained assumptions about the role that race should play in family life. Once we have a more accurate picture of our racial hopes, fears, and expectations in imagining "the family," we will be better equipped to think about how we can achieve racial justice in this unique arena of social life.

There are two major objections to the hypothetical of racial randomization. There are probably more, but I think these two lines of inquiry will cover most of the terrain. First, those who are infertile, unable, or unwilling to engage in traditional biological reproduction may object that they are being unfairly singled out as guinea pigs in a social experiment. Second, and related to the first objection, is the claim that racial randomization violates the constitutional privacy rights of prospective adopters to decide the makeup of their families. Should the constitutional ideas of freedom of association and procreative liberty be interpreted to protect the right of adopters to choose children according to racial classification?

FAIRNESS

Individuals wishing to adopt may charge that racial randomization unfairly discriminates against those who are infertile or otherwise cannot or will not engage in coital reproduction because they are gay, lesbian, single, or uninterested. One might defend race-based adoptive choice as a compensatory liberty that allows people in such circumstances to achieve the semblance of a biologically based family. If fertile heterosexuals may determine the racial composition of their families through the selection of a sexual partner, then fairness would seem to require that infertile individuals be afforded the same latitude in their family planning.

Fertile heterosexual couples are apt to make morally suspect racial choices in their reproductive decision-making. In the interest of fairness, perhaps all opportunities to exercise racial discrimination in reproductive choices ought to be hypothetically banned. This objection from fairness merits attention, especially because "private" racial choices in adoption are interlaced with commonly held assumptions about the proper role that racial classification should play in adult sexual relationships. The race of the person one chooses for a heterosexual partnership is a good, albeit imperfect, predictor of the racial classification of the biological children one might bear.[8] Biologism—the attempt to imitate biological parenting—seeks to transfer this parenting expectation to the adoption context. So, from the position of biologism, the exercise of private racial choice in adoption is perceived as "natural" and "normal." Interracial dating and marriage continue to elicit social disapproval, despite the increased incidence of interracial marriage. In 1980, black-white interracial marriages accounted for 0.3 percent of all marriages. By 1999 this figure had increased to 0.5 percent (U.S. Census Bureau 2000). A 1992 poll by the *Boston Globe* found that only 73 percent of whites and 52 percent of blacks perceived interracial dating as an option (Benning and Bennett 1992, 30–31; cited in Reddy 1994, 8). Future biological parents often make racially risk-averse, consumer-like choices with respect to their children vis-à-vis their selection of a sexual partner. By racial risk-aversion, I mean those decisions based on avoiding the social costs of familial and peer-group disapproval, which is still a likely consequence of interracial romance. Maureen Reddy calls this disapproval a "presumption of pathology." As a white woman married to a black man, she explains the term in the following way:

> Portrayed mostly from the outside by both black and white observers, we find our relationships treated as sick manifestations of deep-seated racial myths or rebellions against our families, background, cultures: the black partner in flight from blackness, a victim of internalized racism and white supremacism; the white partner is running from banality, in search of the exotic. These stereotypes are so ingrained in all of us in the United States that, for both blacks and whites, there is an automatic presumption of underlying pathology in interracial relationships. To most liberal outsiders, such relationships make a retrogressive political statement, while to conservatives, they represent an alarming, sick-by-definition result of integration. (Reddy 1974, 10)

This "presumption of pathology" is especially palpable in perceptions of white-black interracial dating and marriage, and by extension white-black interracial families.

Race-based social aversion in romantic partnerships may simply be an expression of racial differentiation, and not *ipso facto* proof of invidious racial discrimination. Does the person placing a personal advertisement in

---

8. In Nella Larson's novella *Passing,* light-skinned black women agonize over having children because of the possibility of their recessive genes for darker pigmentation will become dominant in their children: "After taking up her own glass she informed them: 'No, I have no boys and I don't think I'll ever have any. I'm afraid. I nearly died of terror the whole nine months before Margery was born for fear that she might be dark. Thank goodness, she turned out all right. But I'll never risk it again. Never! The strain is simply too—too hellish" (Larson 1986, 168).

a magazine or newspaper engage in benign or invidious racial discrimination when he or she lists race as a criterion for a date? We cannot know for certain whether that racial preference stems from racism or idiosyncratic desire. It is nonetheless likely that in a race-conscious society like ours, the persistence of both social and economic racial stratification, coupled with racial stereotypes, will at least contribute to race-based social aversion in dating and beyond.

Parenting expectations stemming from private racial choices in dating emerge in adoption agency practice. Perhaps the most indicting evidence lies in the underreported fact that most domestic white-black adoptions have involved white adults and biracial infants—children with one original parent who self-identifies as black and one original parent who self-identifies as white. And in some cases, children who have two biological parents who self-identify as black but happen to look biracial are placed in white adoptive homes at higher rates than children with "black" phenotypes. These adoption practices underscore the intense drive toward biologism in adoption, for "[t]hese biracial children can be seen as at least a partial racial match with their white adoptive parents" (Bartholet 1991, 1173 8n). Under MEPA, it would be illegal for social workers at federally funded agencies to prevent adoptive placements based on race, but not illegal for prospective adopters to request race-specific children

Should racial randomization be expanded to include other social categories such as sex, ethnicity, physical ability, and religion, as these categories, too, often fuel invidious discrimination? Each of these social designations merits moral inquiry. If, for example, adopters are more likely to select girls than boys, and this has the detrimental consequence of longer waiting periods for boys than girls, then imagining sex-based randomization may illuminate the need to make adoption more sexually just. Issues of sexual justice in adoption are not far-fetched, as Microsort, a trademarked medical technology, allows pregnant women and their partners to determine the sex of their fetuses; it is overwhelmingly being used in U.S. clinical trials to select for female babies.[9]

Other characteristics such as physical and developmental ability pose moral and practical questions about a prospective adopter's capacity and willingness to deal with the special care needs and financial cost of raising such children. Is it morally permissible to avoid adopting a blind child, or a child with Down's syndrome? Is religion a meaningful label for an infant, and thus an acceptable basis for requesting a Muslim, Jewish, or Christian

9. Microsort is a trademarked technology that has been used in cattle breeding for a decade. It is not yet considered safe for human use, but clinical trials are being performed by the Genetics and I.V.F. Institute. In the first 111 uses of Microsort in humans, eighty-three selected for females, and only twenty-eight for males (Belkin 1999, 29).

baby? Racial randomization stirs up these and other questions, but it does not answer them. Ethical concerns about classifying adoptable children based on other social categories call for an assessment of the consequences that a particular sorting mechanism is likely to have on children in need of adoption. Randomization may be used to evaluate the morality of using social categories as the basis for adoption decision-making.

Should the hypothetical of racial randomization be stretched to critically evaluate biological reproductive decisions? I would extend racial randomization to reproductive decisions in the market for new reproductive technologies, because like adoption, these processes necessitate third-party mediation. When a person buys human sperm or ova for in vitro fertilization or assisted insemination, she or he enters a public, or at least less private, domain. Unassisted biological reproduction does not typically involve a mediator. Even though such decisions are motivated by social norms that have public consequences, coital reproduction is mostly a private matter. One could argue that dating services and matchmakers act as third-party mediators in bringing heterosexual men and women together. But these mediators are not directly involved in orchestrating procreation. Randomizing coital reproduction would infringe too much on individual privacy.

Adoption is rightly distinguished from unassisted biological reproduction. Adoptions require state coordination of the interests of those in "the adoptive triangle." Unlike adults, children lack the maturity to articulate their interests in the political arena. Hence social workers and courts must discern and promote the interests of children in need of adoption. Government has a special interest in regulating how racial classification affects children awaiting adoption, because children are constitutional persons. And government also has a legitimate interest in discouraging the racial classification of human gametes because of the potential for such race-based economic transactions to revive discredited notions of discrete biological races (Fogg-Davis 2001).

While racial randomization can help us to imagine a racially just adoption system, its practical implementation would likely discourage many potential adopters from adopting, altogether. The likelihood of large-scale defection is sufficient reason not to treat racial randomization, even in a moderated form, as a policy prescription. But this practical difficulty should not deter further investigation into the morality of race-based adoptive choice. Indeed, the impracticality of racial randomization tells us something about contemporary resistance to racial integration. Racially randomized adoption pushes colorblindness to its logical conclusion. If Americans are truly committed to colorblindness, both legally and morally, then why would so many refuse to submit to a colorblind process that may land them in an interracial adoptive family?

PRIVACY

Linked to the objection that racial randomization discriminates against infertile persons and others who are not engaged in biological reproduction is the objection that prospective adopters, regardless of their reproductive ability, should be free to choose affective ties within the sphere of family life without state interference. This is an argument about privacy and family decisions. And as much as this claim is couched in the socially and religiously conservative rhetoric of "family values," it also harbors a consumerist subtext. Although the privacy objection to my thought experiment is more powerful than the objection based in fairness, it can be refuted on the grounds that it also fails to properly distinguish adoptive families from biological families.

We have already discussed the strong presumption in the United States that adoption is a private act, analogous to the private act of procreation. "Privacy" refers to associative freedom—a freedom that encompasses the freedom to form social bonds with some persons and not others based on a wide range of criteria. If adoption is like biological reproduction in the sense that individuals have the freedom to choose a sexual partner according to any number of personal prejudices, then does it follow that prospective adopters may be equally choosey in their selection of an adoptive child?

Few people question the morality of this discrimination because U.S. constitutional doctrine has maintained that individual acts of racial discrimination, unsupported by government, are beyond the reach of the Fourteenth Amendment. Reva Siegel, discussing affirmative action jurisprudence, shows that the right to privately discriminate on the basis of race has taken on different rhetorical forms since the first judicial constructions of the Fourteenth Amendment. While opponents of civil rights legislation have appealed to associational liberty as a rationale for private racial discrimination since Reconstruction, Siegel observes that "racial discourses of the private are now more commonly couched in a related, but distinct, market idiom that emphasizes individual and/or group competition" (Siegel 1998, 52). In this market idiom, the racial discriminations of adopters become the private decisions of rational consumers.[10]

Treating the family as categorically private is neither accurate nor desirable. As many feminist scholars have pointed out, the division that sets families apart from government intervention can, and too often does, fa-

10. Robin West agrees with Jana Singer that "the denial of the communitarian nature of the family and of marriage has resulted, among much else, in the transformation of family law into a branch of private law within which parenting is construed as the exercise of consumer choice among an array of social, natural, or technological possibilities" (West 1998, 723).

cilitate the domestic subordination of women and children.[11] Moreover, families have never been free of government intervention. From the start, the state issues marriage licenses and alters one's tax status. Parents are legally obligated to provide their children a formal education, either by sending them to an accredited school or providing a state-approved curriculum at home. There are nonetheless many private choices generally associated with family life that we cherish. Chief among these is the freedom to choose with whom one will make a home and create a family. These "fundamental values" are often discussed under the constitutional rubric of freedom of association and procreative liberty.

The Supreme Court has interpreted the Fourteenth Amendment's due-process clause as containing a right to privacy, and the First Amendment as containing a right to associative freedom for the purpose of expression. This theory of constitutional interpretation—alternatively referred to as non-interpretivism and nonoriginalism—holds that "courts should go beyond [the explicit or "clearly implicit" text of the Constitution] and enforce norms that cannot be discovered within the four corners of the document."[12] The doctrinal concepts of both associative freedom and procreative freedom exemplify noninterpretivism, as neither is explicitly mentioned in the Constitution. Noninterpretivism can be traced back to the Court's landmark ruling in the 1905 case *Lochner v. New York* that the due-process clause prohibits the regulation of working hours for bakers, thus establishing a constitutional "liberty of contract" based extra-textually on the Fourteenth Amendment.[13] So-called "substantive due-process" adjudication reached its height in the 1973 *Roe v. Wade* decision, in which the Court held that the Fourteenth Amendment's due-process clause contains a right to privacy broad enough to support a woman's right to procure an abortion during the first trimester of pregnancy without state interference.[14]

---

11. "What is created through the delegation of privacy to the family, in the name of individual autonomy, is not necessarily individual freedom, but at least for many, its opposite: a Hobbesian state of nature, within which the strong control, by virtue of their superior strength, and the weak, Stockholm-syndrome-like, learn to comply." Ibid. Using law to reinforce the privacy of families can also perpetuate an unjust division of labor within households. See Okin (1989).

12. For a discussion of this central debate in public law see Ely (1980). Ely argues that judicial review should be limited to reinforcing the participation of citizens in the democratic process, that courts should not become involved in "the substantive merits of the political choice under attack" (Ely 1980, 181).

13. In his famous dissenting opinion, Justice Oliver Wendell Holmes insisted that the extra-textual basis for the majority's decision was "an economic theory which a large part of the country does not entertain"—namely, laissez-faire capitalism. *Lochner v. New York* , 198 U.S. 45, 25 S.Ct. 539 (1905).

14. Justice Harry A. Blackmun, writing for the Court, notes that "the Constitution does not explicitly mention any right of privacy." Blackmun then points, however, to judicial precedent in which the Court recognized a right to personal privacy in various contexts: "This right of privacy, whether it be founded in the Fourteenth Amendment's concept of personal lib-

The noninterpretivist notions of associative and procreative freedom were most intertwined in the 1965 case *Griswold v. Connecticut* (391 U.S. 145, 85 S.Ct. 1678 [1965]), which struck down a Connecticut statute banning the use of contraceptives by married couples. The majority held that "zones of privacy" emanated from "penumbras" found in the First, Third, Fourth, Fifth, and Ninth amendments. *Griswold* leaned heavily on the assertion that marriage is an inviolable zone of privacy. Writing for the Court, Justice William O. Douglas issued a powerful declaration:

> We deal with a right of privacy older than the Bill of Rights—older than our political parties, older than our school system. Marriage is a coming together for better or for worse, hopefully enduring, and intimate to the degree of being sacred. It is an association that promotes a way of life, not causes; a harmony in living, not political faiths; a bilateral loyalty, not commercial or social projects. Yet it is an association for as noble a purpose as any involved in our prior decisions. (*Griswold v. Connecticut*, 391 U.S. 145, 85 S.Ct. 1678 [1965])

More specifically, Douglas argues that a married couple's sexual relationship is well beyond legislative scope; it is "sacred." At the heart of the majority's opinion, as well as Arthur J. Goldberg and William J. Brennan's concurrence, is visceral outrage at the prospect of police access to "marital bedrooms." That idea, Douglas writes, "is repulsive to the notions of privacy surrounding the marriage relationship." There are real dangers associated with shielding domestic relationships from state intervention, to which I alluded earlier, such as domestic violence and unjust divisions of labor. Although outside the present analysis, these concerns are worth keeping in mind.

The relevant question to be derived from the Court's *Griswold* decision is, "Do these constitutionally based arguments for associative and procreative freedom sustain the objection that adopters should be permitted to assert racial preferences in the adoption placement process?" My answer turns on a prior question: Is adoption analogous to procreation? According to biologism, the answer is yes. The strongest claim in support of biologism is that it downplays the "genetic strangeness" of the adopted child, thus arguably reducing the social stigma that many adopted individuals feel. Likewise, adoptive parents may choose same-race children to avoid the stigma of being identified by others as infertile—a label often associated with personal failure. They may also wish to avoid strangers' rude stares and invasive questioning that racially heterogeneous families en-

---

erty and restrictions upon state action, as we feel it is, or, as the District Court determined, in the Ninth Amendment's reservation of rights to the people, is broad enough to encompass a woman's decision whether or not to terminate her pregnancy." *Roe v. Wade*, 410 U.S. 113, 93 S.Ct. 705 (1973). 391 U.S. 145, 85 S.Ct. 1678 (1965).

counter. One stigma often associated with TRA is the perception of an interracial sexual relationship. Patricia Irwin Johnston, a white adoptive mother of an African American and Hispanic daughter, comments:

> We were shocked to find that when one parent went out with baby, reactions from both black and white people were cold and standoffish. There was a definite unspoken criticism, which we finally came to understand came from the assumption that they were observing an adult involved in a transracial sexual relationship. (Johnston 1992, 129–30)

Social stigma and prejudice are not, however, good reasons for analogizing adoption to procreation. Instead of molding adoptive families to fit the contours of societal prejudice, a thought experiment of racial randomization questions our prior assumptions about race and familial belonging.

An explicit acknowledgment of the nonbiological nature of adoption produces individual and social goods. One of the goods that can result from imagining randomized placement is a constraint on the kind of selfishness that accompanies the seemingly "natural" desire to reproduce oneself or one's partner. Many people harbor some desire to see a "miniature likeness of me" in a child of "my own." Yet this drive does not mean that we are justified in transferring this selfishness to the realm of adoption, and basing our notion of adoptive parenting on biological parenting. Biologism is after all the reason we tend to think of adoption as abnormal, unnatural, and "a choice of last resort" (Bartholet 1993, 164–65).

To have choices suggests some degree of control. Choosing an already born child, rather than giving birth to a child, suggests that prospective adoptive parents can exercise control precisely where "nature"/biology would have held the reins. We may wish for our biological children to resemble us physically, to pursue careers similar to our own, and to share our opinions and outlook. But we also know that recessive genes may render such biological offspring physically dissimilar to both parents, and that biological children are apt to pursue activities and careers divergent from those of their parents. When gaps such as these occur, a common quip is that "I must have been adopted!"

The desire to have the apple fall near to the tree may be an inescapable component of our being. But again, the mere presence of the desire is not an adequate justification for its implementation in adoption. There are larger questions of social justice to consider—questions that may require us not to put our biologism into practice. The larger social concern motivating my thought experiment of racial randomization is the vexing matter of racial justice in the United States. Unrestrained consumer choice in adoption holds tremendous potential for publicly reinforcing racist private choices about what a proper family looks like.

And while our intuitions about justice are tied to constitutionalism, we cannot rely solely on constitutional arguments to fight racism. We may be able to draw a legal distinction between private and public racism, but the picture becomes less clear when we attempt to delineate morally between these two domains. Private racial discrimination in the construction of family life, biological and adoptive, comports with the status quo and thus fails to raise an eyebrow. We think it normal and uninteresting when a white heterosexual couple adopts a healthy white infant. Yet when a white couple adopts a black child, curiosity abounds: "a crazy kind of look from people in a passing car, or a little extra room around our blankets at the beach" (Neufeld 1969, 43). The thought experiment of racial randomization aims to catalyze a rethinking of status quo assumptions about which persons belong together in families. De facto racial segregation in the social and legal construction of family life is an early temporal point in the re-ignition of our structural racism. Antiracist intervention at the point of adoptive placement is a necessary, albeit small, part of a larger project of curbing intergenerational racism.

CHAPTER THIRTEEN

You Mixed? Racial Identity without Racial Biology

SALLY HASLANGER

To set the context for this paper, it will be useful to begin with an anecdote. One recent summer I was in my neighborhood park with my then five-year-old son, Isaac. We live in a racially mixed, though predominantly Black neighborhood. The park consists mainly of a cement basketball court and a play structure set in a huge sandbox. We had been playing basketball for about 45 minutes; for the first part of it I had been helping him with his shots, but eventually a few other kids had joined us and I had stepped to the sidelines to let them negotiate their play on their own. For the time we were there, as is common, I was the only White person in the park; Isaac, my son, is Black. In order to capture the potential import of what follows, it is worth mentioning that in appearance I am quite WASPy looking—straight brown hair, gray eyes, pale skin, and Isaac is dark with nearly black eyes and black (virtually shaved) hair. The time came to leave, and we took our ball and headed down the sidewalk toward home. A boy about nine years old rode up to us on his bike—he wasn't one of the ones we'd been playing with and I didn't recognize him, but let's call him "James"—and asked me a familiar question, "Is he your son?" I replied, "Yes." He looked at me hard with a somewhat puzzled expression and con-

For helpful comments and discussion, thanks to Linda Alcoff, Louise Antony, Margaret Burnham, Ann Cudd, Derek Darby, Jorge Garcia, Robert Gooding-Williams, Diana Henderson, Ishani Maitra, Ruth Perry, Jacqueline Stevens, Ásta Sveinsdottir, Laurence Thomas, Jennifer Uleman, Elizabeth Wood, Stephen Yablo, and members of the audience at colloquia given at Syracuse University, Northwestern University, Smith College, University of Chicago, and the Greater Philadelphia Philosophy Consortium. Special thanks to Charlotte Witt and Lawrence Blum, who each wrote extensive comments on an earlier draft.

tinued, "You mixed?" I paused. I wasn't entirely sure what he was asking. Although I am well aware that African Americans may have straight brown hair, gray eyes, and light complexions, it seemed a huge leap of the imagination for anyone to read my appearance as mixed-race. I suspected that he might be asking whether I am (or was when Isaac was conceived) in an interracial relationship, thus explaining the disparity in Isaac's and my appearance by an absent (Black) father. Sensing that this wasn't one of those times when a long explanation was called for, I replied, somewhat misleadingly (given what I took him to be asking), "I'm not mixed, but my family is mixed." He responded, "Oh, cool," and rode off.

This sort of conversation isn't at all uncommon when you're in a family like mine, and it's the sort that tends to rattle around in the back of your mind for at least a few days, if not weeks or months. What is "a family like mine"? My family consists of me and my husband Steve (also White) and two African American children: Isaac (I've already mentioned) and our daughter Zina (at the time this is being prepared for publication, they are aged nine and seven, respectively). We adopted the children when they were infants. They have different birth families, and their adoptions are "fully open": we have regular contact with their birth families—including phone contact every few weeks, and visits lasting several days where typically we stay in their homes and they stay in ours. The birth families are an important part of our extended family.

Many conversations rattle around in the back of my head because I worry about what they meant, what I should have said (in contrast to what I did say), or what my kids took away from the contact and how I can usefully follow up on it with them; but most of them don't inspire philosophical reflection. However, this conversation puzzled me about a number of issues, and this paper is my most recent effort to sort out what I think about them.

The philosophical questions arise from a tension between certain theoretical claims about race and my own lived experience. Theoretically, I agree with many others in law and the academy that our everyday racial classifications do not track meaningful biological categories: there are no "racial genes" responsible for the different clusters of physical or cultural differences between members of racial groups, and divisions between "racial" groups are a product of social forces that vary across history and culture. But if that's the case, a certain dialectic develops that raises questions about my response to James and opens further ones.

First, if race is not biologically real, then on what basis do I so easily describe myself as White and my son as Black? On what basis can I claim so confidently to James that I'm not "mixed" (even though my family is)? This is not just a question about the facts of my ancestry—although none of my known ancestors are Black, there are many gaps in the record, and for all

I know I may have some fairly recent African roots. The more pressing question for my purposes here, however, is that if race is a biological fiction, then what does it even mean to affirm or deny that I'm "White" or that I'm "mixed"?

Although I reject the idea that there are biological races in which membership is determined by "blood," and along with this reject the idea of "mixed blood," I don't agree with some theorists who conclude that "there is no such thing as race," simply because there are no racial essences or racial genes. I am a social constructionist about race: I believe that races are social categories, and no less real for being social rather than "natural." As a result, I think it is accurate to classify myself socially as White and my son as Black, and to classify others as "mixed race." But I have a rather complicated and non-standard interpretation of what that means that takes races to be social classes defined in a context of what might usefully be called "color" oppression. In the first section of the paper I'll sketch my account of race and say a bit about how it might handle the claims that I am White and Isaac is Black.

But it will become clear that as it stands my account doesn't provide sufficient resources to understand the phenomenon of racial identity, especially in contexts where race and racial identity come apart. So in the middle of the paper I will discuss racial identity with special attention to the phenomenon of life "on the color line" hoping that this discussion may also be of use in thinking about the phenomenon of "passing."[1] I will suggest that there is a sense in which I can claim a "mixed" identity (though certainly not in any of the senses that James probably had in mind) and in which it is probably true that my kids do and will continue to have somewhat "mixed" identities. However, the suggestion that my kids may grow up without the "correct" racial identity—that their identity may be, at least in a certain sense, "mixed" rather than "Black" or "African American"—raises issues that, of course, are one concern in debates over the legitimacy of transracial adoption. So in the final section I will consider briefly what I take to be the import of my arguments regarding the obligation of parents who adopt transracially to raise their children to have the "right" racial identity.[2]

1. Some powerful recent accounts of "life on the color line" include Williams (1995); McBride (1996); Lazarre (1997); Derricotte (1997); Piper (1992); Dalmage (2000). Some recent accounts of living in (Black/White) transracial adoptions include Rush (2000); Thompson (2000); Simon and Roorda (2000). The issue of "passing" has received significant attention recently, and I will not be able to do justice to it here. However, some useful (non-fiction) work beyond that already mentioned includes Ginsberg (1996); Delgado and Stefancic (1997).

2. For a glimpse of the transracial adoption controversy, see NABSW (1972); Bartholet (1991); Bartholet (1993); Perry (1993–94); Howe (1994); NABSW (1994); Simon (1994); Smith (1996); Patton (2000); Neal (n.d.). On the question of the "right identity" see also Allen (1993).

SALLY HASLANGER

RACE AS SOCIAL CLASS

In an earlier paper, "Gender and Race: (What) Are They? (What) Do We Want Them To Be?" (Haslanger 2000), I argue that for the purposes of an antiracist feminist theory, it is important to develop accounts of race and gender that enable us to identify the groups who are targets of racial and sexual oppression.[3] Although it may well be that in the long run ("after the revolution") we may hope that both race and gender will be eliminated, in the short run it would be a mistake not to recognize the ways in which race and sex oppression divide us into hierarchical classes in which membership is "marked" on the body.

In that paper I propose that in order to accommodate the broad variety of ways in which the notions of race and gender are employed (apparently to refer to quite different things, for example, racial norms, racial symbols, racial identities, racial social roles) we should take a "focal meaning" approach to race and gender. A focal analysis undertakes to explain a variety of connected phenomena in terms of their relations to one that is theorized as the central or core phenomenon. As I see it, the core phenomenon to be addressed is the pattern of social relations that constitute certain social classes as racially/sexually dominant and others as racially/sexually subordinate; norms, symbols, and identities are gendered or raced derivatively, by reference to the social relations that constitute the relevant hierarchy of social classes.[4] Although my definitions of race and gender help organize and clarify some of our everyday beliefs (or so I maintain), I do

3. The definitions of race below, and some of the text surrounding them, are taken directly from that paper.
4. To understand the notion of a *social class* as I am using the term, it may be helpful to consider other examples. A social class is a group of individuals who are members of the class (or set) in question by virtue of having a certain social property or standing in a particular social relation. So, for example, the class of husbands is a social class. Men who are legally married are husbands, and their standing in a legal marriage relationship is the basis for their membership. Homeowners constitute a social class: they are those individuals who are legal owners of the property that serves as their domicile. I use legal relations for these examples because they are very straightforward cases of social relations, but other relations, for example, being a neighbor of, being a pastor of, are social but aren't encoded in law. Note especially membership in the sets is not determined by and does not presuppose any common set of beliefs, psychological attitudes, behaviors, etc. among the members. (One can be a homeowner without even being aware of it, for example, if a child inherits the home she or he lives in when the parents die.) E.g., consider the class of scapegoats, or the class of teacher's pets. In these cases membership is determined by the way one is both viewed and treated, though even here, we should not assume that the individuals who fall into the classes are aware that they are scapegoats or that they function as teacher's pets; and likewise, we cannot assume a common subjective experience of being in this position. Yet we may want to say of scapegoats, for example, that some *do* come to have a scapegoat identity. My point is that one might distinguish being a scapegoat from having a scapegoat identity, just as one might distinguish being a member of a race from having a racial identity. On the strategy I will be employing, explaining what it is to have a racial identity will depend on the prior notion of having a race.

268

not offer them as analyses of our *ordinary* concepts of race and gender (whatever they might be). Instead, I offer these accounts in a revisionary spirit as part of an explicitly political project.

My guiding idea is that systems of racial and sexual oppression are alike (in spite of their many differences) in taking certain real or imagined features of the body as markers for oppressive social divisions. Societies structured by racial and/or sexual oppression will produce culture that "helps" us read the body in the requisite ways and will provide narratives or rationalizations linking kinds of bodies to kinds of social positions; they will also be organized so that the roles and activities assigned to certain kinds of bodies systematically disadvantage them (and to other kinds of bodies systematically privilege them) in concrete material ways. Sex and race oppression are structural—institutional—but they are also internalized in our basic interpretations and understandings of our bodies, ourselves, and each other.

Feminists have often used an (albeit contested) slogan to capture the notion of gender: gender is the social meaning of sex. In keeping with the ideas above, materialist feminists have argued that we must understand the use of "social meaning" here along two axes—on one hand, social meaning includes the cultural readings of the body, and on the other hand, the material (economic, political, legal) divisions between the sexes. It is distinctive of materialist feminism that it refuses to prioritize either the cultural or material dimension as (causally) prior. In other words, it is a mistake to suggest that the ultimate source of the problem is "in our heads" (in our conceptual scheme, our language, or our cultural ideals), or alternatively that it is in the unjust structure of our social arrangements, as if it must be one or the other; "culture" and "social/institutional structure" are deeply intertwined, so much so, that they are sometimes inextricable.[5]

On one materialist account of gender (in particular, one I support), men and women are defined as those hierarchical classes of individuals whose membership is determined by culturally variable readings of the reproductive capacities of the human body. In contexts in which the reproductive body is not a site of subordination and privilege (presumably no contexts we know of, but ones we may hope for), there are no men or women, though there still may be other (new) genders.

Is this strategy useful for thinking about race? Perhaps, though off-hand this idea is not easy to develop. It is one thing to acknowledge that race is *socially* real, even if a biological fiction; but it is another thing to capture in racial terms the "social meaning" of the body. There seem to be too many

---

5. The interdependence of the cultural and material is an explicit commitment of materialist feminism as articulated in, for example, Young (1990), 33. See also Delphy (1984), and more generally Hennessey and Ingraham (1997).

different forms that race takes. Note, however, that the same problem
arises for gender: is it possible to provide a unified (cross-cultural, trans-
historical) analysis of "the social meaning of sex"? The materialist feminist
approach offered a helpful strategy: don't look for an analysis that assumes
that the meaning is always and everywhere the same; rather, consider how
members of the group are *socially positioned,* and what *physical markers* serve
in a supposed basis for such treatment. Let this provide the common
framework within which we explore the contextually variable meanings.

To extend this strategy to race it will help first to introduce a technical
notion of "color." What we need is a term for those physical features of individuals taken to mark them as members of a race. One might refer to
them as "racial" features, but to avoid any suggestion of racial essences I
will use the term "color" to refer to the (contextually variable) physical
"markers" of race, just as I use the term "sex" to refer to the (contextually
variable) physical "markers" of gender. Note that I include in "color" more
than just skin tone: common markers also include eye, nose, and lip shape,
hair texture, physique, etc., and it is presumed of the physical markers of
race that the features in question are inherited through an ancestry that
can be traced back to a particular geographical region. Although the term
"people of color" is used to refer to non-Whites, I want to allow that the
markers of "Whiteness" count as "color"; however, I still use the phrases
"people of color" and "children of color" as they are used to refer to non-
Whites.

Transposing the slogan used for gender, then, we might say that race is
the social meaning of color, or more explicitly, of the geographically
marked body. To develop this, I propose the following account (see also
Stevens 1993; Stevens 1999).[6] First definition:

> A group is *racialized* iff$_{df}$ its members are socially positioned as subordinate or
> privileged along some dimension (economic, political, legal, social, etc.), and
> the group is "marked" as a target for this treatment by observed or imagined
> bodily features presumed to be evidence of ancestral links to a certain geo-
> graphical region.

Or in the more elaborate version[7]:

6. Special thanks to Jacqueline Stevens for help in formulating these definitions. My version is quite similar to the one she offers in Stevens (1999), chap. 4. See Omi and Winant
(1994), 53–61.
7. There are aspects of this definition that need further elaboration or qualification. For
details see Haslanger (2000), n. 17. Note also that there may be reasons to claim that a particular group is more racialized than another, depending, for example, on the degree of subordination or privilege, or on the role of physical marks. I would accommodate this by saying
that like many concepts, there are central and peripheral cases depending on the extent to
which something satisfies the conditions.

A group G is *racialized* relative to context C iff$_{df}$ members of G are (all and only) those:

1. who are observed or imagined to have certain bodily features presumed in C to be evidence of ancestral links to a certain geographical region (or regions);

2. whose having (or being imagined to have) these features marks them within the context of the background ideology in C as appropriately occupying certain kinds of social position that are in fact either subordinate or privileged (and so motivates and justifies their occupying such a position); and

3. whose satisfying (1) and (2) plays (or would play) a role in their systematic subordination or privilege in C, that is, who are *along some dimension* systematically subordinated or privileged when in C, and satisfying (1) and (2) plays (or would play) a role in that dimension of subordination or privilege.

In other words, races are those groups demarcated by the geographical associations accompanying perceived body type, when those associations take on (hierarchical) socio-political significance concerning how members of the group should be viewed and treated. It is important to note that the ideology in question need not use physical morphology or geography as the entire or explicit *basis* or *rationale* for the supposed "appropriate" treatment; these features may instead simply be "markers" of other characteristics that the ideology uses to justify the treatment in question.[8]

On this view, whether a group is racialized, and so how and whether an individual is raced, is not an absolute fact, but will depend on context. For example, Blacks, Whites, Asians, Latinos/as, Native Americans, are currently racialized in the United States insofar as these are all groups defined in terms of physical features associated with places of origin, and insofar as membership in the group functions socially as a basis for evaluation. However, some groups are not currently racialized in the United States but have been so in the past and possibly could be again (and in other contexts are), for example, the Italians, the Germans, the Irish.

The definition just provided focuses on races as groups, and this makes sense when we are thinking of group-based oppression. But the analysis as it stands does not do justice to the ways in which an individual's race is negotiated and depends on context. Racialization is definitely more pronounced in some contexts than in others, and in most cases individuals are not simply passive victims of its effects but are agents who are capable of undermining or collaborating in the process. With this in mind, we can we can say that S is of the White (Black, Asian . . .) race iff Whites (Blacks,

---

8. The point here is that the racist ideology that sustains the hierarchy may be a form of either *intrinsic* or *extrinsic* racism in Appiah's sense. Appiah (1992), 13–15.

SALLY HASLANGER

Asians . . .) are a racialized group in S's society, and S is *regularly and for the most part* viewed and treated as a member.[9] Yet we may also want to allow that some people don't have a stable race at all, and that even if some are consistently racialized in the society, there are disruptions in this broad pattern when we consider narrower contexts. To accommodate the contextual racialization of individuals (and not just groups), let's say:

> S *functions as a member* of a racial group R in context C if and only if (by definition)
> 1. S is observed or imagined in C to have certain bodily features presumed to be evidence of ancestral links to a certain geographical region (or regions) where the group R is thought to have originated;
> 2. that S has these features marks S, within the background ideology of C, as someone who ought to occupy certain kinds of social positions that are, in fact, subordinate or privileged (and so motivates and justifies S's occupying such a position); and
> 3. the fact that S satisfies (1) and (2) plays a role in S's systematic subordination or privilege in C, that is, S is systematically subordinated or privileged *along some dimension* when in C, and satisfying (1) and (2) plays (or would play) a role in that dimension of privilege or subordination.

IDENTIFYING OUR RACES

Of course, there are many controversial aspects of this account that merit further discussion. But I hope it is clear that on an account of this sort (in some sense the details don't even really matter for our purposes here), it is possible for individuals to be members of a race even if there is no biological basis for racial classification. On my view, biological ideology is just one of several possible ideologies that might link "color" with social/political hierarchy. For example, in the contemporary United States, even some who grant that race is not a meaningful genetic category believe that "color" is a marker for "culture," and use such color-culture assumptions to justify social/political hierarchy. On my view, groups that are subordinated or privileged on the basis of color-culture assumptions are no less racial groups than those who are subordinated on the basis of color-genetics assumptions. (Hence, it makes sense to speak of "cultural racism.") What's important and interesting about the phenomenon of race, on my account, is not the invocation of biology to justify hierarchy (after all, prior to the development of genetic theory, theology was invoked to

9. As in the case of gender, I recommend that we view membership in a racial/ethnic group in terms of how one is viewed and treated regularly and for the most part in the context in question.

provide a basis for color oppression [Stocking 1993]), but the historically persistent ways in which the marked body—in terms of color-ancestry-geography—takes on meaning and is used to justify and motivate social/political status.

Although on my account *there are races*—understood as social classes—this claim is not directly incompatible with a view that might be stated as, "There are no races." Typically in current discussions those who deny that there are races believe that the concept of race is committed to a naturalistic form of racial essence. I can agree with those who employ the term "race" with such commitments that there are no races—*in their sense*. My disagreement, instead, is with their background philosophical assumptions about language and conceptual analysis. To clarify my point, then, we might want to employ the terminology "*biological* races" and "*social* races." I maintain that there are no biological races, but there are social races, that is, racialized groups. And I not only maintain that the concept of race is sufficiently open-ended to include social races, but that there are philosophical and political reasons to explicate the notion of race in a way that accounts for racialized groups.

Let's return, though, to my conversation with James. Given this account of race, we now have some way of accounting for the idea that I am White and Isaac is Black, even though race is not an adequate biological classification. I count as White because I reap tremendous White privilege by virtue of the ways people regularly interpret my "color"; Isaac, although he reaps some of the benefits of White privilege through my privilege, is already disadvantaged by the interpretation of his "color" and its social implications. Because Isaac is socially "marked" as of African descent, and this is a factor in the disadvantages he experiences, he counts as Black.

However, it is not uncommon in the adoption world to hear people describe the effects of transracial adoption (of children of color by Whites) by saying, "You will become a minority family." The purpose of such comments is not to alert prospective adoptive parents to the fact that interracial families are in the statistical minority, which of course is obvious, but to suggest that a family with children of color counts as a family of color; the strongest version of the claim would be that by virtue of the race of my children, mine is a Black family. I appreciate some of the intentions behind this comment: it is meant to alert the naïve White prospective parents that they will suffer some forms of discrimination hitherto unknown to them once they adopt children of color. This is true. But I strongly resist the idea that my family or I become Black by including Black children, mainly because my family and I retain enormous White privilege. A weaker version of the claim is just that my family becomes an interracial family and so is exposed to some kinds of and some degree of discrimination not felt by White families; to this weak version of the claim I am more sympathetic. If it makes sense to say that a family has a race (as opposed to an individual), it may be that our family is racialized as non-white (our collective "colors" are interpreted as a basis for some forms of subordination/discrimination)—but this must be unpacked in a way that acknowledges the White privilege we, the parents, bring to the family.

However, even if it is true that I am not able to exercise some of my own White privilege when in the company of my family, I maintain that this does not mean that *I* somehow become racialized as Black (or more vaguely as non-White). For me to be a member of the Black race (to any degree), it would have to be that my subordination (or in this case, my diminution of privilege) was due to interpretations of my "color" as linked to recent ancestry in Africa. In those cases in which my privilege is weakened by virtue of my being a parent of Black children, it is not on the basis of anyone viewing me as Black, though my Whiteness may be relevant to my status in their eyes.[10]

But there is also something more I want to say about the possibilities of racial "crossing" in the context of transracial adoption. To put the point bluntly, I believe that my own racial identity has been substantially altered by being a mother of Black children, and although I am White, there are ways of thinking about identity on which my racial identity is better understood as "mixed." But so far the account of race I've offered provides no resources for thinking about this, for although it offers one way of thinking about *race*, as it stands it doesn't begin to address the issue of *racial identity*. Although races as social classes are the central phenomenon to be considered on my approach, a crucial next step is to make the link between race and racial identity.

RACIAL IDENTITY

In the interdisciplinary literature on race and gender there are many different senses of the term "identity." I do not want to argue that there is one true sense of "identity"; I am happy to allow that there are several

10. This is complicated. It may be on the basis of my status as a *White* adoptive mother of *Black* children that my privilege is denied. In this case I would want to say that the subordination is intersectional—racial assumptions are working together with other non-racial assumptions to disadvantage me. What this highlights is that race often does not function (does it ever?) as a single variable in oppression. It may be in contexts such as we are imagining that my Whiteness is diminished, and this in turn may suggest that race, even as I have defined it, is a scalar notion, not all-or-nothing, that is, some individuals as well as some groups of individuals may be more "racialized" than others. (Thanks to Larry Blum for helping me think through some of these complexities; as I understand his view, Blum would argue that this is evidence that I am giving an account of racialization (and racialized groups), but not race. See Blum (2001).

senses that are important. My goal here is modest—to highlight a sense of identity that is often left out of philosophical discussion.[11]

On the approach I've proposed, the social construction of race depends on both a set of symbolic and narrative resources for interpreting human bodies and a set of social and political institutions structured to privilege certain of those bodies, as interpreted. One strategy for thinking about racial identity would be to focus first on the social and political institutions in which racial injustice is materially implemented, and to view racial identities as the normative subjectivities that are deemed appropriate for (and help sustain) those institutions. The relevant analogy would be to see gender identities as the modes of subjective femininity and masculinity that are regarded as suitable to females and males respectively, and whose "proper" or "appropriate" development create subjects who, more or less, function effectively in the institutions constituting gender. Black, White, Asian (etc.) identities are made available to us as part of the process of constituting racial subjects who can function effectively in the institutions constituting race.

There are some advantages to this strategy: societies/cultures have ways of constructing subjects whose lives "unfold" in the sorts of ways that fit within the structure of social life. Racial identity becomes the (idealized) self-understanding of those who are members of racialized groups. Individual members may have the relevant self-understanding to a greater or lesser extent, but the strength of their racial identity is evaluated relative to the "ideal."

This strategy, however, is problematic for several reasons. First, it (at least) appears to prioritize the institutional over the cultural: subjectivity is formed in order to suit the needs of social structures. But we must acknowledge that social structures also mutate in response to cultural shifts in symbolic resources available for the construction of subjectivity. This is a corollary, I believe, of the claim that racism is the joint product of social structures and cultural meanings. On this approach, the shape and evolution of culture, and so of subjectivity, cannot be accounted for by a simple social functionalism.

Second, this strategy appears to make us victims of racial and gender identities: it is unclear to what extent we are agents in constructing our own identities, and it is unclear whether identities that are, admittedly, con-

11. Note that one of the uses of "racial identity" is for the notion of race (or racialized group) as I've defined it above (or for a similar notion). In the context of this paper I use the term "racial identity" to draw a contrast with the notion of race as social class. I don't mean to legislate that the term "racial identity" should not be used to refer to one's racial class membership (one's race); I'm using the term as I do largely because I'm drawing on work in psychology and feminist theory where the more psychological/somatic meaning I am explicating is one of the standard uses.

structed in the context of race or sex oppression, can have emancipatory elements. If one has a racial identity only to the extent that one is a "good" racial subject, that is, a subject whose "identity" enables him or her to "fit" with and so sustain institutions of racial domination, then we have no way to accommodate the importance of racial identity, particularly in subordinated groups, in *resisting* racism.

One possible response is to think of identity, and so racial identity, as a much more self-conscious and potentially political kind of awareness. On this account to have a racial identity is not just to have a certain kind of self-understanding, but for that self-understanding to include as an explicit (and perhaps chosen or at least "owned"?) part that one is a member of a particular race. As an example of an account that leans in this direction, consider Anthony Appiah's account of racial identity in "Race, Culture, Identity: Misunderstood Connections" (Appiah and Gutmann 1996, 30–105). On Appiah's account racial identity involves a process of "identification," and "identification" according to him is defined as

> the process through which an individual intentionally shapes her projects—including her plans for her own life and her conception of the good—by reference to available labels, available identities. (Appiah and Gutmann 1996, 78)

He goes on to define racial identity (roughly) as:

> . . . a label R, associated with *ascriptions* by most people (where ascription involves descriptive criteria for applying the label); and *identifications* by those who fall under it (where identification implies a shaping role for the label in the intentional acts of the possessors, so that they sometimes act *as an R*), where there is a history of associating possessors of the label with an inherited racial essence (even if some who use the label no longer believe in racial essences). (Appiah and Gutmann 1996, 83–84)

As I understand this view, "White", for example, is a racial identity just in case it is a label that has a history of being associated with a racial essence, and it is ascribed to people on the basis of descriptive criteria, and those who are White identify with the label in the sense that they sometimes form intentions to act *as a White person,* and subsequently so act.

The part of this view that is of primary interest for our current purposes concerns what it is for an individual to have a particular racial identity. (The suggestion that the identity is the label puzzles me somewhat.) Taking White identity as our example, Appiah's answer seems to be that X has a White (racial) identity just in case "White" is a racial identity (it is a label of the right sort) and the label "White" plays a role in X's self-understanding, so at least some of X's intentional acts are performed *as a White person.* (Is it also required that X be considered White?)

This account solves several of the problems mentioned above, while also providing a model that could be adapted to my account of race. Appiah makes explicit that he does not view racial identities as (wholly) voluntary (Appiah and Gutmann 1996, 80), but insofar as the main role of racial identity is in the framing of one's intentional action, and this is a primary site of agency, this account frees us from the concern that we are victims of our racial identities. Moreover, the racial labels Appiah has in mind are linked with a history of racial essentialism, but there seems to be no functionalist assumption that requires us to explain the use or evolution of the labels in terms of their role in supporting the background social structure. Admittedly, Appiah counts certain labels as "racial" by virtue of their association with racial essences, and my account of race makes no reference to supposed racial essences; but it would be possible to require instead that the labels count as "racial" by virtue of their association with a hierarchy of "colors," that is, geographically marked (and ranked) bodies.

However, I don't think this captures much of what is at stake in theorizing racial identity. So I want to offer a different notion (perhaps just to add to the collection) that I think is better suited to understanding how race is not just an idea acted upon or acted with, but is deeply embodied. Part of what is motivating me is the sense that most people who I'd locate centrally as having a White identity do not seem to employ the label "White" in the way Appiah's view would require, since Whites, as the privileged group, tend to think of themselves as "raceless," and I suspect that most would find it difficult to point to any actions they perform "as a White person." They don't "identify" as White in the strong sense in question, but they are White, and I would like to claim that they also have a White identity.

What worries me most about Appiah's approach is its hyper-cognitivism, particularly its intentionalism. There are important components of racial identity, I want to argue, that are somatic, largely habitual, regularly unconscious, often ritualized. Our racial identities deeply condition how we live our bodies and relate to other bodies. Individuals are socialized to become embodied subjects, not just rational, cognitive agents; so race and gender socialization isn't just a matter of instilling concepts and indoctrinating beliefs, but are also ways of training the body. Training the body to feel, to see, to touch, to fear, to love. I do not claim that our identities are entirely non-cognitive, but to focus entirely on the cognitive, especially the intentional, is to miss the many ways that we unintentionally and unconsciously participate in racism and sexism.

A further concern that arises in philosophical discussion of identity is that there is a tendency to think of identities as something that either one has or one doesn't, and there is a canonical way of having one. Psychologists, however, tend to see identity formation as a developmental process, as something that happens in stages, that can be disrupted, that can be re-

SALLY HASLANGER

visited (e.g., Tatum 1997). One also finds in the psychological literature a strong interest in disaggregating the elements of identity; for example, in one study (Cross 1991, 42) Black identity has been theorized as having two main components (personal identity and reference group orientation), the first of which (PI) is broken down into nine elements,[12] the second (RGO) into eight.[13] This disaggregation allows, among other things, that an individual's racial identity can be strong along one axis and not another, and can shift with respect to the balance of elements over time.

Although I think that the philosophical and political uses of the notion of "identity" shouldn't bow to the psychologists as experts on the sense we want or need, it is helpful, nonetheless, to bear in mind that identities may not be all or nothing (e.g., racial identities may come in degrees and have different formations), and that a conception of identity that we happen to be focused on may be only one stage of a much broader developmental process. I have a particular interest in the developmental issues, because I am keen to understand the process by which societies construct individuals with particular race and gender identities, and how those identities are lived and unlived, embodied and disembodied. To make this point more vivid, let me turn to some more personal reflections.

Let me emphasize to begin, however, that I am speaking from my own experience and a very small sample of others, and I don't mean to suggest that the phenomena I describe occur in all adoptive families or all inter-racial families. Moreover, I certainly want to allow that some of the experiences I describe can happen in other contexts besides transracial parenting, for example, in close inter-racial friendships and love relationships; further, as our communities become more anti-racist, the boundaries of racial identity—should there be any—will have very different meanings than I describe here and, in fact, one may find important generational differences already. What interests me, however, are the ways that racial identity can be disrupted and transformed, and how.

CROSSING THE COLOR LINE

Begin with the body. Although adoptive parents do not have a biological connection to the bodies of their children, like most (at least female) parents, adoptive parents of infants are intimately involved in the physical being of their baby. Parents learn to read the needs and desires of the baby from cries, facial expressions, body language, and in some cases it is as if

12. Self-esteem, self-worth, self-confidence, self-evaluation, interpersonal competence, ego-ideal, personality traits, introversion-extroversion, level of anxiety.
13. Racial identity, group identity, race awareness, racial ideology, race evaluation, race esteem, race image, racial self-identification.

278

the patterns of the child's hunger and fatigue are programmed into your own body. You know when to expect hunger; and when they are a little older, you know when to suggest that they use the potty or take a nap. In the case of older adoptees from other countries, the same may happen in the early phases of trying to parent across language barriers. This empathetic extension of body awareness, this attentiveness to the minute signals of another's body, does not in any metaphysically real sense make the other body part of your own. But taking on the needs and desires of another body *as if* your own, perhaps especially if the other's body is marked as different, alters your own body sense, or what some have called (following Lacan) the "imaginary body." Moira Gatens has argued, "[The] psychical image of the body is necessary in order for us to have motility in the world, without which we could not be intentional subjects. The imaginary body is developed, learnt, connected to the body image of others, and is not static" (Gatens 1996, 12). In some cases of transracial parenting I think it would be correct to say that one's "imaginary body," that is, the largely unconscious sense of one's own body, becomes racially confused.[14]

The constant attentiveness to the other's body trains one to read it: one is cued to respond to it. But importantly, as a parent, one comes to love it. The child and future adult to which one will have some person-to-person relationship is not there yet, and so parental love often takes the form of a delight in the body of the infant—its shape, movements, warmth, etc. The playful and loving engagement of a White parent with a Black infant, however, disrupts what some theorists have called the "racial social geography" (Mills 1999, 52; Frankenberg 1993). Charles Mills develops this notion: "Conceptions of one's White self map a micro-geography of the acceptable routes through racial space . . . imprinted with domination" (Mills 1999, 52). Among other things, such maps "dictate spaces of intimacy and distance" and carry with them proscriptions and punishments for violation. A White parent's daily routine demands these violations. However, the experience of "trespassing" does not give way just to a sense of neutral ground; the experience of holding and physically cherishing one's child can bring the Black body into one's intimate home space—that space where the boundaries of intimacy expand to encompass others.

Interestingly, the effect is not just to alter one's "micro-geography" of race to accommodate one's relationship to one's children; one's entire so-

---

14. I've heard a story recounted in which a White mother of two Korean-born adoptees returns with them to Korea when they are still children. Upon arriving, she expresses a delight in being somewhere where "everyone looks like us," only registering after receiving some curious and puzzled looks that (in the relevant sense) she doesn't look like those around her. On the "imaginary body" see Gatens (1996), viii and chap. 1; Cornell (1995), chap. 1. Both Gatens and Cornell discuss the gendered imaginary; here I am suggesting that their discussions are relevant to the racial imaginary.

cial map is redrawn.[15] For example, I can find many changes in my physical presence among others: whose faces do I first notice in a group? With whom do I make eye contact? Next to whom do I sit? How close do I stand to others in conversation? Whom do I touch in an affectionate greeting? These questions have different answers than they used to. I am physically at home amongst African Americans in a way I was not before.

It is hard to lovingly parent a child without finding him or her beautiful—sometimes exceptionally beautiful. For a White parent of a Black child, this process also disrupts the dominant society's "somatic norm image" (Mills 1999, 61; Hoetink 1973). Insofar as the dominant society teaches us the aesthetics of racism—which is common, but fortunately not ubiquitous—Black bodies are regarded as less beautiful than White ones; or at least more typically under the current aesthetics of racism only those Black bodies that fulfill certain White stereotypes of Blacks (the exotic, the "natural") count as beautiful. Mills suggests:

> The norming of the individual also involves a specific norming of the *body*, an aesthetic norming. Judgements of moral worth are obviously conceptually distinct from judgements of aesthetic worth, but there is a psychological tendency to conflate the two. . . . (Mills 1999, 61)

But a White parent's (White) somatic norm image cannot remain intact in the face of her child's beauty. One can find lengthy conversations on adoption email lists showing how dramatically the transracial adoptive parent's personal aesthetic does change: White babies come to appear pale, wan, even sickly . . . there's a magnetic pull to babies of color. Although some have suggested that such an aesthetic and emotional response to babies that look like your own is a "conditioned reflex" that parents develop (Register 1990, 45), it isn't just an infant or child aesthetic that changes. One's

15. It is important to think about the similarities and differences between the White parent of a Black child, and the Black nanny of a White child. I argue here that the "trespassing" involved in a White's allowing a Black child into intimate space disrupts some important aspects of White identity. But it would seem that there is an asymmetry in the case of a Black nanny of a White child: the nanny allows the White child into intimate space, but this arguably does not (in most cases?) disrupt her Black identity. How can I account for this? Although I don't have a full answer, I think attention should be devoted to thinking about different modes of intimacy, the specific contours of racial geography, and what counts as racial trespassing: Black caretaking of Whites carries a very different meaning than White caretaking of Blacks. Perry (1998), sec. 1. So the operative factors include not just contact and affection, but power relations and the details of the transgressive relationships. Even with this in mind, it isn't clear that the asymmetries can be accounted for in any simple way. Consider, for example, the relationship between Cora (a Black servant) and Jessie (Cora's white employer's daughter) in Langston Hughes's "Cora Unashamed" (Hughes 1962 [1933], 3–18): "In her heart [Cora] had adopted Jessie." Although the relationship altered Jessie's racial geography to be closer to Cora's, arguably Cora's racial geography was not affected. Is this because the danger to Cora of such a shift would be so clear and present?

response to and "evaluation" of adult bodies and, in my own case, even my own body—my shape, my skin, my hair—can change.

Sometimes, through parenting a child of another race, one is drawn into cultural rituals concerning the body. In the case of White parents of Black children, the most obvious are the rituals of caring for hair and skin. I remember vividly our first trip to a Black barbershop for Isaac's first haircut, our anxiety at crossing an important color line. Having moved several times since Isaac joined our family, each time we've had to negotiate the dynamics of entering with him a predominantly Black male space. And when Isaac met his birth grandparents for the first time (we visited them for a long weekend), one of the most important trips of the weekend was to the barbershop, where we were introduced as family.

The issue of girls' hair is even more laden and contested: a friend and mentor confided in me shortly after our daughter Zina joined our family that when she gave birth the second time and the doctor announced, "It's a girl!" the very first thing that went through her mind was, "Oh my gosh, *three* heads of hair to do each morning!" I had only the vaguest appreciation of what she meant until I found myself trying to comb out my sleeping (toddler) daughter's hair to find myself two hours into it with her awake, screaming, and me in tears. But I have been guided and coached, by friends and acquaintances, by beauty store clerks, the crowd at the barbershop, by Zina herself. It is not just that I have learned various techniques and the use of products I never knew existed, but the hours and hours Zina and I spend together doing her hair have a deep effect on our relationship, and I'm certain that this would have no correlate with a biological daughter of mine. Moreover, this experience has affected my relationship with Black women (both friends and strangers!)—we talk of hair, of the effects of hair rituals on mother-daughter relationships, of aesthetic and political values represented by hair.

Steve and I master the rituals of the body not just for Isaac and Zina's sake, but because norms of appearance vary across race, and we as parents are judged by those norms. Although it is not the case that there is a single unified African American "culture" or set of appearance norms—these vary by class, region of the country, even neighborhood—norms of appearance for children, for example, how the hair should be worn, what sorts of clothes and shoes are appropriate, in most contexts are race-specific. These norms are gradually internalized: I feel anxious at not meeting the standards; I judge others by them, etc. Although I don't uncritically accept the norms of the local Black community in deciding on the appearance or behavior of my children (isn't everyone's relationship to their local norms complex and negotiated?), those norms are ones that I daily consider and respond to.

My own sense of community has dramatically changed. I'm not entirely comfortable anymore in an all-White setting; if I go to a large event that is filled with a sea of White faces, I'm unsettled. Some of the discomfort may come from the wariness that develops when my children are with me in such contexts; I'm concerned about other people's responses to them, their own sense of belonging. This may rub off so that similar feelings arise even when they aren't with me. But it is more than this, for I think it is similar to the discomfort that arises sometimes for those with non-White ancestry who are not distinctively marked physically as a person of color. One carries a background anxiety that someone, not knowing your family, your background, is going to assume that you're White or of a White family and display their racism (Piper 1992; Derricotte 1997). And then you'll have to say something, or not, and you'll have to live with what they said or did. In my own case, it is actually easier for me to bear offensive actions actually directed at me, than to bear them, whether performed knowingly or not, directed at my kids. Racism is no longer just something I find offensive and morally objectionable; I experience it as a personal harm. There is an important sense in which a harm to my kids is a harm to me; by being open to that harm, I am more fully aware of the cost of racial injustice for all of us.[16]

But it isn't just a matter of anxiety around large groups of White strangers; in mixed settings where there is a tendency to group by race or at least by White/non-White, I am drawn to those who aren't White. Often I feel that I have more in common with them, that their life concerns are closer to mine. I am a mother of Black children, my extended family is at least one-third Black. When I want to talk about my kids, their future, our family, there's a lot that I don't think my White friends and family understand.

RACIAL IDENTITY REVISITED

Is there some way to organize these anecdotes toward a more theoretical account? It appears that together they highlight several different dimensions of racial "identity" we might want to capture:

---

16. Sharon Rush (2000) suggests the concept of "transformative love" for this experience:

Transformative love . . . moves beyond racial empathy because it does not depend on Whites' imaginations. A person who experiences transformative love literally *feels* some of the direct pain caused by racism. . . . Importantly, I am not saying that I *know* what Blacks feel when racism hits them; I don't and never will. I am saying that I used to think empathy was as close as one could get to understanding another's pain. Loving across the color line, I am feeling something that is deeper and more personal than empathetic pain. Ironically, this new feeling, although situated in feeling the pain of racial injustice, is more empowering than empathy when it is mixed with love. (169)

- unconscious somatic (routine behaviors, skills and "know-hows")
- unconscious imaginary (unconscious self-image/somatic image)
- tacit cognitive (tacit understandings, tacit evaluations)
- perceptual (perceptional selectivity, recognitional capacities)
- conscious cognitive (fear, apprehension, attraction, sense of community)
- normative (aesthetic judgments, judgments of suitability or appropriateness, internalized or not?)

Many of these, I believe, cannot be captured in the kind of intentionalist account Appiah offers (Rorty and Wong 1990). And plausibly we will need a quite complex model to do justice to all of them. At this point we may have to make do with metaphors that point to a model.

In his book on African American identity, William E. Cross provides a compelling account of the development of racial identity. According to him,

> In a generic sense, one's identity is a maze or map that functions in a multitude of ways to guide and direct exchanges with one's social and material realities. (Cross 1991, 214)

(Remember, the map image was also present in Mills.) Does the image of an internal map help in rethinking racial identity? In the context of feminist work on gender, the image of a map is more often replaced with the image of a script. But the map image might be preferable insofar as it need not be understood linguistically, and may involve a "map" of one's own body. Some may prefer the notion of a "program," since it seems even less cognitive than a map—but it can also invoke the specter of determinism.

There are some advantages to the metaphor of a map: map boundaries vary—what's included and what's not; their design is responsive to different concerns (contrast road maps with topographical maps) and different values (what's central, what's marginal); they vary in scale and effectiveness. Maps also function to guide the body: they are a basis for exercising "know-how," they provide information on the basis of which we can form intentions and act. And yet, the image of a map suggests that one's racial identity is something conscious (to be consulted?) and still rather cognitive (e.g., the idea that one knows how to ride a bike because one employs an internal "map" is not plausible). Moreover, we need racial identity not only to guide social interactions but also to frame in a much more basic way our perceptions and evaluations of ourselves and others. (Yet when navigating in unfamiliar locations, don't we sometimes fail to see what is not included on our map?) Perhaps the solution is to think of "maps" as sometimes tacit and unconscious, sometimes more explicit and conscious.

283

Interestingly, it is plausible that in crossing "the color line," as in transracial adoption, the tacit racial maps are forced into consciousness and made explicit.[17]

Nonetheless, keeping in mind these limitations of the metaphor (and perhaps drawing on Cross's other suggestion of an internal "maze"—a framework or structure of thought), is there some way to distinguish different racial maps that function as different racial identities? And is there a way to do it without assuming that all Blacks, or all Whites, or all Asians have the same substantive identity, that is, that their identities have the very same content?

Here is a proposal. The account of race I offered above gives some way of identifying the "social and material realities of race" for particular groups: the social and material realities of Whiteness, for example, concern the cultural process of marking the body as apparently descended (predominantly) from Europeans, and the structural privileging of those so marked. Given this, however, we can then focus on those aspects of our overall identity, that is, our broad map—perhaps our atlas?—that guides and directs exchanges with the racial dimension of our lives. So, someone has a White racial identity just in case their map is formed to guide someone marked as White through the social and material realities that are (in that context) characteristic of Whites as a group. More generally, one has an X racial identity just in case their map is formed to guide someone marked as X through the social and material realities that are (in that context) characteristic of Xs as a group.[18] Note that on this account a White person who resists the privileges of Whiteness—and so works from a map that navigates them *around* those privileges, rather than *toward* them— nonetheless has a White identity, for their map is formed in response to (though not necessarily accepting) the material realities of being White. Likewise, a Black person who resists the disadvantages of Blackness—navigating around those disadvantages in any number of different ways—has a Black identity.

Note that this proposal addresses the two concerns raised before: it does not entail that a White racial identity is constructed to sustain White privilege (or that the identity of a person of color must be constructed to sus-

17. So, anticipating what is yet to come, not only is a transracial adoptee's (and transracial parent's) racial identity different from other racial "typicals," by being "mixed," but is also different in being less tacit and taken for granted, and more conscious and navigated. Thanks to Charlotte Witt for helping me think through this point.

18. Note that this analysis depends on the prior definition of race or racialized groups insofar as it presupposes that we can specify the markings and social/material realities of particular racialized groups. But because I am offering a focal analysis in which racial identity is the derivative notion and race the central or focal notion, this is not problematic. It is in fact an important feature of the project that the derived notions depend in this way on the central notion.

tain their subordination); the point is rather that the identity is formed in navigating the social and material impact of one's race. In special cases, one's identity is formed or reformed in navigating the impact of one's loved one's race, or perhaps a race one wants or needs to have; it can also be formed or reformed through a conscious commitment to anti-racism. This account allows that, at least insofar as it is possible to have some critical agency with respect to the maps that guide us, we are not helpless victims of racial socialization. Moreover, it allows that racial identity comes in degrees: we vary in the extent to which our lives and self-understandings are formed in response to the social frameworks of race. Let me conclude this section, however, by saying that although I am hopeful that uses of the notion of a map by Cross and Mills will be helpful in developing further this account of racial identity, I think quite a bit more work needs to be done in explicating it.

"MIXED" IDENTITIES

Earlier I suggested that there is at least one sense of identity in which my racial identity has changed tremendously through the experience of parenting Black children. It would be wrong, I think, to say that I am Black, or that I see myself as Black, or that I intend sometimes to act "as a Black person"; I don't even think it is correct to say in a much weaker sense that I have a Black identity. But I do think that my map for navigating the social and material realities of race has adjusted so that I'm now navigating much more often as if my social and material realities are determined by being "marked" as of African descent. As I've emphasized, I am not marked as of African descent. But as a parent of children who are, my day-to-day life is filled with their physical being and social reality, and by extension, the reality of their extended families and their racial community. And their realities have in an important sense become mine.

But it is also the case that there is much of my life in which I continue to rely on old (White) maps, and in which I work to contest and challenge the realities of my Whiteness from the position of being White. As a result, I'm tempted to conclude that my racial identity, in at least the specific sense I've outlined, should count as "mixed." I have, in an important sense, been resocialized by my kids, and although I do not share their "blood," I have "inherited" some aspects of their race.[19]

It may be worth taking a moment, however, to consider different ways in which racial identity might count as "mixed." The term "mixed" is typically used to refer to individuals whose recent ancestors are differently marked

19. Thanks to Jackie Stevens for pointing out this inversion.

racially. And in contemporary racial politics, there is a movement to affirm the identities of those who count as "mixed" (note the recent change on the U.S. Census to include a biracial category). My point here is not to claim a mixed identity in this sense:

> X has a racially "mixed" identity₁ just in case (and to the extent that) X's internal "map" is formed to guide someone marked as of "mixed" ancestry through the social and material realities that structure (in that context) the lives of those of "mixed" ancestry as a group.

But there is an alternative notion that may also, at least in some contexts, characterize those of "mixed" ancestry:

> X has a racially "mixed" identity₂ just in case (and to the extent that) X's internal "map" is substantially fragmented, that is, is formed to guide, in some contexts and along some dimensions, someone marked as of one race, and in other contexts and other dimensions, a person marked as of a different race.

In contexts where it is important to keep our terminology clear, we might speak of racially "mixed" identity (the first sense) and racially "aggregated" (or fragmented?) identity (in the second sense).

But what of my kids? What is their racial identity? Of course the racial identity of young children is a very different matter than the racial identity of adults. But what are the prospects for their racial identities? Given that neither have any prospect for passing as White, they will grow up with the realities of racism and will develop identities that are responsive to those realities. A more pressing question, however, is whether they can, as our children, develop healthy Black identities. Living in a Black neighborhood, attending integrated schools and a Black church, having Black friends and extended family, I think it is almost certain that they will have resources for developing strong and healthy Black identities, that is, it will be possible for them to construct maps that guide them in self-affirming and racial group-affirming ways. But no doubt they will also be sheltered from certain aspects of racism by living with us, they will learn by our example some patterns of social interaction that are responsive to White privilege, and they will develop some primary somatic connections to White bodies. So it is arguable that their identities will also be, at least to some extent, "mixed" (i.e., "aggregated"). But is this a problem? Is this by itself grounds for doubting that transracial adoption is acceptable?

To begin, let me note that there are many different reasons for questioning the practice of transracial adoption, especially as it occurs under current social conditions.[20] Even if one believes that in many cases trans-

---

20. The term "transracial adoption," although sometimes used to refer to international

racial adoption is permissible, one might object to the child welfare policies and broader context of economic injustice that make transracial adoption appear to be the best option for some birth families and children of color (Perry 1998; cf. Bartholet 1999). It is important to keep in mind that the debate over transracial adoption is not *just* about "identity" but also concerns questions of power (racial, sexual, cultural, and economic) and autonomy (individual, community, and national).

With this in mind, I want to maintain that the fact that transracial adoptees plausibly develop "mixed" ("aggregated") racial identities is not a basis for opposing transracial adoption. First, it is plausible that many middle-class Blacks have similarly "mixed" identities, and it is problematic, I think, to insist that there is a form of "pure" Black (or other raced) identity that should be the ideal for anyone, including adopted children. Second, although there is much of value to be found in racialized communities, I would argue that organizing ourselves (both psychically and as communities) primarily around race—rather than, for example, values, histories, cultures—should not be our long-term objective. It is politically important to recognize that race is real and has a profound effect on our lives, but it is also important to resist being racialized and participating in racial forms of life. (Recall that on my view, race is inherently hierarchical; ethnicity is its non-hierarchical counterpart [Haslanger 2000]). To this end, the formation of "aggregate" or "fragmented" identities is one strategy (of many) for disrupting the embodiment of racial hierarchy and the hegemony of current racial categories. Another (not incompatible) strategy might involve working against racial hierarchy (and so, on my view, against race) in a way that maintains extensional equivalents of racial categories that function more like ethnicities: by re-valuing racialized traits, reconfiguring racialized practices to be more egalitarian, eliminating racist institutions.

But perhaps my argument does not address the real issues. The more common objections to transracial adoption are not to cases in which children of color are part of an integrated community in open adoptions. The cases of greater concern are those in which the parents' identity does not shift, because the ordinary somatic norms and racialized maps are entrenched, or in which the children are given little or no resources for forming the kinds of identity that will enable them to integrate into a Black

---

adoptions in which the adoptee's race differs from that of the adoptive parents, tends to be used more often in the context of domestic Black-White adoptions, specifically where the adoptees are Black and the adoptive parents are White. ("Cross-cultural" adoption is more commonly used for international adoptions of children of color by White parents.) Throughout this paper I have focused on the domestic Black-White "transracial adoption," mostly because I've been explicitly drawing on my personal experience in such a family. However, I intend the points I am making here to apply under the broader sense of the term. See Perry (1998).

community (or a community of individuals "marked" in relevantly similar ways as the child), or to form adequate defenses against racism. This can happen, no doubt about it. And it certainly would be a horror to be brought up by parents whose racial identities cast you, their child, as a racialized Other. If it can be determined in advance that particular prospective adoptive parents would be incapable of a loving attachment to a child of a different race, this is obviously a good reason not to allow a transracial adoption in the particular case. Whether placement would be absolutely precluded would have to depend, I think, on what the other options for the child are. But I hope that the anecdotal evidence offered above shows at least that it is possible for the racial identities of White parents to shift in significant ways, for their racial "maps" to be profoundly altered.[21] This is crucial in order for parents to mirror back to the child the kind of affirmation and love that enables self-love, and that one demands of healthy parenting.[22]

It does seem possible for White parents to overcome some of those aspects of their identity that would make transracial parenting only a poor imitation of same-race parenting; and it does seem possible for White parents to provide a context in which children of color can form healthy racial identities. This is not easy; it is a challenge for any parent (biological or adoptive) of a child of color to raise a child with secure self-esteem and effective strategies to combat racism. White parents of a child of color will no doubt have to depend on the skills and knowledge of the child's racial community in order to succeed.

But a further question is whether and to what extent encouraging the development of a racial identity is a good thing. If, after all, race is a system of dominance and subordination, shouldn't we be attempting to bring up children who do not identify with one race or another, shouldn't we foster color blindness? And aren't transracial families the ideal place to do this?

On the rough account I've given of racial identities, they are responsive to the realities of race and racial subordination/privilege, but they don't necessarily sustain those realities, for the maps we use to navigate our racial positions may also guide us in resisting them. I would argue that it would be irresponsible to bring up kids who will inevitably face racism without the resources to handle it and identities that provide a defense against it. This requires attention to the social differences between White parents and children of color and, I think, over time, requires providing children the tools to construct their own political analysis of those differences. But

---

21. In fact, Cross cites one study in which the RGO of transracially adopted children at age four is "stronger" and more "Black oriented" that that of their inracially adopted peers. See Cross (1991), 111.

22. On the development of self-love in a context of injustice, see Thomas (2000).

the sense of race they develop need not be essentialist and can be pragmatic. My hope is that ultimately cultural/ethnic differences will replace racial differences. In the terms of my account, that cultural/ethnic difference will not be marked as a site of subordination and privilege. When that time comes, I think we will no longer have the need of racial identities; that is to say that we will no longer need maps that guide us in navigating the social and material injustices of race. I am deeply committed to bringing about that day, but clearly it is not today, nor will it be tomorrow. Until then, the best I can do is to navigate the racial spaces of my life with maps that support and guide me in resisting racial dominance and subordination, and to offer my children resources for constructing maps that will sustain them in the face of it.

References

ACLU Lesbian and Gay Rights Project. 2002. *Too High a Price: The Case against Restricting Gay Parenting.* New York: ACLU. http://www.lethimstay.com/pdfs/gayadoptionbook .pdf (accessed: 8 December 2003).

Administration for Children and Families. United States Department of Health & Human Services. 2000. *Child Maltreatment 1998: Reports from the States to the National Child Abuse and Neglect Data System.* Washington, DC: U.S. Government Printing Office.

——. 2003. "The AFCARS Report: Preliminary FY 2001 Estimates." http://www.acf.hhs .gov/programs/cb/publications/afcars/report8.htm (accessed: March 2003).

Aiken, William, and Hugh LaFollette. 1980. *Whose Child? Children's Rights, Parental Authority, and State Power.* Totowa, NJ: Littlefield Adams.

Alexander, M. Jacqui. 1994. "Not (Any) Body Can Be a Citizen: The Politics of Law, Sexuality, and Postcoloniality in Trinidad and Tobago and the Bahamas." *Feminist Review* no. 48 (Autumn).

——. 1997. "Erotic Autonomy as a Politics of Decolonization: An Anatomy of Feminist and State Practice in the Bahamas Tourist Economy." In *Feminist Genealogies, Colonial Legacies, Democratic Futures,* edited by M. Jacqui Alexander and Chandra Talpade Mohanty, 76–77. New York: Routledge.

Allen, Anita L. 1988. "Privacy, Surrogacy, and the Baby M Case." *Georgetown Law Journal* 76: 1759–1792.

——. 1992–1993. "Do Children Have a Right to a Certain Identity?" *Rechtstheorie* 15: 109–19.

——. 1997. "Genetic Privacy." In *Genetic Secrets: Protecting Privacy and Confidentiality in the Genetic Era,* edited by Mark A. Rothstein, 31–59. New Haven, CT: Yale University Press.

Allen, Jennifer. 1984. "Motherhood: The Annihilation of Women." In *Feminist Frameworks: Alternative Theoretical Accounts of the Relations between Women and Men,* edited by Alison M. Jaggar and Paula S. Rothenberg, 380–85. 3rd ed. New York: McGraw-Hill.

REFERENCES

Alliance for Children, Massachusetts. 2001. http://www.allforchildren.org (accessed: 20 May 2001).

Alton, Kristine. 2000. "Casenote: In re Adoption of Kelsey S." *Journal of Contemporary Legal Issues* 11: 547–53.

Anderlik, Mary R., and Mark A. Rothstein. 2002. "The Genetics Revolution: Conflicts, Challenges, and Conundra: DNA-Based Identity Testing and the Future of the Family: A Research Agenda." *American Journal of Law and Medicine* 28: 215.

Anderson, Elizabeth. 1990. "Is Women's Labor a Commodity?" *Philosophy and Public Affairs* 19: 71–92.

———. 1993. *Value in Ethics and Economics*. Cambridge, MA: Harvard University Press.

———. 1995. "Feminist Epistemology: An Interpretation and Defense." *Hypatia* 10: 50–84.

———. 2002. "Feminist Epistemology and Philosophy of Science." In *The Stanford Encyclopedia of Philosophy*, edited by Edward N. Zalta. http://plato.stanford.edu/archives/fall2002/entries/feminism-epistemology/.

Anna J. v. Mark C., 286 Cal. Rptr. 369 (Cal. App. 1991), review granted, 822 p.2d.1317 (Cal. 1992).

Appell, Annette R. 1995. "Blending Families through Adoption: Implications for Collaborative Adoption Law and Practice." *Boston University Law Review* 75: 997–1061.

Appiah, Kwame Anthony. 1992. *In My Father's House*. New York: Oxford University Press.

Appiah, Kwame Anthony, and Amy Gutmann. 1996. *Color Conscious: The Political Morality of Race*. Princeton, NJ: Princeton University Press.

Aristotle. 1985. *Nicomachean Ethics*. Translated by Terence Irwin. 2nd ed. Indianapolis: Hackett.

Ashe, Marie. 1995. "Postmodernism, Legal Ethics, and Representation of 'Bad Mothers.'" In *Mothers in Law: Feminist Theory and the Legal Regulation of Motherhood*, edited by Martha A. Fineman and Isbel Karpin, 142–66. New York: Routledge.

Associated Services for International Adoption. 2001. http://www.asiadopt.org (accessed: 20 May 2001).

Austin, Carol. 1995. "Latent Tendencies and Covert Acts." In *The Adoption Reader: Birth Mothers, Adoptive Mothers, and Adoptive Daughters Tell Their Stories*, edited by Susan Wadia-Ellis, 105–13. Seattle: Seal.

Badgett, M. V. Lee. 2001. *Money, Myths, and Change*. Chicago: University of Chicago Press.

Baher v. Miike. 1996. WL 694235 (Hawai'i Cir.Ct.).

Baker v. Vermont. 744 A.2d 864.

Bakhtin, Mikhail M. 1981. "Discourse in the Novel." In *The Dialogic Imagination*, edited by M. Holquist, 259–422. Austin: University of Texas Press.

Banks, Richard. 1998. "The Color of Desire: Fulfilling Adoptive Parents' Racial Preferences through Discriminatory State Action." *Yale Law Journal* 107: 875–964.

Barber, Elinor. 1955. *The Bourgeoisie in 18th-Century France*. Princeton, NJ: Princeton University Press.

Bartholet, Elizabeth. 1991. "Where Do Black Children Belong? The Politics of Race Matching in Adoption." *University of Pennsylvania Law Review* 139: 1163–1256.

———. 1993. *Family Bonds: Adoption and the Politics of Parenting*. New York: Houghton Mifflin.

———. 1999a. *Nobody's Children: Abuse and Neglect, Foster Drift, and the Adoption Alternative*. Boston: Beacon.

———. 1999b. "Taking Adoption Seriously: Radical Revolution or Modest Revisionism." *Capital University Law Review* 28: 85.

Bartlett, Katharine. 1984. "Rethinking Parenthood as an Exclusive Status." *Virginia Law Review* 70: 837–1012.

Beauchamp, Thomas, and J. Childress. 2001. *Principles of Biomedical Ethics.* New York: Oxford University Press.

Beauvoir, Simone de. 1974 [1952]. *The Second Sex.* Translated by H. M. Parshley. New York: Alfred A. Knopf.

Becker, Lawrence. 1977. *Property Rights: Philosophic Foundations.* Boston: Routledge.

Belkin, Lisa. 1999. "Getting the Girl." *New York Times Magazine,* 25 July 1999, 29.

Benning, Victoria, and Philip Bennett. 1992. "Racial Lines Shadow New Generation." *Boston Globe,* 13 September 1992.

Berkner, Lutz. 1973. "Recent Research on the History of the Family in Western Europe." *Journal of Marriage and the Family* 35: 395–405.

Bernard, Diane. 1992. "The Dark Side of Family Preservation." *Affilia* 7(2): 156–59.

Bishop, Donna M., and Charles E. Frazier. 1996. "Race Effects in Juvenile Justice Decision-Making: Findings of a Statewide Analysis." *Journal of Criminal Law & Criminology* 86:392.

Blackstone, William. 1966. *Commentaries on the Law of England.* 3rd ed. New York: Oxford University Press.

Blum, Lawrence. 1997. *Multicultural Education as Values Education.* Harvard Project on Schooling and Children, Working Paper.

———. 2001. *"I'm Not a Racist, But . . .": The Moral Quandary of Race.* Ithaca, NY: Cornell University Press.

Blustein, Jeffrey. 1982. *Parents and Children: The Ethics of the Family.* New York: Oxford University Press.

Boggis, Terry. 2001. "Affording Our Families: Class Issues in Family Formation." In *Queer Families, Queer Politics,* edited by M. Bernstein and R. Reimann, 175–200. New York: Columbia University Press.

Bowen, James, S. 1987–88. "Cultural Convergences and Divergences: The Nexus between Putative African American Family Values and the Best Interest of the Child." *Journal of Family Law,* 1987–88: 487–544.

Bowlby, John. 1969. *Attachment.* Vol. 1 of *Attachment and Loss.* New York: Basic Books.

Brand, Ann E., and Paul M. Brinich. 1999. "Behavior Problems and Mental Health Contacts in Adopted, Foster, and Nonadopted Children." *Journal of Child Psychology and Psychiatry and Allied Disciplines* 40: 1221–29.

Bright Futures Adoption Agency. 2001. http://www.bright-futures.org (accessed: 20 May 2001).

British Medical Association. 2001. Organ Transplant Ethics. http://web.bma.org.uk (accessed: 20 May 2001).

Brooks, Susan L. 2001. "The Case for Adoption Alternatives." *Family and Conciliation Courts Review* 39: 43–53.

Butler, Judith. 1991. "Imitation and Gender Insubordination." In *Inside/Out: Lesbian and Gay Theories,* edited by Diana Fuss, 13–31. New York: Routledge.

———. 1997. *The Psychic Life of Power: Theories in Subjection.* Stanford, CA: Stanford University Press.

Buzawa, Eve S., and Carl G. Buzawa. 1996. *Domestic Violence: The Criminal Justice Response.* 2nd ed. Thousand Oaks, CA: Sage.

Cahill, Sean, Ellen Mitra, and Sarah Tobias. 2002. *Family Policy: Issues Affecting Gay, Lesbian, Bisexual, and Transgender Families.* New York: The National Gay and Lesbian Taskforce Policy Institute.

Cahill, Sean, and Kenneth T. Jones, 2001. *Leaving Our Children Behind: Welfare Reform and the Gay, Lesbian, Bisexual, and Transgender Community.* New York: National Gay and Lesbian Taskforce Policy Institute.

Cahn, Naomi, R. 1994. "Family Issue(s)." *University of Chicago Law Review* 61: 325.

———. 1999. "Models of Family Privacy." *George Washington Law Review* 67: 1225–46.

Cahn, Naomi, and Jana Singer. 1999. "Adoption, Identity, and the Constitution: The Case for Opening Closed Records." *University of Pennsylvania Journal of Constitutional Law* 2: 150.

Calhoun, Cheshire. 2000. *Feminism, the Family, and the Politics of the Closet: Lesbian and Gay Displacement.* New York: Oxford University Press.

California Family Code. Division 12, Part 3, Chapter 2, § 7611.

Cannon, Janell. 1993. *Stellaluna.* New York: Scholastic Books.

Carby, Hazel. "White Women Listen!: Black Feminism and the Boundaries of Sisterhood." In *Black British Cultural Studies: A Reader,* edited by Houston A. Baker Jr., Manthia Diawara, and Ruth H. Lindeborg, 61–86. Chicago: University of Chicago Press.

Carp, E. Wayne. 1998. *Family Matters: Secrecy and Disclosure in the History of Adoption.* Cambridge, MA: Harvard University Press.

Caulfield, Timothy. 2000. "Canadian Family Law and the Genetic Revolution: A Survey of Cases Involving Paternity Testing." *Queen's Law Journal* 26: 67.

Center for an Urban Future. 1998. "Race, Bias, and Power in Child Welfare." *Child Welfare Watch* (Spring/Summer): 1.

Chambers, David. 1996. "What If: The Legal Consequences of Marriage and the Legal Needs of Lesbian and Gay Male Couples." *Michigan Law Review* 95: 447–91.

Chesler, Phyllis. 1986. *Mothers on Trial: The Battle for Children and Custody.* San Diego, CA: McGraw-Hill.

———. 1988. *The Sacred Bond: The Legacy of Baby M.* New York: Random House.

Children's Home Society, Washington. 2001. Adoption Rules. http://www.cshs.org (accessed: 20 May 2001).

Cloud, Dana. 1992. "The Possibility of a Liberating Narrative: *Woman on the Edge of Time* as Radical, Mythic, Moral Argument." In *Constructing and Reconstructing Gender: The Links among Communication, Language, and Gender,* edited by Linda A. M. Perry, Lynn H. Turner, and Helen M. Sterk. Albany: State University of New York Press.

Code, Lorraine. 1995. *Rhetorical Spaces: Essays on Gendered Locations.* New York: Routledge.

Cohen, Felix. 1954. "Dialogue on Private Property." *Rutgers Law Review* 9: 357–406.

Collins, Patricia Hill. 1991. *Black Feminist Thought.* New York: Routledge.

Colonial Laws of Massachusetts. 1660. Vol. 2. Reprint, Boston 1889. Edited by Robert H. Bremner et al. Cambridge, MA: 1971.

Colorado Department of Human Services. Rules: Adoption Code. 7.500.2. http://www.cdhs.state.co.us (accessed: 20 May 2001).

Comparison of the Experiences of Adult Korean and Black Transracial Adoptees. Lanham, MD: Rowman and Littlefield.

Cooper, John. 1980. "Aristotle on Friendship." In *Essays on Aristotle's Ethics,* edited by Amélie Oksenberg Rorty, 301–40. Berkeley: University of California Press.

Corbett, Sara. 2002. "Where Do Babies Come From?: Complex Origins of Cambodian 'Orphans.'" *New York Times Magazine,* 16 June 2002, 42–85.

Cornell, Drucilla. 1991. *Beyond Accommodation: Ethical Feminism, Deconstruction, and the Law.* New York: Routledge.

——. 1995. *The Imaginary Domain: Abortion, Pornography, and Sexual Harassment.* New York: Routledge.

——. 1998. *The Heart of Freedom: Feminism, Sex, and Equality.* Princeton, NJ: Princeton University Press.

Cornell Law School Legal Information Institute. 2003. Adoption Laws of the Fifty States, District of Columbia, and Puerto Rico. http://www.law.cornell.edu/topics/Table_Adoption.htm (accessed: 30 December 2003).

Costin, Lela B., Jacob Karger, and David Stoesz. 1996. *The Politics of Child Abuse in America.* New York: Oxford University Press.

Cott, Nancy. 1977. *The Bonds of True Womanhood: "Women's Sphere" in New England, 1780–1835.* New Haven, CT: Yale University Press.

Courtney, Mark. 1997. "The Politics and Realities of Transracial Adoption." *Child Welfare* 76 (6): 749–79.

——. 1998. "The Costs of Child Protection in the Context of Welfare Reform." *Future of Children* 8 (1): 88–103.

Courtney, Mark E., and Irene Vin-Ling Wong. 1996. "Comparing the Timing of Exits from Substitute Care." *Child and Youth Services Review* 18: 307.

Crenshaw, Kimberle. 1991. "Mapping the Margins: Intersectionality, Identity Politics, and Violence against Women of Color." *Stanford Law Review* 43: 1241–99.

Cross, William E. Jr. 1991. *Shades of Black: Diversity in African-American Identity.* Philadelphia: Temple University Press.

Dailey, Timothy J. 2002. "Homosexual Parenting: Placing Children at Risk." http://www.orthodoxytoday.org/articles/DaileyGayAdopt.htm (accessed: 8 December 2003).

Dalmage, Heather M. 2000. *Tripping on the Color Line: Black-White Multiracial Families in a Racially Divided World.* New Brunswick, NJ: Rutgers University Press.

Dalton, Susan E. 2001. "Protecting Our Parent Child Relationships: Understanding the Strengths and Weaknesses of Second-Parent Adoption." In *Queer Families, Queer Politics,* edited by M. Bernstein and R. Reimann, 201–11. New York: Columbia University Press.

Daly, Martin, and Margo Wilson. 1988. "Evolutionary Social Psychology and Family Homicide." *Science* 242: 519–24.

Daniel, E. Valentine. 1996. *Charred Lullabies: Chapters in an Anthropology of Violence.* Princeton, NJ: Princeton University Press.

Daro, Deborah. 1988. *Confronting Child Abuse: Research for Effective Program Design.* New York: Free Press.

Davis, Angela. 2000. "Keynote Address to Color of Violence Conference." Quoted in Donna Coker, "Feminism and the Criminal Law: Crime Control and Feminist Law Reform in Domestic Violence Law: A Critical Review." *Buffalo Criminal Law Review* 4: 801, 808, 2001.

Dawson, Michael C. 1994. *Behind the Mule: Race and Class in African-American Politics.* Princeton, NJ: Princeton University Press.

Delgado, Richard. 1992. "Shadowboxing: An Essay on Power." *Cornell Law Review* 77: 813.

Delgado, Richard, and Jean Stefancic. 1997. *Critical White Studies: Looking behind the Mirror.* Philadelphia: Temple University Press.

Delphy, Christine. 1984. *Closer to Home: A Materialist Analysis of Women's Oppression.* Translated by Diana Leonard. Amherst: University of Massachusetts Press.

Derricotte, Toi. 1997. *The Black Notebooks: An Interior Journey.* New York: W. W. Norton.

Dowd, Nancy E. 1994. "A Feminist Analysis of Adoption." *Harvard Law Review* 107: 913.

Due, Linnea. 1996. *Joining the Tribe: Growing Up Gay and Lesbian in the Nineties.* New York: Doubleday.

Duggan, Lisa. 1994. "Queering the State." *Social Text* 39: 1–14.

Durkheim, Emile. 1965. *Elementary Forms of Religious Life.* Translated by Joseph Swain. New York: Free Press.

Dusky, Lorraine. 1979. *Birthmark.* New York: M. Evans.

——. 1982. "Brave New Babies?" *Newsweek,* 6 December 1982.

——. 1992. "The Daughter I Gave Away." *Newsweek,* 30 March 1992.

Duster, Troy. 1990. *Backdoor to Eugenics.* New York: Routledge.

Eastman, P. D. 1960. *Are You My Mother?* New York: Random House.

Edlin, Gordon. 1982. "Inappropriate Use of Genetic Terminology in Medical Research: A Public Health Issue." *Perspectives in Biology and Medicine* 31: 47–56.

Ely, John Hart. 1980. *Democracy and Distrust: A Theory of Judicial Review.* Cambridge, MA: Harvard University Press.

Engle, Diane. 1995. "In Search of What Is Real." In *The Adoption Reader,* edited by Susan Wadia-Ellis, 128–34. Seattle: Seal.

The Evan B. Donaldson Adoption Institute. 2002a. "International Adoption Facts." http://www.adoptioninstitute.org/FactOverview/international.html (accessed: 13 June 2003).

——. 2002b. "Overview of Adoption in the United States." http://www.adoptioninstitute.org/FactOverview.html (accessed: 13 June 2003).

Evans-Pritchard, E. E. 1959. *Kinship and Marriage among the Nuer.* New York: Oxford University Press.

Fein, Esther B. 1998. "Secrecy and Stigma No Longer Clouding Adoptions." *New York Times,* 25 October 1998, 1.

Feinberg, Joel. 1992. "The Child's Right to an Open Future." In *Freedom and Fulfillment: Philosophical Essays,* edited by William Aiken and Hugh LaFollette, 297–330. Princeton, NJ: Princeton University Press.

Felder, Raoul, and Barbara Victor. 1996. *Getting Away with Murder.* New York: Simon and Schuster.

Ferguson, Ann. 1989. "A Feminist Aspect Theory of the Self." In *Women, Knowledge, and Reality: Explorations in Feminist Philosophy,* edited by Ann Garry and Marilyn Pearsall, 93–108. Boston: Unwin Hyman.

Fields, Jason. 2001. "Living Arrangements of Children." P70–74, U.S. Census Bureau (Apr.).

Fineman, Martha. 1991. *The Illusion of Equality.* Chicago: University of Chicago Press.

——. 1995a. "Images of Mothers in Poverty Discourse." In *Mothers in Law: Feminist Theory and the Legal Regulation of Motherhood,* edited by Martha A. Fineman and Isbel Karpin, 205–23. New York: Routledge.

——. 1995b. *The Neutered Mother, the Sexual Family, and Other Twentieth-Century Tragedies.* New York: Routledge.

——. 1999. "What Place for Family Privacy?" *George Washington Law Review,* 67: 1207–24.

Firestone, Shulamith. 2003 [1970]. *The Dialectic of Sex.* New York: Farrar, Straus & Giroux.

Florida. 2001. Title VI, Ch. 63.042. http://www.leg.state.fl.us/Statutes (accessed: 20 May 2001).

Fogg-Davis, Hawley. 2001. "Navigating Race in the Market for Human Gametes." *Hastings Center Report* 31 (5): 13–21.

Foucault, Michel. 1997. "Subjectivity and Truth." In *The Politics of Truth*, edited by Sylvere Lotringer and Lysa Hochroth, 171–98. New York: Semiotext(e).

Frankenberg, Ruth. 1993. *White Women, Race Matters: The Social Construction of Whiteness.* Minneapolis: University of Minnesota Press.

Frankfurt, Harry. 1988. "Freedom of the Will and the Concept of the Person." In *The Importance of What We Care About.* Cambridge: Cambridge University Press. Originally published in *Journal of Philosophy* 68, no. 1 (1971).

———. 1999. "Autonomy, Necessity, and Love." In *Necessity, Volition, and Love.* Cambridge: Cambridge University Press. Originally published in *Vernunftbegriffe in der Moderne*, edited by Hans Fulda and Rolf-Peter Horstmann, Stuttgarter Hegel-Kongreß. Kletta-Cotta Sonderdruck, 1994. All references are to the reprinted version.

Freud, Sigmund. 1957. "On Narcissism." In *The Standard Edition of the Complete Psychological Works of Sigmund Freud,* translated by James Strachey. London: Hogarth.

Freudberg, Judy, and Tony Geiss. 1986. *Susan and Gordon Adopt a Baby.* Toronto: Random House.

Freundlich, Madelyn. 1999. "Expediting Termination of Parental Rights: Solving a Problem or Sowing the Seeds of a New Predicament?" *Capital University Law Review* 28: 97–110.

Frye, Marilyn. 1983. *The Politics of Reality: Essays in Feminist Theory.* Trumansburg, NY: Crossing.

Gallagher, Maggie. 1996. *The Abolition of Marriage: How We Destroy Lasting Love.* Washington, DC: Regnery.

Gatens, Moira. 1996. *Imaginary Bodies: Ethics, Power, and Corporeality.* New York: Routledge.

Gawronski, Stacia. 2000. "Termination of the Absent or Unknown Putative Father's Rights." *Journal of Contemporary Legal Issues* 11: 554.

Gelles, Richard J. 1987. *Family Violence.* Thousand Oaks, CA.: Sage.

Gelles, Richard J., and Murray A. Strauss. 1988. *Intimate Violence.* New York: Simon and Schuster.

Gilder, George. 1973. *Sexual Suicide.* New York: Quadrangle.

Gilligan, Carol. 1982. *In A Different Voice: Psychological Theory and Women's Development.* Cambridge, MA: Harvard University Press.

Gilman, Lois, and Susan Freivalds. 2002. "Adopting Smart." http://www.adoptivefamilies.com/articles.php?aid=286 (accessed: 16 June 2003).

Ginsberg, Elaine K. 1996. *Passing and the Fictions of Identity.* Durham, NC: Duke University Press.

Goldstein, Joseph, Anna Freud, and Albert Solnit. 1973. *Beyond the Best Interests of the Child.* New York: Free Press.

———. 1979. *Before the Best Interests of the Child.* New York: Free Press.

Gomes-Schwartz, Beverly, Jonathan Horowitz, and Albert P. Cardarelli. 1990. *Child Sexual Abuse.* Thousand Oaks, CA: Sage.

Gómez, Laura E. 1997. *Misconceiving Mothers: Legislators, Prosecutors, and the Politics of Prenatal Drug Exposure.* Philadelphia: Temple University Press.

Göpfert, Rebekka. 2000. "The Jewish Kindertransport from Germany to England, 1938–39." In *The Dynamics of Adoption: Social and Personal Perspectives*, edited by Amal Treacher and Ilan Katz, 45–52. London: Jessica Kingsley.

Gordon, Linda. 1994. *Pitied But Not Entitled: Single Mothers and the History of Welfare, 1890–1935.* Cambridge, MA: Harvard University Press.

Gould, Stephen Jay. 1996. *The Mismeasure of Man.* New York: Norton.

Griswold v. Connecticut. 1965. 391 U.S. 145.

Grossberg, Michael. 1985. *Governing the Hearth: Law and Family in Nineteenth-Century America.* Chapel Hill: University of North Carolina Press.

Grotevant, Harold D., and Ruth McRoy. 1998. *Openness in Adoption: Exploring Family Connections.* Thousand Oaks, CA: Sage.

Guardianship of Aston H. v. Sofia D. 1995. 635 N.Y.S.2d. 418 (N.Y. Family Court).

Guardianship of Phillip B, a Minor. 188 California Reporter 781 (Ct. App. 1983). 2000. In *Child, Family, and State,* edited by Robert Mnookin and D. Kelly Weisberg. 4th ed. New York: Aspen Law & Business.

Halley, Janet. 1994. "The Construction of Heterosexuality." In *Fear of a Queer Planet,* edited by Michael Warner, 82–104. Minneapolis: University of Minnesota Press.

Harvard Law Review. 1990. "Developments in the Law—Medical Technology and the Law." *Harvard Law Review* 103: 1519.

Haslanger, Sally. 1996. "Objective Reality, Male Reality, and Social Construction." In *Women, Knowledge, and Reality,* edited by Ann Garry and Marilyn Pearsall, 84–107. 2nd ed. New York: Routledge.

———. 2000. "Gender and Race: (What) Are They? (What) Do We Want Them To Be?" *Noûs* 34(1): 31–55.

Haugaard, Jeffrey J. 1998. "Is Adoption a Risk Factor for the Development of Adjustment Problem?" *Clinical Psychology Review* 18: 47–69.

Hegel, G. W. F. 1976. *The Philosophy of Right.* Translated by T. M. Knox. Oxford: Oxford University Press.

Henderson, Lynne. 1997. "Without Narrative: Child Sexual Abuse." *Virginia Journal of Social Policy & the Law* 4: 479.

Hennessey, Rosemary, and Chrys Ingraham. 1997. *Materialist Feminism: A Reader in Class, Difference, and Women's Lives.* New York: Routledge.

Hoetink, Harry. 1973. *Slavery and Race Relations in the Americas.* New York: Harper Torchbooks.

Holmes, Gilbert A. 1995. "The Extended Family System in the Black Community: A Child Centered Model for Adoption Policy." *Temple Law Review* 68: 1649–1685.

Hollinger, Joan Heifetz, ed. 1990. *Adoption Law and Practice.* 2 Vols. Supplement, 1996. New York: Matthew Bender.

Hollinger, Joan Heifetz. 2001. "A Guide to The Multiethnic Placement Act of 1994 as Amended by the Interethnic Adoption Provisions of 1996." Administration for Children and Families, United States Department of Health and Human Services. http://www.acf.hhs.gov/programs/cb/publications/mepa94/ (accessed: 14 June 2003).

Hollinger, Joan, et al. 1998. *Adoption Law and Practice.* New York: Matthew Bender.

Honore, A. M. 1961. "Ownership." In *Oxford Essays in Jurisprudence,* edited by A. G. Guest, 107–47. Oxford: Clarendon.

hooks, bell. 1984. *Feminist Theory: From Margin to Center.* Boston: Southend.

Hoopes, Janet. 1982. *Prediction in Child Development: A Longitudinal Study of Adoptive and Nonadoptive Families.* New York: Child Welfare League of America.

Houlgate, Lawrence. 1988. *Family and State: The Philosophy of Family Law.* Lanham, MD: Rowman & Littlefield.

Howe, Ruth-Arlene. 1994. "Redefining the Transracial Adoption Controversy." *Duke Journal of Gender Law and Policy* 1 (3): 131–164.

———. 1999. "Adoption Law and Practices in 2000: Serving Whose Interests?" *Family Law Quarterly* 33: 677–89.

Hughes, Judith. 1996. "The Philosopher's Child." In *Children's Rights Re-visioned*, edited by Rosalind Ekman Ladd, 15–28. New York: Wadsworth.

Hughes, Langston. 1962. "Cora Unashamed." In *The Ways of White Folks: Stories*. New York: Random House.

Human Rights Campaign Foundation. 2003. Laws by State. http://www.hrc.org/familynet (accessed: 26 January 2003).

Hunt, Alan. 1993. *Explorations in Law and Society: Toward a Constitutive Theory of Law*. New York: Routledge.

International Mission of Hope. 2001. www.childrenshopeint.org (accessed: 20 May 2001).

Irigaray, Luce. 1994. *Thinking the Difference: For a Peaceful Revolution*. Translated by Karin Montin. New York: Routledge.

———. 1996. *I Love to You: Sketch for a Possible Felicity within History*. Translated by Alison Martin. New York: Routledge.

Jaggar, Alison M. 1983. *Feminist Politics and Human Nature*. Sussex: Harvester.

Jagger, Gill, and Caroline Wright. 2000. *Changing Family Values*. New York: Routledge.

Jefferies, David. 1998. "The Body as Commodity: The Use of Markets to Cure the Organ Deficit." *Indiana Journal of Global Legal Studies* 5: 621. http://www.law.indiana.edu/glsj/vol5/no2/13jeffer.html.

Jenny, Carole, et al. 1999. "Analysis of Missed Cases of Abusive Head Trauma." *Journal of the American Medical Association* 281: 621–626.

Johnson, Dirk. 1999. "Former Cocaine User Regains Child in Racial Custody Case." *New York Times,* 9 March 1999, A18.

Johnston, Patricia Irwin. 1992. *Adopting after Fertility*. Indianapolis: Perspectives.

Jones, Ann. 1994. *Next Time She'll Be Dead: Battering and How to Stop It*. Boston: Beacon.

Jones, Loring P. 1997. "Social Class, Ethnicity, and Child Welfare." *Journal of Multicultural Social Work* 6:123.

Kamin, Leon. 1974. *The Science and Politics of IQ*. Potomac: L. Erlbaum Associates.

Kamin, Leon, and H. J. Eysenck. 1981. *The Intelligence Controversy*. New York: Wiley.

Kant, Immanuel. 1956. *Critique of Practical Reason*. Translated by Lewis White Beck. Indianapolis: Bobbs-Merrill.

Kaplan, Morris. 1997. *Sexual Justice*. New York: Routledge.

Kasza, Keiko. 1992. *A Mother for Choco*. New York: G. P. Putnam's Sons.

Katz, Mitchell H., et al. 1986. "Returning Children Home: Clinical Decision Making in Cases of Child Abuse and Neglect." *American Journal of Orthopsychiatry* 56: 253–63.

Keller, Holly. 1991. *Horace*. New York: William Morrow.

Kirk, David. 1981. *Adoptive Kinship*. Washington: Ben-Simon.

Kittay, Eva Feder. 1999. *Love's Labor: Essays on Women, Equality, and Dependency*. New York: Routledge.

Kleinpenning, Gerard, and Louk Hagendoorn. 1993. "Forms of Racism and the Cumulative Dimension of Ethnic Attitudes." *Social Psychology Quarterly* 56 (1): 21–36.

Klibanoff, Susan, and Elton Klibanoff. 1973. *Let's Talk about Adoption*. Boston: Little, Brown.

Kline, Marlee. 1995. "Complicating the Ideology of Motherhood: Child Welfare Law and First Nation Women." In *Mothers in Law: Feminist Theory and the Legal Regulation of Motherhood,* edited by Martha A. Fineman and Isbel Karpin, 118–41. New York: Routledge.

Koehler, Phoebe. 1990. *The Day We Met You.* New York: Simon and Schuster.

Kovel, Joel. 1970. *White Racism: A Psychohistory.* New York: Vintage.

Kripke, Saul. 1980. *Naming and Necessity.* Cambridge: Harvard University Press.

Ladd, Rosalind Ekman. 1996. *Children's Rights Re-visioned: Philosophical Readings.* Belmont, CA: Wadsworth.

Lambda Legal Defense and Education Fund. 1996. "Lesbian and Gay Men Seeking Custody and Visitation: An Overview of the State and the Law." New York: Lambda Legal Defense and Education Fund.

Lane, Wendy G., et al. 2002. "Racial Differences in the Evaluation of Pediatric Fractures for Physical Abuse." *Journal of the American Medical Association* 288: 1603.

Larner, Mary B., Carol S. Stevenson, and Richard E. Behrman. 1998. "Protecting Children from Abuse and Neglect: Analysis and Recommendations." *Future of Children* 8:1 (Spring): 4–22.

Larson, Nella. 1986. *Quicksand and Passing.* Edited by Deborah McDowell. New Brunswick, NJ: Rutgers University Press.

Lawrence v. Texas. 2003. 539 U.S.

Lazarre, Jane. 1997. *Beyond the Whiteness of Whiteness: Memoir of a White Mother of Black Sons.* Durham, NC: Duke University Press.

Le Guin, Ursula K. 1995. *Four Ways to Forgiveness.* New York: Harper Collins.

Leites, Edmund. 1979. "Locke's Liberal Theory of Fatherhood." In *Having Children: Philosophical and Legal Reflections on Parenthood,* edited by Onora O'Neill and William Ruddick. New York: Oxford University Press.

LeRoy, Dan. 2001. "West Virginia Gives $100 Welfare Marriage Bonus." http://www.womensenews.org/article.cfm/dyn/aid/255/context/archive (accessed: 8 December 2003).

Lévi-Strauss, Claude. 1969. *Elementary Structures of Kinship.* Translated by James Bell. Boston: Beacon.

Lewin, Ellen. 1993. *Lesbian Mothers : Accounts of Gender in American Culture.* Ithaca, NY: Cornell University Press.

Lewontin, R. C., Steven Rose, and Leon J. Kamin. 1984. *Not in Our Genes: Biology, Ideology, and Human Nature.* New York: Pantheon.

Liem, Deann Borshay. 2000. "Adoption History: Transracial Adoption." National Asian-American Telecommunications Association and PBS: First Person Plural. http://www.pbs.org/pov/pov2000/firstpersonplural/historical/transracial.html (accessed: 16 June 2003).

Lifton, Betty. 1979. *Lost and Found: The Adoption Experience.* New York: Harper & Row.

Lipman, Allen, David R. Offord, Michael H. Boyle, and Yvonne A. Racine. 1993. "Follow-up of Psychiatric and Educational Morbidity among Adopted Children." *Journal of the American Academy of Child and Adolescent Psychiatry* 32(5): 1007–12.

Lochner v. New York. 1905. 198 U.S. 45.

Locke, John. 1979. "Paternal Power." In *Having Children: Philosophical and Legal Reflections on Parenthood,* edited by Onora O'Neill and William Ruddick. New York: Oxford University Press.

———. 1988 [1689]. *The Two Treatises of Government.* Edited by Peter Laslett. Cambridge: Cambridge University Press.

Loving v. Virginia. 1967. 388 U.S. 1.

Lugones, María. 1989. "Playfulness, 'World'-traveling, and Loving Perception." In *Women, Knowledge, and Reality: Explorations in Feminist Philosophy,* edited by Ann Garry and Marilyn Pearsall, 275–90. Boston: Unwin Hyman.

Lugones, María C., and Elizabeth V. Spelman. 1983. "Have We Got a Theory For You! Feminist Theory, Cultural Imperialism, and the Demand for 'The Woman's Voice.' " In *Feminist Theory,* edited by Wendy Kolmar and Frances Bartkowski, 17–27. Mountain View, CA: Mayfield.

MacKinnon, Catharine A. 1989. *Toward a Feminist Theory of the State.* Cambridge, MA: Harvard University Press.

Maclean, Doug. 1994. "Cost-Benefit Analysis and Procedural Values." *Analyse and Kritik* 16:166–80.

Mahoney, Joan. 1995. "Adoption as a Feminist Alternative to Reproductive Technologies." In *Reproduction, Ethics, and the Law: Feminist Perspectives,* edited by Joan C. Callahan, 35–54. Bloomington: Indiana University Press.

Mansbridge, Jane. 1996. "Using Power/Fighting Power: The Polity." In *Democracy and Difference: Contesting the Boundaries of the Political,* edited by Seyla Benhabib, 46–66. Princeton, NJ: Princeton University Press.

Mason, Mary Ann. 1994. *From Father's Property to Children's Rights.* New York: Columbia University Press.

Massachusetts. 2001. General Laws of Massachusetts, Part 2, Title 3, Ch. 210, Sect. 5B. http://www.state.ma.us/legis/laws/mgl/210–5B.htm (accessed: 20 May 2001).

Maxwell, Nancy G. 2000. "Opening Civil Marriage to Same-Gender Couples: A Netherlands–United States Comparison." *Electronic Journal of Comparative Law* 4.3. http://www.law/kub.nl/ejcl (accessed: 20 May 2001).

Maxwell, Nancy G., Astrid A. M. Mattijssen, and Charlene Smith. 2000. "Legal Protection for All the Children: Dutch–United States Comparison of Lesbian and Gay Parent Adoptions." *Arizona Journal of International and Comparative Law* 17: 309.

McBride, James. 1996. *The Color of Water: A Black Man's Tribute to His White Mother.* New York: Riverhead Books.

McLanahan and Sandefur. 1994. *Growing Up with a Single Parent: What Hurts? What Helps?* Cambridge: Harvard University Press.

McCulley, Melanie G. 1999. "The Male Abortion: The Putative Father's Right to Terminate His Interests in and Obligations to the Unborn Child." *Missouri Law Review* 64: 517.

McGuffin v. Overton. 1995. 542 N.W.2d 288 (Mich. Ct. App.).

McKelvey, Carole, and JoEllen Stevens. 1994. *Adoption Crisis: The Truth behind Adoption and Foster Care.* Golden, CO: Fulcrum.

McLarin Kim. 1998. "Primary Colors: The Mother Is Black; Her Interracial Daughter Is Fair-Skinned. Society Has Trouble Seeing Their Connection." *New York Times Magazine,* 24 May 1998, 58.

Meyers, Diana Tietjens. 1994. *Subjection and Subjectivity: Psychoanalytic Feminism and Moral Philosophy.* New York: Routledge.

——. 1997. *Feminists Rethink the Self.* Boulder: Westview.

Micek, Jana. 2000. "Termination of Parental Rights Based on a Felony Conviction." *Journal of Contemporary Legal Issues* 11: 565–69.

Miller, Jean Baker. 1976. *Toward a New Psychology of Women.* Boston: Beacon.

Miller, Nancy. 1995. "Mothers, Daughters, and Autobiography: Maternal Legacies and Cultural Criticism." In *Mothers in Law: Feminist Theory and the Legal Regulation of Motherhood,* edited by Martha A. Fineman and Isbel Karpin, 3–26. New York: Routledge.

REFERENCES

Mills, Linda. 1999. "Killing Her Softly: Intimate Abuse and the Violence of State Intervention." *Harvard Law Review* 113: 550–613.

Mink, Gwendolyn. 1998. *Welfare's End*. Ithaca, NY: Cornell University Press.

Minnesota. 2001. Chapter 260C.193 subd. 3. http://www.revisor.leg.state.mn.us/stats/260C/193.html (accessed: 20 May 2001).

Minow, Martha. 1995. "What Ever Happened to Children's Rights?" *Minnesota Law Review* 80: 267.

Minow, Martha, and Richard Weissbourd. 1993. "Social Movements for Children." *Daedalus* 122: 1–29.

Mississippi. Adoption Law. §93–17–3 based on Codes, 1942 §1269–02; Laws, 1955, Ex. ch. 34 §2; Laws, 1973, ch. 361, § 1; Laws, 1994, ch. 437, §1; Laws, 2000, ch 535, §1. http://198.187.128.12/mississippi/lpext.dll?f=templates&fn=main-hit.h.htm&2.0 (accessed: 20 May 2001).

Mnookin, Robert, and D. Kelly Weisberg, eds. 2000. *Child, Family, and State: Problems and Materials on Children and the Law*. 4th ed. New York: Aspen Law & Business.

Modell, Judith S. 1994. *Kinship with Strangers: Adoption and Interpretations of Kinship in American Culture*. Berkeley: University of California Press.

Modell, Judith, and Naomi Dambacher. 1997. "Making a 'Real' Family: Matching and Cultural Biologism in American Adoption." *Adoption Quarterly* 1(2): 3–20.

Mongold, Susan Vivian. 2000. "Extending Non-Exclusive Parenting and the Right to Protection for Older Foster Children: Creating Third Options in Permanency Planning." *Buffalo Law Review* 48: 835–79.

Moody Adams, Michelle M. 1999. "Self/Other." In *A Companion to Feminist Philosophy*, edited by Alison M. Jaggar and Iris Marion Young, 255–63. Oxford: Blackwell.

Moore, Janette, and Eric Fombonne. 1999. "Psychopathology in Adopted and Nonadopted Children: A Clinical Sample." *American Journal of Orthopsychiatry*. 69(3): 403–9.

Moran, Rachel F. 2001. *Interracial Intimacy: The Regulation of Race and Romance*. Chicago: University of Chicago Press.

Munsch, Robert. 1982. *Murmel, Murmel, Murmel*. Toronto: Annick.

Murray, Thomas. 1996. *The Worth of the Child*. Berkeley: University of California Press.

Narayan, Uma. 1999. "Family Ties: Rethinking Parental Claims in the Light of Surrogacy and Custody." In *Having and Raising Children: Unconventional Families, Hard Choices, and the Social Good*, edited by Uma Narayan and Julia J. Bartkowiak, 65–86. University Park: Pennsylvania State University Press.

National Adoption Information Clearinghouse, United States Department of Health and Human Services. 2000a. "The Adoption Homestudy Process." http://naic.acf.hhs.gov/pubs/f_homestu.cfm (accessed: 20 May 20 2001).

——. 2000b. "Gay and Lesbian Adoptive Parents: Resources for Professionals and Parents." http://naic.acf.hhs.gov/pubs/f_gay.cfm (accessed: 16 June 2003).

——. 2002a. "Single Adoptive Parents." http://naic.acf.hhs.gov/pubs/s_single.cfm (accessed: 16 June 2003).

——. 2002b. "State Laws Regarding Adoption by Gay and Lesbian Parents." http://naic.acf.hhs.gov/pubs/l_same.cfm (accessed: 13 June 2003).

——. 2002c. "Adoption: Numbers and Trends." http://naic.acf.hhs.gov/pubs/s_number.cfm (accessed: 13 June 2003).

——. 2003. "The Cost of Adopting." http://naic.acf.hhs.gov/pubs/s_cost.cfm (accessed: 13 June 2003).

National Association of Black Social Workers. 1972. Position Paper: "Transracial Adoption." New York.

——. 1994. Position Statement: "Preserving African-American Families." Detroit, MI.

The National Center for Lesbian Rights. 2003. "Second Parent Adoptions: A Snapshot of Current Law." http://www.nclrights.org/publications/2ndparentadoptions.htm (accessed: 8 December 2003).

National Research Council and Institute of Medicine. 1998. Washington, DC: National Academy Press.

Neal, Leora. n.d. "The Case against Transracial Adoption." Regional Research Institute for Human Services. http://www.puaf.umd.edu/courses/puaf650/Transracial%20 Adoption-Neal.htm (accessed: 23 December 2003).

Neufeld, John. 1969. *Edgar Allen*. New York: Signet.

Nevada Adoption Code. Chapter 127.40. http://www.leg.state.nv.usregister/98Register/ R067–99_IN.html (accessed: 20 May 2001).

——. Chapter 127.240.http://www.legl.state.nv.usregister/99Register/R067–99_IN .html (accessed: 20 May 2001).

Newman, Beth. 1998. "Frequency of Breast Cancer Attributable to BRCA1 in a Population-Based Series of American Women." *Journal of the American Medical Association* 279: 915.

Nicholas, Barry. 1962. *Introduction to Roman Law*. Oxford: Clarendon.

Nicholson v. Scoppetta. 2001. 202 F.R.D. 377, Eastern District of New York.

Noddings, Nel. 1986. *Caring: A Feminine Approach to Ethics and Moral Education*. Berkeley: University of California Press.

Novkov, Julie. 2002. "Racial Constructions: The Legal Regulation of Miscegenation in Alabama, 1890–1934." *Law and History Review* 20.2: 135 pars. http://www.historyco-operative.org/journals/lhr/20.2/novkov.html (accessed: 16 June 2003).

Office of Children's Issues, United States Department of State. N.d. "Immigrant Visas Issued to Orphans Coming to the U.S." http://travel.state.gov/ orphan_numbers .html (accessed: 13 June 2003).

Okin, Susan. 1984. *Justice, Gender, and the Family*. New York: Basic Books.

Oliver, Kelly. 1997. *Family Values: Subjects between Nature and Culture*. New York: Routledge.

Omi, Michael, and Howard Winant. 1994. *Racial Formation in the United States*. New York: Routledge.

O'Neill, Onora. 1979. "Begetting, Bearing, and Rearing." In *Having Children: Philosophical and Legal Reflections on Parenthood*, edited by Onora O'Neill and William Ruddick, 25–38. New York: Oxford University Press.

Open Door Adoption. Information Packet. [online document]. www.opendooradoption.com/infopacket.pdf. (accessed: 20 May 2001).

Pannor, Rueben, and Annette Baran. 1993. "Perspectives in Open Adoption." *Future of Children* 3(1). http://www.futureofchildren.org/information2826/information_show .htm?doc_id=77498 (accessed: 21 January 2004).

Pardo, Natalie. 1999. "Losing Their Children." *Chicago Reporter* 28: 1.

Park, Shelley. 1996. "Mothering across Racial and Cultural Boundaries." In *Everyday Acts against Racism: Raising Children in a Multiracial World*, edited by Maureen T. Reddy, 223–37. Seattle: Seal.

Park, Shelley, and Cheryl Green. 2000. "Is Transracial Adoption in the Best Interests of Ethnic Minority Children? Some Questions concerning Legal and Scientific Conceptions of a Child's Best Interests." *Adoption Quarterly* 3(4): 5–34.

Patterson, Charlotte J. 1995. "Lesbian and Gay Parenting." http://www.apa.org/pi/ parent.html (accessed: 8 December 2003).

Patton, Sandra Lee. 2000. *Birthmarks: Transracial Adoption in Contemporary America.* New York: New York University Press.

Pelton, LeRoy H. 1989. *For Reasons of Poverty: A Critical Analysis of the Public Child Welfare System in the United States.* New York: Praeger.

Pennsylvania Title 23, Chapter 25, Subchapter D, §2530.

Perry, Twila L. 1993–94. "The Transracial Adoption Controversy: An Analysis of Discourse and Subordination." *New York University Review of Law and Social Change* 21: 33–108.

———. 1998. "Transracial and International Adoption: Mothers, Hierarchy, Race, and Feminist Legal Theory." *Yale Journal of Law and Feminism* 10: 101.

Pertman, Adam. 1998. "U.S. Adoptees May Approach 6 Million." http://search. boston.com/globe/metro/packages/adoption/us_adoptees.htm (accessed: 13 June 2003).

Peters, B. R., M. S. Atkins, and M. M. McKay. 1999. "Adopted Children's Behavior Problems: a Review of Five Explanatory Models." *Clinical Psychology Review* 19(3): 297–328.

Piasecki, Marlene. 1987. "Who Adopts Special Needs Children." Philadelphia, PA: National Adoption Center.

Piper, Adrian. 1992. "Passing for White, Passing for Black." *Transition* 58: 4–32.

Plato. 1974. *Republic.* Translated by G. M. A. Grube. Indianapolis: Hackett.

Pollitt, Katha. 1994. "Subject to Debate: Republican Party and Unwed Mothers." *Nation,* 12 December 1994, 717.

Poster, Mark. 1978. *Critical Theory of the Family.* New York: Seabury.

Radcliffe-Brown, A. R. 1963. *African Systems of Kinship and Marriage.* New York: Oxford University Press.

Radin, Margaret Jane. 1987. "Market Inalienability." *Harvard Law Review* 100: 1849–1937.

———. 1996. *Contested Commodities.* Cambridge, MA: Harvard University Press.

Rainwater, Lee, and William L. Yancey, eds. 1975. *The Moynihan Report and the Politics of Controversy.* Cambridge, MA: MIT Press.

Rawls, John. 1972. *A Theory of Justice.* Cambridge, MA: Harvard University Press.

Reddy, Maureen T. 1994. *Crossing the Color Line: Race, Parenting, and Culture.* New Brunswick, NJ: Rutgers University Press.

Regan, Donald H. 1979. "Rewriting *Roe v. Wade.*" *Michigan Law Review* 77: 1569.

Register, Cherrie. 1990. *Are Those Kids Yours?: American Families with Children Adopted from Other Countries.* New York: Free Press.

Rich, Adrienne, 1986. "Compulsory Heterosexuality and the Lesbian Continuum." In *Blood, Bread, and Poetry: Selected Prose, 1979–1985.* New York: Norton.

Richie, Beth E. 2000. "A Black Feminist Reflection on the Antiviolence Movement." *Signs* 25: 1133–37.

Roberts, Dorothy. 1991. "Punishing Drug Addicts Who Have Babies: Women of Color, Equality, and the Right of Privacy." *Harvard Law Review* 104: 1419–82.

———. 1995. "The Genetic Tie." *University of Chicago Law Review* 62 (1): 209–73.

———. 1997. *Killing the Black Body: Race, Reproduction, and the Meaning of Liberty.* New York: Pantheon.

———. 2000. *Shattered Bonds: The Color of Child Welfare.* New York: Basic Books/Civitas.

———. 2001. "Kinship Care and the Price of State Support for Children." *Chicago-Kent Law Review* 76: 1619.

Robinson, Elise L. E., Hilde Lindemann Nelson, and James Lindemann Nelson. 1997. "Fluid Families: The Role of Children in Custody Arrangements." In *Feminism and Families,* edited by Hilde Lindemann Nelson, 90–101. New York: Routledge.

Robson, Ruthann. 2000. "Making Mothers: Lesbian Legal Theory & the Judicial Construction of Lesbian Mothers." *Women's Rights Law Reporter* 22(1): 15.

Roe v. Wade. 1973. 410 U.S. 113.

Rohwer, Sievert, Jon Herron, and Martin Daly. 1999. "Step-parental Behavior as Matin Effort in Birds and Other Mammals." *Evolution and Social Behavior* 20: 367–90.

Rorty, Amélie, and David Wong. 1990. "Aspects of Identity and Agency." In *Identity, Character, and Morality: Essays in Moral Psychology,* edited by Owen Flanagan and Amélie Rorty, 19–36. Cambridge, MA: MIT Press.

Rosenau, Pauline Marie. 1992. *Postmodernism and the Social Sciences: Insights, Inroads, and Intrusions.* Princeton, NJ: Princeton University Press.

Rousseau, Jean Jacques. 1911 [1762]. *Emile.* Translated by Barbara Foxley. Everyman's Library. New York: Random House.

Ruddick, Sara. 1989. *Maternal Thinking.* Boston, MA: Beacon.

Ruddick, William. 1979. "Parents and Life Prospects." In *Having Children: Philosophical and Legal Reflections on Parenthood,* edited by Onora O'Neill and William Ruddick, 123–37. New York: Oxford University Press.

Rush, Sharon. 2000. *Loving Across the Color Line: A White Adoptive Mother Learns about Race.* Lanham, MD: Rowman and Littlefield.

Sanger, Carol. 1996. "Separating from Children." *Columbia Law Review* 96: 375–492.

Sappho. N.d. "Excerpts from the Poems of Sappho." Translated by Emma Bianchi. Unpublished manuscript.

Sarkar, Sohotra. 1999. *Genetics and Reductionism.* Cambridge: Cambridge University Press.

Scheffler, Samuel. 1997. "Relationships and Responsibilities." *Philosophy and Public Affairs* 26 (3): 189–209.

Scheman, Naomi. 1997. "Though This Be Method, Yet There Is Madness in It: Paranoia and Liberal Epistemology." In *Feminist Social Thought: A Reader,* edited by Diana Tietjens Meyers, 342–67. New York: Routledge.

Schemo, Diana Jean. 1996. "The Baby Trail: A Special Report; Adoptions in Paraguay: Mothers Cry Theft." *New York Times,* 19 March 1996, A1.

Schneider, David Murray. 1984. *A Critique of the Study of Kinship.* Ann Arbor: University of Michigan Press.

Schneider, Elizabeth. 2000. *Battered Women and Feminist Lawmaking.* New Haven: Yale University Press.

Schorr, Lisbeth B. 1997. *Common Purpose: Strengthening Families and Neighborhoods to Rebuild America.* New York: Anchor Books.

———. 1998. *Within Our Reach: Breaking the Cycle of Disadvantage.* New York: Anchor.

Scott, Joan Wallach. 1996. *Only Paradoxes to Offer: French Feminists and the Rights of Man.* Cambridge, MA: Harvard University Press.

Sen, Amartya. 1992. *Inequality Reexamined.* Cambridge, MA: Harvard University Press.

Sengupta, Somini. 2000. "Parents in Poor Neighborhoods Wary of Child Welfare Agency." *New York Times,* 31 May 2000, A27.

Seuss, Dr. 1940. *Horton Hatches the Egg.* New York: Random House.

Shakespeare, William. 1965. *The Merchant of Venice.* New York: Signet Classics.

———. 1970. *King Lear.* New York: Pelican Books.

Shalev, Carmel. 1989. *Birth Power: The Case for Surrogacy.* New Haven, CT: Yale University Press.

Shanley, Mary Lyndon. 2001. *Making Babies, Making Families: What Matters Most in an Age of Reproductive Technologies, Surrogacy, Adoption, and Same-Sex and Unwed Parents.* Boston: Beacon.

Sherman, Lawrence, et al. 1992. "The Variable Effect of Arrests on Criminal Careers: The Milwaukee Domestic Violence Experiment." *Journal of Criminal Law and Criminology* 83: 137.

Siegel, Reva. 1998. "The Racial Rhetorics of Colorblind Constitutionalism: The Case of *Hopwood v. Texas.*" In *Race and Representation: Affirmative Action,* edited by Robert Post and Michael Rogin, 29–72. New York: Zone.

Simon, Rita James. 1999. "Transracial Adoptions: Does the Law Matter?" *American Experiment Quarterly* Fall: 89.

——. 2000. "A Comparison of the Experiences of Adult Korean and Black Transracial Adoptees." In *Adoption Across Borders: Serving the Children in Transracial and Intercountry Adoptions,* 117–26. Lanham, MD: Rowman and Littlefield.

Simon, Rita James, and Howard Alstein. 2000. "The Case against Transracial Adoption." In *Adoption Across Borders: Serving the Children in Transracial and Intercounty Adoptions,* ed. Rita James Simon, 37–48. Lanham, MD: Rowman & Littlefield.

Simon, Rita James, Howard Altstein, and Marygold Shire Melli. 1994. *The Case for Transracial Adoption.* Lanham, MD: American University Press.

Simon, Rita James, and Rhonda M. Roorda. 2000. *In Their Own Voices: Transracial Adoptees Tell Their Stories.* New York: Columbia University Press.

Simon, Stephanie. 2002. "Judges Push for Abused to Follow the Law." *Los Angeles Times,* 22 January 2002, A12.

Sklar, Kathryn Kish. 1973. *Catharine Beecher: A Study in American Domesticity.* New Haven, CT: Yale University Press.

Smith, Anna Marie. 2002. "The Sexual Regulation Dimension of Contemporary Welfare Law: A 50-State Overview." *Michigan Journal of Gender and Law* 8: 121.

Smith, Janet Farrell. 1983. "Parenting and Property." In *Mothering,* edited by J. Trebilcot. Totowa, NJ: Littlefield Adams.

——. 1996. "Analyzing Ethical Conflict in the Transracial Adoption Debate: Three Conflicts Involving Community." *Hypatia: A Journal of Feminist Philosophy* 11(2): 1–33.

——. 2002. "Genetic Testing: A Cautionary Tale of Foster and Pre-Adoptive Children." *New England Journal of Public Policy* 17(2): 55–75.

Smolowe, Jill. 1995. "Adoption in Black and White: An Odd Coalition Takes Aim at the Decades-Old Prejudice against Transracial Placements." *Time,* 14 August 1995.

Sober, Elliott. 1994. "Models of Cultural Evolution." In *Conceptual Issues in Evolutionary Biology* 2, edited by Elliott Sober. Cambridge, MA: MIT Press.

Solinger, Rickie. 2001. *Beggars and Choosers: How the Politics of Choice Shapes Adoption, Abortion, and Welfare in the United States.* New York: Hill and Wang.

Spake, Amanda. 1998. "Adoption Gridlock." *U.S. News and World Report,* 22 June 1998, 30.

Stacey, Judith. 1996. *In the Name of the Family: Rethinking Family Values in the Postmodern Age.* Boston: Beacon.

Stack, Carol. 1974. *All Our Kin: Strategies for Survival in a Black Community.* New York: Harper and Row.

Stanworth, Michelle, ed. 1987. *Reproductive Technologies: Gender, Motherhood, and Medicine.* Minneapolis: University of Minnesota Press.

Stanworth, Michelle. 2000. "Birth Pangs: Conceptive Technologies and the Threat to Motherhood." In *Feminist Theory,* edited by Wendy Kolman and Francis Barkowski, 449–64. Mountainview, CA: Mayfield.

Steiner, Hillel. 1994. *An Essay on Rights.* Oxford: Blackwell.

Stevens, Jacqueline. 1993. "The Politics of Identity: From Property to Empathy." PhD diss., University of California, Berkeley.

——. 1999. *Reproducing the State.* Princeton, NJ: Princeton University Press.

——. 2002. "Symbolic Matter: DNA and Other Linguistic Stuff." *Social Text* 20(1): 105–36.

——. 2003. "Racial and Ethnic Classifications: Policy Proposals for NIH-sponsored Research Reporting Human Variation." *Journal of Health Policy, Politics, and Law* 28: 1033–1098.

——. 2004. Introduction to *States without Nations.* http://www.agoraxchange.net (accessed: 21 January 2004).

Stocking, George W. 1993. "The Turn of the Century Concept of Race." *Modernism/ Modernity* 1(1): 4–16.

Stolley, Kathy S. 1993. "Statistics on Adoption in the United States." *Future of Children* 3(1): 26–42.

Stone, Lawrence. 1975. "The Rise of the Nuclear Family in Early Modern England." In *The Family in History,* edited by C. Rosenberg, 13–57. Philadelphia: University of Pennsylvania Press.

Sullivan, P. F., J. E. Wells, and J. A. Bushnell. 1995. "Adoption as a Risk Factor for Mental Disorders." *Acta Psychiatrica Scandinavica* 92: 119–24.

Tan, Amy. 1989. *The Joy Luck Club.* New York: Putnam.

——. 1991. *The Kitchen God's Wife.* New York: Putnam.

Tatum, Beverly. 1997. *Why Are All the Black Kids Sitting Together in the Cafeteria? And Other Conversations about Race.* New York: Basic Books.

Temrin, Hans, Susanne Buchmayer, and Magnus Enquist. 2000. "Step-parents and Infanticide: New Data Conradict Evolutionary Predictions." *Proceedings of the Royal Society B* 267: 943–45.

Terry, Don. 2000. "U.S. Child Poverty Rate Fell as Economy Grew, But Is Above 1979 Level." *New York Times,* 11 August 2000, 10.

Testa, Mark. 2000. Presentation at Conference on the Impact of the Adoption and Safe Families Act on Minority Communities, Child Welfare League of America, Chicago Illinois. 13 November 2000.

Thomas, Laurence. 2000. "Moral Health: Living in an Unjust World." In *African-Americans and Social Justice: Essays in Honor of Bernard Boxill,* edited by Tommy L. Lott. Lanham, MD: Rowman and Littlefield.

Thompson, Becky. 2000. *Mothering without a Compass: White Mother's Love, Black Son's Courage.* Minneapolis: University of Minnesota Press.

Tiffin, Susan. 1982. *In Whose Best Interests?: Child Welfare Reform in the Progressive Era.* Westport, CT: Greenwood.

Tobias, Sarah. 2001. *Coexisting with Cacophony: Affirming Discordant Voices in Feminist Ethics and Politics.* PhD diss., Columbia University, New York.

Treacher, Amal, and Ilan Katz. 2000. "The Jewish Kindertransport from Germany to England, 1938–39." In *The Dynamics of Adoption,* edited by Amal Treacher and Ilan Katz, 45–52. London: Jessica Kingsley.

Trimble v. Gordon. 1977. 430 U.S. 762.

Turner, Ann. 1990. *Through Moon and Stars and Night Skills.* New York: Harper Collins.

United States Census Bureau. 2001a. Percentage of Children under Age 18 Living in Various Family Arrangements. Table POP5.B. http://www.childstats.gov/ac2000/surveys.asp#sipp (accessed: 20 May 2001).

——. 2001b. SIPPS Data Source Description. http://www.childstats.gov/ac2000/poptxt.asp (accessed: 20 May 2001).

United States Congress. 1994. Multi-ethnic Placement Act of 1994, Public Law 104–88.

REFERENCES

———. 2000. Child Citizenship Act. Title III, Ch. 2—INA, Sec. 322. [8 U.S.C. 1433]. http://www.ins.usdoj.gov/graphics/lawsregs/INA.htm (accessed: 20 May 2001).

United States Department of Health and Human Services, Administration for Children and Families, Administration on Children, Youth, and Families, National Center on Child Abuse and Neglect. 1996a. "Executive Summary of the Third National Incidence Study of Child Abuse and Neglect (NIS-3)." Washington, DC.

———. 1996b. "The Third National Incidence Study of Child Abuse and Neglect, Final Report (NIS-3)." Washington, DC.

United States Department of Health and Human Services. 1997. National Study of Protective, Preventive, and Reunification Services Delivered to Children and Their Families. Washington, DC: U.S. Government Printing Office.

Utah Adoption Law, Title 78, Chapter 30.

Vanamo, T., et al. 2001. "Infra-familial child homicide in Finland, 1970–1994: Incidence, causes of death, and characteristics." *Forensic Science International* 117: 199–204.

Vlastos, Gregory. 1981. "The Individual as Object of Love in Plato." In *Platonic Studies*. 2nd ed. Princeton, NJ: Princeton University Press.

Wald, Alexandra. 1997. "What's Rightfully Ours: Toward a Property Theory of Rape." *Columbia Journal of Law and Social Problems* 30: 459.

Wambaugh, Carrie L. 1999. "Biology Is Important, But Does Not Necessarily Always Constitute a 'Family': A Brief Survey of the Uniform Adoption Act." *Akron Law Review* 32: 791–832.

Watson, Gary. 1982. "Free Agency." In *Free Will*, edited by Gary Watson, 337–51. New York: Oxford University Press.

Weinberg, Joanna K. 1995. "Older Mothers and Adult Children: Toward an Alternative Construction of Care." In *Mothers in Law: Feminist Theory and the Legal Regulation of Motherhood*, edited by Martha A. Fineman and Isbel Karpin, 328–45. New York: Routledge.

Welter, Barbara. 1982. "Cult of True Womanhood: 1820–1860." In *The American Family in Social Historical Perspective*, edited by Michael Gordon, 372–92. New York: St. Martin's.

West, Robin. 1998. "Universalism, Liberal Theory, and the Problem of Gay Marriage." *Florida State University Law Review* 25: 705–730.

Weston, Kath. 1991. *Families We Choose: Lesbians, Gays, Kinship*. New York: Columbia University Press.

Whitbeck, Caroline. 1989. "A Different Reality: Feminist Ontology." In *Women, Knowledge, and Reality: Explorations in Feminist Philosophy*, edited by Ann Garry and Marilyn Pearsall, 51–76. Boston: Unwin Hyman.

Williams, Gregory Howard. 1995. *Life on the Color Line: The True Story of a White Boy Who Discovered He Was Black*. New York: Penguin Books.

Williams, Margery. 1995. *The Velveteen Rabbit*. New York: Smithmark.

Wilson, William Julius. 1987. *The Truly Disadvantaged: The Inner City, the Underclass, and Public Policy*. Chicago: University of Chicago Press.

Winter, Steven L. 1989. "The Cognitive Dimension of the Agon: Between Legal Power and Narrative Meaning." *Michigan Law Review* 87: 2225.

Wolf, Susan. 2001. "The True, the Good, and the Lovable: Frankfurt's Avoidance of Objectivity." In *Contours of Agency: Essays on Themes from Harry Frankfurt*, edited by Sarah Buss and Lee Overton, 227–44. Cambridge, MA: MIT Press.

Wood, Allen. 1999. *Kant's Ethical Thought*. Cambridge: Cambridge University Press.

Woodhouse, Barbara B. 1992. "Who Owns the Child?: Meyer and Pierce and the Child as Property." *William and Mary Law Review* 33: 995.

——. 1993. "Hatching the Egg: A Child-Centered Perspective on Parents' Rights." *Cardoza Law Review* 14: 1814–20.

——. 1994. "Out of Children's Needs, Children's Rights: The Child's Voice in Defining the Family." *BYU Law Journal* 8: 321–24.

——. 1995. "Are You My Mother? Conceptualizing Children's Identity Rights in Transracial Adoptions." *Duke Journal of Gender, Law, and Policy* 2:1–21.

——. 1999. "The Dark Side of Family Privacy." *George Washington Law Review* 67:1247–1262.

Wriggins, Jennifer. 1997. "Genetics, IQ, Determinism, and Torts: The Example of Discovery in Lead Exposure Litigation." *Boston University Law Review* 77: 1025.

——. 2000. "Parental Rights Termination Jurisprudence: Questioning the Framework." *South Carolina Law Review* 52: 241–268.

Wu, Jean Yu-Wen Shen, and Min Song. 2000. *Asian-American Studies: A Reader.* New Brunswick, NJ: Rutgers University Press.

Ynvesson, Barbara. 1997. "Negotiating Motherhood: Identity and Difference in 'Open' Adoptions." *Law and Society Review* 31(1): 33–67.

Young, Alison H. 1998. "Reconceiving the Family: Challenging the Paradigm of the Exclusive Family." *The American University Journal of Gender and Law* 6: 505–556.

Young, Iris. 1990. *Justice and the Politics of Difference.* Princeton, NJ: Princeton University Press.

Zainaldin, Jamail. 1979. "The Emergence of a Modern American Family Law: Child Custody, Adoption, and the Courts, 1796–1851." *Northwestern University Law Review* 72: 1038–89.

Zelizer, Viviana A. 1985. *Pricing the Priceless Child: The Changing Social Value of Children.* Princeton, NJ: Princeton University Press.

Index

INDEX

Adult adoptees (*continued*)
as not adopted, 155–58, 168–69; original name, 161–62. *See also* Adopted children; Children; Desire to know
Affirmative action jurisprudence, 260
African American adopters, 248–49, 251, 252
African American children, 234–35; juvenile offenders, 236; low rates of adoption, 248–49; over-represented in adoption market, 235, 240; at risk of removal, 231, 235–37, 241–42
African American families: mother's attempts to regain custody, 241–42; punitive responses to, 239–40, 244; state disruption of, 237–41; stereotypes of mothers, 238–39
African Americans: gay and lesbian parents, 106; informal adoptions, 22; opposition to transracial adoption, 64, 202n, 211–12; transracial adoption by whites, 5–6
Agency, 173, 275–77
Aid for Families with Dependent Children (AFDC), 227–28
Alexander, Jacqui, 31–32, 36
Allen, Anita L., 121n
Alternative methods of adoption. *See* Methods of adoption
American Psychiatric Association, 107
American Psychological Association, 107–8
Anderson, Elizabeth, 254n
Anna J. v. Mark C., 45n
Appiah, Anthony, 276–77
Apprenticeships/indentured servitude, 115, 126
A priori ground, 204
Are You My Mother? (Eastman), 175, 177–78
Argentina, 24–25
Aristotle, 196–97, 198, 204, 212
Arrogant perceiver, 187, 192
Austin, Carol, 26–27
Autonomy, 53–54, 59–60
"Autonomy, Necessity, and Love" (Frankfurt), 195–97

Baher v. Milke, 42n
Baker v. Vermont, 135n
Banks, Richard, 247–48, 250
Bare relations of love, 196–99
Bartholet, Elizabeth, 14, 79–80, 178, 245–46
Battered women's movement, 228–32; adoption policies and, 242–45; children neglected by, 230–31
Beauvoir, Simone de, 45
Beneficence, 53–54, 60, 64

Best interests of child, 51–52, 172, 228; genetic issues and, 73, 84
Bioethics model, 53–55
Biological cause-effect relations, 72–73
Biological families: abdication in, 202–3; adoptive families as copy of, 68, 76–77; biology as identity, 153–56; feminist support of, 136–37; as ideal, 29, 68, 76–77, 123, 135–37. *See also* Genetic families; Parenting, biological
Biological mother, as term, 20
Biological parent, definition, 70–71
Biologism, 248, 257, 262–63
Biracial children, 258
Birth certificates, sealed, 4, 63, 176
Birth family: exclusion of, 22, 49–57; as moral equal of adoptive family, 54–55; transracial adoption and, 266. *See also* Birth mother
Birth mother, 5, 19–21; becoming real for child, 190–91; economic issues and, 26–27; equal protection of imaginary domain, 29–30; erasure of, 179–80n; fear of return of, 30, 42; hope for return of, 184; institution of heterosexual family and, 24–25; legally defined as mother, 89–90; primary custody and, 22, 29, 30, 55; rights of, 26–30; as trope for self, 162; trust for adoptive family, 75–76. *See also* Pregnancy; Real mother
Bishop, Donna, 238
Blackmun, Harry A., 261–62n
Blum, Lawrence, 253
Bodily, 152; denial of, 154–55; knowledge of, 163–64
Body, 152; epistemic authority and, 167; imaginary, 279; of infant, in transracial adoption, 278–79; physical markers of race, 268–72, 277; social meaning of, 269–70; somatic norm image, 280–81; training of, 277–78
Boggis, Terry, 100
Brave New World (Huxley), 43–44
Brennan, William J., 262
Bryant, Anita, 95
Butler, Judith, 76

California Family Code, 75–76n
Capability rights, 35
Caretaking, 33–34
Certainty, desire for, 158–60, 162–67
Chambers, David, 91n
Chesler, Phyllis, 44–45n
Chicago, 237–38, 240
Child abuse, 223; in genetic families, 78–79; neglect related to poverty, 237, 243;

312

"Gender and Race: (What) Are They? (What) Do We Want Them to Be?" (Haslanger), 268
Gene pool, 81
Genetic essentialism, 12, 137–38
Genetic families: abuse in, 78–79; hazards of gene expression, 81–83; legal bias in favor of, 72–75; as legal construct, 68–69; statistics, 77–78; U.S.-American family, 77–80; U.S. law, 80–83. *See also* Biological families
Gestational mother, 44–45 n
Gilligan, Carol, 104–5
Gingrich, Newt, 241
Goldberg, Arthur J., 262
Good child/bad child dichotomy, 182–83
Good mother/bad mother dichotomy, 181–85
Goods, 199, 263
Good Samaritan laws, 88, 94
Good will, 199–200
Griswold v. Connecticut, 262
Grotevant, Harold D., 48
Guardianship, subsidized, 227

Hades myth, 37, 46
Hahn, Songsuk, 13
Harlem, 240
Haslanger, Sally, 14–15
Heart of Freedom, The (Cornell), 85–86
Hegel, G. W. F., 22–23, 38–39
Heritage, genetic component, 29, 86 n
Heterosexual families, 21, 23–25; racial choices, 256–57
Heterosexuality: duties of, 24–25, 31–32; gay and lesbian relationships as copy of, 40–41, 76–77, 84–85; as normative, 105–7
Hobbes, Thomas, 127
Holmes, Oliver Wendell, 261 n
Homicide rate, 79
Homosexuality, as copy of heterosexuality, 76–77, 84–85. *See also* Gay and lesbian adoption
hooks, bell, 190
Horton Hatches the Egg (Seuss), 175, 183–85
Human flourishing model, 119
Huxley, Aldous, 43–44

Identification, 276–77
Identity, 7, 11–13, 28–29, 185, 278; adopted, 146–48, 166–70; aporias, 147, 150, 162, 167; of biological organisms, 140; biology as, 153–56; desire for certainty, 158–60, 162–67; as essence, 137–38, 148, 155–56; family resemblances and, 138–39, 141–42; full human

parentage, 44–45; genetic essentialism, 12, 137–38; as given, 153 n, 154–55; illegitimacy/bastardy, trope of, 151, 155, 160–61 n, 169; impossibility of articulation, 153, 156, 160; legal, of women, 22–23; logic of, 154, 159, 162, 164; manipulation of difference, 153–54; mother/child dyad as central to, 144–45; motherhood as biological, 175–78; motherhood as social, 175, 177–78; as ontology, 153 n, 154; open adoption and, 64–66; otherness as threat to, 163–64; performance of, 155; possibility and, 147, 156, 169–70; sameness and, 151–56, 165–66; self-understanding, 138–39; social aspects, 147–48, 167–68, 210. *See also* Racial identity; Self
Illegitimacy/bastardy, trope of, 151, 155, 160–61 n, 169
Illinois Department of Children and Family Services, 237–38
Imaginary body, 279
Imaginary domain, 46; of adopted child, 29–30; equal protection of, 21–22, 25–26, 29–30; family law reform and, 30–32
Independent adoption, 3, 4, 254
Indian Child Welfare Act (1978), 120
Individual, 14
Individuation, 35
Informal adoption, 22
Inner-city neighborhoods, 237–38, 240
Institutions, 7–8, 275; heterosexual family as, 23–25; marriage as, 8, 110
Intensive Family Preservation Services (IFPS), 226
International adoption, 5, 20, 29, 48, 57, 163–64 n, 199 n
Interpretational communities, 103
Interracial relationships, 256–58, 263
Intimacy, sexuality conflated with, 33–34, 85–86 n
Intra-family adoption, 3. *See also* Step-parent adoption
Irigaray, Luce, 26, 32, 37–39, 42

Jaggar, Alison M., 102
Jessica, baby, 19
Johnston, Patricia Irwin, 263
Joint adoption, 96–97
Joint custody, 30, 42
Joy Luck Club, The (Tan), 190
Judgments, 102–3
Justice, 60, 64, 105
Juvenile justice authorities, 238–39

Kant, Immanuel, 199–200, 219
Kindertransport program, 214

Plato, 212
Pollitt, Katha, 241
Postcolonial nations, 20, 29, 30–32
Post-placement contact, 48, 56
Poverty, 84, 94, 238; neglect related to, 237, 243; systemic reasons for, 236–37; welfare reform and, 227–28, 235–36
Power: of knowledge, 163–64; narrative ethics and, 103–4
Pregnancy, 28, 86–89, 93. See also Birth mother
Preservation of family. See Family preservation policies
Prima facie rights and obligations, 51, 54, 55, 65–66
Primary custody, 22, 29, 30, 55
Privacy, 121n, 249; associative freedom, 260–62; entity-privacy, 33, 46; open adoption and, 59–61; public/private distinction, 101–2, 123; racial randomization and, 256, 259, 260–64
Private agency adoption, 3, 4
Private/public spheres, 123
Privilege, situated knowledge and, 8–9
Property, as bundle of rights, 116–18
Property-based parent-child relations, 11, 43, 112–13, 130; moral assessment of property concepts, 114–21; worth of child, 114–17
Prospective adopters, 56–59, 63, 66–67; African American, 248–49, 251, 252; race-based aversion, 248–49, 252, 258
Public adoption. See Foster care adoption
Public-agency adoption, racial randomization and, 254–55
Public/private distinction, 101–2, 123
Pure will, 204

Race: culture and, 252–53; identifying, 272–74; physical markers of, 268–72, 277; sameness and, 212–13; as social category, 13, 267; as social class, 268–73; as social meaning of color, 270–71
"Race, Culture, Identity: Misunderstood Connections" (Appiah and Gutmann), 276–77
Race-based aversion, 14, 248–49, 252; in romantic partnerships, 256–58
Racial essentialism, 276–77
Racial identity, 13–15, 265–66, 274–78; agency and, 275–77; children in transracial adoption, 286–88; development of, 277–78, 283; identification and, 276–77; map image, 283–84, 286; mixed, 274, 285–89; parents in transracial adoption, 287–88; self-understanding and, 275–76; social and material realities, 284–85;

286; training of body and, 277–78. See also Identity
Racialization, 270–72
Racial preferences in adoption, 14, 56–57, 248–49, 252
Racial purity fantasy, 29
Racial randomization, 14, 248, 250–51; fairness and, 256–59; imagining comprehensive change, 254–55; objections to, 255–56; privacy and, 256, 259, 260–64; strict nonaccommodation and, 250, 252–53. See also Transracial adoption
Racial social geography, 279–80
Racism, 13–14, 238–40, 280, 287–88
Radin, Jane, 254
Rape, 104, 229
Real family, 76
Reality: asymmetrical, 188–90; as function of being seen lovingly, 186–91; interactive model of, 184–85
Real mother, 19–20, 171–72; adoptive mother as, 183–84; birth mother as, 182; birth mother becoming real for child, 190–91; as contested notion, 175–76; media view of, 19–20; real-for-child, 173, 190–91, 193–94. See also Children's literature
Reciprocal rights, 43
Recognition, 186–89
Reddy, Maureen, 257
Reference group orientation, 278
Religion, 258–59
Reproductive technologies, 44, 57, 60, 82, 136, 175n, 258–59
Responsibility, 32–33, 93–94, 112, 127, 130–31
Rights, as property-based, 116–18
Right-wing groups, 224–25
Roberts, Dorothy, 14, 29, 136–37
Robinson, Elise L. E., 173
Roe v. Wade, 261–62n
Role-responsibility, 127
Roorda, Rhonda, 248
Ruddick, Sara, 187n
Ruse, Sharon, 282n

Sameness, love conditional upon, 211–16
Same-sex couple adoption. See Gay and lesbian adoption
Sandefur, Gary, 79
Sanger, Carol, 57
Sappho, 36
Scalia, Antonin, 80–81
Scheffler, Samuel, 196n, 206n
Scheman, Naomi, 164–65
Second-parent adoption, 3, 98–101, 110
Secrecy, 26–27, 63